Beginning HTML5 Games with CreateJS

Brad Manderscheid

Apress®

Beginning HTML5 Games with CreateJS

ISBN-13 (pbk): 978-1-4302-6340-1

ISBN-13 (electronic): 978-1-4302-6341-8

President and Publisher: Paul Manning
Lead Editor: Ben Renow-Clarke
Technical Reviewer: Sebastian DeRossi
Editorial Board: Steve Anglin, Mark Beckner, Ewan Buckingham, Gary Cornell, Louise Corrigan, Jim DeWolf, Jonathan Gennick, Jonathan Hassell, Robert Hutchinson, Michelle Lowman, James Markham, Matthew Moodie, Jeff Olson, Jeffrey Pepper, Douglas Pundick, Ben Renow-Clarke, Dominic Shakeshaft, Gwenan Spearing, Matt Wade, Steve Weiss
Coordinating Editor: Christine Ricketts
Copy Editor: Mary Behr
Compositor: SPi Global
Indexer: SPi Global
Artist: SPi Global
Cover Designer: Anna Ishchenko

Distributed to the book trade worldwide by Springer Science+Business Media New York, 233 Spring Street, 6th Floor, New York, NY 10013. Phone 1-800-SPRINGER, fax (201) 348-4505, e-mail orders-ny@springer-sbm.com, or visit www.springeronline.com. Apress Media, LLC is a California LLC and the sole member (owner) is Springer Science + Business Media Finance Inc (SSBM Finance Inc). SSBM Finance Inc is a Delaware corporation.

For information on translations, please e-mail rights@apress.com, or visit www.apress.com.

Apress and friends of ED books may be purchased in bulk for academic, corporate, or promotional use. eBook versions and licenses are also available for most titles. For more information, reference our Special Bulk Sales–eBook Licensing web page at www.apress.com/bulk-sales.

Any source code or other supplementary material referenced by the author in this text is available to readers at www.apress.com. For detailed information about how to locate your book's source code, go to www.apress.com/source-code/.

For my wife, Jennifer

Contents at a Glance

Contents

About the Author

Brad Manderscheid is currently a Sr. Developer for the agency Bader Rutter and lives in Milwaukee, WI. He specializes in mobile and games, and has a strong passion for creating rich, interactive experiences for both desktop and mobile. He previously spent the better part of a decade making documentaries, working as a freelance developer and consultant for large companies and agencies across the country, and has built everything from mobile applications to large CMS applications and multi-player games for the Web. You can find him on Twitter @bmanderscheid, or on Google+, where he is most active at http://plus.google.com/u/0/+BradManderscheid.

About the Technical Reviewer

Sebastian De Rossi is a senior software developer working at gskinner.com. During this time, most of his efforts have been in developing web- and mobile-based applications. Serving as the Community Evangelist for CreateJS and one of the two @createjs posters on Twitter, he finds himself answering a ton of great questions from community members.

You can see what Sebastian is up to with his latest experiments on Twitter @derossi_s, https://github.com/sebastianderossi/amusement, and https://plus.google.com/+SebastianDeRossi.

Outside the office, you'll find him racking up the miles on his treadmill or planning his next travel adventure with his wife, Shelagh.

Sebastian currently lives in Edmonton, Alberta.

Acknowledgments

First and foremost, I'd like to thank my close friends and mentors for helping me become the developer that I am today. Adam Dansky taught me so much when I was starting out as a Flash developer in San Diego back in 2005. He was not only my first boss in this field, but he became a close friend and mentor. Jason Reynolds played a huge roll in some of the examples and projects in this book, and continues to use CreateJS every day to make fun and amazing things; we'll be teaming up on many more projects in the future. Other friends and colleagues that continue to motivate and inspire me include Zach Nelson, Dustin Dupree, Jourdan Laik, Dirk Watkins and Steven Fischer. I'd also like to acknowledge the endless support I've gotten my entire life from my Mom and brother Tony.

Design and custom art were essential in accomplishing the many examples and projects in this book. My good friend Taylor Martens of *Robots Made It* was a key factor in both designing and acquiring art for this book; I couldn't have done it without him. Other people who have generously created or donated custom art include Spencer Nelsen, Chris Georgenes, Damon Sanchez, The Milwaukee Art Museum, and opengameart.org.

I'd also like to thank the people that make up the amazing developer community that was spawned by Flash. These guys have helped, and continue to help, motivate so many people to create new and exciting things through art and code. Their tireless activity on Twitter and Google+ make it all the more enjoyable to be a part of this field. These folks include Terry Paton, Keith Peters, Jesse Warden, Grant Skinner, Joseph Labrecque, Joseph Burchett, John Hattan, Andreas Rønning, Shawn Blais, Fabio Biondi, Gregg Williams, Richard Davey, Paul Trani and many more.

Last but not least, a huge thanks to Sebastian DeRossi for his technical review of this book. His knowledge and technical advice far exceeded what I could have possibly fit into this book.

Introduction

CreateJS is not a game engine. It was written to create rich, interactive experiences of all kinds by providing tools for HTML5 applications. EaselJS, the library in the suite upon which all games in this book are based, helps manage and control graphics in HTML5 Canvas. Because the very nature of Canvas lends itself nicely to both performance and the technical procedures of classic game development, EaselJS very much feels like it's *meant* for games in many ways. Although this is not entirely true, EaselJS, along with the other tools in the CreateJS suite, are a perfect combination of tools to do just that. The low level, heavy lifting of drawing and management of your game graphics are taken care of, which gives you more freedom to concentrate on the game logic itself. Tools for preloading assets, playing and managing audio, and creating complicated tweens are also included in CreateJS, and can also be used extensively to build engaging games.

A large advantage of using CreateJS for games, as opposed to the other *game-specific* HTML5 libraries out there, is the freedom to create and fine-tune your own game framework. In many popular markets, primarily casual, board, and turn-based games, the overhead of a framework built for tiling, heavy collision, and physics is not necessary. Simply utilizing a tool to draw and sort graphics on the canvas is all that is needed. That's where this book comes in. It puts you right in the middle between complicated native canvas management and being tied down to a specific framework to build your games. This is not to say these other frameworks are bad. In fact they are quite good, especially Phaser and ImpactJS. Depending on the type of game you are building, they can often be the better choice. The purpose of this book is to not only teach you to write these game development techniques yourself, but to give you the skills to mold your own workflow and frameworks using the CreateJS tools. What's more, the skills learned in this book will fully prepare you to create endless, rich HTML5 applications that extend far beyond games.

The book itself is split up into two parts. The first half of the book concentrates on learning the APIs of the suite. Game development techniques will be introduced, focusing on how they can be used with EaselJS and TweenJS. The second half of the book will take your new CreateJS skills to the next level by learning more advanced, objected-oriented JavaScript, asset loading and management, and code organization. More advanced game development techniques will also be learned, which will result in performance gains; mobile optimization will be introduced as well.

You'll find that the libraries in CreateJS are powerful and extremely easy to use. You'll also learn the best tools and applications used to create the graphical assets needed for your games, and how to best use them in conjunction with EaselJS. There are several small exercises, including four full game project chapters. I hope you find this book both fun and educational, and that it will encourage you to create new and exciting applications using CreateJS.

For support, updates on code APIS, and general discussion on this book, please visit the public forum at **https://plus.google.com/u/0/communities/109922548905806388011**.

CHAPTER 1

■■■

Getting to Know CreateJS

Before you can start building your games, you need to get familiar with the CreateJS suite. I'll take a look at each library in the suite and give a brief overview on how to use them. A few JavaScript techniques will also be examined in effort to learn best practices when working with CreateJS, and the final code example will show the harmony that can easily be achieved with the entire suite at work.

Getting Started

The best place to get started is to head over to the official web site, `http://createjs.com`, shown in Figure 1-1.

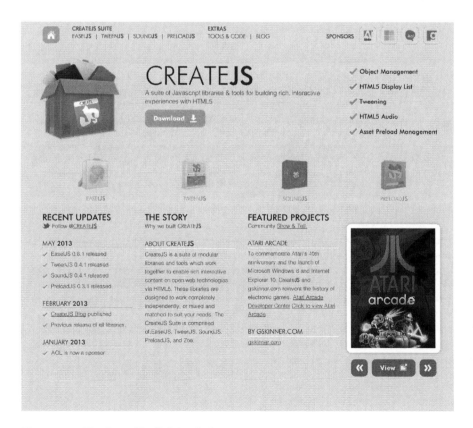

Figure 1-1. *The CreateJS official web site*

Here you can gain access to the latest builds of the suite, as well as view official tutorials and a showcase of recent projects using the suite. Be sure to view this showcase to get an idea of the cool things you can do with CreateJS. You'll also notice the highly-detailed documentation that is available for each library in the suite. Along with being one of the largest JavaScript libraries out there today, CreateJS has amazing documentation to go with it. As you progress in your learning of the suite, these documents will prove to be priceless in extending your skills and optimizing your code.

To acquire the necessary libraries, click the download button on the home page of the site. You'll be taken to https://github.com/CreateJS/ where you can download all of the latest builds. For this book you'll need all four libraries in the toolset.

At the time of writing this book, the following versions were used:

- TweenJS version 0.5

- PreloadJS version 0.4

- EaselJS version 0.7

- SoundJS version 0.5

These four libraries are everything you need to draw and animate graphics, play sound effects and music, and preload your game assets. You'll be using one or more of these libraries throughout the code examples that you'll build in this book. Place them in an area where you can easily include them in your documents while following along with the exercises. I suggest creating a project directory and placing these libraries in a folder named lib so that you can easily set up your files for each exercise to match the code listings.

Let's start by taking a look at the most important tool in the suite when building HTML5 games.

EaselJS

EaselJS is by far the most frequently used tool in the suite when building games. It's where all graphics and interactivity are managed and drawn to an HTML5 Canvas element. The API is based on a hierarchal display list that should be very familiar to anyone that has worked with Flash and ActionScript 3.0. Along with a core interaction model and various helper classes, EaselJS makes working with canvas a lot more manageable than going it alone.

Since EaselJS relies entirely on HTML5 Canvas, it's important to understand what it is and how it works. If you are already familiar with techniques such as blitting and/or working with Flash Stage3D, you already have a pretty good idea of how it works. If not, then you might find the concept a bit complicated at first, but rest assured that EaselJS will smooth out those learning curves almost instantly. In any case, let's start this section by diving into the basics of what Canvas is and how to work with it natively.

HTML5 Canvas

Canvas is an HTML5 element that creates a rectangle in your document used for drawing graphics on the fly with JavaScript. It contains very few attributes or applicable styles. It's quite literally an empty canvas.

Although this programmatically driven graphics environment makes it a powerful tool with many opportunities for rich interactive creation, it's a low-level system that requires a lot of manual drawing management. You are responsible for both drawing and erasing all pixels, and no graphics on the canvas are directly tied to any properties or objects.

The best analogy I've come up with to describe this concept is as follows. Imagine you have a magnet board hanging on the wall, and to the right of it is a dry erase board. The magnet board consists of three butterfly magnets laid out horizontally. The dry erase board has the same three butterflies but are drawn on the board with a marker.

If I were to tell you to change the position of the second butterfly on the magnet board by moving it down two inches, you wouldn't need much thought on how to accomplish this. You would simply grab the butterfly with your finger and pull it down two inches. You simply *changed* its position.

In a typical scripting language it may look something like this:

```
butterfly.y += 200;
```

Now imagine I told you to do the same thing on the dry erase board. You might pause for a minute but you'd ultimately come to only one solution. You would need to erase it, and then draw it again at its new desired position. This is precisely how Canvas works. It's not enough to manage and update the next position of every sprite in your game; you need to manually erase and redraw them as well. These visual graphics are not collectively retainable, but are simply pixels *painted* on to the canvas with no other reference to what they are or represent.

To demonstrate how this looks in action, let's look at a simple example of how you would do this in JavaScript using the Canvas API (see Listing 1-1). The result is demonstrated in Figure 1-2.

Listing 1-1. Drawing and Moving Graphics with the Canvas API

```
var canvas = document.getElementById("canvas");
var ctx = canvas.getContext("2d");

var butterfly = new Image();
butterfly.src = "images/butterfly.png";
butterfly.onload = drawButterflies;

function drawButterflies() {
        ctx.drawImage(butterfly, 0, 0, 200, 138, 0, 0, 200, 138);
        ctx.drawImage(butterfly, 0, 0, 200, 138, 200, 0, 200, 138);
        ctx.drawImage(butterfly, 0, 0, 200, 138, 400, 0, 200, 138);
        setTimeout(moveButterfly,1000);
        }
    function moveButterfly(){
        ctx.clearRect(0,0, canvas.width,canvas.height);
        ctx.drawImage(butterfly, 0, 0, 200, 138, 0, 0, 200, 138);
        ctx.drawImage(butterfly, 0, 0, 200, 138, 200, 200, 200, 138);
        ctx.drawImage(butterfly, 0, 0, 200, 138, 400, 0, 200, 138);
    }
```

Figure 1-2. *Bitmaps drawn onto the canvas using the Canvas API*

At first glance, the initial drawing of the graphics doesn't seem too complicated. You draw your graphic by passing in a reference to the loaded image plus some coordinates and dimensions that dictate what you grab from the loaded bitmap and where to draw it on the canvas.

Now take a look at the function that moves your second butterfly. You are responsible for not only redrawing your graphics again with newly calculated positions, but clearing all of your previous graphics as well. If you didn't first clear the canvas before redrawing your butterfly in its new position, you'd end up with four butterflies (see Figure 1-3).

Figure 1-3. *Results when not first clearing your canvas before drawing new positions*

In this example, you are simply hardcoding the new position of the second butterfly, but as you add more and more sprites to your games, the management of what gets drawn, when you draw, and where you draw it becomes increasingly difficult to maintain.

EaselJS with HTML5 Canvas

Elegant canvas management is where EaselJS comes in. It handles the heavy lifting of managing and drawing graphics so you can concentrate on your game logic, thus making your games as fun and enjoyable as possible. You can rest assured that your sprite objects will be properly drawn and moved appropriately so you can focus on the shelf life and behavior of these game assets while remaining completely decoupled from the rendering process.

Let's take a quick look at what this code might look like if you were doing the exact same thing using EaselJS (see Listing 1-2).

Listing 1-2. Drawing and Moving Graphics with EaselJS

```
function drawButterflies() {
        var imgPath = 'images/butterfly.png';
        butterfly1 = new createjs.Bitmap(imgPath);
        butterfly2 = new createjs.Bitmap(imgPath);
        butterfly3 = new createjs.Bitmap(imgPath);
        butterfly2.x = 200;
        butterfly3.x = 400;
        stage.addChild(butterfly1,butterfly2,butterfly3);
        stage.update();
        setTimeout(moveButterfly, 1000);
    }
    function moveButterfly(){
        butterfly2.y += 200;
        stage.update();
    }
```

As you can see, the EaselJS API makes your code much more clean and manageable. You can refer to and transform what you see on screen as if they were retainable objects, and not get bogged down with the details of what actually connects your graphics with the logical display objects that are created to represent them. Again, the things you see on the canvas are never the same as an object that holds its properties, but merely a graphical representation of it. But you don't need to worry about this because EaselJS will manage that for you. If you tell the butterfly to move, it will move. Much nicer!

You'll also notice that you are adding graphics to and updating an object named stage. This is a reference to Stage, the root display object in which all graphics are drawn to with EaselJS. I will be covering this in depth before starting the actual exercises, which will begin in the next chapter.

Let's take one more look at the power of EaselJS before moving on with the rest of the suite. As you can imagine, layers will be playing a large role in your graphics management when it comes to game development. With Canvas, any pixel drawn in the same coordinates of another will completely erase and replace it. By now that should seem clear so its no surprise that controlling graphics that overlay each other can quickly become difficult to manage.

Luckily, EaselJS consists of the concept referred to as the *display list.* With it you are able to easily add and remove graphics, manipulate the order in which they are drawn, access them by their index in the list, and a whole lot more. I will be covering the display list in more detail later in this section.

Using the previous dry erase board analogy, let's consider one more scenario. This time, each board consists of two butterflies, each with one butterfly slightly overlapping another. Imagine swapping the depths of the butterflies on the magnet board. Once again you're able to quickly accomplish this, this time by simply grabbing both butterflies and replacing one's layer with the other.

Using DOM and jQuery, you might do something like this:

```
$('#butterfly1').css('z-index',1);
$('#butterfly2').css('z-index',2);
```

Simple enough; just move your butterflies. But with the dry erase board you'd have no other choice but to erase both butterflies and redraw them. Again, this is exactly how you would do it with Canvas. You'd draw your two butterflies slightly overlapping using the drawing techniques in the previous Canvas API example. Then, when it comes time to swap their layers, you'd have to erase the current graphics and redraw your butterflies. Only this time you'd change the *order* in which you drew them (see Figure 1-4). This provides the illusion of depth swapping. To manage those depths, and the depths of every graphic in your game, you'd need to come up with a system to factor the order in which your graphics are drawn and execute the code accordingly when drawing.

Figure 1-4. Image depth swapping on Canvas

It's no surprise that this can be handled in a much simpler way using the EaselJS API. Since all of your drawing is taken care of, including the depths of those drawings, this is accomplished with one simple line of code.

```
stage.swapChildren(butterfly1,butterfly2);
```

This is a fine example of the power we have in graphic management and it's all due to the concept of a display list, which EaselJS is built upon. Anything in a display list is referred to as a *child,* and the collective items in that stack are referred to as *children.* In the examples so far, your butterflies are *children* of the stage object.

There are several handy methods that let you quickly access, manipulate, and remove these "stacked" children on your stage. The following are a few of these key methods and they will be used in depth throughout the examples and games in this book:

- addChild
- removeChild
- removeAllChildren
- getChildAt
- setChildIndex

These are just to name a few but are probably the most used when it comes to game development. A full list of methods used to control the display list can be found at www.createjs.com/Docs/EaselJS/classes/Container.html. Because of this display list and the API to control it, you can completely ignore the tedious tasks of drawing management and concentrate on what, when, and why your graphics should appear or go away. It's the one key concept that makes EaselJS such a powerful and easy-to-use library for drawing to the canvas.

You'll see much more EaselJS magic as you progress in the book and start making your games, but let's look at the rest of the suite. We'll move on to animation.

TweenJS

TweenJS is a powerful, lightweight tweening engine that helps you easily animate your display objects in Easel.JS. In fact, you can use TweenJS to tween just about anything, including DOM elements and even sounds. Since you are only concerned about EaselJS and how to use it for games, I will only be covering its use with your easel graphics.

Animating with TweenJS

One final time, take a moment to imagine how you would animate your butterfly using only the Canvas API. I'll spare you the code you'd need to accomplish this, but as a quick reference, you would most likely do something similar to the following.

1. Draw your butterfly image.

2. Create a timer that would execute until a desired increment is reached.

3. At each interval, clear your butterfly graphics.

4. Redraw your butterfly with a new, slightly incremented y value.

5. Check if the number of ticks or desired butterfly y position is reached.

6. Clear your timer.

As you can imagine, with several game graphics and animations, the actual code for this can quickly become convoluted. You're not even accounting for the extra calculations it would take to simultaneously handle duration and distance, easing formulas, and what you want to do after your animation is finished.

It should be no surprise that TweenJS makes this animation process a lot simpler. You can accomplish the previous example, and much more, within a single line of code. Using the same butterfly, let's take a quick look at how you would handle this using TweenJS.

```
createjs.Tween.get(butterfly).to({y:butterfly.y + 20},1000);
```

That's all there is to animating graphics with TweenJS. Let's break this up a bit. First, you access the static class Tween and call its get method. This method takes one parameter, its *target*, which is the object you want to animate. Next, you call the to method on the returned target and pass it an object of properties you want to tween. Lastly, in this method you set the desired duration of the animation using milliseconds. In this case, you want the animation to take exactly one second.

It's really as simple as that. You can optionally pass even more properties to tween by simply adding on to the object. Say you wanted to do a similar animation but also have the butterfly fade out.

```
createjs.Tween.get(butterfly).to({y:butterfly.y + 20,alpha:0},1000);
```

▓ **Note**   The above code example demonstrates the practice of combining methods know as *chaining*. Many techniques used in the CreateJS suite utilize this functionality. It's a handy technique for creating shorter, more concise code.

Easing

One of the coolest things about tweening engines is the built-in equations for handling several animation types, such as easing in and out, bouncing, curving, and more. To give your animation a more natural feel, a typical animation is an ease-out effect. This gradually slows down your animation speed as the tween progresses. The easing equations used in TweenJS were developed by the well-known programmer Robert Penner. These equations are used in many of the tweening engines today and in a wide variety of languages.

Let's add some easing to your butterfly, which is now the third argument in your to method:

```
createjs.Tween.get(butterfly).to({y:butterfly.y + 20},1000,createjs.Ease.QuadOut);
```

There are several animation effects at your disposal, many of which are quite silly but may come in handy in dramatic situations. Play around with different options to get the effect you are looking for. For more information and examples of the included tween animations, check out the Spark Table that is available from the TweenJS web page (see Figure 1-5).

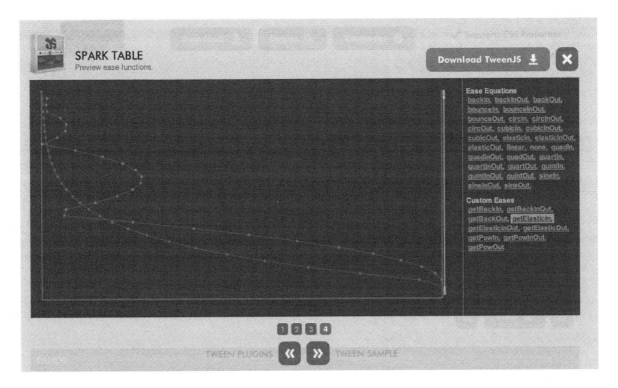

Figure 1-5. Spark Table with animated samples of Ease equations

There are two more important things you need to look into with TweenJS, the wait and call methods.

The wait method allows you to specify a desired time to delay before executing your animation. The following example waits 2 seconds before animating your butterfly:

```
createjs.Tween.get(butterfly).wait(2000).to({y:butterfly.y + 20},1000);
```

The call method allows you to call on a function when your animation is complete. This is referred to as a callback, which is simply a function that will be called asynchronously from other executing commands. This is an important feature in game development but can quickly get confusing because of the nature of JavaScript scope.

Callbacks and Scope

Before fully explaining JavaScript callbacks, let's take one more look at a Tween command that utilizes the call method.

```
create.js.Tween.get(butterfly).to({alpha:0,1000 ).call(butterflyGone);
```

```
function butterflyGone(){
    stage.removeChild(this);
}
```

Here your butterfly fades out, and when complete, calls a function named butterflyGone, which then removes it from the stage. You can already see how this will be important to your game development. This function might also be used to remove a reference from an object pool, add points to a scoreboard, and/or determine if the user has caught enough to advance to the next level.

Callbacks are common in JavaScript programming. What differentiate them from regular functions is that the time in which they are called is completely independent from other surrounding code that is being executed. In other words it's out of order, or *asynchronous*.

An example would be when using AJAX to fetch data from a server. You need a function to process that data and execute other commands when the service is complete. With your butterfly animation, you need to know when that animation is complete so you can handle it while still carrying on with your game logic.

Notice that by default the callback function is scoped to the Tween's target, butterfly. This may not always be the behavior you want. In the examples so far, you are working directly in the global scope of window, so it's easy for you to continue referencing any other global variable or function in your application. But as your games progress you won't be working in this *global* manner, but instead inside other objects and instances. You'll often times need to access to an object's properties and functions within your callbacks, and in many situations you'll lose sight of them completely.

There a few other helpful arguments you can pass into call to help you manage with scope in asynchronous situations. Take a look at the example shown in Listing 1-3.

Listing 1-3. Setting Callback Scope in Tweeners call Method

```
var Game = {
        score:0,
        init:function () {
            this.drawButterfly();
        },
        drawButterfly:function () {
            var imgPath = 'images/butterfly.png';
            var butterfly = new createjs.Bitmap(imgPath);
            stage.addChild(butterfly);
            createjs.Tween.get(butterfly).to({y:100},  1000).call(this.butterflyGone,
                [butterfly],this);
        },
        butterflyGone:function (butterfly) {
            stage.removeChild(butterfly);
            this.score += 10;
            this.gameOver();
        },
        gameOver:function () {
            alert('score: ' + this.score);
        }
    }
```

This example's code is all encapsulated into an object named Game. When you get to the callback function, you need to maintain a reference to the object it's contained in so you can set its score property and reach its other methods. You managed to do this by first passing a reference to your butterfly instance to the callback through the second argument in call. You do this instead of keeping it the default scope that calls the callback function. This argument takes an array where you can pass as many values as you want to the callback.

Lastly, and most importantly, you use the third argument to set the scope to call the callback function in. By passing in this (Game), it will remain in scope when the animation is complete. This can be very important in many programming situations.

■ **Note**   If I've lost you, don't worry. We'll get back into encapsulating code and scope as you build your games later on in the book. This approach is an important one when dealing with game programming in JavaScript, so I felt it necessary to briefly cover it as applied to animations using TweenJS.

You can see how powerful and easy-to-use TweenJS can be. In fact, you could actually get pretty far with EaselJS and TweenJS alone when making games, but there a few more tools you need to check out that will polish your games and help them perform more reliably.

SoundJS

One of the biggest gripes about HTML5 when it comes to games is audio. Browsers all have their own ways of dealing with audio. There is heavy fragmentation when it comes to file types, playback control, volume, and a few other annoyances that make HTML5 games that much more difficult to master. And it all gets worse when you move to mobile.

SoundJS makes an effort to bridge these gaps and it does a pretty good job at doing so. It prevents you from doing endless conditionals each time you want to handle a sound object and provides the concept of *ids* to reference these loaded audio files for quick access and playback control. A simple demo will show you the ease in working with audio with SoundJS.

```
createjs.Sound.registerSound("audio/boom.mp3", "boom",5);
var boom = createjs.Sound.play("boom");
```

The first thing you need to do with a sound file is to register it. This is essential for working with any sound asset. This puts a reference to the sound into memory and allows you to assign an id for quick access to it when you need it, regardless of scope in your game. The third parameter is optional and specifies how many concurrently playing instances of the same sound can be played. Once your sound is registered, you can play it by passing in the registered id string to the *play* method.

Although these two lines are about all you need to play a sound, it is important that your sounds are loaded before attempting to access them. If a sound has even the slightest delay, especially in games, your application will appear off or even broken. You can preload and register all sounds using PreloadJS, which you'll see in action in the next section. But before you move on, let's take a look at a few more features of SoundJS.

Events

There are a handful of useful events that will trigger from a SoundJS instance. These can come in handy when you need to know information about the sound in question, such as when it's loaded, ready to play, finished, and so on. The following is an example of how to listen for when the sound file has finished playing:

```
mySound.addEventListener ("complete", function(mySound) {
        alert('sound has finished')
});
```

Plugins

Plugins are optional additions to help us deal with known audio problems in today's browsers. There are currently three official plugins available: HTMLAudio plugin, WebAudio plugin, and Flash plugin. You'll be learning what these plugins are and how you can use them throughout the book, but let's take a quick look at the Flash plugin.

When the Flash plugin is registered, it will embed the provided FlashAudioPlugin.swf into your HTML document and will act as a fallback when HTML5 audio is not supported. This is a common practice with many desktop HTML5 games and is often used as the primary source of audio. This ensures that the user has the best audio experience possible when in a browser where Flash is supported.

Here is an example of how to register the Flash plugin:

```
createjs.FlashPlugin.BASE_PATH = '../plugins';
createjs.Sound.registerPlugins([createjs.FlashPlugin]);
```

The base path is first assigned and dictates where your swf file is located. Next, you call the registerPlugins method, which accepts an array of available plugins. In this example, you are only registering one, but you can register as many plugins that you have available by adding to the array.

▓ **Note** The easing methods you used in the "TweenJS" section are examples of utilizing plugins within CreateJS. Ease itself is also referred to as a plugin, although it does not need to be registered.

You'll be playing a lot more with SoundJS in your final game, and a bit more in the next section. There's only one more tool to discuss and you'll see how you can use it to wrap everything up into a complete, working example.

PreloadJS

As you probably guessed, PreloadJS is a tool for preloading all of your assets in your game or application. PreloadJS is by no means exclusively tied to the rest of the suite and can be used in any HTML environment where you need to preload the files used in your project. The implementation of PreloadJS is fairly straightforward so it doesn't take much to learn. You can easily wait for loading assets and listen to their progress with minimal amounts of code.

PreloadJS is centered around the LoadQueue class, which manages file loading and events. Take a look at the following example shown in Listing 1-4 and then we'll discuss what's going on.

Listing 1-4. Using LoadQueue Class to Preload Assets

```
var queue = new createjs.LoadQueue();
queue.installPlugin(createjs.Sound);
queue.addEventListener("complete", onComplete);
queue.loadManifest([
    {id: "butterfly", src:"/img/butterfly.png"},
    {id: "poof", src:"/snd/poof.mp3"}
]);
function onComplete () {
    alert('all files loaded');
}
```

After creating an instance of the LoadQueue class, you instantly install the Sound plugin. This is necessary for handling the loading of sound files. Next, you register an event listener so you can tell your application that all files are ready and it's safe to start. A manifest is next built, as opposed to loading each file independently, by invoking the loadManifest method and passing it an array of objects.

These objects should include two properties, the path to the file and an id so you can quickly access them when needed. You can use these ids for both playing audio files and accessing image files.

Now that you've seen this in action, let's combine everything you've learned in this chapter into a quick butterfly application that will encompass all tools in the CreateJS suite. Before you start writing code to build your games throughout this book, you'll first formulate descriptions and simple outlines of what it is you want to accomplish. The next example is extremely simple but this outline will give you an idea of all functionality necessary to complete your goal.

Dancing Butterflies

Dancing butterflies is a simple application that animates three butterflies down the screen in sequential order while playing sound effects as each float down and a final chime sound at the end.

- Create three butterfly graphics.

- Animate each butterfly in sequence, starting at the left.

- Play a sound effect as each butterfly animates.

- Remove each butterfly when it has finished animating.

- Play a sound effect when all butterflies have finished animating.

With the exception of the stage setup, the code in Listing 1-5 should all seem familiar to you. It's a simple example of how all of the tools in CreateJS can nicely work together.

Listing 1-5. Complete Code Example Using All Four CreateJS Libraries

```
<!DOCTYPE html>
<html>
<head>
    <title></title>
    <script src="lib/easeljs-0.7.1.min.js"></script>
    <script src="lib/tweenjs-0.5.1.min.js"></script>
    <script src="lib/soundjs-0.5.2.min.js"></script>
    <script src="lib/preloadjs-0.4.1.min.js"></script>
</head>

<body onload="init()">

<canvas id="canvas" width="1000" height="800" style="border: black solid 1px"></canvas>

</body>

<script>
    var stage;
    var queue;
    function init() {
        queue = new createjs.LoadQueue();
        queue.installPlugin(createjs.Sound);
```

```
        queue.addEventListener("complete", loadComplete);
        queue.loadManifest([
            {id:"butterfly", src:"images/butterfly.png"},
            {id:"woosh", src:"sounds/woosh.mp3"},
            {id:"chime", src:"sounds/chime.mp3"}
        ]);
    }
    function loadComplete() {
        setupStage();
        buildButterflies();
    }
    function setupStage() {
        stage = new createjs.Stage(document.getElementById('canvas'));
        createjs.Ticker.setFPS(60);
        createjs.Ticker.addEventListener("tick", function(){
            stage.update();
        });
    }
    function buildButterflies() {
        var img = queue.getResult("butterfly");
        var i, sound, butterfly;
        for (i = 0; i < 3; i++) {
            butterfly = new createjs.Bitmap(img);
            butterfly.x = i * 200;
            stage.addChild(butterfly);
            createjs.Tween.get(butterfly).wait(i * 1000).to({y:100}, 1000,
                createjs.Ease.quadOut).call(butterflyComplete);
            sound = createjs.Sound.play('woosh',createjs.Sound.INTERRUPT_NONE,i * 1000);
        }
    }
    function butterflyComplete(){
        stage.removeChild(this);
        if(!stage.getNumChildren()){
            createjs.Sound.play('chime');
        }
    }
}

</script>
</html>
```

This code calls a function named init when the body loads. This begins your preload process, which will then fire the function loadComplete when everything is loaded and ready to go. Before you can start using your assets, your stage is set up in the setupStage function. This process, along with creating a *ticker* to constantly update your stage, is an important procedure, and will be the first thing I cover in the next chapter.

After the stage is set up, you animate each butterfly, which will then call the butterflyComplete function to remove itself from the stage when its tween is complete. Lastly, when all children have been removed from the stage, you play a *chime* sound effect.

Summary

Much information was covered in this introductory chapter. You've seen the power of EaselJS by comparing it to the extensive, low-level approach needed with native canvas development; you can now see how the ease of adding animations and sound makes CreateJS an excellent choice for game development. Some programming principles and roadblocks were introduced to prepare you for some of the challenges that lie ahead when managing JavaScript applications. Finally, you managed to squeeze all four toolsets into a short, working example that demonstrates how quickly you can build HTML5 games and applications.

Now that you've gotten acquainted with the suite, you can move on to more detailed examples and begin your exercises using the EaselJS API. You'll learn how to start implementing these techniques into fully functional games. Let's start by learning how to create graphics using EaselJS.

CHAPTER 2

■ ■ ■

Making and Animating Graphics

As you start building your games, you'll be loading in several graphical assets prepared externally in other graphics and drawing applications. However, EaselJS comes bundled with a Graphics class that is built up of a drawing API that you can use to create on-the-fly graphics.

In this chapter, we'll be taking a close look at how you can accomplish these graphics and the kinds of things you can do with them when building your games. But before you start drawing, you need to get a bit more acquainted with what you are drawing them *to*. In the previous chapter, you saw the use of a stage object in many situations, but you don't yet know what it is and how to set it up. Let's do that now.

Stage

Stage is the root level of your EaselJS application. Any display object you add directly to stage becomes a child of the stage's display list. You've seen this in action already with your butterflies.

Setting Up the Stage

Before you can start using EaselJS, you need to set up your stage. This is done by creating an instance of Stage and assigning it to an existing canvas element within your document. The following are some examples of how you set up a stage instance for your games:

```
stage = new createjs.Stage(document.getElementById('canvas'));
```

Alternatively, you can simply pass in the id of the canvas element.

```
stage = new createjs.Stage('canvas');
```

These examples are really all there is to setting up your stage. You're now ready to start adding display objects to it and start building your game. But before anything will be rendered to it and displayed, you need to invoke its update method.

```
stage.update();
```

This method will render all descendants of the stage to the display list. Any time you add or update a child to the stage, or any of its descendants, you need to update the stage to see the changes. Of course, calling this method every time you make an update to a display object would quickly become tedious. It's a much better idea to centralize the stage updates in one function. A typical approach to this would be a timer that would constantly do this at a specified rate. You can accomplish this by utilizing the built-in Ticker class.

Ticker

The Ticker class provides a main interval that is crucial to games development. Its primary purpose is to be that centralized area that calls your code to update the stage, which will reflect upon all added, deleted, and updated sprites that exist in the game. The frequency in which this occurs is referred to as the game's *frame rate*.

A typical desirable frame rate is around 60 frames per second, or 60fps. This means that the stage would need to be updated 60 times every second. This rate can be adjusted accordingly depending on the complexity and speed of your game. You typically want to get away with the smallest *fps* as you can without visually hampering the look and feel of the gameplay. Just remember that the higher your frame rate is, the more taxing it will be on the memory of your computer or device, which can be detrimental to the performance of your game.

Let's take a look at Listing 2-1 to see this in action.

Listing 2-1. Setting Up the Stage and Ticker

```
var stage;

// called when the body is loaded
function setupStage() {
    stage = new createjs.Stage(document.getElementById('canvas'));
    createjs.Ticker.setFPS(60);
    createjs.Ticker.addEventListener("tick", tick);
}

function tick(e) {
    stage.update();
}
```

This is the bare-bones setup that you'll be using for most of the upcoming examples and games you'll be building in this book. This Ticker function can also be used to manage what is known as a *game loop* and can be used for other things such as managing game states. You'll be getting into those game techniques later in the book, but for now you'll use this simple approach to assure that your graphics will render appropriately when updating your children in the stage's display list.

▓ **Note** When using TweenJS, it is essential that the stage is constantly updated by using this or a similar approach.

Before you finally move on to creating graphics and adding them to the stage, let's consider one more performance technique. As convenient as it may be for you to update the stage at a constant rate, it might not always be necessary. If nothing is changing on the screen, such as a static Game Over screen, why clear and redraw it on every tick? The fact is you really don't need to. There is no internal management within the Easel framework to prevent redrawing unchanged properties on any existing display objects so you need to manage this yourself. This can easily be achieved by setting the Ticker to paused.

Take a look at the following example, which sets the Ticker to paused, and how it's handled in the Ticker's handler function:

```
createjs.Ticker.setPaused(false);

function runGame(e){
    if(!e.paused){
        stage.update();
    }
}
```

As you can see, this paused property can be accessed via the event passed into the event handler. You simply only update the stage when the Ticker is *not* set to paused. This is a handy feature to prevent unnecessary rendering in static moments in your game, or when you simply want to pause the level.

You can also retrieve this property directly from the Ticker class.

```
var paused = createjs.Ticker.getPaused();
```

Now that you see how the stage is set up you can finally move on to creating fun and exciting things to add on to it. Unlike the main game chapters in this book, many examples will assume that you have a global stage set up and are running its updates. If at any time you try to replicate an example and nothing shows up, there's a good chance your stage is either not set up correctly or it's not being updated.

Creating Graphics

Now that you've got your stage properly set up, let's start adding some graphics to it. Graphics in EaselJS are either vector or bitmaps. Vectors can be easily drawn with code and used in many gaming and application scenarios. In this section, you'll learn how to create and animate vector graphics. You'll also explore a handy tool that can convert your Illustrator drawings into code, which can then easily be brought into your application.

Graphics

The Graphics class consists of an API for generating vector drawings. It's extremely easy to use and comes with shape drawing methods as well as path building functionality. The following example shows how easy it is to create a red square with a black stroke:

```
var g = new createjs.Graphics();
g.beginStroke('#000');
g.beginFill('#FF0000');
g.drawRect(0,0,100,100);
```

Much like the previous Tween examples, the Graphics methods all return the instance so you can conveniently chain them together.

```
var g = new createjs.Graphics().beginStroke('#000').beginFill('#FF0000').drawRect(0,0,100,100);
```

Once you have your graphics constructed, you need to display them. Since Graphics is not a display object, you are not able to simply add it to the stage. The vessel used to hold and display your created graphics is a simple display object called Shape.

Shapes

The Shape class is used to display vector graphics in the display list. Once you've created a graphics instance, you can pass it directly into the constructor of Shape. The following code creates a square and passes it in through the constructor of a new Shape object, which then gets added to the stage. Figure 2-1 shows the result.

```
var g = new createjs.Graphics().beginStroke('#000').beginFill('#FF0000').drawRect(0,0,100,100);

var square = new createjs.Shape(g);
square.x = square.y = 100;
stage.addChild(square);
```

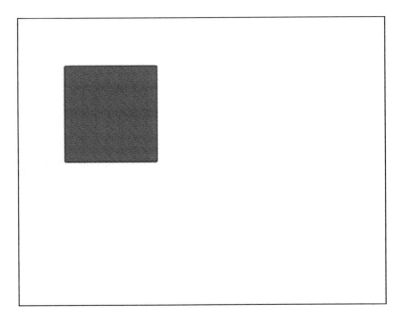

Figure 2-1. *Square drawn with the Graphics API*

Now that your graphic is in a display object, you can add it to the stage and move it around appropriately. Any instance of Shape will have a Graphics instance named graphics, whether you pass one in through its constructor or not.

You can alternatively create graphics and display them via Shape objects by directly accessing its graphics property, as opposed to passing a new instance *into* it. The following code demonstrates how you can use this approach by creating a semi-transparent screen that covers the entire stage:

```
var screen = new createjs.Shape();
screen.graphics.beginFill(createjs.Graphics.getRGB(0, 0, 0, .6));
screen.graphics.drawRect(0, 0, stage.canvas.width, stage.canvas.height);
stage.addChild(screen);
```

Notice that you can control the transparency of any color by using the getRGB static method, allowing you to also specify an alpha property. You'll also notice that the stage itself doesn't have any properties specifying its size so you access its width and height via its canvas property, which is a reference to the HTML Canvas element that it is tied to.

Let's take a look at some of the other shapes that you can quickly build via the Graphics class (see Listing 2-2). The shapes are shown in Figure 2-2.

Listing 2-2. Various Shapes Drawn with the EaselJS Graphics Class

```
//RECTANGLE
var rectangle = new createjs.Shape();
rectangle.graphics.beginStroke('#000');
rectangle.graphics.beginFill('#FF0000');
rectangle.graphics.drawRect(0, 0, 150, 100);
rectangle.x = rectangle.y = 20;
stage.addChild(rectangle);
```

```
//CIRCLE
var circle = new createjs.Shape();
circle.graphics.beginStroke('#000');
circle.graphics.beginFill('#FFF000');
circle.graphics.drawCircle(0, 0, 50);
circle.x = 250;
circle.y = 70;
stage.addChild(circle);

//STAR
var poly = new createjs.Shape();
poly.graphics.beginStroke('#000');
poly.graphics.beginFill('#90ABC2');
poly.graphics.drawPolyStar(0, 0, 60, 6, 0.6);
poly.x = 400;
poly.y = 70;
stage.addChild(poly);

//TRIANGLE
var tri = new createjs.Shape();
tri.graphics.beginStroke('#000');
tri.graphics.beginFill('#00FF00');
tri.graphics.moveTo(50, 0)
    .lineTo(0, 100)
    .lineTo(100, 100)
    .lineTo(50, 0);
tri.x = 20;
tri.y = 150;
stage.addChild(tri);

//ROUNDED RECTANGLE
var roundedRectangle = new createjs.Shape();
roundedRectangle.graphics.beginStroke('#000');
roundedRectangle.graphics.beginFill('#F7D0D1');
roundedRectangle.graphics.drawRoundRect(0,0,400,100,10);
roundedRectangle.x = roundedRectangle.y = 150;
stage.addChild(roundedRectangle);

stage.update();
```

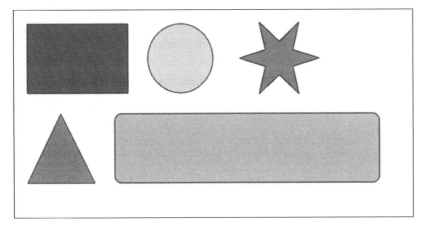

Figure 2-2. *Various shapes using Graphics API*

Some of the shapes in Listing 2-2 are drawn via the built-in shape-drawing methods, but the triangle shows how you can build custom shapes by creating paths. The moveTo method positions your path's starting point and the lineTo draws the path to the specified *x* and *y* positions. Closing a path will use your previously defined fill color to fill it in.

You can essentially draw any shape you can imagine, but manually drawing these path coordinates can be pretty tedious and complicated. If you plan on using some more interesting shapes in your game, you might want to check out this really neat tool that will do the graphics code for you.

Drawscript

Drawscript is an extension that can be used to export graphics code from vector shapes drawn in Illustrator. It was developed by Adobe gaming evangelist Tom Krcha and can be downloaded for free via the web site drawscri.pt (see Figure 2-3). At the time of writing this book, Drawscript is in beta and is actively being updated with more features.

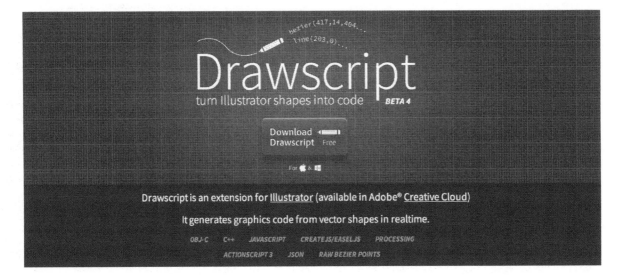

Figure 2-3. *Web site for Drawscript, an Ilustrator extenstion*

Drawscript exports code for several platforms, including EaselJS. Because it handles the complex math and code needed for drawing detailed shapes, you aren't as limited as you might be if you were to write the code yourself.

After you install the extension, open the Drawscript window under Extensions. With it open, make sure you select the shape you've drawn and click Generate in the Drawscript window. This will generate the necessary code that you can then copy and bring into your EaselJS project (see Figure 2-4).

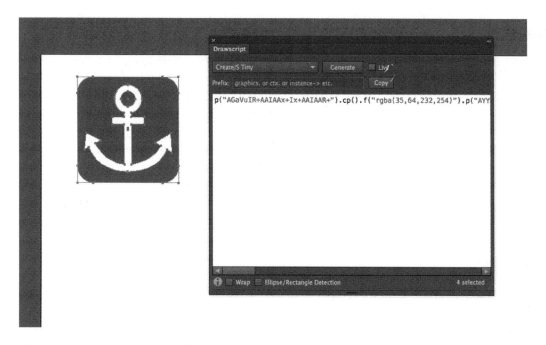

Figure 2-4. *Drawscript in use in Illustrator*

The code generated looks a bit different than what you've seen so far when creating graphics. For starters, it utilizes an API called tiny API that is included in the Graphics class. This is essentially one- or two-letter method names that act as shortcuts when writing graphics code (see Figure 2-5). You can find the complete chart of shortcuts in the documentation for Graphics.

Tiny	Method	Tiny	Method
mt	moveTo	lt	lineTo
at	arcTo	bt	bezierCurveTo
qt	quadraticCurveTo (also curveTo)	r	rect
cp	closePath	c	clear
f	beginFill	lf	beginLinearGradientFill
rf	beginRadialGradientFill	bf	beginBitmapFill
ef	endFill	ss	setStrokeStyle
s	beginStroke	ls	beginLinearGradientStroke
rs	beginRadialGradientStroke	bs	beginBitmapStroke
es	endStroke	dr	drawRect
rr	drawRoundRect	rc	drawRoundRectComplex
dc	drawCircle	de	drawEllipse
dp	drawPolyStar	p	decodePath

Figure 2-5. *Graphics Tiny API cheat sheet*

Along with utilizing this tiny API, Drawscript uses the *decodePath* API also included in `Graphics`. This dramatically shortens and encodes the code needed for drawing paths. The following example shows the code generated by the anchor shape in Illustrator:

```
p("AGaVuIR+AAIAAx+Ix+AAIAAR+").p().f("rgba(35,64,232,254)").p("AYYS6YAABkhaBQhkAAIsMAAYhkAAhQhQ
AAhkIAAsWYAAhkBQhQBkAAIMMAAYBkAABaBQAABkIAAMW").cp().ef().f("rgba(255,255,255,254)").p("AOsLuIiM
AAIAAhQICMAAIAAAAIAAgoYg8gUgyg8AAhGYAAhaBGhGBQAAYBaAABGBGAABaYAABGgyA8hGAUIAAAoIAAAAICWAAIAABQIi
WAAIAAAAIAAG4YAAAADmgUBkioIg8goICOhkIAKDSIg8geYAAAAhQDwloAAYloAAhQkOAAAAIg8AeIAei+ICgBQIg8AoYAAA
ABaDSDwAUIAAm4IAAAA").cp().ef().f("rgba(35,64,232,254)").p("AQuHgYAAAogoAogyAAYgoAAgogoAAgoYAAgy
AogeAoAAYAyAAAoAeAAAy").cp().ef();
```

The generated code begins a series of chained methods, which are intended to be called from a `Graphics` object. You then pass that along to a `Shape` object and add it to the stage as you would with any other graphics example that you've learned so far. Figure 2-6 shows the image after its been exported.

```
var g = new createjs.Graphics();

g.p("AGaVuIR+AAIAAx+Ix+AAIAAR+").cp().f..........ef();
var s = new createjs.Shape(g);
stage.addChild(s);
```

Figure 2-6. *Anchor shape drawn in Illustrator and exported via Drawscript*

The result is a vector shape, completely drawn with code. Because of this, you can scale and manipulate this shape in many ways without pixelating it. Although this approach can be useful in some situations, the overuse of vector shapes can be extremely taxing for your processor. Bitmap graphics, which will be fully explored in Chapter 5, are the preferred format for complex graphics in most gaming environments. Be sure to weigh your options when deciding on the graphics format for your game or application.

Animating Shapes

You've now successfully drawn and added shapes to the stage, but shapes that just sit there are no fun. This is a games book, after all. As with the Bitmap example in the previous chapter, you can use the same tweening methods to a shape because it too is a display object. Let's tween a square by rotating it 360 degrees (see Listing 2-3). The rotating shape is shown in Figure 2-7.

Listing 2-3. Rotating a Square 360 Degrees Using Tween

```
var g = new createjs.Graphics();
g.beginStroke('#000').beginFill('#FF0000').drawRect(0, 0, 100, 100);
var square = new createjs.Shape(g);
square.x = 150;
square.y = 100;
stage.addChild(square);
createjs.Tween.get(square).to({rotation:360},3000);
```

Figure 2-7. Square rotating on upper left axis

You first draw your square and center it on the stage. You are able to quickly rotate it just fine but there is a clear problem. Your goal is to have your square spin dead center in the middle of the stage. The issue is that the registration point defaults to the upper left corner of the square, which acts as its axis point for the rotation. This can be an undesirable effect on many of your game sprites so it's best in most situations to have your registration points in the center (see Listing 2-4). This results in a centered rotating shape like the one in Figure 2-8.

Listing 2-4. Rotating a Square with a Centered Registration Point

```
var g = new createjs.Graphics();
g.beginStroke('#000').beginFill('#FF0000').drawRect(0, 0, 100, 100);
var square = new createjs.Shape(g);
square.regX = square.regY = 50;
square.x = stage.canvas.width / 2;
square.y = stage.canvas.height / 2;
stage.addChild(square);
createjs.Tween.get(square).to({rotation:360},3000);
```

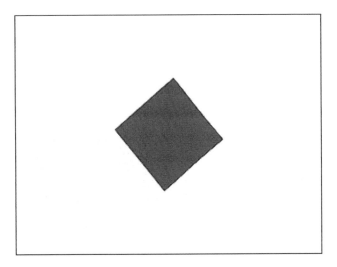

Figure 2-8. *Square rotating on center axis*

Using regX and regY on your shape object forces the graphics registration point to be where you specify it. In this case, you know that your square is 100 pixels tall and 100 pixels wide, so hard-coding its new registration point is easy to accomplish.

▓ **Note**   When it comes to drawing shapes, you can alternatively accomplish this by offsetting the *x* and *y* position of where you start drawing your graphics.

This gives you a much better result. You also have a more exact measurement on where you want to position your sprites. Because your 0 x and y values are now in the center, you can easily position the sprite in the center of the stage by factoring in the width and height of the canvas.

You've just seen how easy and convenient tweening custom shapes can be but it's not always an ideal situation when animating game sprites around the stage. For example, imagine that you have several random power pellets bouncing around your level. A tween is great for one-off animations but not for the continual motion needed for many game elements.

A typical technique for animating game sprites is to utilize the game loop by setting up an update/render process. This technique usually first calls some sort of update method that evaluates your sprites' current positions and sets them up with new properties for rendering to the next desired locations. The render method then simply renders the sprites by using the new temporary properties, typically assigned to each sprite during the update process.

You can use the tick method created by Ticker to call on these two functions. In this example, you have a circle that simply moves across the stage.

```
function updateCircle () {
    var nextX = circle.x + 5;
    circle.nextX = nextX;
}

function renderCircle () {
    circle.x = nextX;
}
```

```
function tick(e) {
   if(!e.paused){
      updateCircle();
      renderCircle();
      stage.update();
   }
}
```

This simple game loop example will gradually move the circle across the screen horizontally. The update and render methods get called on each *game tick,* followed by the update call on stage to finalize the actual rendering of your graphics.

▨ **Note**   Because of the dynamic nature of JavaScript, you can easily "dynamically inject" properties and methods into any object. In the previous example, nextX is a custom property injected into your circle shape. This approach will be used many times in this book as a way to quickly extend display objects by giving them extra, useful values.

You might be wondering why you didn't simply change the x position in your update method. The reason you want to keep these calls separated is because you rarely change the sprite's next position without first evaluating its current locations and/or the game's current situation. You handle all of your physics logic within these update methods, separated from the function that ultimately *moves* them. In an even more complex game loop, you might call on several *other* update methods from here as well, where sprites or containers might handle calculations within themselves.

Listing 2-5 shows an example of this process in action. Albeit a simple demonstration, it should give you an idea on how the update/render cycle is executed within a game loop.

Listing 2-5. Bouncing a Ball Against the Walls Using a Simple Update/Render Cycle

```
var stage = new createjs.Stage(document.getElementById('canvas'));
var direction = 1;
var speed = 10;
var circle = new createjs.Shape();
circle.graphics.beginStroke('#000');
circle.graphics.beginFill('#FFF000');
circle.graphics.drawCircle(0, 0, 50);
circle.radius = 50;
circle.x = 100;
circle.y = 300;

stage.addChild(circle);

createjs.Ticker.addEventListener("tick", tick);
createjs.Ticker.setFPS(60);

function updateCircle() {
   var nextX = circle.x + (speed * direction);
   if (nextX > stage.canvas.width - circle.radius) {
      nextX = stage.canvas.width - circle.radius;
      direction *= -1;
   }
   else if (nextX < circle.radius) {
```

```
        nextX = circle.radius;
        direction *= -1;
    }
    circle.nextX = nextX;
}
function renderCircle() {
    circle.x = circle.nextX;
}

function tick(e) {
    updateCircle();
    renderCircle();
    stage.update();
}
```

Here you have a ball that bounces back and forth between the walls of the stage. In the update function, you first check what the location of the ball will be if you were to change its x position by factoring in the current speed and direction. You set this value to a temporary variable. If this value is beyond the bounds of either side of the stage, you set that value so that it would set the ball directly against the wall in its path; in other words, it won't let it extend past your boundaries. You then assign your ball a variable that stores what its new location should be the next time it's rendered. The render function is then called, where you then assign the new x position to the ball.

Drawing UI Elements

Another great way you can use the power of the drawing API is for drawing UI elements in your games and applications. This can be useful when creating screens, modals, buttons, and a lot more.

A common use for drawing graphics on the fly is for building a preloader bar. You'll need to show some sort of indication that your game is loading as it takes more and more time for your assets to load. PreloadJS provides events that you can use to indicate progress in your load process so drawing a preloader to accompany that process is ideal.

Let's wrap up this chapter by building a quick prototype of how this might be accomplished. You'll be building a self-contained, encapsulated preloader object in Chapter 8, but before you learn some of those advanced coding techniques, you can manually call an update function on the preloader. This will allow you to see how this UI component is drawn and how it works.

Preloader Prototype

Preloader Prototype will be built to demonstrate how you can use code-written graphics to create UI elements, and how you can use animation for updating them. This preloader will consist of an outline graphic with a fill, which will animate to simulate a load progress.

- Draw a preloader bar with an outline and fill shape to represent load progress.

- Manually update the bar with a statically incremented value.

- Remove preloader when load has reached 100%.

Start by creating an HTML file that includes the necessary CreateJS libraries, and a canvas element. You'll be writing your JavaScript right in the document so you don't need to include any custom scripts. Listing 2-6 shows the HTML file so far.

Listing 2-6. HTML Elements for the Preloader

```
<!DOCTYPE html>
<html>
<head>
    <title></title>
    <script src="lib/easeljs-0.7.1.min.js"></script>
    <script src="lib/tweenjs-0.5.1.min.js"></script>
</head>
<body onload="init()" style="margin: 20px">
<canvas id="canvas" width="1024" height="768" style="border: black solid 1px"></canvas>
</body>
</html>
```

Next, open a script block by adding a `script` element. You will write all of your code here. A few variables are first declared, as shown in Listing 2-7.

Listing 2-7. Variables Declared for the Preloader

```
<script>
    const LOADER_WIDTH = 400;
    var stage, loaderBar, loadInterval;
    var percentLoaded = 0;
```

A constant is created to hold the size of the preloader. Then the stage reference is declared, along with a few other variables. A final value of 0 is set to `percentLoaded` so that the bar graphic starts out at a width of 0. The first function that is called is `init`, which is triggered when the body is finished loading (see Listing 2-8).

Listing 2-8. The init Function, Called when Body is Loaded

```
function init() {
    setupStage();
    buildLoaderBar();
    startLoad();
}
```

The `init` function initializes the application by calling a series of functions. The first few are used for preparing the stage and drawing your preloader graphics to it (see Listing 2-9).

Listing 2-9. Setting Up the Stage and Drawing an Empty Loader

```
function setupStage() {
    stage = new createjs.Stage(document.getElementById('canvas'));
    createjs.Ticker.setFPS(60);
    createjs.Ticker.addEventListener("tick", function(e){
        stage.update();
    });
}
function buildLoaderBar() {
    loaderBar = new createjs.Shape();
    loaderBar.x = loaderBar.y = 100;
    loaderBar.graphics.setStrokeStyle(2);
    loaderBar.graphics.beginStroke("#000");
```

```
    loaderBar.graphics.drawRect(0, 0, LOADER_WIDTH, 40);
    stage.addChild(loaderBar);
}
```

The setupStage function does your typical stage setup. The stage variable is set for global reference, and the Ticker is set to fire 60 times per second, which will update the stage on every tick. The next function, buildLoaderBar, draws an empty loader bar to the stage, which is now just a black stroke with no fill. These graphics will be cleared and redrawn each time you have a progress update. This is done in the updateLoaderBar function, shown in Listing 2-10.

Listing 2-10. Rotating a Square 360 Degrees Using Tween

```
function updateLoaderBar() {
    loaderBar.graphics.clear();
    loaderBar.graphics.beginFill('#00ff00');
    loaderBar.graphics.drawRect(0, 0, LOADER_WIDTH * percentLoaded, 40);
    loaderBar.graphics.endFill();
    loaderBar.graphics.setStrokeStyle(2);
    loaderBar.graphics.beginStroke("#000");
    loaderBar.graphics.drawRect(0, 0, LOADER_WIDTH, 40);
    loaderBar.graphics.endStroke();
}
```

The first thing that is done in this function is the clearing of all existing graphics. Next, you start with creating the loader fill by using the current percentLoaded value. This percentage is multiplied against the predetermined width of the preloader. You create the stroke afterwards so it sits nicely on top of the fill.

In this prototype, you are manually updating the load percentage in an interval, which is set up in the final function called in the init function startLoad. This interval will repeatedly update your percentage in the function updateLoad. Both functions are shown in Listing 2-11.

Listing 2-11. An Interval is Created to Update the Percentange for the Preloader Graphics

```
    function startLoad() {
        loadInterval = setInterval(updateLoad, 50);
    }
    function updateLoad() {
        percentLoaded += .005;
        updateLoaderBar();
        if (percentLoaded >= 1) {
            clearInterval(loadInterval);
            stage.removeChild(loaderBar);
        }
    }
```

```
</script>
```

The interval function updateLoad simply updates the percentage by .005 and calls on the updateLoaderBar function to update the graphics. If you've reached the end of the load, you clear the interval and remove the graphics from the stage. Finally, you close your script block. The final result, shown in Figure 2-9, demonstrates the load progress at about 60 percent.

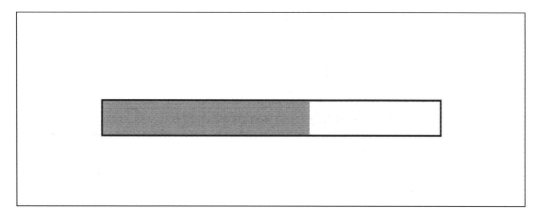

Figure 2-9. *Preloader animating to mimic load progress*

This preloader is a nice, practical example of what you can do with graphics in EaselJS. You managed to create a visually rich feature using nothing but a little math and the built-in drawing API. You'll be wrapping this preloader up nicely in its own reusable object in Chapter 8, but the drawing techniques will remain the same.

Summary

This chapter demonstrates the amount of visual development that you can accomplish without loading a single asset. The drawing API gives you the power to create visuals, from primitive shapes to complex paths and gradients. With a little help from Drawscript, your shapes and colors can get even more detailed by allowing you to draw them inside of Illustrator and pasting the code into your application. We also took a quick look at animations using both TweenJS and more advanced, manual approaches achieved by tapping into the interval fired from the `Ticker` class.

Lastly, you used your newly learned drawing skills to create a practical UI element that will give visual feedback that can be used with PreloadJS or other situations where the user needs to wait for action.

Now that you have custom graphics added to the stage, the next logical step in game development is making them react to user input, as well as give the user feedback on their progress.

CHAPTER 3

■ ■ ■

Capturing User Input

Now that you have a solid understanding of how graphics are created and how you can animate them, some player interaction is in order to turn your visuals into playable, interactive content.

I'll discuss using both mouse and keyboard controls to capture user input, and you'll view a few practical examples that show how to accomplish some common gaming features. Text will also be introduced to display the necessary messaging to provide feedback to the player.

Mouse Events

EaselJS not only handles your canvas drawing, but also the management of mouse positions and actions, and whether they intersect with any of your display objects. This allows you to mimic mouse interactions. Starting with the utmost basics of all interactivity, we'll start by handling some clicks on some simple shape objects.

Mouse Clicks

A mouse event is set up and handled like many other typical interactive environments you might already be used to, such as Flash or HMTL DOM. An *event listener* is applied to the display object for a specific type of mouse interaction, and an *event handler* is written to accept and handle it.

```
troll.addEventListener('click',trollAttacked);

function trollAttacked(e){
    alert('ouch');
}
```

In this troll attacking example, you add the event listener directly on your display object, and you write your function to handle it.

Another way to achieve this would be to use an anonymous function as your event handler.

```
troll.addEventListener('click', function (e) {
    alert('ouch');
});
```

This approach is typical in JavaScript development. Depending on the length and complexity of your function's code, there will be times when you'll want to keep your handler function explicitly defined, but anonymous functions can be handy for many reasons. Not only can they simplify the flow of your code for management and readability, but they can also be crucial when managing scope in many situations.

As previously promised, you'll be diving deep into scope management as your games become more difficult, but for now you can simply take a look at how you can obtain a reference to the object that triggered the event.

```
troll.addEventListener('click', function (e) {
    stage.removeChild(e.target);
});
```

This approach uses the event object passed into the handler. This event object contains many properties that can help you identify what was clicked and where on the stage, or on the object, the mouse pointer was when the event was fired. You are able to kill the appropriate troll by using the target property in the event object, which is a reference to the clicked display object.

You can similarly use the dblclick event to achieve the same effect for double-clicks. Listing 3-1 is an example that uses this event to alert a message when the circle was double-clicked (see Figure 3-1).

Listing 3-1. Registering for Double-Click Events

```
var circle = new createjs.Shape();
circle.graphics.beginFill('#0000FF').drawCircle(0, 0, 50);
circle.x = stage.canvas.width / 2;
circle.y = stage.canvas.height / 2;
circle.name = 'Blue Circle';
stage.addChild(circle);
stage.update();

circle.addEventListener('dblclick', function (e) {
    alert(e.target + ' was double clicked!');
});
```

Figure 3-1. Alert message when the circle was double-clicked

You can also register for rollover and rollout events on display objects. As you can probably imagine, the legwork needed to constantly monitor the mouse location and compare it to the position of any display object can be taxing. Therefore, it should probably be used as sparingly as possible in the Canvas environment. Because of this, EaselJS doesn't allow this functionality by default. You can turn it on by calling the following method:

```
stage.enableMouseOver();
```

After invoking this method on stage, you can now register and properly handle mouseover and mouseout events. Notice that you can also easily change the cursor of the mouse by using any valid CSS style. Figure 3-2 shows your circle's alpha value decrease when the mouse is hovering it.

```
circle.cursor = 'pointer';

circle.addEventListener("mouseover", function (e) {
   circle.alpha = 1;
});

circle.addEventListener("mouseout", function (e) {
   circle.alpha = .5;
});
```

Figure 3-2. *Display object rollover effect and cursor change*

Drag and Drop

EaselJS does not come with built-in functionality for dragging and dropping display objects but you can easily set this up with a combination of a few mouse events. Take a look at the code in Listing 3-2, which accomplishes drag-and-drop functionality.

Listing 3-2. Creating Drag-and-Drop Functionality

```
circle.addEventListener('mousedown',function(e){
    stage.addEventListener('stagemousemove',function(e){
        circle.x = stage.mouseX;
        circle.y = stage.mouseY;
    });

    stage.addEventListener('stagemouseup',function(e){
        e.target.removeAllEventListeners();
    });
});
```

First, you register for a mousedown event on your circle. This differs from the click event as it is fired as soon as you click down, where the click event will fire only after quickly releasing your mouse button over the object. Once you press down on the circle, you immediately listen for every update of the mouse position by setting a listener for stagemousemove, directly on the stage.

In the stagemousemove handler, you change the position of your circle to match that of the mouse, which will give you the illusion of grabbing and dragging that item. In addition to registering for these mouse updates, you also want to listen for when you let go of your circle (i.e., drop it). The stagemouseup will work nicely for this, as it will be triggered as soon as you let go of the mouse button.

Once you do this, you can easily remove both the mousemove and mouseup event listeners on your stage by calling its removeAllEventListeners. Since you are no longer registered for mouse move events, the circle ceases to follow your mouse and is dropped when you let go.

With this drag-and-drop approach with display objects, let's put together a full example that puts this into action, and then add a little bit of game logic to determine if you are dropping your shapes in the appropriate, predetermined locations.

■ **Note** As some of the examples get longer and more complex, I'll be taking a function-by-function approach to explaining the code.

Color Drop

Color Drop is a simple color-matching game where the player must drop each game piece in the correct slot by matching their colors.

- Four square slots are displayed on the top of the screen.

- Four blocks are randomly placed on the bottom of the screen, each with a color that matches a slot at the top of the screen.

- The player must drag each block into its corresponding slot, which is accomplished by matching their colors.

- If a player drops it in the wrong slot, the block will animate back to where it was grabbed.

- If a player drops it in the correct slot, it should animate to snap in place of the slot.

- Once the player fills all four slots, alert the user that they have won the game.

First, set up the HTML document that includes a Canvas element and the necessary CreateJS file includes (see Listing 3-3). The game code will be written in a separate script (see Listing 3-4), so be sure to create this file and include it in the document.

Listing 3-3. HTML Document for Color Drop

```
<!DOCTYPE html>
<html>
<head>
<title>Color Drop Game</title>

<script src="js/lib/easeljs-0.7.1.min.js"></script>
<script src="js/lib/tweenjs-0.5.1.min.js"></script>
<script src="js/colorDrop.js"></script>
</head>

<body onload="init()">

<canvas id="canvas" width="1000" height="800" style="border: black solid 1px"></canvas>

</body>

</html>
```

Listing 3-4. colorDrop.js - Game Variables and init Function

```
var stage;
var shapes = [];
var slots = [];
var score = 0;
```

```
function init() {
    stage = new createjs.Stage("canvas");
    buildShapes();
    setBlocks();
    startGame();
}
```

First, some variables are declared to hold values that you'll need throughout your game code. The first is the stage reference and the second two are arrays that will hold the blocks you drag, as well as the slots that you drop them on. Lastly, a score variable is declared to hold the game score.

The init function is called when your body loads and kicks off your game. The Stage object is created and set to the stage variable.

Next is a series of functions that set up and start the game, the first being a function (see Listing 3-5) used to create all of the shape objects that you will be using in the game.

Listing 3-5. colorDrop.js – buildShapes Function

```
function buildShapes() {
    var colors = ['blue', 'red', 'green', 'yellow'];
    var i, shape, slot;
    for (i = 0; i < colors.length; i++) {
        //slots
        slot = new createjs.Shape();
        slot.graphics.beginStroke(colors[i]);
        slot.graphics.beginFill('#FFF');
        slot.graphics.drawRect(0, 0, 100, 100);
        slot.regX = slot.regY = 50;
        slot.key = i;
        slot.y = 80;
        slot.x = (i * 130) + 100;
        stage.addChild(slot);
        slots.push(slot);
        //shapes
        shape = new createjs.Shape();
        shape.graphics.beginFill(colors[i]);
        shape.graphics.drawRect(0, 0, 100, 100);
        shape.regX = shape.regY = 50;
        shape.key = i;
        shapes.push(shape);
    }
}
```

The buildShapes function creates all of the visual assets needed for the game. You start by creating an array that holds the colors used for building the blocks. A series of reusable variables are also declared for loop iterations, as well as the display objects that you'll create throughout the function.

■ **Note**   It's good practice to declare reusable variables to prevent unnecessarily creating new ones each time you simply need a temporary holder to represent an object. It's also a good idea to declare all local variables at the top of your function for easy reference.

The rest of the function will consist of one loop that creates the game assets and assigns them their necessary properties, for both display and logic. Using the loop's iterator value you can both build and position the slots in a horizontal line at the top of the stage. While the slots are actually drawn to the stage in this loop, the blocks are simply instantiated and pushed to an array so you can draw them later at random positions.

A key property is assigned to each slot and block using the iterator value, and can be used later in the game to determine matches when you drop blocks on the slots.

With the slots drawn on the stage and your block objects instantiated, you are ready to draw the blocks in random positions (see Listing 3-6).

Listing 3-6. colorDrop.js – setBlocks Function

```
function setBlocks() {
    var i, r, shape;
    var l = shapes.length;
    for (i = 0; i < l; i++) {
        r = Math.floor(Math.random() * shapes.length);
        shape = shapes[r];
        shape.homeY = 320;
        shape.homeX = (i * 130) + 100;
        shape.y = shape.homeY;
        shape.x = shape.homeX;
        shape.addEventListener("mousedown", startDrag);
        stage.addChild(shape);
        shapes.splice(r, 1);
    }
}
```

A similar loop is created to position the blocks, this time along the bottom. Each iteration grabs a random index out of the shapes array before placing it on the screen. After you add it, you remove it from the array so you don't grab the same object again. This makes the array length shorter so it's imperative that you first declare that initial array length and use it to write your loop. Otherwise, you would get undesired results.

As you randomly choose and draw each block, you also set a few properties to them for reference on where it was initially drawn. This lets you put it back to this position if you incorrectly drop it somewhere else on the stage.

Finally, a mousedown event listener is registered to each shape so you can create its dragging functionality. This handler has a good amount of code so you'll avoid writing this function anonymously to preserve legibility.

The last function you call from init sets up a simple game loop to continuously update the stage (see Listing 3-7). At this point, your game objects are drawn on the stage and registered to fire a function for handling their drags. Figure 3-3 shows the game elements drawn on the stage and ready for interaction.

Listing 3-7. colorDrop.js – startGame Function

```
function startGame() {
    createjs.Ticker.setFPS(60);
    createjs.Ticker.addEventListener("tick", function(e){
        stage.update();
    });
}
```

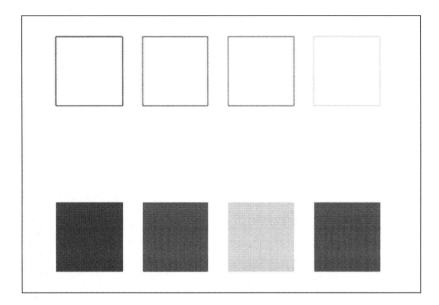

Figure 3-3. *All boxes and slots added to the stage*

Now that all game elements are added to the stage and the mouse event listeners are attached to the boxes, you need to write the game logic that will fire when the pieces are grabbed. Listing 3-8 shows this function and how you use it to handle dragging, dropping, and determining if the player's moves are correct.

Listing 3-8. colorDrop.js – startDrag Function Used to Set Up Your Game Logic

```
function startDrag(e) {
   var shape = e.target;
   var slot = slots[shape.key];

   stage.setChildIndex(shape, stage.getNumChildren() - 1);
   stage.addEventListener('stagemousemove', function (e) {
      shape.x = e.stageX;
      shape.y = e.stageY;
   });

   stage.addEventListener('stagemouseup', function (e) {
      stage.removeAllEventListeners();
      var pt = slot.globalToLocal(stage.mouseX, stage.mouseY);
      if (shape.hitTest(pt.x, pt.y)) {
         shape.removeEventListener("mousedown",startDrag);
         score++;
         createjs.Tween.get(shape).to({x:slot.x, y:slot.y}, 200,
            createjs.Ease.quadOut).call(checkGame);
      }
      else {
         createjs.Tween.get(shape).to({x:shape.homeX, y:shape.homeY}, 200,
            createjs.Ease.quadOut);
      }
   });
}
```

This function acts as the event handler when a block has been grabbed and also handles the entirety of the game logic. Let's break this down to examine what is going on.

A variable is first created to hold a reference to the instance of the block that was grabbed, as well as a reference to the slot that it actually belongs to by using its key property. Since the slots were never shuffled, their keys match their index in the array that holds the reference to them.

The next line uses a method that lets you assign objects in the display list to a specific display index. In other words, you can reorder the layers of displays object by using this handy function:

```
stage.setChildIndex(shape, stage.getNumChildren() - 1);
```

Since all of the blocks are directly in the stage's display list, you call this method on stage. The first parameter is the child you want to access, and the second is the "layer" in which you want to move it to. You can access the top layer by referencing the number of children the stage currently has and forcing your grabbed block to take that place. Similar to arrays, the display list is zero-based so you need to subtract 1 from the length returned to reference the desired index. The object it replaces in the list is then pushed down one index and the others beneath it follow suit. This assures you that the blocks won't render underneath any other shapes as you drag them around the stage.

You then proceed with the drag-and-drop functionality that was covered earlier. The drop function removes the dragging of the block and then moves right into the game logic to determine if it was dropped on the appropriate slot. A Point object is first assigned to a variable to hold the x and y values of where your mouse cursor was when you released the mouse button. You'll need this to determine if the correct slot was under the mouse when you dropped the block. In a drag-and-drop scenario, you can get away with simply evaluating your mouse point, which is also the center of your dragged object, to determine if it was over a drop target. You then invoke the hitTest method on the slot to determine if any of its displayable area intersected with the mouse point when it was let go. If it did, you know you have dropped it on the correct slot and you increase the score. You also take away its dragging functionality by removing its mousedown listener. It is then tweened to snap in place with the slot by using the slot's x and y positions. If the hit test was not passed, you tween the block back to its original position where the player can pick it up and try again. Both tween callbacks are assigned to your last function, checkGame (see Listing 3-9).

Listing 3-9. colorDrop.js – checkGame Function

```
function checkGame(){
    if(score == 4){
        alert('You Win!');
    }
}
```

The final function checks if the player has reached four matches, and if they have, alerts them that they have won. Figure 3-4 shows the alert window displayed when the player wins the game.

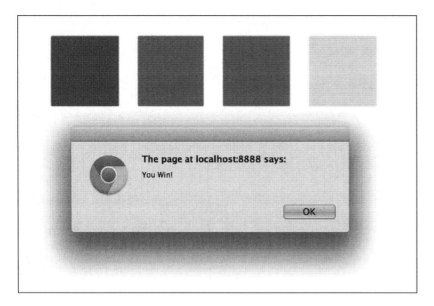

Figure 3-4. *Color Drop win message*

This was your first real game-like example so far, and although extremely basic, you're starting use your newly learned skills to create interactive content. You have a few more things to learn to improve the interactive experience in games, one of which is the keyboard and how you can use it to control game objects.

Keyboard Events

The keyboard is a crucial component to computer game development. It's the next best, tactical piece of hardware after the video game controller. Many would argue it's even better.

Many of the games in this book will be mobile friendly so mouse events, which double as *tap* events, will often times be your only choice in creating an interactive experience. Desktop games, however, don't have that limitation and plenty of game developers have no desire to even reach the mobile space at all. That developer might be you, so let's dive into the keyboard controls that you'll be using in the game project in the next chapter.

Keyboard events are similar to mouse events and you set them up pretty much identically. The difference is that you typically add the keyboard event listeners to the HTML document or window object, as opposed to display objects directly. The following are two approaches to handling keyboard events:

```
//approach 1
window.addEventListener('keydown',function(e){
    //move hero
});

//approach 2
window.onkeydown = moveHero;

function moveHero(e){
    //move hero
};
```

A crucial piece of information needed is to determine what key was pressed so you can take the appropriate actions. You can access this by the keyboard event passed into the handler, which holds a reference to the key that triggered it.

```
window.onkeydown = moveHero;

function moveHero(e){
    alert(e.keyCode + ' was pressed!');
}
```

It's your job to decipher what key code corresponds with what key and how to react to it. To make this a bit more readable, creating some string constants for the key codes you need can be worth the setup. Listing 3-10 is an example of a simple directional pad using the keyboard arrow keys and constants to represent the key codes.

Listing 3-10. *Determining Key Pressed by keyCode*

```
const ARROW_KEY_LEFT = 37;
const ARROW_KEY_UP = 38;
const ARROW_KEY_RIGHT = 39;
const ARROW_KEY_DOWN = 40;

window.onkeydown = onDPad;

function onDPad(e){
    switch (e.keyCode){
        case ARROW_KEY_LEFT:
            console.log('move left');
            break;
        case ARROW_KEY_UP:
            console.log('move up');
            break;
        case ARROW_KEY_RIGHT:
            console.log('move right');
            break;
        case ARROW_KEY_DOWN:
            console.log('move down');
            break;
    }
}
```

▩ **Note** The const keyword is not supported in all browsers, primarily Internet Explorer. Although this keyword is extremely helpful, you may need to simply declare these values as variables, knowing that the all-caps naming convention means they should never be altered.

Let's put this to use in an example with a bit more detail. You'll draw a paddle that the player can control with the arrow keys by moving it left and right along the bottom of the screen (see Listing 3-11).

Listing 3-11. Controlling a Game Paddle Using Arrow Keys

```
const ARROW_KEY_LEFT = 37;
const ARROW_KEY_RIGHT = 39;

var stage,padel;
var leftKeyDown,rightKeyDown = false;

function init() {
    stage = new createjs.Stage(document.getElementById('canvas'));
    createjs.Ticker.addEventListener("tick", tick);
    createjs.Ticker.setFPS(60);
    startGame();
}

function startGame() {
    padel = new createjs.Shape();
    padel.width = 100;
    padel.graphics.beginFill('#0000FF').drawRect(0, 0, padel.width, 20);
    padel.x = padel.nextX = 0;
    padel.y = stage.canvas.height - 20;
    stage.addChild(padel);
    //handle keys
    window.onkeydown = movePadel;
    window.onkeyup = stopPadel;
}

function movePadel(e) {
    e = !e ? window.event : e;
    switch (e.keyCode) {
        case ARROW_KEY_LEFT:
            leftKeyDown = true;
            break;
        case ARROW_KEY_RIGHT:
            rightKeyDown = true;
            break;
        }
}

function stopPadel(e) {
    e = !e ? window.event : e;
    switch (e.keyCode) {
        case 37:
            leftKeyDown = false;
            break;
        case 39:
            rightKeyDown = false;
            break;
    }
}
```

```
function update() {
    var nextX = padel.x;
    if (leftKeyDown) {
        nextX = padel.x - 10;
        if(nextX < 0){
            nextX = 0;
        }
    }
    else if (rightKeyDown) {
        nextX = padel.x + 10;
        if(nextX > stage.canvas.width - padel.width){
            nextX = stage.canvas.width - padel.width;
        }
    }
    padel.nextX = nextX;
}

function render() {
    padel.x = padel.nextX;
}

function tick(e) {
    update();
    render();
    stage.update();
}
```

To keep the movement more smooth while holding down your arrow keys, a few variables are used to store the current direction based on what key was pressed. When you let go, you remove that value to prevent the paddle from moving on the next update cycle. This makes for a much more fluid movement by using the update/render cycle to move the sprites as opposed to moving them directly in the keyboard event handlers. Figure 3-5 shows the paddle drawn and moved on the bottom of the stage.

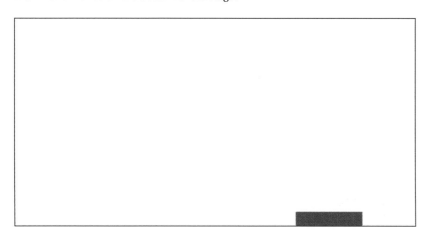

Figure 3-5. *A game paddle drawn and controlled with arrow keys*

Now that some interactivity has been accomplished by user input, some output will be necessary to give your players some feedback on how they are doing.

Text

In your games, you'll often need to provide messaging to the player. Whether as simple as static instructions, or dynamic text for scoreboards, it is essential that you provide the player with textual feedback. EaselJS comes bundled with a Text class that allows you to easily draw and manipulate text on the canvas.

Creating Text

Creating text with EaselJS is done by creating a new Text object and optionally passing it some initial values for its appearance. The following code is an example of how you create a new Text object:

```
var txt = new createjs.Text("Game Over", "20px Arial", "#ff7700");
```

Three parameters can be initially passed into the constructor. The first is the text value you want to set to it. The second is any style you wish to add to the font, such as font family, size, bold, etc. Any valid CSS style for font will be accepted. You can also use non-system fonts if they are properly embedded into your document. The third is the color of your font; again, any valid CSS property for color will work.

Since Text is a display object, you can position and add it to the stage like you can with graphics. There are also a few alignment properties (see Listing 3-12) on Text to help you properly position text on the stage, which is demonstrated in Figure 3-6.

Listing 3-12. Using a Text Object to Display a Game Over Message

```
var txt = new createjs.Text("Game Over", "20px Arial", "#ff7700");
txt.textBaseline = "middle";
txt.textAlign = "center";
txt.x = stage.canvas.width / 2;
txt.y = stage.canvas.height / 2;
stage.addChild(txt);
stage.update();
```

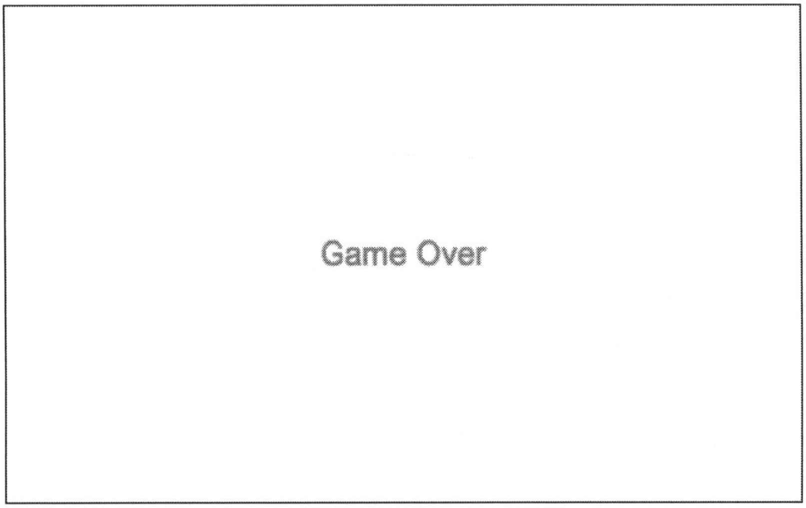

Figure 3-6. *A Game Over message drawn on the screen using a Text object*

You can later change or concatenate the text value by accessing its `text` property.

```
var txt = new createjs.Text("0", "20px Arial", "#ff7700");
txt.text = "Score: ";
txt.text += 1000;
stage.addChild(txt);
stage.update();
```

An important thing to remember when working with EaselJS text is that it is basically no different than drawing any other type of graphic to the `Canvas`. Once it's drawn, there is no direct way of selecting it. Inline styles are also impossible with EaselJS text, so if you need to format specific words or characters within your text, you'll have to create new text objects and position them appropriately.

This type of formatting is not often needed with game elements, so for the most part you'll get by just fine with Text. However, if you need more control over formatting, EaselJS provides a cool way to build and position a DOM element within your application.

DOMElement Class

The `DOMElement` class can be added to the stage and act as if it were an actual child of the parent. Since it's actually a DOM element, it is placed above your canvas and positioned relative to the container you added it to.

```
var domElement = new createjs.DOMElement(htmlElementID);
domElement.x = domElement.y = 50;
stage.addChild(domElement);
```

As you can see, you treat this object like any other display object when adding to the stage in EaselJS. This can be handy when coding tooltips that need to extend past the canvas, or in an instructions screen for a game.

Let's look at this in action by building some HTML text, shown in Listing 3-13, which can be added to a game screen within an Easel application, shown in Listing 3-14.

Listing 3-13. HTML Elements to be Displayed Within Your Easel Application

```
<div id="gameHolder">

    <div id="instructions" style="width: 400px;height: 300px;border: dashed 2
        #008b8b;text-align: center;">
      <h3 style="font-family:arial;">Game Instructions</h3>
      <p><strong>Click</strong> on the <span style="color:red">RED</span>
        balloons as they fall from the sky.</p>
      <p>Make sure you click them <span style="text-decoration:
        underline">all</span> before time runs out!</p>
      <p>Rack up <i>as many points</i> as you can to reach the <span
        style="color:blue">BLUE</span> level.</p>
      <h2 style="font-weight: bold;margin-top:30px">GOOD LUCK!</h2>
    </div>

    <canvas id="canvas" width="500" height="400" style="border: black solid
      1px"></canvas>

</div>
```

Listing 3-14. DOMElement Class Used to Add HTML Text to Your Game Screen

```
var el = new createjs.DOMElement(instructions);
el.alpha = 0;
el.regX = 200;
el.x = stage.canvas.width / 2;
stage.addChild(el);
createjs.Tween.get(el).wait(1000).to({y:40, alpha:1},2000,
    createjs.Ease.quadOut);
```

The id of the div is what gets passed into the DOMElement constructor. Notice that the visibility style for this div is set to hidden. This is done so it is initially hidden and you don't get any unwanted flickers before it's "added" to the stage and positioned. Once you update the DOMElement's alpha property, the DOM element will adhere and become visible. In the example here, the alpha is tweened up while it animates slightly down the screen.

Figure 3-7 shows how much more control you have over text formatting by using HTML elements and the DOMElement class.

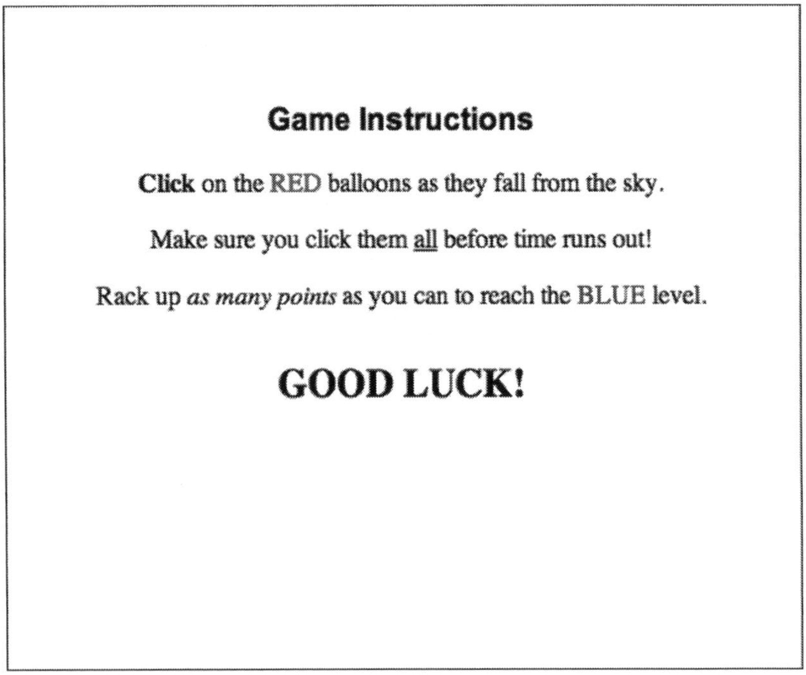

Game Instructions

Click on the RED balloons as they fall from the sky.

Make sure you click them <u>all</u> before time runs out!

Rack up *as many points* as you can to reach the BLUE level.

GOOD LUCK!

Figure 3-7. *HTML elements using HTMLElement*

■ **Note**   It is recommended that you wrap any elements you wish to include using DOMElement within the same div as your EaselJS Canvas element. This will ensure best results for positioning in your application.

Let's wrap up the chapter with another simple game example. Using interaction and text objects, a Hangman-like game will make a perfect demonstration of utilizing the skills you've learn in this chapter.

Word Game

Word Game is a game similar to Hangman, where the player must choose letters to guess a phrase displayed as hidden letters.

- A series of empty slots that represent blank letters are positioned on the screen.

- These letters form a phrase that the player needs to guess.

- A board of letter buttons are available for choosing a letter.

- Fill in all slots of the puzzle before losing your five lives to win the game.

Create an HTML file and include your canvas, CreateJS scripts, and a JavaScript file for your game code. Name this JavaScript file, wordGame.js. Be sure to fire the init function on body load. Open the wordGame.js file and start by declaring the game variables and init function (see Listing 3-15).

Listing 3-15. wordGame.js – Game Variables and init Function

```
var stage, livesTxt, gameOverTxt, win;
var answer = "CREATEJS IS&AWESOME"
var abc = "ABCDEFGHIJKLMNOPQRSTUVWXYZ";
var lives = 5;
var lettersNeeded = 0;

function init() {
    stage = new createjs.Stage(document.getElementById('canvas'));
    drawBoard();
    drawLetters();
    drawMessages();
    startGame();
}
```

As usual, you declare a stage variable to use throughout the game. Others are declared as well, including a few that will be used to reference some text objects. These are followed by a list of variables that contain some initial values, such as how many lives the player has left and how many matches are needed to win the game. The actual answer to the puzzle is also created. An *ampersand* symbol is used to indicate when there should be a line break when creating the empty letter slots.

■ **Note** It's pretty easy to cheat when playing word games for the browser—one only needs to view the page source to get the answers to the puzzle. Although this is true, it doesn't take away from the techniques learned in this lesson. If you decide to get serious about a game of this nature, you'll want to handle some of your game logic on a web server.

In typical fashion, the init function sets up the stage and calls a series of functions to start the game. Let's take a look at the first three functions, which are laid out in Listing 3-16.

Listing 3-16. wordGame.js – drawBoard, drawLetters, and drawMessages Functions Used to Draw and Position Your Game Display Objects

```
function drawBoard() {
    var i, char, box;
    var xPos = 20;
```

```
    var yPos = 90;
    for (i = 0; i < answer.length; i++) {
        char = answer[i];
        if (char != ' ' && char != '&') {
            lettersNeeded++;
            box = new createjs.Shape();
            box.graphics.beginStroke("#000");
            box.graphics.drawRect(0, 0, 20, 24);
            box.regX = 10;
            box.regY = 12;
            box.x = xPos;
            box.y = yPos;
            box.name = 'box_' + i;
            box.key = char;
            stage.addChild(box);
        }
        xPos += 26;
        if (char == '&') {
            yPos += 40;
            xPos = 20;
        }
    }
}

function drawLetters() {
    var i, char, txt, btn;
    var cnt = 0;
    var xPos = 20;
    var yPos = 200;
    for (i = 0; i < abc.length; i++) {
        char = abc[i];
        btn = new createjs.Shape();
        btn.graphics.beginFill("#000");
        btn.graphics.beginStroke("#000");
        btn.graphics.drawRect(0, 0, 20, 24);
        btn.regX = 10;
        btn.regY = 12;
        btn.x = xPos;
        btn.y = yPos;
        stage.addChild(btn);
        //create text
        txt = new createjs.Text(char);
        txt.color = "#FFF";
        txt.textAlign = 'center';
        txt.textBaseline = 'middle';
        txt.x = xPos;
        txt.y = yPos;
        stage.addChild(txt);
        btn.txt = txt;
        btn.addEventListener('click', onLetterClick);
        //adjust positions
```

```
          xPos += 24;
          cnt++;
          if (cnt == 13) {
              yPos += 30;
              xPos = 20;
          }
      }
  }
}

function drawMessages() {
    var txt = new createjs.Text("WORD GAME", "26px Arial");
    txt.color = "#99000";
    txt.x = txt.y = 10;
    stage.addChild(txt);
    livesTxt = new createjs.Text("LIVES: " + lives, "16px Arial");
    livesTxt.textAlign = 'right';
    livesTxt.y = 16;
    livesTxt.x = stage.canvas.width - 10;
    stage.addChild(livesTxt);
}
```

The drawBoard function is used to build the empty letter slots by using the answer variable. A loop runs through each letter in the answer and builds simple box shapes in the process. Some positioning is determined in each iteration, and you use the *ampersand* character to know when to start a new line for the slots. A letter value stores what letter it represents, and a name is given to each slot so you can easily reference it when checking for matches later.

Next, the drawLetters function is used to build the letter buttons for guessing letters in the puzzle. It draws and positions boxes similar to your previous function, while also creating text labels as you loop through the abc variable. The abc variable is a string that simply has every letter in the alphabet. Since you are assigning the click events to each button, a reference to these corresponding text objects are assigned to them. You do this so you can use them later in the handler function to evaluate the puzzle.

Finally, drawMessages adds simple text objects to the stage. One displays the title of the game, and another displays the number of lives the player has during gameplay.

Figure 3-8 shows the results on the stage after you call the drawing functions.

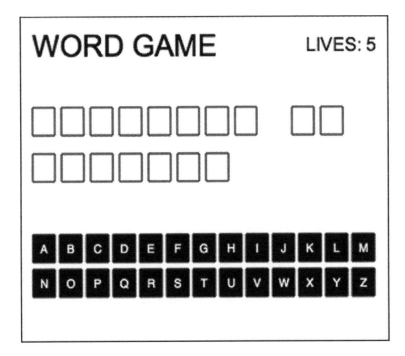

Figure 3-8. Messages and game objects added to your stage

Now that each button has been registered for a mouse `click` event, you need to create the handler function that will determine what action is needed when a player chooses a letter. Listing 3-17 shows this handler function.

Listing 3-17. wordGame.js – onLetterClick Function to Handle Button Clicks

```
function onLetterClick(e) {
    var btn = e.target;
    var txt = btn.txt;
    btn.removeEventListener('click', onLetterClick);
    checkForMatches(txt);
    checkGame();
}
```

A reference to both the button that was clicked and the text object that it's tied to are held in local variables. The mouse events are immediately removed to prevent the player from clicking the same letter twice, and a few functions (see Listing 3-18) are then called to factor the result of the latest letter choice.

Listing 3-18. wordGame.js – checkForMatches and checkGame Functions Used to Check Letter Matches and Game Status

```
function checkForMatches(txt) {
    var letter = txt.text
    var i, char, box, txtClone;
    var match = false;
    var l = answer.length;
```

```
    for (i = 0; i < l; i++) {
        char = answer[i];
        if (char == ' ' || char == '&') {
            continue;
        }
        box = stage.getChildByName('box_' + i);
        if (box.key == letter) {
            lettersNeeded--;
            match = true;
            txtClone= txt.clone();
            txtClone.color = "#000";
            txtClone.x = box.x;
            txtClone.y = box.y;
            stage.addChild(txtClone);
        }
    }
    stage.removeChild(txt);
    if (!match) {
        lives--;
        livesTxt.text = "LIVES: " + lives;
    }
}

function checkGame() {
    if (lettersNeeded == 0) {
        win = true;
        gameOver();
    }
    else if (lives == 0) {
        win = false;
        gameOver();
    }
}
```

A reference to the button's corresponding text object is passed to checkForMatches, and its text value will be used to check for matches in the puzzle. You then create a variable defaulted to false that will be updated to true if you find any matches in the function's loop. This loop is set up to iterate through each letter in the answer while checking for a match in each puzzle box. If that character is either a space or a symbol used for formatting, you ignore it and continue on with the loop. Using your iterator, you can reference each box in the puzzle and the keys you assigned to them.

If you find a match, you first subtract the amount of letters needed to win the game and set the match variable to *true*. You need to then display this letter on the appropriate box to indicate that a match was made and further reveal the secret phrase (see Figure 3-9). The Text object has a clone method that will create a new text instance, using all of the same properties assigned to it. This is much faster than having to create a new one from scratch. After changing its color and coordinates, it's added to the stage in the center of the appropriate box.

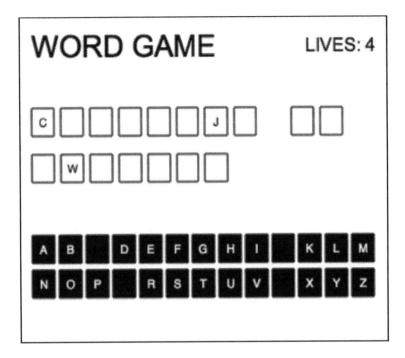

Figure 3-9. *Correct letters chosen and placed in empty boxes*

After the loop, you remove the button's text object from the stage to indicate that this letter is no longer available to choose from. If you made it through the loop with no matches, you subtract the player's lives and update the livesTxt text object.

At this point, your checkGame function is called to check on the player's progress. If the player got all of the letters, win is set to true and gameOver is called. Similarly, if the player is out of lives, win is set to false and gameOver is fired.

If the game is declared over after checking on the game's progress, you end the game by calling the gameOver function to determine the game's outcome (see Listing 3-19).

Listing 3-19. wordGame.js – gameOver Function for Winning or Losing the Game

```
function gameOver() {
    stage.removeAllChildren();
    var msg = win ? "YOU WIN!" : "YOU LOSE";
    gameOverTxt = new createjs.Text(msg, "36px Arial");
    gameOverTxt.alpha = 0;
    gameOverTxt.color = win ? 'blue' : 'red';
    gameOverTxt.textAlign = 'center';
    gameOverTxt.textBaseline = 'middle';
    gameOverTxt.x = stage.canvas.width / 2;
    gameOverTxt.y = stage.canvas.height / 2;
    stage.addChild(gameOverTxt);
    createjs.Tween.get(gameOverTxt).to({alpha:1},1000);
}
```

This final game logic function is used to handle the end of the game, whether the player wins or loses. All display objects can easily be removed by calling removeAllChildren on the stage. A message string is then created, based on if the puzzle was solved or if all lives were lost. This message is displayed with a new text object that is formatted, positioned, and faded up on the stage. Figure 3-10 shows the outcome when a player wins the game.

Figure 3-10. *Game Win message*

Finally, the startGame function is written to set up the Ticker and stage updates; it is the last function called in the init function. Listing 3-20 shows this final function that is used as the heartbeat of the game.

Listing 3-20. wordGame.js – startGame Function to Set Up Ticker and Stage Updates

```
function startGame() {
    createjs.Ticker.setFPS(60);
    createjs.Ticker.addEventListener("tick", function (e) {
        stage.update();
    });
}
```

Summary

In this chapter, you started to see your game graphics really come alive by adding interactivity with user input. You learned how to use both mouse and keyboard events to control game elements on the stage. You also started creating messages by using the EaselJS Text and DOMElement classes. A few examples and short games demonstrated how quickly you can build canvas games using the EaselJS drawing API and its core interaction model.

User input and messaging are crucial aspects to any game, and the lessons learned in this chapter should already give you the ground needed to start building engaging games using EaselJS graphics. Now that you can create, animate, and control graphics and text, the next chapter will be a full game project using the skills you've learned so far.

CHAPTER 4

Game Project: Progressive Break-it

For your first game project, you'll be building a version of the Atari classic, Breakout. You'll be building your game in the *progressive* mode, which will continuously add rows of bricks as the game progresses. A few new twists will be added to the classic to make it a bit more fun, and to fully utilize your new skills.

The graphics for the game will be fully built using EaselJS's drawing API and Text objects. A game loop will be created, which will be used to animate the puck around the stage, and the TweenJS library will be utilized to animate some of the bonus text during gameplay. All controls will be handled by the keyboard, which will control the paddle and pause or play the game.

As usual, let's start by describing and outlining the project by listing the features you'll accomplish in the game.

Progressive Break-it

Progressive Break-it is a game where the player must control a game paddle that moves horizontally across the bottom of the screen. The player must prevent the puck from getting past the paddle, while busting the bricks laid out above it.

- Draw a paddle, puck, and bricks using drawing API.

- Control the paddle by using left and right arrow keys.

- Create level data for brick colors and points for each level.

- Add a new row of bricks every five hits of the paddle.

- Create one random free life brick with every new level added.

- Award bonus points for long, sequential brick hits.

- Display animated text for both free lives and combo bonuses.

- Allow player to pause/resume game by hitting the spacebar.

- End the game when the player runs out of lives or the bricks reach the bottom of the screen.

Figure 4-1 shows the game in its complete state.

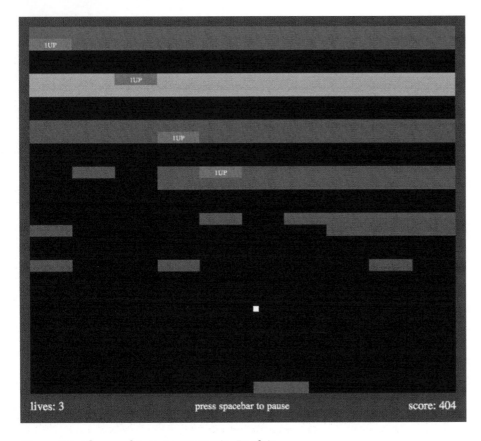

Figure 4-1. *The complete game, Progressive Break-it*

Setting Up the Project Files

Now that a solid understanding has been established for what you want to accomplish, let's move right into setting up the project. Start by setting up the usual HMTL file, which should include the EaselJS and TweenJS libraries, as well as a new JavaScript file for the game code. Name this file breakit.js. Finally, add the Canvas element, giving it a width of 800, a height of 700, and a background color of black.

```
<!DOCTYPE html>
<html>
<head>
    <title></title>
    <script src="../lib/easeljs-0.7.1.min.js"></script>
    <script src="../lib/tweenjs-0.5.1.min.js"></script>
    <script src="breakit.js"></script>
    <style>
      canvas{
          background-color:black;
      }
    </style>
</head>
```

```
<body onload="init()">

<canvas id="canvas" width="800" height="700"></canvas>

</body>

</html>
```

Beginning the Game Code

Now that the HTML is set up, let's start digging into the game code. Open up breakit.js to begin the game programming. Start by declaring all of the game variables that will be used in the game.

Declaring the Game Constants and Variables

Several constants and variables will be used throughout the game. As usual, these are declared at the the top of the script. Start by listing the game constants (see Listing 4-1). I prefer to lay these out first, as they are often the most tweaked during programming to adjust the look and feel of the game.

Listing 4-1. Game Constants

```
const WALL_THICKNESS = 20;
const PADDLE_WIDTH = 100;
const PADDLE_SPEED = 16;
const PUCK_SPEED = 5;
const PADDLE_HITS_FOR_NEW_LEVEL = 5;
const SCORE_BOARD_HEIGHT = 50;
const ARROW_KEY_LEFT = 37;
const ARROW_KEY_RIGHT = 39;
const SPACE_KEY = 32;
```

These constants represent the values that won't change during gameplay, and they play a crucial part in building the game. As you get further into the game code, it becomes a lot easier to adjust these values at the top of your script, as opposed to chasing down hard-coded values in your game functions. Since this particular game doesn't progressively adjust speed, you can add these values to the list of constants. Also included are some values that will be needed to draw the game assets; they will factor into calculating the graphics positions during gameplay. The final three are meant to help with the keyboard keyCodes (you saw this in a few examples in Chapter 3). Listing 4-2 lists the game variables.

Listing 4-2. Game Variables

```
var canvas, stage, paddle, puck, board, scoreTxt, livesTxt, messageTxt, messageInterval;
var leftWall, rightWall, ceiling, floor;

var leftKeyDown = false;
var rightKeyDown = false;

var bricks = [];
var paddleHits = 0;
var combo = 0;
```

```
var lives = 5;
var score = 0;
var level = 0;

var gameRunning = true;
```

The first set of variables is created for the stage and most of the visuals in the game, including messaging. Some variables are also set up that will be used to reference the bounds of the screen. The next two, leftKeyDown and rightKeyDown, are used to help with the game controls.

Next is a series of variables that are declared with initial values. These are grouped for easy reference for all values that should be reset when restarting the game.

The bricks array will start empty and eventually be used to reference all bricks created in the game. You'll add and remove bricks to this array during gameplay. The paddleHits variable will increase in value on each hit of the paddle, and is used to determine when a new level should be added to the board. The combo value similarly gets increased during play and represents the number of bricks busted in a row before hitting the paddle. This gives the player combo bonuses. The number of remaining lives, the score, and current level are also declared with initial values.

The gameRunning variable is used for some very simple state logic. This game has a pause feature that can be triggered via the spacebar. This key is also used to replay the game after losing, so this simple Boolean value can be used to determine what state the game is in when the user hits the spacebar. When gameRunning is true, it should toggle the pause feature. When it's false, it will simply call a function to restart the game.

Finally, the data is created to be used when creating the levels (see Listing 4-3). Each index in the levels array holds an object that determines the color of bricks and the points each one is worth when busted.

Listing 4-3. Creating the Level Data

```
var levels = [
    {color:'#705000', points:1},
    {color:'#743fab', points:2},
    {color:'#4f5e04', points:3},
    {color:'#1b5b97', points:4},
    {color:'#c6c43b', points:5},
    {color:'#1a6d68', points:6},
    {color:'#aa7223', points:7},
    {color:'#743fab', points:8},
    {color:'#4f5e04', points:9},
    {color:'#1b5b97', points:10},
    {color:'#c6c43b', points:11},
    {color:'#1a6d68', points:12}
];
```

With the game variables declared, it's time to move on to initializing the game.

Initializing the Game

Initializing the game is usually called within some sort of init function and is often called when the document and/or game assets are completely finished loading. You've seen this done already in previous examples. All graphics will be created with code in this game project so you don't need to load in any graphics or sounds. Because of this, the onload event will be used within the body of the document to call the init function. Listing 4-4 shows this function.

Listing 4-4. The init Function Is Called when the Document Has Loaded

```
function init() {
    canvas = document.getElementById('canvas');
    stage = new createjs.Stage(canvas);
    newGame();
    startGame();
}
```

A reference to the canvas is stored and the stage object is created. This is followed by a few methods, the first being newGame, which is used to call its own series of functions used to set up the game. The final function, startGame, will kick off the game loop, which will trigger all animation and gameplay into action. Both of these functions are shown in Listing 4-5.

Listing 4-5. The newGame and startGame Functions

```
function newGame() {
    buildWalls();
    buildMessageBoard();
    buildPaddle();
    buildPuck();
    setControls();
    newLevel();
    newLevel();
}
function startGame() {
    createjs.Ticker.setFPS(60);
    createjs.Ticker.addEventListener("tick", function (e) {
        if (!e.paused) {
            stage.update();
        }
    });
}
```

You'll be taking a close look at each function fired from the newGame function shortly, but first let's get a broad overview of what is accomplished when they are executed. The first four functions draw the essential game elements in the game. The controls are then set up, and finally a few levels are added to the board.

After the new game is initialized, it's started by setting up Ticker to update the stage at a frame rate of 60 frames per second. You'll be adding much more to this game loop after the setup of the game, so you'll be revisiting this function later. I prefer to keep this function at the bottom of my script, closer to the run game functions we will build later, but feel free to leave it where it is for now.

Let's break down these initializing functions now. The first four are used for building and drawing the game elements.

Building the Game Elements

It's now time to draw the elements that will be used in the game play. In this section, a series of functions are written to draw the walls, a message board, and the puck and paddle.

Creating the Walls

These first sets of graphics drawn to the board are the walls that make up the bounds of the game (see Listing 4-6). You want a wall drawn on the left, top, and right sides of the stage for the puck to bounce off of. The bottom is left alone so the puck can pass through if the player fails to hit it with the paddle.

Listing 4-6. The buildWalls Function Creates the Bounds of Your Game

```
function buildWalls() {
    var wall = new createjs.Shape();
    wall.graphics.beginFill('#333');
    wall.graphics.drawRect(0, 0, WALL_THICKNESS, canvas.height);
    stage.addChild(wall);
    wall = new createjs.Shape();
    wall.graphics.beginFill('#333');
    wall.graphics.drawRect(0, 0, WALL_THICKNESS, canvas.height);
    wall.x = canvas.width - WALL_THICKNESS;
    stage.addChild(wall);
    wall = new createjs.Shape();
    wall.graphics.beginFill('#333');
    wall.graphics.drawRect(0, 0, canvas.width, WALL_THICKNESS);
    stage.addChild(wall);
    leftWall = WALL_THICKNESS;
    rightWall = canvas.width - WALL_THICKNESS;
    ceiling = WALL_THICKNESS;
}
```

A reusable wall variable is first created to build all of the shapes for the walls. The WALL_THICKNESS constant is used, along with the stage size to build the shapes and position them around the screen. The game variables leftWall and rightWall, which were previously declared for the bounds, are then given their values using some of the same values that were used to build the walls. Since the edges of the stage are not the actual walls of the playing field, you can't simply reference the size of the stage to determine the bounds of the stage like in previous examples. These properties also prevent you from having to continuously calculate these areas on every game tick.

Creating the Message Board

An area for text will be needed to display various game messaging. This message board will be placed on the bottom of the screen, right under the floor where the paddle will rest. The buildMessageBoard sets this up and is shown in Listing 4-7.

Listing 4-7. The buildMessageBoard Function Sets Up all Game Messaging

```
function buildMessageBoard() {
    board = new createjs.Shape();
    board.graphics.beginFill('#333');
    board.graphics.drawRect(0, 0, canvas.width, SCORE_BOARD_HEIGHT);
    board.y = canvas.height - SCORE_BOARD_HEIGHT;
```

```
    stage.addChild(board);
    livesTxt = new createjs.Text('lives: ' + lives, '20px Times', '#fff');
    livesTxt.y = board.y + 10;
    livesTxt.x = WALL_THICKNESS;
    stage.addChild(livesTxt);
    scoreTxt = new createjs.Text('score: ' + score, '20px Times', '#fff');
    scoreTxt.textAlign = "right";
    scoreTxt.y = board.y + 10;
    scoreTxt.x = canvas.width - WALL_THICKNESS;
    stage.addChild(scoreTxt);
    messageTxt = new createjs.Text('press spacebar to pause', '18px Times',
        '#fff');
    messageTxt.textAlign = 'center';
    messageTxt.y = board.y + 10;
    messageTxt.x = canvas.width / 2;
    stage.addChild(messageTxt);
}
```

Similarly to the walls, the message board is drawn at the very bottom edge of the stage. The text objects are then drawn above this shape and positioned at the edges and center of the board. The score and lives text values will be updated during the game loop, but are initially set to help with positioning and styling. Figure 4-2 demonstrates the walls and game message board.

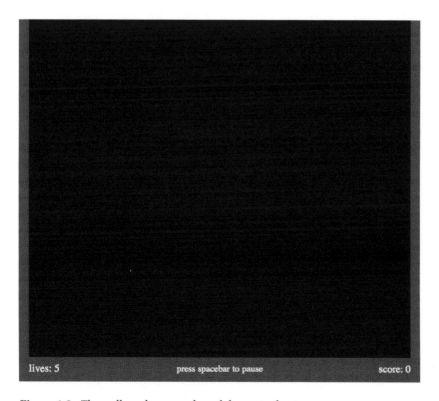

Figure 4-2. *The walls and message board drawn to the stage*

Creating the Paddle and Puck

Directly above the message board will be the floor for the paddle and represent the bottom bounds of the board where the puck can pass through. Let's draw those game elements next (see Listing 4-8).

Listing 4-8. Drawing and Adding the Paddle and Puck

```
function buildPaddle() {
    paddle = new createjs.Shape();
    paddle.width = PADDLE_WIDTH;
    paddle.height = 20;
    paddle.graphics.beginFill('#3e6dc0').drawRect(0, 0, paddle.width, paddle.height);
    paddle.nextX = 0;
    paddle.x = 20;
    paddle.y = canvas.height - paddle.height - SCORE_BOARD_HEIGHT;
    stage.addChild(paddle);
}
function buildPuck() {
    puck = new createjs.Shape();
    puck.graphics.beginFill('#FFFFFF').drawRect(0, 0, 10, 10);
    puck.width = 10;
    puck.height = 10;
    puck.x = canvas.width - 100;
    puck.y = 160;
    puck.velX = PUCK_SPEED;
    puck.velY = PUCK_SPEED;
    puck.isAlive = true;
    stage.addChildAt(puck, 0);
}
```

The game paddle is drawn and positioned appropriately by using the board's height and y position, as well as its own height. The puck is then drawn in the following function and positioned near the center of the stage. You then assign it some properties to determine its velocity, and if it is currently in play. Its velocity determines how fast it should travel and in what direction it should move. By assigning both velX and velY to positive values, it will begin to travel right and down by an increase of the PUCK_SPEED value on every game tick. Lastly, the addChildAt method is used to add it to the bottom layer of the stage. This is to ensure that the puck will travel under the scoreboard when it flies out of bounds beneath the floor.

Adding the Controls

To add interactivity to the game, you need to set up the keyboard event listeners to move the paddle, and to both pause and start the game. Listing 4-9 shows the registering and handling of these event listeners.

Listing 4-9. Setting Up the Game Controls

```
function setControls() {
    window.onkeydown = handleKeyDown;
    window.onkeyup = handleKeyUp;
    }
```

```
function handleKeyDown (e) {
    switch (e.keyCode) {
        case ARROW_KEY_LEFT:
            leftKeyDown = true;
            break;
        case ARROW_KEY_RIGHT:
            rightKeyDown = true;
            break;
    }
}
function handleKeyUp(e) {
    switch (e.keyCode) {
        case ARROW_KEY_LEFT:
            leftKeyDown = false;
            break;
        case ARROW_KEY_RIGHT:
            rightKeyDown = false;
            break;
        case SPACE_KEY:
            if (gameRunning) {
                createjs.Ticker.setPaused(createjs.Ticker.getPaused() ? false
                    : true);
            }
            else {
                resetGame();
            }
            break;
    }
}
```

The setControls function adds a few keyboard listeners to the window object. These handlers are written immediately after and handle events fired when a key is pressed and when it's released.

The rightKeyDown and leftKeyDown variables are set accordingly and used to control the paddle during the update/render cycle that will be set up shortly. The paddle control is set up exactly how it was demonstrated in Chapter 3. If you need to review this process, please refer to Listing 3-11.

If the key that was pressed is the spacebar, you want to do one of two things. If the game is currently in a running state, it should pause or un-pause the game. The game can easily be paused by pausing the Ticker, which will essentially shut down the game loop, freezing everything in its place. If the Ticker is already paused, it is un-paused to resume the game.

If the game is not in a running state (i.e., the *game over* state), this action will completely reset the game by calling a function that will also be examined later in the "Evaluating the Game" section.

At this point, the walls, message board, game puck, and paddle are finished and ready to review. Figure 4-3 demonstrates how the game looks in its current state.

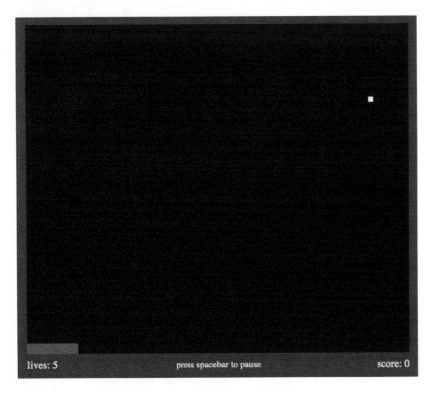

Figure 4-3. *The walls, puck, paddle, and message board drawn to the stage*

Creating Levels

A level in this game consists of adding a new set of bricks to the game after a predetermined amount of paddle hits. The game continues in play, and all subsequent rows of bricks move down on the screen, making it increasingly difficult to hit the puck.

Adding Levels

One more function remains in the initialization process. The newLevel function (see Listing 4-10) creates two new rows of bricks, which make up a level. The game begins with two sets of bricks, so this function is initially called twice and essentially starts the player on level 2.

Listing 4-10. Adding a New Level of Bricks to the Game

```
function newLevel() {
    var i, brick, freeLifeTxt;
    var data = levels[level];
    var xPos = WALL_THICKNESS;
    var yPos = WALL_THICKNESS;
    var freeLife = Math.round(Math.random() * 20);
    paddleHits = 0;
    shiftBricksDown();
```

```
for (i = 0; i < 20; i++) {
    brick = new createjs.Shape();
    brick.graphics.beginFill(i == freeLife ? '#009900' : data.color);
    brick.graphics.drawRect(0, 0, 76, 20);
    brick.graphics.endFill();
    brick.width = 76;
    brick.height = 20;
    brick.x = xPos;
    brick.y = yPos;
    brick.points = data.points;
    brick.freeLife = false;
    bricks.push(brick);
    stage.addChild(brick);
    if (i == freeLife) {
        freeLifeTxt = new createjs.Text('1UP', '12px Times', '#fff');
        freeLifeTxt.x = brick.x + (brick.width / 2);
        freeLifeTxt.y = brick.y + 4;
        freeLifeTxt.width = brick.width;
        freeLifeTxt.textAlign = 'center';
        brick.freeLife = freeLifeTxt;
        stage.addChild(freeLifeTxt);
    }
    xPos += 76;
    if (xPos > (brick.width * 10)) {
        xPos = WALL_THICKNESS
        yPos += brick.height;
    }
}
level++;
if (level == levels.length) {
    level--;
}
}
```

A few reusable variables are first declared for the loop and display objects. Next, level data is accessed by using the level value, which grabs the appropriate level object from the levels array. This data is used to assign each brick the appropriate properties.

The bricks will be laid out in a loop by incrementing the function's xPos and yPos values, which are set to lay the first brick snug in the upper left corner of the left wall and ceiling. As you build these blocks, a random one is chosen to act as a free player bonus. Each level consists of 20 bricks, so a random number between 0 and 19 is assigned to freeLife.

The advancement of levels is determined by the amount of times the paddle hits the puck, which is declared from the game constant PADDLE_HITS_FOR_NEW_LEVEL. The number of paddle hits is reset to zero when building this new level. Before the upcoming brick-building loop, you call on the shiftBricksDown function so that that all previous rows of bricks shift down to make room for the new level. Let's finish the new level by examining the loop.

The loop builds 20 bricks, in two rows of 10, to make up the new level. A basic shape is created and colored by referencing the level data object. When coloring the brick, you first determine if the current iteration value matches the randomly generated number for the bonus brick. If a match was found, the brick is colored green so it stands out as special.

Next, the bricks are positioned using the position values that are evaluated and incremented with each iteration. Before ultimately adding them to the stage, a set of properties is given to each brick. Remember that a display object does not inherently contain a width and height property, but they can be added dynamically by using the values that were used to draw them. These properties will be crucial when writing the collision tests. The number of points that will be given when busted is set as points, and the status of freeLife is declared and defaulted to false.

A few more things are needed to complete the function. Earlier, a random number was set to determine if the current iteration should draw a bonus brick. Along with coloring the brick green, a simple text object will be added to help indicate what the prize will be when busting it. A white text object with the value of '1UP' is centered above the brick. A reference to this text object is assigned to the brick so it can be properly disposed of when the brick is hit. The text object is then added to the stage.

The last piece of code in this loop is a simple conditional to check if a new row should start in the two-row level. And finally, to end the function, the level is increased. There are only so many levels in the levels array, so you continue to use the last data object for the remainder of the game by decreasing the level by one. Figure 4-4 shows the first two levels of bricks added to the game.

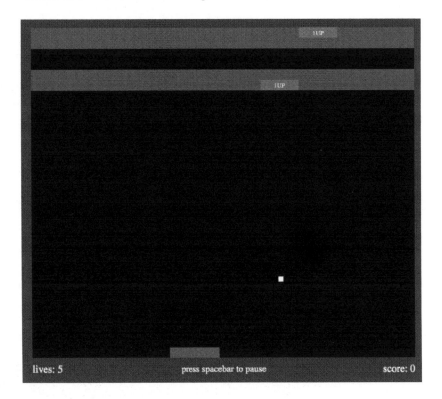

Figure 4-4. *The game and bonus bricks for the first two levels*

Shifting the Bricks

Shifting all existing bricks makes room for the next level. This is done before adding the new level, and is shown in Listing 4-11.

Listing 4-11. The shiftBricksDown Function Moves all Bricks Down when Adding a New Level

```
function shiftBricksDown() {
    var i, brick;
    var shiftHeight = 80;
    var len = bricks.length;
    for (i = 0; i < len; i++) {
        brick = bricks[i];
        brick.y += shiftHeight;
```

```
      if (brick.freeLife) {
         brick.freeLife.y += shiftHeight;
      }
   }
}
```

Immediately before creating the new rows of bricks, the function shiftBricksDown is called to clear the way for the new level. In this function, you loop through all of the current bricks, which are stored in the bricks array. Each brick is shifted down 80 pixels, along with any free life text object that it may be tied to. Figure 4-5 shows a new row of bricks added to the game after reaching a new level.

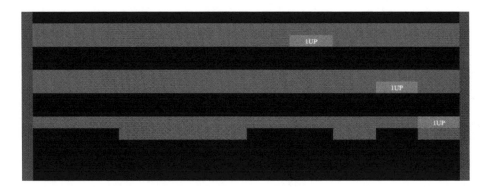

Figure 4-5. *A new level of bricks, pushing the first two rows down*

With the initialization process complete, and the game graphics drawn to the stage, it's time to start setting the game in motion. Let's take a look at setting up the game loop.

Setting Up the Game Loop

Understanding the process of a game loop is an important concept for any game developer. A game with constant motion has a constant heartbeat, and its speed is determined by its frame rate. I briefly touched on this process in Chapter 2; it's now time to see this cycle in full action.

To set up the game loop, return to the startGame function. If you haven't already, move this function to the end of the script where you will set up the game loop. Add the function called runGame just before the stage is updated. Listing 4-12 shows this update and the runGame function.

Listing 4-12. Revisiting the startGame Function and Running the Game

```
function startGame() {
   createjs.Ticker.setFPS(60);
   createjs.Ticker.addEventListener("tick", function (e) {
      if (!e.paused) {
         runGame();
         stage.update();
      }
   });
}
```

```
function runGame() {
    update();
    render();
    evalPuck();
    evalGame();
}
```

As you can see, the runGame function is called on every tick of the game. This function executes the update/render cycle. It also runs a few functions that determine end level and/or end game scenarios.

Updating Game Elements in the Game Loop

The update cycle will evaluate the next position of the puck and paddle, and how they will affect the game in regards of collisions and bounds. Let's take a quick look at update before analyzing each of the functions it calls (see Listing 4-13).

Listing 4-13. The Update Cycle

```
function update() {
    updatePaddle();
    updatePuck();
    checkPaddle();
    checkBricks();
}
```

The update function calls a series of functions used to evaluate and update display objects in motion. A series of functions is also called to check if a brick is about to be busted, or if the puck is about to hit the paddle. You want to do this before ultimately updating the stage. Let's go over each of these functions in detail, starting with updatePaddle (see Listing 4-14).

Listing 4-14. Updating the Paddle

```
function updatePaddle() {
    var nextX = paddle.x;
    if (leftKeyDown) {
        nextX = paddle.x - PADDLE_SPEED;
        if (nextX < leftWall) {
            nextX = leftWall;
        }
    }
    else if (rightKeyDown) {
        nextX = paddle.x + PADDLE_SPEED;
        if (nextX > rightWall - paddle.width) {
            nextX = rightWall - paddle.width;
        }
    }
    paddle.nextX = nextX;
}
```

This should look familiar to you from Chapter 3. Depending on which arrow key is currently pressed down, the next position of the paddle is assigned to it, and determines where it should be drawn during the next render cycle. A quick check against the left and right walls assures that you can't extend past them when controlling it. The next update function will move the puck. Listing 4-15 shows the updatePuck function.

Listing 4-15. Updating the Puck

```
function updatePuck() {
    var nextX = puck.x + puck.velX;
    var nextY = puck.y + puck.velY;
    if (nextX < leftWall) {
        nextX = leftWall;
        puck.velX *= -1;
    }
    else if (nextX > (rightWall - puck.width)) {
        nextX = rightWall - puck.width;
        puck.velX *= -1;
    }
    if (nextY < (ceiling)) {
        nextY = ceiling;
        puck.velY *= -1;
    }
    puck.nextX = nextX;
    puck.nextY = nextY;
}
```

Using the puck's x and y velocity, a few temporary values are set up to determine its next location by adding to its current point values. Similar to the paddle, collisions against the walls and ceiling are considered, and values are adjusted appropriately to prevent the puck from moving out of bounds. In the case of the puck, and its constant motion, a collision with a wall should reverse its x velocity, and its y velocity is reversed when hitting the ceiling. Lastly, the puck is assigned its next x and y positions for the next render cycle.

Checking for Collisions

With the paddle controls set, and the puck in motion, some evaluations need to be made on what is about to happen with these new positions, and what they might collide with. The next function in Listing 4-16 determines if the puck is about to collide with the paddle.

Listing 4-16. Checking the Puck for a Collision with the Paddle

```
function checkPaddle () {
    if (puck.velY > 0 && puck.isAlive && puck.nextY > (paddle.y -
        paddle.height) && puck.nextX >= paddle.x && puck.nextX <=
        (paddle.x + paddle.width)) {
        puck.nextY = paddle.y - puck.height;
        combo = 0;
        paddleHits++;
        puck.velY *= -1;
    }
}
```

The puck's collision with the paddle is handled in the same way as the ceiling in that its y velocity is reversed when hitting. Only the paddle is a moving target, so the collision detection is a bit more complicated. You need to detect the x and y position of both the paddle and the puck to determine if they are about to intersect. This detection really only needs to run when the puck is moving downwards, so first check its velY value. The puck also has an isAlive property that is set to false when it's beneath and beyond the reach of the paddle. This prevents you from running its brick and paddle collision calculations during the time it travels beyond and below the stage.

Continue with the conditional by comparing the position and size values of both the puck and the paddle to see if the rectangles intersect. If all conditions are met, then you know that the puck must be covering the paddle and a collision is successfully detected. Updating the puck's nextY property to sit snuggly on top of the paddle, similar to the walls and ceiling, gives it a much more natural look when bouncing up and away.

A few of the game variables need to be updated when the paddle hits the puck. The combo variable is used to count consecutive brick hits before reaching the paddle again. This is used for the combo bonuses that are awarded to the player. When the puck hits the paddle, this value is reset back to zero to restart the consecutive brick count. The paddleHits variable is used to count the number of times the puck hit the paddle. This count is how you determine if you should add a new level of bricks to the board. Finally, the y velocity is reversed, which will set the puck flying back up towards the bricks. Figure 4-6 demonstrates the puck ricocheting off of the paddle.

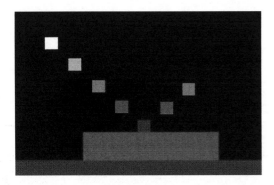

Figure 4-6. *The puck colliding with the paddle and bouncing away to the left*

The next function (see Listing 4-17) handles the coolest part of the game, the brick busting! This function is one of the most complex functions yet and consists of one giant loop. This loop checks all bricks in the game for a puck collision, and a few conditionals are then written to factor in the bonus features.

Listing 4-17. Checking the Puck for Brick Collisions

```
function checkBricks() {
   if(!puck.isAlive){
      return;
   }
   var i, brick;
   for (i = 0; i < bricks.length; i++) {
      brick = bricks[i];
      if (puck.nextY >= brick.y && puck.nextY <= (brick.y + brick.height)
            && puck.nextX >= brick.x && puck.nextX <= (brick.x +
            brick.width)) {
         score += brick.points;
         combo++;
```

```
        if (brick.freeLife) {
            lives++;
            createjs.Tween.get(brick.freeLife)
                .to({alpha:0, y:brick.freeLife.y - 100}, 1000)
                .call(function () {
                    stage.removeChild(this);
                });
        }
        if (combo > 4) {
            score += (combo * 10);
            var comboTxt = new createjs.Text('COMBO X' + (combo * 10),
                '14px Times', '#FF0000');
            comboTxt.x = brick.x;
            comboTxt.y = brick.y;
            comboTxt.regX = brick.width / 2;
            comboTxt.regY = brick.height / 2;
            comboTxt.alpha = 0;
            stage.addChild(comboTxt);
            createjs.Tween.get(comboTxt)
                .to({alpha:1, scaleX:2, scaleY:2, y:comboTxt.y - 60}, 1000)
                .call(function () {
                    stage.removeChild(this);
                });
        }
        stage.removeChild(brick);
        bricks.splice(i, 1);
        puck.velY *= -1;
        break;
    }
  }
}
```

The loop is set to cycle through the bricks array, which holds every brick visible on the stage. The same collision detection that was used on the paddle is used on each brick. If a hit is found, several things are then considered.

First, the score is increased by the number of points that were assigned to the brick during the building of its level, and the combo count is incremented by one. If the brick was a bonus brick, the player is awarded a new life. When this brick was created, it was assigned a reference to the '1UP' text object so it could be removed later. Before doing this, it is given a classic up-and-fade animation, and is ultimately removed from the stage when the tween is complete.

The combo bonuses are next determined by checking if the combo count is over four. For every one of these hits, the current score is increased by the value of the combo count times 10. To add dramatic effect for these combo points, a text object is created on the fly, added to the stage above the brick, and then animated up while growing in size. Adding a short delay prevents too much overlapping of text as the bonus messages populate the screen. When the animation is complete, the text object is removed from the stage. Figure 4-7 shows the visuals during a combo streak.

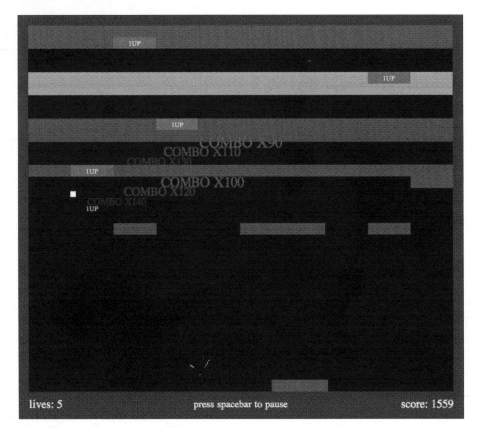

Figure 4-7. Combo and Free Player text animations

This loop is still not quite complete. The brick needs to be removed from the stage so it will disappear when it is next updated. Setting these busted bricks to null helps keep the game clean, and invokes garbage collection on objects no longer in use. It's also important to splice this object out of the bricks array so it's no longer factored in this loop during the next update cycle.

At last, the puck's y velocity is reversed and the loop is broken. You only need to detect one brick collision per update cycle, so breaking the loop prevents unnecessary code execution.

Rendering the Game Elements

The puck's and paddle's next positions have been calculated, and the fate of each brick has been determined. All points and lives have been properly added or subtracted from the game. Now it's finally time to officially assign these new properties to these display objects (see Listing 4-18), which will take effect once the stage is updated.

Listing 4-18. The Render Cycle

```
function render() {
    paddle.x = paddle.nextX;
    puck.x = puck.nextX;
    puck.y = puck.nextY;
```

```
        livesTxt.text = "lives: " + lives;
        scoreTxt.text = "score: " + score;
}
```

The render function assigns the puck and paddle their new positions using the temporary values that were injected into them during the update process. The messaging is also updated by assigning their text values using the score and lives game variables that may or may not have been changed during the update cycle.

Evaluating the Game

A few functions are left to run at the end of the game loop to evaluate the game. Listing 4-19 shows the code used to determine a few key scenarios in the game, which could result in a loss of a life, a new level, or the end of the game completely.

Listing 4-19. Evaluating Game Progress

```
function evalPuck() {
    if (puck.y > paddle.y) {
        puck.isAlive = false;
    }
    if (puck.y > canvas.height + 200) {
        puck.y = bricks[0].y + bricks[0].height + 40;
        puck.x = canvas.width / 2;
        puck.velX *= -1;
        puck.isAlive = true;
        combo = 0;
        lives--;
    }
}
function evalGame() {
    if (lives < 0 || bricks[0].y > board.y) {
        gameOver();
    }
    if (paddleHits == PADDLE_HITS_FOR_NEW_LEVEL) {
        newLevel();
    }
}
```

The current position of the puck is first examined in evalPuck. If it's below the top of the paddle, you know it has no chance of being hit in the next iterations of the game loop so its isAlive property is set to false. You also want to see if it has traveled enough distance below the stage so you can reset its position and put it back in play. This gives the player a bit of time to prepare for the puck being thrown back into the game. The position of the puck when reset is determined by the bottom row of bricks by accessing the first index in the bricks array. The first brick in this array will always be the lowest or one of the lowest positioned bricks on the screen. The puck's x position is always set near the center of the stage to give the player a chance to get into position as the rows become lower and increasingly more difficult to reach after a puck is reset.

During this puck reset, a few more properties need to be updated. The puck's x velocity is reversed, and its isAlive property is set back to true. The combo game variable is reset to zero, and the number of lives is decreased by one.

The game's progress is determined by whether a new level should be added, or if the game should end completely. The evalGame will check for both. First, it checks if the game should be over by checking two scenarios.

The first is when a player has completely run out of lives, and the second is when the bottom row of bricks has reached past the floor. Each of these situations should end the game immediately by executing the gameOver function.

A new level is determined by checking on the number of hits the puck has made with the paddle. It was decided that five hits should make a new level when you declared the constant PADDLE_HITS_FOR_NEW_LEVEL. Now on every fifth paddle hit, a new level of bricks is thrown into gameplay.

Ending the Game

You are now officially finished with the game loop functions. During this cycle, the game was constantly checking to see if the game should be over, and if so, to call on gameOver. Listing 4-20 shows this as one of the final three functions in the game, all of them handling the end-game scenario.

Listing 4-20. The gameOver Function

```
function gameOver() {
    createjs.Ticker.setPaused(true);
    gameRunning = false;
    messageTxt.text = "press spacebar to play";
    puck.visible = false;
    paddle.visible = false;
    stage.update();
    messageInterval = setInterval(function () {
        messageTxt.visible = messageTxt.visible ? false : true;
        stage.update();
    }, 1000);
}
```

The game should immediately be paused in the gameOver function to prevent the game loop from carrying on, and gameRunning is set to false. Then, the paddle and puck are hidden and the message below is changed to instruct the player how to restart the game. After this, the stage needs to be manually updated since the update/render cycle has been paused. To draw attention to this new message, a simple interval is set up to blink these instructions on and off, and is set to the messageInterval game variable. This is done so it can be referenced and stopped when the game is restarted.

Resetting the Game

As simple as the game state logic is in this game, it's enough to determine if the game is in motion or if it's waiting to be restarted. Because the gameRunning variable is now set to false, the hit of the spacebar will no longer simply pause the game, but will run a function to completely reset all game values and start it over (see Listing 4-21).

Listing 4-21. Resetting the Game Variables and Starting the Game Over

```
function resetGame() {
    clearInterval(messageInterval);
    level = 0;
    score = 0;
    lives = 5;
    paddleHits = 0;
    puck.y = 160;
    puck.velY = PUCK_SPEED;
    puck.visible = true;
```

```
        paddle.visible = true;
        messageTxt.visible = true;
        gameRunning = true;
        messageTxt.text = "press spacebar to pause";
        stage.update();
        removeBricks();
        newLevel();
        newLevel();
        createjs.Ticker.setPaused(false);
}
function removeBricks() {
        var i, brick;
        for (i = 0; i < bricks.length; i++) {
                brick = bricks[i];
                if (brick.freeLife) {
                        stage.removeChild(brick.freeLife);
                }
                stage.removeChild(brick);
        }
        bricks = [];
}
```

To reset the game, several of the key game variables are reset to the values they were assigned at the beginning of the game. All remaining bricks, and their corresponding '1UP' text objects are removed from the stage. Finally, two new levels are added to the game and the game loop is resumed by unpausing the Ticker.

The Progressive Break-it game is now finished. The complete game code is available in the breakit.js file that you can find with the other source code for this book. You can download it from the Source Code/Downloads tab on the book's Apress product page (www.apress.com/9781430263401).

Summary

In this chapter, we made a complete game using nothing but code and the magic of EaselJS. All graphics and messaging were accomplished without loading in a single graphical asset, and by utilizing a game loop we were able to create a game that involves constant movement. We even took advantage of TweenJS by using it for one-off animations. Player control was made possible by listening for keyboard events, and assigning them to move the paddle and pause the game. Simple collision detection techniques were also introduced.

With some key game and drawing techniques now in your arsenal, it's time to start adding much more polish to your games. The drawing API in EaselJS can be extremely efficient and easy to use, but your graphics really need some serious upgrading. Loading bitmaps and managing groups of graphics by using *containers* will be covered in the next chapter. If you're ready, let's start making your games look a lot more professional.

CHAPTER 5

Using and Managing Bitmap Images

You've made it this far without loading in a single asset for the visuals in your games, but a nicely polished game is going to need some better graphics. Drawing to the canvas from loaded bitmap graphics is a breeze with EaselJS and will instantly start making your games look professional. We'll be covering the use of bitmaps in this chapter.

We'll also dive into the management of bitmaps, along with other display objects. As your game elements get more complex, it becomes extremely difficult to manage them all on the stage. Grouping these assets into containers will make the world of difference when managing your visual assets.

Bitmaps

When drawing a single loaded bitmap onto the stage, you use the Bitmap class. An instance of Bitmap is a display object and will be treated the same as your shapes when altering properties and animating. For instance, you could easily update your Progressive Break-it game to use loaded bitmap graphics, instead of drawing shapes, and all of the game code would work just fine. EaselJS includes many interesting methods for manipulating bitmaps, which allows us to do many cool effects on the pixels. You'll learn about these and other cool effects, but first, you must get the bitmap on to the stage.

Adding Bitmaps to the Stage

There are a few different ways of getting bitmaps on to the stage. The first, and simplest, approach is to simply pass the path to the image as a string into the new **Bitmap** instance.

```
var frank = new createjs.Bitmap('img/frank.png');
```

With this new bitmap object, you can add it to the stage and manipulate it like any other display object. Listing 5-1 shows the bitmap positioned on the stage, with an alpha of 50 percent.

Listing 5-1. Bitmap Object Added and Faded on the Stage

```
var frank = new createjs.Bitmap('img/frank.png');
stage.addChild(frank);
frank.x = 100;
frank.y = 40;
frank.alpha = .5;
stage.update();
```

A new, semi-transparent bitmap is shown in Figure 5-1.

Figure 5-1. *Bitmap object added to stage and faded*

With this approach, EaselJS will load in the image from the path you pass into it. This approach might work in some situations, but if the image was not yet loaded, it won't appear until the next stage update. In games, the slightest delay in graphic rendering can make your game look pretty bad. It's better if you already know that your asset is loaded before attempting to create and add a bitmap to your game.

Let's try another approach, where you will pass an Image JavaScript object into the constructor, as opposed to a string. Listing 5-2 shows this alternative approach.

Listing 5-2. Image Object Used to Create Bitmap Object

```
var img = new Image();
img.addEventListener('load', drawFrank);
img.src = 'img/frank.png';

function drawFrank(e){
    var frank = new createjs.Bitmap(e.target);
    stage.addChild(frank);
    stage.update();
}
```

With the bitmap loaded, you can be assured that it will show the moment you add it to the stage. However, you can do even better by using PreloadJS to load in the assets, and using their ids to pass into the new bitmap objects. Listing 5-3 loads in three bitmap assets and aligns them along the stage.

Listing 5-3. Three Bitmap Objects Created Using PreloadJS

```
var stage, queue;

// onload
function preload() {
    queue = new createjs.LoadQueue();
    queue.addEventListener("complete", drawCharacters);
```

```
    queue.loadManifest([
        {id:"frank", src:"img/frank.png"},
        {id:"v1", src:"img/villager1.png"},
        {id:"v2", src:"img/villager2.png"}
    ]);
}

function drawCharacters(){
    stage = new createjs.Stage('canvas');
    var frank = new createjs.Bitmap(queue.getResult('frank'));
    var villager1 = new createjs.Bitmap(queue.getResult('v1'));
    var villager2 = new createjs.Bitmap(queue.getResult('v2'));
    frank.y = villager1.y = villager2.y = 40;
    frank.x = 20;
    villager1.x = 190;
    villager2.x = 360;
    stage.addChild(frank,villager1,villager2);
    stage.update();
}
```

As you can see in the previous example, the ids that were assigned to the assets when loading them via PreloadJS are accessible when creating new bitmap objects. Figure 5-2 shows this result, which lines the bitmap characters up across the stage.

Figure 5-2. *Three bitmap objects added to the stage*

Adding Effects

You can add some interesting effects to bitmaps using EaselJS. Although these effects are not exclusive to bitmaps, we'll discuss how you can use them by applying them to the previously used characters. A pretty common effect is a drop shadow, which can easily be applied to bitmaps. Listing 5-4 shows the updates in bold. The result is shown in Figure 5-3.

Listing 5-4. Drop Shadow Effect on Bitmap Object

```
function drawCharacters() {
    var frank = new createjs.Bitmap(queue.getResult('frank'));
    var villager1 = new createjs.Bitmap(queue.getResult('v1'));
    var villager2 = new createjs.Bitmap(queue.getResult('v2'));
    frank.y = villager1.y = villager2.y = 40;
    frank.x = 20;
    villager1.x = 190;
    villager2.x = 360;
    stage.addChild(frank, villager1, villager2);
    villager1.shadow = new createjs.Shadow('#000', 5, 5, 8);
    stage.update();
}
```

Figure 5-3. *Drop shadow effect applied to second character*

Now the first villager has a nice drop shadow applied to it, which gives it a little more depth. There are a handful of other interesting effects that are bundled in with CreateJS as well. Unlike shadow, which is a direct property of display objects, these other effects are applied via the filters property. This property is an array, so you can apply more than one filter to the object. To apply a filter, you must first instantiate one of the handful of filter objects included in EaselJS. Let's start with a blur effect on Frank (see Listing 5-5).

Listing 5-5. Blur Effect on Bitmap Object

```
function drawCharacters() {
    var frank = new createjs.Bitmap(queue.getResult('frank'));
    var villager1 = new createjs.Bitmap(queue.getResult('v1'));
    var villager2 = new createjs.Bitmap(queue.getResult('v2'));
    frank.y = villager1.y = villager2.y = 40;
    frank.x = 20;
    villager1.x = 190;
    villager2.x = 360;
    stage.addChild(frank, villager1, villager2);
    villager1.shadow = new createjs.Shadow('#000', 5, 5, 8);
```

```
    var w = frank.image.width;
    var h = frank.image.height;
    var blur = new createjs.BoxBlurFilter(5, 5, 1);
    frank.filters = [blur];
    frank.cache(0, 0, w, h);
    stage.update();
}
```

▨ **Note**   The filter classes are not included in the single EaselJS file. They are all contained in a separate folder called `filters` and must be individually included in your document. This folder was included in your downloading of EaselJS.

An important thing to note when it comes to filtering is that the display object must be cached for the effect to take place. To use caching, you need to provide the bounds of the cache, which is supplied here by the `frank` bitmap image. By caching the bitmap, it is drawn into a new canvas, which will be used for its future drawing to the stage. Because of this, the caching must come *after* you assign the filter. If at any time you wish to update your display object, the update method must be called on `cache` so your updates will be seen in subsequent draws. This blur effect on Frank is shown in Figure 5-4.

Figure 5-4. *Blur effect applied to first character*

▨ **Note**   It is recommended that you never cache a simple bitmap; however, it is essential when applying filters.

As previously mentioned, the `filters` property is actually an array. Even if you only apply one filter, it must be assigned as an array. When you applied the `blur` filter to Frank, it was built as an array that contained one filter.

```
frank.filters = [blur];
```

The final effects example will demonstrate how you can apply multiple filters to a bitmap. The same `blur` filter will be used to go along with a new effect using the `ColorFilter` class. Listing 5-6 adds some filters to the final characters.

Listing 5-6. Color and Blur Effect on Bitmap Object

```
function drawCharacters() {
    var frank = new createjs.Bitmap(queue.getResult('frank'));
    var villager1 = new createjs.Bitmap(queue.getResult('v1'));
    var villager2 = new createjs.Bitmap(queue.getResult('v2'));
    frank.y = villager1.y = villager2.y = 40;
    frank.x = 20;
    villager1.x = 190;
    villager2.x = 360;
    stage.addChild(frank, villager1, villager2);
    var w = frank.image.width;
    var h = frank.image.height;
    villager1.shadow = new createjs.Shadow('#000', 5, 5, 8);
    var blur = new createjs.BoxBlurFilter(5, 5, 1);
    frank.filters = [blur];
    frank.cache(0, 0, w, h);
    var color = new createjs.ColorFilter(1, 0, 0, 1, 0, 0, 0, 0);
    villager2.filters = [color, blur];
    villager2.cache(0, 0, w + 10, h + 10);
    stage.update();
}
```

In the color filter, the first three RGB parameters are used to build the color. Each value accepts a value between 0 and 1. By setting the red multiplier to 1, and the rest to 0, the red color is created. The fourth parameter is alpha and is set to 1, and the final three are for offset color values, which will be left at 0. Along with the blur effect, the final result is shown in Figure 5-5.

Figure 5-5. *Blur and color effects applied to third character*

There are more filters available, along with endless combinations and techniques that can be used for adding effects and transforming bitmaps. These can be made to fit many types of games and applications; however, be careful not to go too crazy with these effects. Filtering can be pretty taxing on the computer and could slow down performance. In games, it's often best to render your effects in your image processor, and load those bitmaps into your game. We'll cover these techniques when discussing sprites and sprite sheets in Chapter 6.

Masking and Clipping

Along with filters, you can also apply masking and clipping to bitmaps. To use masking, simply use a Shape object, and apply it to the display object's mask property.

```
myBitmap.mask = myShape;
```

Listing 5-7 shows how you can apply a circle shape as the mask for a loaded photograph.

Listing 5-7. Masking a Photo Using a Shape

```
var bmp = new createjs.Bitmap('img/mam.png');
var circle = new createjs.Shape(new createjs.Graphics().drawCircle(0,0,250));
circle.x = 620;
circle.y = 300;
stage.addChild(bmp);
bmp.mask = circle;
stage.update();
```

The shape is simply positioned and set as the mask for the photograph. You can use any shape, simple like this circle or as complex as a star, to mask display objects. Figure 5-6 shows your masked photograph.

Figure 5-6. *Photograph with a circular mask using a shape object*

Masking can be extremely handy in a lot of situations. Take a look at a simple, yet clever example where masking is used to see the inside of a teddy bear (see Listing 5-8). Some controls will be added to the mask as well to give it some fun interaction.

Listing 5-8. Creating an Interactive Mask to Create an X-ray Effect

```
var stage;

// onload
function init() {
   stage = new createjs.Stage('canvas');
   buildBears();
   startGame();
}

function buildBears() {
   var bear = new createjs.Bitmap('img/bear.png');
   var bearUnder = new createjs.Bitmap('img/bearUnder.png');
   var mask = new createjs.Shape(new createjs.Graphics().drawCircle(0, 0, 50));
   bearUnder.mask = mask;
   stage.addChild(mask,bear, bearUnder);
   mask.addEventListener('tick', function (e) {
      e.currentTarget.x = stage.mouseX;
      e.currentTarget.y = stage.mouseY;
   })
}

function startGame() {
   createjs.Ticker.setFPS(60);
   createjs.Ticker.addEventListener("tick", function (e) {
      stage.update();
   });
}
```

In this example, two bear graphics are stacked directly on top of each other. The skeleton version is laid on top so it can be masked, which will reveal a small portion and give it the illusion of an x-ray feature. The event tick can be used on any display object to tap into the game's ticker. In this example, it is being used to update the position of the mask to match the mouse pointer. Figure 5-7 shows this feature in action.

Figure 5-7. *X-ray bear, using two bitmaps and a moveable mask*

Clipping is another technique that can be used with bitmaps. When you create a new bitmap and add it to the stage, the entire bounds of that bitmap are used. However, you don't need to use the entire image if you wish to only display a portion of it. This can be accomplished by using the sourceRect property, which takes a Rectangle object. The following is a sample of this technique being used:

```
var piece = new createjs.Bitmap('img/mam.png');
var rect = new createjs.Rectangle(100, 100, 100, 100);
piece.sourceRect = rect;
```

The Rectangle object is part of the EaselJS API, and takes four parameters: x, y, width, and height. These values will be used as the area of the bitmap image that you want to display in the bitmap object. This is accomplished simply by assigning the bitmap objects sourceRect to the rectangle.

Let's take this a bit further and create two bitmaps from the same image, and add them to the stage, shown in Listing 5-9. Figure 5-8 demonstrates the final result.

Listing 5-9. Using sourceRect to Clip Bitmap Graphics

```
var bmp1 = new createjs.Bitmap('img/mam.png');
var bmp2 = new createjs.Bitmap('img/mam.png');
var rect = new createjs.Rectangle(0, 0, 200, 200);
bmp1.sourceRect = rect;
rect = new createjs.Rectangle(200, 400, 200, 200);
bmp2.sourceRect = rect;
bmp1.x = 20;
bmp2.x = 240;
bmp1.y = bmp2.y = 20;
stage.addChild(bmp1, bmp2);
stage.update();
```

Figure 5-8. *Two bitmap objects using different portions of the same source*

This technique leads us to the first exercise in this chapter. It will use clipping, along with some simple filter effects, to create a puzzle game using a single photograph image.

Puzzle Swap

Puzzle Swap is a puzzle game where the player moves pieces by selecting the puzzle pieces they wish to swap. Once all pieces are in their appropriate locations, the image is revealed and the player wins.

- Load in a single bitmap image.
- Create multiple bitmap objects that contain only pieces of the full bitmap.
- Display all bitmap pieces in place for three seconds at the start of game.
- Explode pieces by shuffling them all to random places.
- Allow users to swap pieces until all pieces are in place.
- Selected puzzle pieces are indicated by a color filter that is applied when the piece is selected.

Setting up the Game Files

First, set up the HTML document that includes a canvas element and the necessary CreateJS file includes (see Listing 5-10). You will be using some color filters, so remember to include the appropriate filter scripts as well. The game code will be written in a separate file named puzzle.js. Be sure to create this file and include it in the document.

Listing 5-10. HTML File for Puzzle Swap

```html
<!DOCTYPE html>
<html>
<head>
    <title></title>
    <script src="lib/easeljs-0.7.1.min.js"></script>
    <script src="lib/tweenjs-0.5.1.min.js"></script>
    <script src="lib/filters/ColorMatrix.js"></script>
    <script src="lib/filters/ColorMatrixFilter.js"></script>
    <script src="puzzle.js"></script>
</head>

<body onload="init()">

<canvas id="canvas" width="1000" height="600" style="border: black solid 1px"></canvas>

</body>

</html>
```

Initializing the Game

Moving over to the puzzle.js file, some game constants and variables are first declared. Following this, the init function is written (see Listing 5-11), which is fired on the onload body event.

Listing 5-11. puzzle.js Game Variable and init Function

```javascript
const PUZZLE_COLUMNS = 5;
const PUZZLE_ROWS = 3;
const PUZZLE_SIZE = 200;

var stage;
var pieces = [];
var selectedPieces = [];

function init() {
    stage = new createjs.Stage(document.getElementById('canvas'));
    buildPuzzle();
    startGame();
    setTimeout(shufflePuzzle, 3000);
}
```

The constants created will be used in creating the graphics for the puzzle pieces and creating the grid to lay them out on. A couple of arrays are created to store all of the puzzle pieces, and another for the pieces that are selected to swap. The init function sets up the stage, and then calls a list of functions. The function buildPuzzle is first called to set up the puzzle pieces.

Building the Puzzle Pieces

The puzzle pieces are created by slicing out chunks of graphics from a complete bitmap file. This process is shown in Listing 5-12.

Listing 5-12. Building the Puzzle Pieces from a Loaded Bitmap Graphic

```
function buildPuzzle() {
    var i, piece;
    var l = PUZZLE_COLUMNS * PUZZLE_ROWS;
    var col = 0;
    var row = 0;
    for (i = 0; i < l; i++) {
        piece = new createjs.Bitmap('img/mam.png');
        piece.sourceRect = new createjs.Rectangle(col * PUZZLE_SIZE, row * PUZZLE_SIZE,
            PUZZLE_SIZE, PUZZLE_SIZE);
        piece.homePoint = {x: col * PUZZLE_SIZE, y: row * PUZZLE_SIZE};
        piece.x = piece.homePoint.x;
        piece.y = piece.homePoint.y;
        stage.addChild(piece);
        pieces[i] =  piece;
        col ++;
        if (col === PUZZLE_COLUMNS) {
            col = 0;
            row ++;
        }
    }
}
```

The pieces in the puzzle are all created in a loop that has the length of the total pieces. Multiplying the number of columns by the number of rows, declared in the game constants, determines this total number. Starting with column 0 and row 0, the col and row variables are set to represent these values.

The first thing you do in the loop is create a bitmap object using the png file used for the puzzle. Since only a specific portion of the graphic is wanted for each piece, a Rectangle object is created by using the current column and row, and the size of the puzzle pieces. Using these values, the areas of the bitmap can be calculated for each piece.

```
piece.sourceRect = new createjs.Rectangle(col * PUZZLE_SIZE, row * PUZZLE_SIZE,  PUZZLE_SIZE,
    PUZZLE_SIZE);
```

Next, each piece is assigned a point object, which holds the location of each piece's home coordinates. The x and y values are immediately assigned to each bitmap so the puzzle starts out intact. This gives the player a view of the puzzle at its complete state. They are each then added to the stage and pushed to the pieces array.

Lastly, the current column is increased by one so the start location of the bitmap is adjusted in the next iteration. If you've reached the end of the total columns, it's reset back to 0, and the current row is increased by one.

The result is shown in Figure 5-9. Although it looks as though you have a single bitmap, there are actually a total of 15 bitmap objects, perfectly placed on the stage.

Figure 5-9. *Fifteen bitmap objects perfectly placed to form a complete image*

Shuffling the Puzzle Pieces

The puzzle will appear intact for three seconds before its pieces shuffle. With the three-second timeout you created in the init function, shufflePuzzle is called to shuffle the order of each puzzle piece (see Listing 5-13).

Listing 5-13. *Randomly Placing the Bitmap Objects into New Locations*

```
function shufflePuzzle() {
   var i, piece, randomIndex;
   var col = 0;
   var row = 0;
   var p = [];
   p = p.concat(pieces);
   var l = p.length;
   for (i = 0; i < l; i++) {
      randomIndex= Math.floor(Math.random() * p.length)
      piece = p[randomIndex];
      p.splice(randomIndex, 1);
      createjs.Tween.get(piece).to({x:col * PUZZLE_SIZE, y: row * PUZZLE_SIZE},200);
      piece.addEventListener('click', onPieceClick);
      col++;
      if (col === PUZZLE_COLUMNS) {
         col = 0;
         row++;
      }
   }
}
```

To shuffle the bitmap objects into new locations, a loop is set up, similar to the one that was used to create them. Since you want to keep the game array `pieces` intact for game evaluations, a clone of it is made to use for the loop.

```
var p = [];
p = p.concat(pieces);
```

You'll be randomly grabbing and splicing out objects for the shuffling, so this cloning process is essential. The length of this array is stored away in the variable l for the loop length. This is done because of the splicing that will be taking place. A random value is generated and is used to find a puzzle piece in the array, which is immediately taken out to prevent being chosen again. The new location for each piece is then determined, using the same grid calculations used when the pieces were first created. The pieces are then tweened to this location.

Figure 5-10 demonstrates the puzzle pieces being shuffled to new locations.

Figure 5-10. *The puzzle pieces shuffled to random locations*

Moving Puzzle Pieces

Before evaluating the current column in the loop, a click event listener is set, which will call the function `onPieceClick` and is shown in Listing 5-14.

Listing 5-14. Selecting the Puzzle Pieces

```
function onPieceClick(e) {
    if (selectedPieces === 2) {
        return;
    }
```

```
    var piece = e.target;
    var matrix = new createjs.ColorMatrix().adjustColor(15, 10, 100, 180);
    piece.filters = [
        new createjs.ColorMatrixFilter(matrix)
    ];
    piece.cache(0, 0, PUZZLE_SIZE, PUZZLE_SIZE);
    selectedPieces.push(piece);
    if (selectedPieces.length === 2) {
        evalSelectedPieces();
    }
}
```

The selected pieces are pushed to the selectedPieces array, so a quick check is written to prevent more than two pieces from being selected. If still under two, a reference to the bitmap clicked is set to the local variable piece.

For visual indication that a puzzle piece was chosen, a color filter will be created and applied to the bitmap. Using some of the techniques learned in the "Adding Effects" section, a single filter is applied to the bitmap when clicked and is pushed into the selectedPieces array.

Finally, you check if there have been two bitmaps that have been selected, and if so, the swapPieces function is called (see Listing 5-15).

Listing 5-15. Swapping the Locations of the Bitmap Objects when Two Are Selected

```
function swapPieces() {
    var piece1 = selectedPieces[0];
    var piece2 = selectedPieces[1];
    createjs.Tween.get(piece1).wait(300).to({x:piece2.x, y:piece2.y},200);
    createjs.Tween.get(piece2).wait(300).to({x:piece1.x, y:piece1.y},200).call(function(){
        setTimeout(evalPuzzle,200);
    });
}
```

A reference to each piece is first assigned to a few variables. A few tweens are then created to swap the location of each piece. The call method is used on the second tween to call on the function evalPuzzle, which will determine if the puzzle is complete (see Listing 5-16). A short timeout is set to fire this function as a safety precaution to assure that the pieces are in their new locations before evaluating them.

Listing 5-16. Evaluating the Puzzle to See Whether All Pieces Are in Place

```
function evalPuzzle() {
    var win = true;
    var i, piece;
    selectedPieces[0].uncache();
    selectedPieces[1].uncache();
    for (i = 0; i < pieces.length; i++) {
        piece = pieces[i];
        if (piece.x != piece.homePoint.x || piece.y != piece.homePoint.y) {
            win = false;
            break;
        }
    }
```

```
    if (win) {
       setTimeout(function () {
          alert('YOU DID IT!');
       }, 200);
    }
    else {
       selectedPieces = [];
    }
}
```

Before looping through and evaluating each puzzle piece's location, the bitmaps are uncached, which will remove the effect filter applied to them. In the loop, you simply check each piece to see if either their x or y position does *not* match their "home" location. If this is the case at any time during the loop, you know that the puzzle cannot be complete. The local win variable will then be set to false, and the loop is broken.

The win value is checked, and if true, a simple alert is called to award the user with a message. If not, the selectedPieces array is emptied, allowing the player to continue swapping puzzle pieces.

Lastly, the typical startGame function (shown in Listing 5-17) is used to run the stage updates.

Listing 5-17. Ticker and Stage Update Function

```
function startGame() {
   createjs.Ticker.addEventListener("tick", function(){
      stage.update();
   });
   createjs.Ticker.setFPS(60);
}
```

The Complete Puzzle Swap Code

The complete code for the puzzle game is shown in Listing 5-18.

Listing 5-18. The Complete Code for puzzle.js

```
const PUZZLE_COLUMNS = 5;
const PUZZLE_ROWS = 3;
const PUZZLE_SIZE = 200;

var stage;
var pieces = [];
var selectedPieces = [];

function init() {
   stage = new createjs.Stage('canvas');
   buildPuzzle();
   startGame();
   setTimeout(shufflePuzzle, 2000);
}
function buildPuzzle() {
   var i, piece;
   var l = PUZZLE_COLUMNS * PUZZLE_ROWS;
   var col = 0;
   var row = 0;
```

```
    for (i = 0; i < l; i++) {
        piece = new createjs.Bitmap('img/mam.png');
        piece.sourceRect = new createjs.Rectangle(col * PUZZLE_SIZE,
            row * PUZZLE_SIZE, PUZZLE_SIZE, PUZZLE_SIZE);
        piece.homePoint = {x:col * PUZZLE_SIZE, y: row * PUZZLE_SIZE};
        piece.x = piece.homePoint.x;
        piece.y = piece.homePoint.y;
        stage.addChild(piece);
        pieces[i] = piece;
        col ++;
        if (col === PUZZLE_COLUMNS) {
            col = 0;
            row ++;
        }
    }
}
function shufflePuzzle() {
    var i, piece, randomIndex;
    var col = 0;
    var row = 0;
    var p = [];
    p = p.concat(pieces);
    var l = p.length;
    for (i = 0; i < l; i++) {
        randomIndex= Math.floor(Math.random() * p.length)
        piece = p[randomIndex];
        p.splice(randomIndex, 1);
        createjs.Tween.get(piece).to({x:col * PUZZLE_SIZE, y:row * PUZZLE_SIZE},200);
        piece.addEventListener('click', onPieceClick);
        col++;
        if (col === PUZZLE_COLUMNS) {
            col = 0;
            row++;
        }
    }
}
function onPieceClick(e) {
    if (selectedPieces === 2) {
        return;
    }
    var piece = e.target;
    var matrix = new createjs.ColorMatrix().adjustColor(15, 10, 100, 180);
    piece.filters = [
        new createjs.ColorMatrixFilter(matrix)
    ];
    piece.cache(0, 0, PUZZLE_SIZE, PUZZLE_SIZE);
    selectedPieces.push(piece);
    if (selectedPieces.length === 2) {
        swapPieces();
    }
}
```

```
function swapPieces() {
    var piece1 = selectedPieces[0];
    var piece2 = selectedPieces[1];
    createjs.Tween.get(piece1).wait(300).to({x:piece2.x, y:piece2.y},200);
    createjs.Tween.get(piece2).wait(300).to({x:piece1.x, y:piece1.y},200).call(function(){
        setTimeout(evalPuzzle,200);
    });
}
function evalPuzzle() {
    var win = true;
    var i, piece;
    selectedPieces[0].uncache();
    selectedPieces[1].uncache();
    for (i = 0; i < pieces.length; i++) {
        piece = pieces[i];
        if (piece.x != piece.homePoint.x || piece.y != piece.homePoint.y) {
            win = false;
            break;
        }
    }
    if (win) {
        setTimeout(function () {
            alert('YOU DID IT!');
        }, 200);
    }
    else {
        selectedPieces = [];
    }
}
function startGame() {
    createjs.Ticker.addEventListener("tick", function(){
        stage.update();
    });
    createjs.Ticker.setFPS(60);
}
```

Now that you've seen how to load and manipulate loaded bitmap graphics in your games, you'll next learn how you can properly manage them using containers.

Containers

Containers are used to group multiple display objects into a single, contained group, which can be positioned and manipulated as a single display object. These containers have their own display list. In fact, Stage is actually a container itself that merely resides at the root of your application. You'll quickly see the benefits in using containers, which are built by using the Container class.

Building Containers

The Container class is used to build container objects. Once a container is made, you can add and remove children to it exactly in the same manner as you have been with Stage. The following is an example of how to create a container, add a few shapes to it, and ultimately add it to the stage:

```
var group = new createjs.Container();
group.addChild(shape1);
group.addChild(shape2);
group.x = container.y = 100;
stage.addChild(group);
```

In this code, the new group object has two children added to it, shape1 and shape2. It is then added to the stage, which now has group as its only child. The stage is now the parent of group, and can be accessed via the group's parent property. Likewise, group is now the parent of both shape1 and shape2.

```
var parent = group.parent; //Stage
parent = shape1.parent;    //group
```

Let's put this into a working example, which creates two containers and is shown in Listing 5-19.

Listing 5-19. Two containers, Populated with Various Display Objects

```
var container1 = new createjs.Container();
var container2 = new createjs.Container();
var pepper = new createjs.Bitmap('img/pepper.png')
var circle = new createjs.Shape(new createjs.Graphics().beginFill('#FF0000')
    .drawCircle(0, 0, 50));
var square = new createjs.Shape(new createjs.Graphics().beginFill('#00FF00')
    .drawRect(0, 0, 50, 50));
var txt = new createjs.Text("Hello Containers", "20px Arial", "#000");
var bg = new createjs.Shape(new createjs.Graphics().beginStroke('#000')
    .drawRect(0, 0, 250, 250));
container1.addChild(bg);
bg = new createjs.Shape(new createjs.Graphics().beginStroke('#000')
    .drawRect(0, 0, 250, 250));
container2.addChild(bg);
txt.x = txt.y = 10;
circle.x = circle.y = 125;
container1.addChild(txt, circle);
square.x = square.y = 10;
pepper.x = pepper.y = 100;
container2.addChild(square, pepper);
container1.x = 20;
container2.x = 320;
container1.y = container2.y = 40;
stage.addChild(container1, container2);
stage.update();
```

Two containers are created and then populated with various display objects, including shapes, text, and bitmaps. Each container shares the same background shape, which acts as its visual bounds. The result is shown in Figure 5-11.

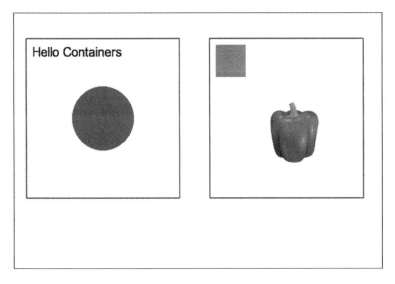

Figure 5-11. *Two containers with shapes, bitmaps, and text added to their display lists*

The result is two containers on the stage, each acting as one, unified group with its own display list. You can position and even animate each container as a whole, and access their children using the same methods you've been using on stage.

Animating and Cloning Containers

When animating containers, you treat them like any other display object. You can easily target a container when using tweens in your application. Listing 5-20 is an example of how you would accomplish this.

Listing 5-20. Rotating a Container Around its Center Axis

```
var container = new createjs.Container();
var pepper = new createjs.Bitmap('img/pepper.png')
var txt = new createjs.Text("Green Pepper", "20px Arial", "#000");
var bg = new createjs.Shape(new createjs.Graphics().beginStroke('#000')
    .drawRect(0, 0, 250, 250));
txt.x = txt.y = 10;
pepper.x = pepper.y = 80;
container.regX = container.regY = 125;
container.x = 300;
container.y = 200;
container.addChild(bg, txt, pepper);
stage.addChild(container);
createjs.Tween.get(container).to({rotation:360},4000);
```

As you can see from the previous example, you can also set the registration point on a container, which allows you to spin them around their center point. Figure 5-12 demonstrates this in action.

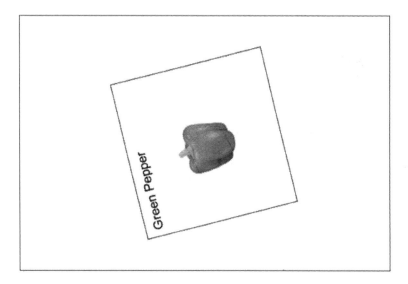

Figure 5-12. *Rotating animation applied to a container*

Figure 5-12 should give you an idea on how helpful containers can be in your games. In fact, they are actually pretty essential. You'll also run into to situations where you may need several containers that that contain the same visuals. The clone method can be used to accomplish this.

If you recall, the clone method was used on a text object during the word game in Chapter 3. This was very helpful in that it prevented you from having to recreate the styles and properties needed to create the same text object. With containers, there will often times be several objects added and positioned inside it. You really only need to build this once and then take advantage of the clone method to duplicate it. Listing 5-21 shows this being done.

Listing 5-21. Cloning a Container

```
var container = new createjs.Container();
var pepper = new createjs.Bitmap('img/pepper.png')
var txt = new createjs.Text("Green Pepper", "20px Arial", "#000");
var bg = new createjs.Shape(new createjs.Graphics().beginStroke('#000')
  .drawRect(0, 0, 250, 250));
txt.x = txt.y = 10;
pepper.x = pepper.y = 80;
container.regX = container.regY = 125;
container.x = 150;
container.y = 200;
container.addChild(bg, txt, pepper);
container2 = container.clone(true);
container2.x = 430;
container2.y = 200;
stage.addChild(container,container2);
```

The first container is built by populating its display objects. A new container is then built and is created by using the clone method on the first container. Its positioning is set, and both containers are then added to the stage. Figure 5-13 shows two identical containers on the stage.

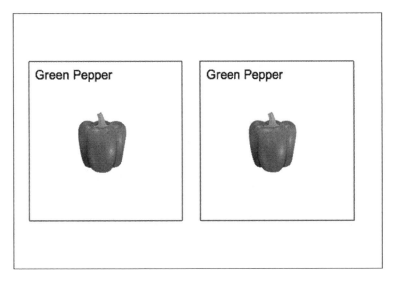

Figure 5-13. *Cloning a container*

One thing you'll notice, unlike the text-cloning example, is that you pass in the value of true to the clone method. This is so it will be executed in *recursive* mode, which will clone all children within the container, as well as its children's children. To duplicate all objects in your container, be sure to pass this value in when using clone.

Now that you've learned how to group and manipulate display objects into containers, it's time to put them into a game. A great example for the use of containers in games is when using them for creating playing cards. Let's do that now in the next exercise, which will demonstrate the true power in containers.

Veggie Match

Veggie Match is a simple memory game where the player tries to match cards by revealing them two at a time.

- Preload images needed to build card containers.
- Build cards using Container, and add a card shell, card back, food graphic, and a text object.
- Apply a drop shadow to each card object.
- Flip each card on click by hiding the *back* bitmap in the container.
- Flip back over if guessed wrong by revealing the card's *back* bitmap.
- End the game when all cards are successfully flipped over.

Setting Up the Game Files

First, set up the HTML document that includes a canvas element and the necessary CreateJS file includes (see Listing 5-22). The game code will be written in a separate file and named memory.js. Be sure to create this file and include it in the document.

Listing 5-22. HTML File for Veggie Match

```html
<!DOCTYPE html>
<html>
<head>
    <title></title>
    <script src="../../lib/easeljs-0.7.1.min.js"></script>
    <script src="../../lib/preloadjs-NEXT.min.js"></script>
    <script src="../../lib/tweenjs-0.5.1.min.js"></script>
    <script src="memory.js"></script>
</head>

<body onload="preload()">

<canvas id="canvas" width="650" height="650" style="border: black solid 1px"></canvas>

</body>

</html>
```

Initializing the Game

A series of game variables is first declared, and a preload function is used to load in bitmaps before initializing the game (see Listing 5-23).

Listing 5-23. Game Variables and Preload Function to Load in all Graphics

```javascript
var stage, queue;

var faces = ['garlic', 'onion', 'pepper', 'potato', 'spinach', 'tomato'];
var cards = [];
var cardsFlipped = [];
var matches = 0;

function preload() {
    queue = new createjs.LoadQueue();
    queue.addEventListener("complete", init);
    queue.loadManifest([
        {id:"shell", src:"img/card.png"},
        {id:"back", src:"img/back.png"},
        {id:"garlic", src:"img/garlic.png"},
        {id:"onion", src:"img/onion.png"},
        {id:"pepper", src:"img/pepper.png"},
        {id:"potato", src:"img/potato.png"},
        {id:"spinach", src:"img/spinach.png"},
        {id:"tomato", src:"img/tomato.png"}
    ]);
}
```

The faces array is used for both creating ids for loaded bitmaps, and to write the label on each card. Similar to the puzzle pieces, an array is created to hold each card, and another to hold reference to the cards flipped over when a player is making their guesses.

The preload function is used to set up the loading of all of the bitmap graphics that will be used in the game. A new LoadQueue object is created and set to the game variable queue, which will give global access to the ids that were assigned to each bitmap in the manifest. When the files are successfully loaded, the game is initialized by calling init (see Listing 5-24).

Listing 5-24. The init Function Sets Up the Canvas and Calls a Series of Functions

```
function init() {
    stage = new createjs.Stage(document.getElementById('canvas'));
    buildCards();
    shuffleCards();
    dealCards();
    startGame();
}
```

The stage is created and a series of functions is then called, starting with buildCards, which is used to create the cards.

Creating the Cards

The cards are created by adding a series of display objects to containers. This process is shown in Listing 5-25.

Listing 5-25. Building and Cloning Containers for Each Card in the Game

```
function buildCards() {
    var i, card, card2, bmp, label, face;
    for (i = 0; i < faces.length; i++) {
        card = new createjs.Container();
        bmp = new createjs.Bitmap(queue.getResult('shell'));
        card.regX = bmp.image.width / 2;
        card.regY = bmp.image.height / 2;
        card.addChild(bmp);
        face = faces[i];
        bmp = new createjs.Bitmap(queue.getResult(face));
        bmp.regX = bmp.image.width / 2;
        bmp.regY = bmp.image.height / 2;
        bmp.x = card.regX;
        bmp.y = 70;
        card.addChild(bmp);
        label = new createjs.Text(faces[i].toUpperCase(), "20px Arial", "#FFF");
        label.textAlign = 'center';
        label.x = card.regX;
        label.y = 144;
        card.addChild(label);
        bmp = new createjs.Bitmap(queue.getResult('back'));
        bmp.name = 'back';
        card.addChild(bmp);
```

```
        card2 = card.clone(true);
        card.key = card2.key = faces[i];
        cards.push(card, card2);
        card.shadow = card2.shadow = new createjs.Shadow("#333", 3, 3, 5);
    }
}
```

This card-creating function consists of a single loop, which will build each container. The container is immediately created, which will hold all assets that make up the card. The base of each container will be the shell graphic. The registration point is set to be centered by using the width and height of the shell image, which is then added to the container.

Next, the food graphic is determined by using the loop count and the faces array. This bitmap is then horizontally centered, given a y value of 70, and then added to the container. The cards will also contain a text object to display the name of the food. This text value is also determined by the faces array and is assigned to a new text object, which is positioned and finally added to the card container. Figure 5-14 shows an example of a complete card container.

Figure 5-14. *A card container using text and bitmap objects*

The top-most graphic in each card is the back graphic, which will be shown or hidden to indicate the current state of the card. This bitmap will start out visible, and will be turned invisible to reveal the cards properties when it's selected during gameplay.

Two cards of each food item are needed, so this is a perfect opportunity to utilize the clone method on the card container. Be sure to pass true into the constructor so it is *recursively* cloned, which will duplicate all children in the container. A key value is assigned to each card, which will be used to determine if the selected cards are matching. You can simply use the unique *face* value for this property. Finally, a drop shadow is assigned to the card.

Shuffling the Cards

Before adding the cards to the stage, the cards need to be shuffled. The shuffleCards function will do this next (see Listing 5-26).

Listing 5-26. Shuffling the Cards Array and Animating Them on a Grid

```
function shuffleCards() {
    var i, card, randomIndex;
    var l = cards.length;
    var shuffledCards = [];
    for (i = 0; i < l; i++) {
        randomIndex = Math.floor(Math.random() * cards.length);
        shuffledCards.push(cards[randomIndex]);
        cards.splice(randomIndex, 1);
    }
    cards = cards.concat(shuffledCards);
}
function dealCards() {
    var i, card;
    var xPos = 100;
    var yPos = 100;
    var count = 0;
    for (i = 0; i < cards.length; i++) {
        card = cards[i];
        card.x = -200;
        card.y = 400;
        card.rotation = Math.random() * 600;
        card.addEventListener('click', flipCard);
        stage.addChild(card);
        createjs.Tween.get(card)
            .wait(i * 100)
            .to({x:xPos, y:yPos, rotation:0}, 300);
        xPos += 150;
        count++;
        if (count === 4) {
            count = 0;
            xPos = 100;
            yPos += 220;
        }
    }
}
```

Similar to the puzzle pieces shuffle, the cards array is used to shuffle the deck. It's handled a bit differently here to show an alternative way to shuffle object arrays. A local array named shuffledCards is first declared and set to empty. As you loop through the array cards, you select and splice out random card objects and push them to the local array shuffleCards. After the loop, simply give them back by concatenating the local array with the now-empty cards array.

```
cards = cards.concat(shuffledCards);
```

The result is a freshly shuffled deck of cards. Now it's time to deal them out in a grid on the stage. A loop is set up to add each card to the stage, starting off screen and randomly rotated. Each card is then ultimately animated to the locations determined in the loop. The result is shown in Figure 5-15.

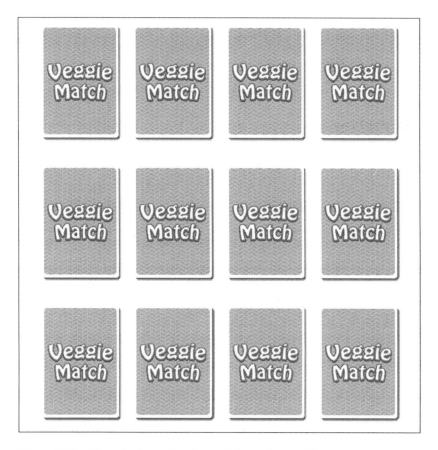

Figure 5-15. *All cards after animating to their random positions*

Flipping the Cards

Before adding the cards to the stage, a click event listener was added that will fire the function `flipCard`. When two cards are flipped, they are evaluated in the function `evalCardsFlipped`. These functions are shown in Listing 5-27.

Listing 5-27. *Flipping the Cards and Checking for Matches*

```
function flipCard(e) {
   if (cardsFlipped.length === 2) {
      return;
   }
   var card = e.target
   card.mouseEnabled = false;
   card.getChildByName('back').visible = false;
   cardsFlipped.push(card);
   if (cardsFlipped.length === 2) {
      evalCardsFlipped();
   }
}
```

```
function evalCardsFlipped() {
    if (cardsFlipped[0].key === cardsFlipped[1].key) {
        matches++;
        evalGame();
    }
    else {
        setTimeout(resetFlippedCards, 1000);
    }
}
```

Flipping a card is simple. As previously mentioned, the card is revealed by simply hiding its top-most graphic, which was named *back*. A conditional is first set to see if there are currently two cards already being evaluated; if not, the mouse events are immediately disabled on the card that was clicked. This prevents clicking the same card twice. Figure 5-16 shows the first two cards after they have been clicked.

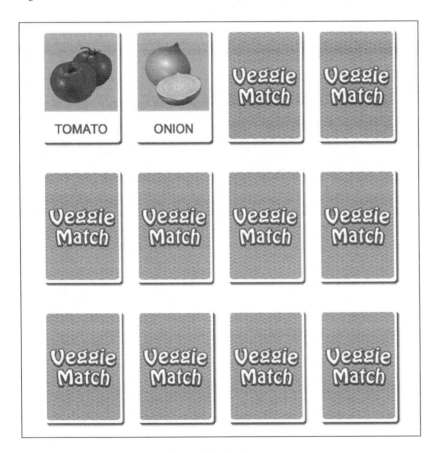

Figure 5-16. *Two cards after being clicked to flip over*

Once two cards are flipped, the evalCardsFlipped function is called to check if they match. The key properties on each card are used to determine this, and if a match was found, the match count is increased and the game is evaluated with the function evalGame. If they don't match, a small timeout is created to reset the flipped cards. Listing 5-28 shows these two functions, resetCardsFlipped and evalGame.

Listing 5-28. Resetting Cards when They Don't Match and Evaluating the Game when They Do

```
function resetFlippedCards() {
    cardsFlipped[0].mouseEnabled = cardsFlipped[1].mouseEnabled = true;
    cardsFlipped[0].getChildByName('back').visible = true;
    cardsFlipped[1].getChildByName('back').visible = true;
    cardsFlipped = [];
}
function evalGame() {
    if (matches === faces.length) {
        setTimeout(function () {
            alert('YOU WIN!')
        }, 300)
    }
    else {
        cardsFlipped = [];
    }
}
```

When the two cards flipped are not the same, the resetFlippedCards function is called to put them back in play. These cards were stored in the cardsFlipped array and are referenced here to reset each card. First, the mouseEnabled properties are set back to true so they can be chosen again. The back bitmaps are hidden, and finally the cardsFlipped array is emptied. At this point, the game is back in play.

When a match is made, you need to evaluate the game to see if all matches were made. The length of the faces array is the number of matches you need, and if it is reached, an alert message is displayed. If the game should carry on, simply leave the flipped cards alone and empty the cardsFlipped array, which will resume the game.

Finally, the typical startGame function is called to set up the Ticker to update the stage (see Listing 5-29).

Listing 5-29. The Ticker and Stage Update Function

```
function startGame() {
    createjs.Ticker.setFPS(60);
    createjs.Ticker.addEventListener("tick", function(e){
        stage.update();
    });
}
```

The Complete Veggie Match Code

The complete code for Veggie Match is shown in Listing 5-30.

Listing 5-30. The Complete Code for memory.js

```
var stage, queue;

var faces = ['garlic', 'onion', 'pepper', 'potato', 'spinach', 'tomato'];
var cards = [];
var cardsFlipped = [];
var matches = 0;
```

```
function preload() {
    queue = new createjs.LoadQueue();
    queue.addEventListener("complete", init);
    queue.loadManifest([
        {id:"shell", src:"img/card.png"},
        {id:"back", src:"img/back.png"},
        {id:"garlic", src:"img/garlic.png"},
        {id:"onion", src:"img/onion.png"},
        {id:"pepper", src:"img/pepper.png"},
        {id:"potato", src:"img/potato.png"},
        {id:"spinach", src:"img/spinach.png"},
        {id:"tomato", src:"img/tomato.png"}
    ]);
}

function init() {
    stage = new createjs.Stage(document.getElementById('canvas'));
    startGame();
    buildCards();
    shuffleCards();
    dealCards();
}
function buildCards() {
    var i, card, card2, bmp, label, face;
    for (i = 0; i < faces.length; i++) {
        card = new createjs.Container();
        bmp = new createjs.Bitmap(queue.getResult('shell'));
        bmp.shadow = new createjs.Shadow("#666", 3, 3, 5);
        card.regX = bmp.image.width / 2;
        card.regY = bmp.image.height / 2;
        card.addChild(bmp);
        face = faces[i];
        bmp = new createjs.Bitmap(queue.getResult(face));
        bmp.regX = bmp.image.width / 2;
        bmp.regY = bmp.image.height / 2;
        bmp.x = card.regX;
        bmp.y = 70;
        card.addChild(bmp);
        label = new createjs.Text(faces[i].toUpperCase(), "20px Arial", "#009900");
        label.textAlign = 'center';
        label.x = card.regX;
        label.y = 144;
        card.addChild(label);
        bmp = new createjs.Bitmap(queue.getResult('back'));
        bmp.name = 'back';
        card.addChild(bmp);
        card2 = card.clone(true);
        card.key = card2.key = faces[i];
        cards.push(card, card2);
    }
}
```

```
function shuffleCards() {
    var i, card, randomIndex;
    var l = cards.length;
    var shuffledCards = [];
    for (i = 0; i < l; i++) {
        randomIndex = Math.floor(Math.random() * cards.length);
        shuffledCards.push(cards[randomIndex]);
        cards.splice(randomIndex, 1);
    }
    cards = cards.concat(shuffledCards);
}
function dealCards() {
    var i, card;
    var xPos = 100;
    var yPos = 100;
    var count = 0;
    for (i = 0; i < cards.length; i++) {
        card = cards[i];
        card.x = -200;
        card.y = 400;
        card.rotation = Math.random() * 600;
        card.addEventListener('click', flipCard);
        stage.addChild(card);
        createjs.Tween.get(card)
            .wait(i * 100)
            .to({x:xPos, y:yPos, rotation:0}, 300);
        xPos += 150;
        count++;
        if (count === 4) {
            count = 0;
            xPos = 100;
            yPos += 220;
        }
    }
}
function flipCard(e) {
    if (cardsFlipped.length === 2) {
        return;
    }
    var card = e.target
    card.mouseEnabled = false;
    card.getChildByName('back').visible = false;
    cardsFlipped.push(card);
    if (cardsFlipped.length === 2) {
        evalCardsFlipped();
    }
}
```

```
function evalCardsFlipped() {
    if (cardsFlipped[0].key === cardsFlipped[1].key) {
        matches++;
        evalGame();
    }
    else {
        setTimeout(resetFlippedCards, 1000);
    }
}
function resetFlippedCards() {
    cardsFlipped[0].mouseEnabled = cardsFlipped[1].mouseEnabled = true;
    cardsFlipped[0].getChildByName('back').visible = true;
    cardsFlipped[1].getChildByName('back').visible = true;
    cardsFlipped = [];
}
function evalGame() {
    if (matches === faces.length) {
        setTimeout(function () {
            alert('YOU WIN!')
        }, 300)
    }
    else {
        cardsFlipped = [];
    }
}
function startGame() {
    createjs.Ticker.setFPS(60);
    createjs.Ticker.addEventListener("tick", function (e) {
        stage.update();
    });
}
```

These cards should give you an idea of the importance of creating containers. You'll be using them quite a bit as you move forward with more games. They can quickly become essential to graphic management in game development, and although this section on containers was rather short, most of your previously learned knowledge on Stage and the display list carries over.

Summary

In this chapter, you've taken a large step forward in making games look more polished by loading in graphics. The Bitmap object allows you to easily draw these graphics to the stage, and with some effects and filtering, you can create some cool and interesting features. You also learned the essential technique of grouping display objects by using the Container class.

In the next chapter, you will learn how to build sprite sheets, which will pack all bitmaps into a single file. These sprite sheets will be used to create *sprites*, which can be simple, static graphics, or full-blown animated sequences.

■ ■ ■

CHAPTER 6

Sprites and Sprite Sheet Animations

Loading in bitmap graphics is a necessary procedure and gives you the ability to further style and polish your games, but as your games require more and more graphics, it's not ideal to load them all individually. In this chapter, you'll learn how to better optimize your load times, and how to achieve even better performance by using sprite sheets. Using sprite sheets with EaselJS, you'll also see the benefit of using bitmap fonts, and how animated sprites can bring your characters to life.

Animation and sprite sheet applications will be covered and compared, and you'll see how you can use them to prepare your assets for single frame or animated sprites for EaselJS. These procedures all revolve around the sprite sheet.

Sprite Sheets

Sprite sheets are images that contain many images within a single file. They are usually accompanied by a corresponding data file that specifies the regions for each image. A sprite sheet can be built to specify both images and image sequences, or *sprite animations*. Figure 6-1 shows an example of what a sprite sheet might look like when creating the assets for a mancala game.

Figure 6-1. *Sprite sheet using graphics for a mancala game*

As you can see from Figure 6-1, all of your graphics are crammed into a single, bitmap file. The benefit of this is that you only need to load in one image, as opposed to every single .png file individually. In a simple game with static graphics, such as this mancala example, you would most likely be fine with separate graphics. But as your games get larger and require more graphics, sprite sheets are the way to go to decrease load times and increase performance.

Before getting into the creation of these sprite sheet images and their corresponding data, let's take a look at how you will be using them in EaselJS.

SpriteSheet Class

The SpriteSheet class is used to create the data necessary to extract the graphics from a sprite sheet. You can use this for both single sprites and sprite animations. A SpriteSheet object needs data passed into it to properly instantiate. This data requires the following information:

- images: This property is an array that will take the image, or images that will be used. These images can be ids from PreloadJS or paths to the files.

- frames: This property can be a complex array or a simple object. The array approach will hold several arrays, one for each frame in the sprite sheet graphic. These arrays hold the rectangle data (x, y, width, and height) of each frame. If all frames are actually the same size, a single object can be used to specify the width and height of all frames.

- animations: This property is an object, which will contain animation objects for each sprite or sprite animation.

Listing 6-1 is an example of the data that would be used for a SpriteSheet object, using the sprite sheet image show in in Figure 6-1.

Listing 6-1. Data Format for SpriteSheet Objects

```
var data = {
    "images":["mancala.png"],
    "frames":[
        [2, 2, 903, 331],
        [826, 409, 59, 51],
        [356, 335, 117, 150],
        [588, 335, 117, 133],
        [707, 335, 117, 124],
        [2, 335, 118, 170],
        [239, 335, 115, 152],
        [122, 335, 115, 142],
        [475, 335, 111, 146],
        [826, 335, 75, 72],
        [142, 479, 16, 25],
        [122, 482, 18, 22],
        [160, 482, 18, 19],
        [907, 242, 127, 238],
        [907, 2, 127, 238]
    ],
    "animations":{
        "board":[0],
        "bubble":[1],
        "chooseCPU1":[2],
        "chooseCPU2":[3],
```

```
        "chooseCPU3":[4],
        "cpu1":[5],
        "cpu2":[6],
        "cpu3":[7],
        "frank":[8],
        "scoreBrick":[9],
        "stone_0":[10],
        "stone_1":[11],
        "stone_2":[12],
        "stone_3":[13],
        "window":[14],
        "windowOn":[15]
    }
};
```

In this example, only one image is used for your data, `mancala.png`. The second object, `frames`, defines the bounds of each frame in the image. There are 15 frames in this particular sprite sheet.

The `animations` property is an object that holds the frames, by index for single or multi-frame sprites. For each of these animation properties, the key string will be used to access it when creating a new sprite, and its value is an array of frames you wish to use. This array can be written to do a few different things in the animations, and will be covered more in depth in the "Sprite Sheet Animations" section later in this chapter. For now, you'll be focusing on single-frame sprites, which are shown in the example data above.

With the data object written, it can then be passed into a new `SpriteSheet` object.

```
var spritesheet = new createjs.SpriteSheet(data);
```

Creating the sprite sheet image and its corresponding data can often be complicated or laborious. For this, you would typically use an application that specializes in creating both the sprite sheet image and the sprite sheet data by importing a series of images. Let's see how this can be accomplished by using the popular application Texture Packer.

Creating Sprite Sheets with Texture Packer

Texture Packer is an application that makes it easy to create sprite sheets. It supports a wide range of platforms for data formatting, including EaselJS. To get started, download and install a trial version, which can be located at `www.codeandweb.com/texturepacker` (see Figure 6-2).

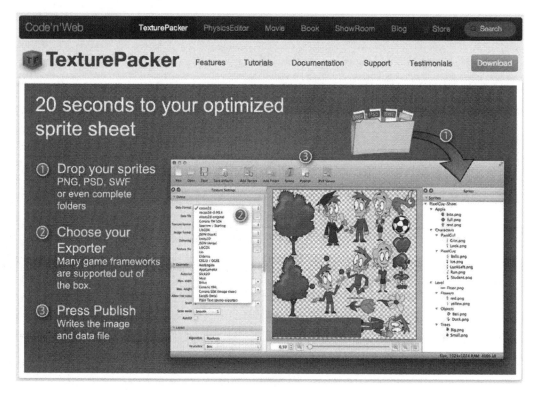

Figure 6-2. *TexturePacker web site*

With the application installed, a new project will be open and ready for your bitmap files. Figure 6-3 demonstrates a project with the .png files from the hypothetical mancala game, dragged into the right side panel.

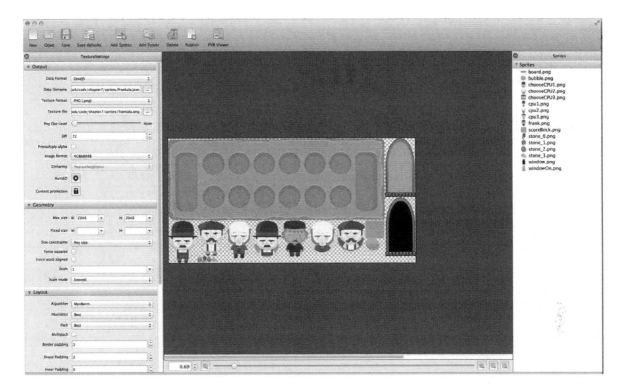

Figure 6-3. *Texture Packer with mancala assets imported*

There are several options available in the left side panel to choose from when creating sprite sheets. As you become more familiar with the tool, you'll want to explore these options, which can further optimize your sprite sheets. Depending on the data type chosen, several of these options will be set for you. For your purposes now, these defaults settings will work great.

The top four settings are the most crucial. By opening the *Data Format* drop-down menu, you'll see the many platforms it supports (see Figure 6-4).

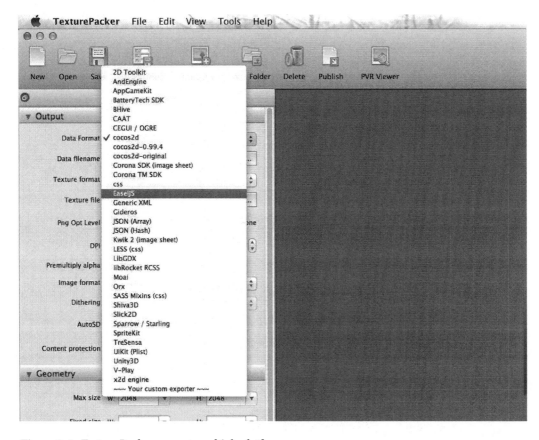

Figure 6-4. *Texture Packer supports multiple platforms*

The next options are for naming and exporting your texture and data filenames, and an option for choosing the texture file type, which will be defaulted to .png. You can then publish your files by selecting *File* ➤ *Publish,* or by selecting the *Publish* button in the top tool bar. The result will be what you saw in Listing 6-1 and Figure 6-1.

You've already seen how these assets are used to create a SpriteSheet object. Now you need to actually *do* something with this object and start displaying your sprites on the stage. This is done by using the Sprite class.

Sprite Class

The Sprite class is a display object that is used to display a frame, or a sequence of frames defined in a SpriteSheet object. The following is an example of how to create a sprite and add it to the stage:

```
var spritesheet = new createjs.SpriteSheet(data);
var frank = new createjs.Sprite(spritesheet,'frank');
stage.addChild(frank);
stage.update();
```

By passing the `spritesheet` object into the sprite, you have access to all of its frames. The second, optional parameter passed into `Sprite` is a shortcut that will display that particular animation. The following example omits this parameter and will result in the same results:

```
var spritesheet = new createjs.SpriteSheet(data);
var frank = new createjs.Sprite(spritesheet);
frank.gotoAndStop('frank');
stage.addChild(frank);
stage.update();
```

Let's put this all into a working example. Listing 6-2 demonstrates three sprites being added to the stage from the image and JSON data created from Texture Packer.

Listing 6-2. Sprite Objects Added to Stage Using Files from Texture Packer

```
var stage, spritesheet;

// body onload
function init() {
    stage = new createjs.Stage(document.getElementById('canvas'));
    createjs.Ticker.addEventListener("tick", stage);
    drawSprites();
}
function drawSprites() {
    var data = {
        "images":["mancala.png"],
        "frames":[
            [2, 2, 903, 331],
            [826, 409, 59, 51],
            [356, 335, 117, 150],
            [588, 335, 117, 133],
            [707, 335, 117, 124],
            [2, 335, 118, 170],
            [239, 335, 115, 152],
            [122, 335, 115, 142],
            [475, 335, 111, 146],
            [826, 335, 75, 72],
            [142, 479, 16, 25],
            [122, 482, 18, 22],
            [160, 482, 18, 19],
            [907, 242, 127, 238],
            [907, 2, 127, 238]
        ],
        "animations":{
            "board":[0],
            "bubble":[1],
            "chooseCPU1":[2],
            "chooseCPU2":[3],
            "chooseCPU3":[4],
            "cpu1":[5],
            "cpu2":[6],
            "cpu3":[7],
```

```
            "frank":[8],
            "scoreBrick":[9],
            "stone_0":[10],
            "stone_1":[11],
            "stone_2":[12],
            "stone_3":[13],
            "window":[14],
            "windowOn":[15]
        }
    };
    var spritesheet = new createjs.SpriteSheet(data);
    var frank = new createjs.Sprite(spritesheet,'frank');
    frank.regY = frank.getBounds().height;
    var villager1 = new createjs.Sprite(spritesheet,'cpu1');
    villager1.regY = villager1.getBounds().height;
    var villager2 = new createjs.Sprite(spritesheet,'cpu2');
    villager2.regY = villager2.getBounds().height;
    frank.y = v1.y = v2.y = 200;
    villager1.x = 150;
    villager2.x = 300;
    stage.addChild(frank, villager1, villager2);
}
```

One new technique you'll notice in the init function is the shortcut that can be used on Ticker to update the stage. This can be convenient when you only need to update the stage on the tick event.

```
createjs.Ticker.addEventListener("tick", stage);
```

The drawSprites function starts by creating the data for the sprite sheet object. Next, a series of sprites are created, positioned, and added to the stage. This is done in the same way as any other display object. However, to set the registration point on a Sprite, getBounds is the method used to receive its width and height. Figure 6-5 shows these results.

Figure 6-5. *Graphics using the Sprite class*

Given the previous example, it should seem clear to you that you could easily substitute `Bitmaps` with `Sprites` when creating the games that were built in Chapter 6. Since those games had no frame animations, loading in simple bitmaps versus using sprite sheets is probably trivial; however, a game with several more graphics would be better served with sprites.

Before diving into sprite sheet animations, let's take a look at another useful class that utilizes sprite sheets. This class allows you to write text on the stage using bitmap graphics.

Bitmap Fonts

Font bitmapping is the process of using bitmap graphics to write out messaging, usually from a sprite sheet. This technique can be accomplished by using the class `BitmapText`, which was written to work with EaselJS.

BitmapText Class

The `BitmapText` class is a display object that uses a `SpriteSheet` object built out of frames for each available character. This can be beneficial in that it guarantees that your dynamic text will look exactly how you want it to. Some computers might not embed or correctly display the font you are using, which can have a negative effect on your intended design style. A `BitmapText` object is built by passing in the text you want to display and the sprite sheet you wish to use.

```
var txt = new createjs.BitmapText("12345", spritesheet);
stage.addChild(txt);
stage.update();
```

The `spritesheet` object used in this example consists of a series of single frame animations. The animation labels must correspond to the characters they represent. Listing 6-3 shows an example of this data.

Listing 6-3. Data Example for a Font Sprite Sheet

```
var data = {
    "images":["letters.png"],
    "frames":[
        [2, 2, 34, 41],
        [34, 176, 22, 43],
        [36, 45, 26, 41],
        [34, 88, 24, 41],
        [2, 45, 32, 41],
        [34, 131, 22, 43],
        [2, 174, 30, 41],
        [38, 2, 24, 41],
        [2, 131, 30, 41],
        [2, 88, 30, 41]
    ],
    "animations":{
        "0":[0],
        "1":[1],
        "2":[2],
        "3":[3],
        "4":[4],
        "5":[5],
```

```
        "6":[6],
        "7":[7],
        "8":[8],
        "9":[9]
    }
}
```

Creating the graphics to create these sprite sheets can be a bit tricky. There are amazing bitmap font generators, a lot of them free, but at the time of writing this book they don't support EaselJS. However, there are few different approaches that can be taken to generate the character graphics you need for use with bitmap fonts.

Creating Bitmap Font Sprite Sheets

The first approach is the utilization of a bitmap font editor. As previously mentioned, EaselJS is not available in any of these popular tools as of this date, but you can still utilize the assets generated to manually create the data.

Depending on the software chosen, there will be several options and features for you to choose from while creating your font sprite sheet, much like Texture Packer. Instead of importing bitmap files, you'll typically be given a menu to choose your desired font. We won't be covering any of these applications specifically since they don't support EaselJS, but the following is an example of some XML data that would be generated from the application Glyph Designer:

```
<char id="65" x="51" y="158" width="50" height="45" xoffset="-1" yoffset="13"
    xadvance="48" page="0" chnl="0" letter="A"/>

<char id="66" x="382" y="158" width="41" height="45" xoffset="1" yoffset="13"
    xadvance="44" page="0" chnl="0" letter="B"/>

<char id="67" x="37" y="65" width="37" height="47" xoffset="2" yoffset="12"
    xadvance="41" page="0" chnl="0" letter="C"/>
```

This will correspond with the sprite sheet image generated by the application. As you can see, the rectangle information you need to create your EaselJS SpriteSheet data is in each XML node. The necessary frame label is included as well in the attribute letter. The rest of the data will not be used, as BitmapText will not support them. Listing 6-4 shows what your sprite sheet data will look like after converting it from the XML.

Listing 6-4. Data Converted to EaselJS Format from XML

```
var data = {
    "images":["letters.png"],
    "frames":[
        [51, 158, 50, 45],
        [382, 1158, 41, 45],
        [37, 65, 37, 47]
    ],
    "animations":{
        "A":[0],
        "B":[1],
        "C":[2],
    }
}
```

The conversion of this data can be done manually, or by building a simple application that will convert it for you. This is situation when custom tools can be built to help you be more productive when creating game assets and data.

The next approach is to manually lay out each character in a Flash timeline, which will then export the .png files to be used in Texture Packer. Figure 6-6 shows a timeline in Flash being used to generate a series of numbers that could be used in a scoreboard in EaselJS.

Figure 6-6. *Number characters on the Flash timeline*

The movieclip in Figure 6-6 has a center-aligned text field on the stage. By advancing down the timeline's keyframes, the text value is updated. This results in a series of numbers using a special font in each frame, all sharing the same spacing. The keyframes can be exported to a .png sequence by right-clicking on the movieclip in the library and choosing *Export PNG Sequence* (see Figure 6-7).

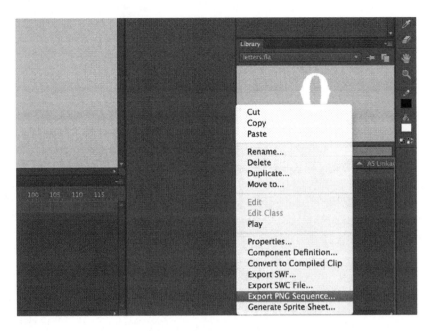

Figure 6-7. *Export PNG Sequence option in the Flash library*

The result will be 10 .png files that can be brought into Texture Packer. You can then proceed to export the sprite sheet assets for EaselJS. Let's put this into a working example. Listing 6-5 shows how bitmap text can be created using the assets from Flash and Texture Packer.

Listing 6-5. Adding and Updating Bitmap Text Using BitmapText

```
var stage, scoreContainer, scoreTxt;
var score = 0;

var data = {
    "images":["letters.png"],
    "frames":[
        [2, 2, 34, 41],
        [34, 176, 22, 43],
        [36, 45, 26, 41],
        [34, 88, 24, 41],
        [2, 45, 32, 41],
        [34, 131, 22, 43],
        [2, 174, 30, 41],
        [38, 2, 24, 41],
        [2, 131, 30, 41],
        [2, 88, 30, 41]
    ],
    "animations":{

        "0":[0],
        "1":[1],
        "2":[2],
```

```
            "3":[3],
            "4":[4],
            "5":[5],
            "6":[6],
            "7":[7],
            "8":[8],
            "9":[9]
        }
    }
}
function init() {
    stage = new createjs.Stage(document.getElementById('canvas'));
    createjs.Ticker.setFPS(60);
    createjs.Ticker.addEventListener("tick", stage);
    var img = new Image();
    img.src = "letters.png";
    img.onload = function () {
        addScore();
    }
}
function addScore() {
    scoreContainer = new createjs.Container()
    scoreContainer.x = scoreContainer.y = 30;
    spritesheet = new createjs.SpriteSheet(data);
    scoreTxt = new createjs.BitmapText(score.toString(), spritesheet);
    scoreContainer.addChild(scoreTxt);
    scoreContainer.updateText = function (text) {
        this.removeChildAt(0);
        scoreTxt = new createjs.BitmapText(text, spritesheet);
        scoreTxt.letterSpacing = 6;
        this.addChild(scoreTxt);
    }
    stage.addChild(scoreContainer);
    setInterval(updateScore, 100);
}
function updateScore() {
    score += 1;
    scoreContainer.updateText(score.toString());
}
```

At the time of writing this book, BitmapText does not contain a public update method, so a new one needs to be created if the message needs to updated. In the case of a scoreboard, it absolutely needs to update on a regular basis. Wrapping the text object in a container makes it easy to remove its only child and add a new one when needed. This is done by assigning it an *update* method. This method, udpateText, accepts one parameter, which is the text you want to display.

The first thing this method does is remove the current text object, which is the only child and located at index 0. A new one is immediately created to replace it and is given the text value passed into the method. The letter spacing can also be adjusted to give you the desired spacing between letters.

A simple interval is then created to demonstrate the update process. Figure 6-8 demonstrates the bitmap text for a scoreboard after letting the interval run for a while.

421

Figure 6-8. BitmapText class displaying bitmap fonts on the stage

Sprite Sheet Animations

Sprite sheet animations are built using the Sprite class and using multi-frame animation data to display a sequence of images. There are a few different approaches to creating this data, which we will go over next.

Animations Data

You've already built animation data to create single frame sprites. Let's pick back up on this area and extend it to create animations. The following is an example of animation data that consists of one sprite animation labeled run:

```
animations: {
    run: [0, 1, 2, 3, 4, 5]
}
```

In this example, there is one declared animation named run, which contains six frames. To run this animation, you would create a sprite object exactly the same way as before.

```
var runner = new createjs.Sprite(spritesheet,'run');
stage.addChild(runner);
```

This will run through and loop the frames defined in the run animation. You can optionally make the sprite initially paused on the first frame. This can be useful if you want to only display the first frame and later dictate when the animation should play.

```
var runner = new createjs.Sprite(spritesheet,'run');
runner.paused = true;
stage.addChild(runner);
```

A handful of methods are available for animated sprites. The following demonstrates a few of these:

```
runner.play();
runner.stop();
runner.gotoAndStop(2); //stops at the third frame
runner.gotoAndPlay(3); //advances to the fourth frame and plays
```

The animations property can be alternatively set up as an object, which can give you more options on how you want your sprites to play. The following example sets up an animation object with a few new properties, in addition to the required frames array:

```
animations: {
    run: {
        frames:[0, 1, 2, 3, 4, 5],
        next:'jump',
        speed:.5
    }
```

```
jump:{
    frames:[6, 7, 8, 9, 10],
    speed:.5
  }
}
```

The next property lets you define an animation that should play at the end of the frame cycle. In this example, the sprite will play its run sequence, then play jump. The speed property was set on both animations to control the speed in which the animation will play. By setting it to .5, the animations will play at half the speed of the Ticker's current FPS playback.

Let's get into a working example. Before adding and playing an animated sprite to the stage, you need to create the animation's frames and its corresponding data. An excellent tool for creating animation is Flash, which you will use to create a .swf file for use with Zoe.

Animated Sprite Sheets Using Zoe

Zoe, a tool created by the makers of CreateJS, is used to convert timeline animations created in Flash to sprite sheets for use in EaselJS. The application is free and can be downloaded at www.createjs.com/#!/Zoe (see Figure 6-9).

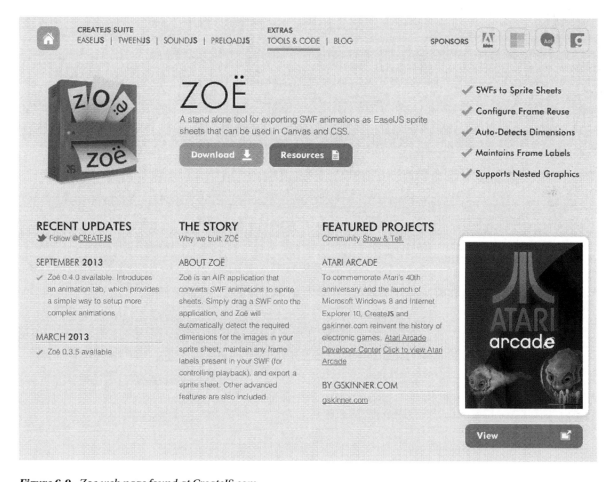

Figure 6-9. *Zoe web page found at CreateJS.com*

123

A pre-existing Flash project will be used in your Zoe example. Figure 6-10 is an example of a fairly detailed timeline animation in Flash CC.

Figure 6-10. *Pig animation in Flash CC*

This animation has several frames and is laid out in Flash's main timeline. After publishing the Flash file into a .swf file, it is then ready to bring into Zoe for building its sprite sheet. You can use the .swf provided in this book's project folder on the *Source Code/Downloads* tab on the book's product page, www.apress.com/9781430263401. You can alternatively use any published animation you have available. Begin by opening Zoe. You'll be presented with an empty project, as shown in Figure 6-11.

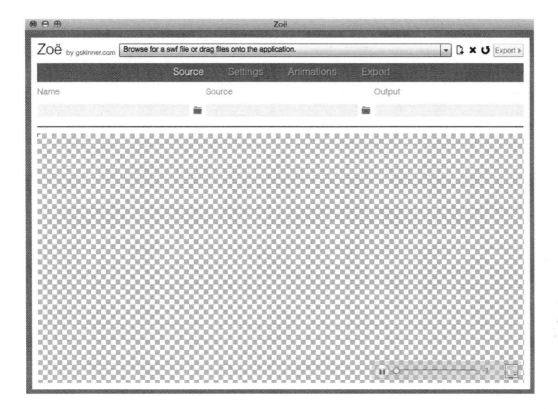

Figure 6-11. *Blank Zoe project*

To bring a .swf file into Zoe, you can browse for a file on your computer, or simply drag it into the application. Once a file is brought into the application, Zoe will process the file by calculating the bounds of each frame and immediately play the animation at the selected frame rate, which is defaulted to the frame rate defined in Flash when creating the animation. Figure 6-12 shows the pig animation .swf after it's been imported into Zoe.

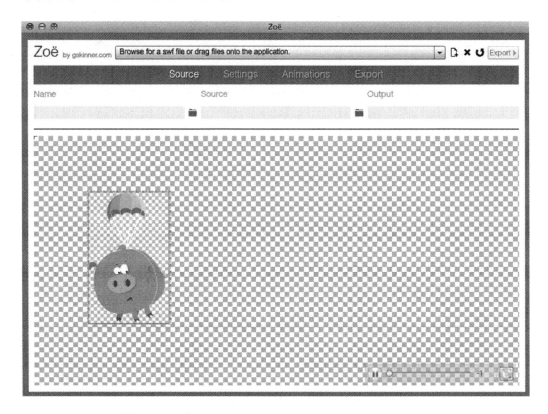

Figure 6-12. Pig swf file imported into Zoe

There are several options for you to play around with to best optimize your output. You can leave everything at its default now, but I encourage you to try and tweak the options to get an idea on what you can do. Along with many other features, you have the ability to specify registration points, adjust speed, specify the animations that should play when one is finished, and even scale the exported sprite sheet. It's even smart enough to reuse duplicate frames, which will result in smaller sprite sheets.

Hitting *Export* will create the sprite image or images (see Figure 6-13) and the data object. Listing 6-6 shows this generated object.

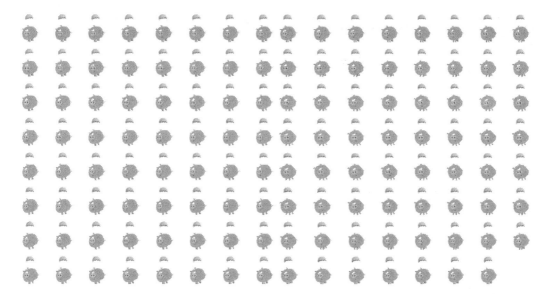

Figure 6-13. *Pig sprite sheet frames, generated from Zoe*

Listing 6-6. JSON Data Generated from Zoe

```
{
    "images": ["pig_0.png", "pig_1.png"],
    "frames": [
        [2, 2, 252, 252, 0, -61, -127],
        [258, 2, 252, 252, 0, -61, -127],
        [514, 2, 252, 252, 0, -61, -127],
        [770, 2, 252, 252, 0, -61, -127],
        [1026, 2, 252, 252, 0, -61, -127],
        [1282, 2, 252, 252, 0, -61, -127],
        [1538, 2, 252, 252, 0, -61, -127],
        [1794, 2, 252, 252, 0, -61, -127],
        [2, 258, 252, 252, 0, -61, -127],
        [258, 258, 252, 252, 0, -61, -127],
        [514, 258, 252, 252, 0, -61, -127],
        [770, 258, 252, 252, 0, -61, -127],
        [1026, 258, 252, 252, 0, -61, -127],
        [1282, 258, 252, 252, 0, -61, -127],
        [1538, 258, 252, 252, 0, -61, -127],
        [1794, 258, 252, 252, 0, -61, -127],
        [2, 514, 252, 252, 0, -61, -127],
        [258, 514, 252, 252, 0, -61, -127],
        [514, 514, 252, 252, 0, -61, -127],
        [770, 514, 252, 252, 0, -61, -127],
        [1026, 514, 252, 252, 0, -61, -127],
        [1282, 514, 252, 252, 0, -61, -127],
        [1538, 514, 252, 252, 0, -61, -127],
        [1794, 514, 252, 252, 0, -61, -127],
        [2, 770, 252, 252, 0, -61, -127],
```

```
        [258, 770, 252, 252, 0, -61, -127],
        [514, 770, 252, 252, 0, -61, -127],
        [770, 770, 252, 252, 0, -61, -127],
        [1026, 770, 252, 252, 0, -61, -127],
        [1282, 770, 252, 252, 0, -61, -127],
        [1538, 770, 252, 252, 0, -61, -127],
        [1794, 770, 252, 252, 0, -61, -127],

        . . . . . . . .

        [2, 1538, 252, 252, 1, -61, -127],
        [258, 1538, 252, 252, 1, -61, -127],
        [514, 1538, 252, 252, 1, -61, -127],
        [770, 1538, 252, 252, 1, -61, -127],
        [1026, 1538, 252, 252, 1, -61, -127],
        [1282, 1538, 252, 252, 1, -61, -127],
        [1538, 1538, 252, 252, 1, -61, -127],
        [1794, 1538, 252, 252, 1, -61, -127],
        [2, 1794, 252, 252, 1, -61, -127],
        [258, 1794, 252, 252, 1, -61, -127],
        [514, 1794, 252, 252, 1, -61, -127],
        [770, 1794, 252, 252, 1, -61, -127],
        [1026, 1794, 252, 252, 1, -61, -127],
        [1282, 1794, 252, 252, 1, -61, -127],
        [1538, 1794, 252, 252, 1, -61, -127]
    ],
    "animations": {
      "all": {
        "frames": [0, 1, 2, 3, 4, 5, 6, 7, 8, 9, 10, 11, 12, 13, 14, 15, 16,
          17, 18, 19, 20, 21, 22, 23, 24, 25, 26, 27, 28, 29, 30, 31, 32, 33,
          34, 35, 36, 37, 38, 39, 40, 41, 42, 43, 44, 45, 46, 47, 48, 49, 50,
          51, 52, 53, 54, 55, 56, 57, 58, 59, 60, 61, 62, 63, 64, 65, 66, 67,
          68, 69, 70, 71, 72, 73, 74, 75, 76, 77, 78, 79, 80, 81, 82, 83, 84,
          85, 86, 87, 88, 89, 90, 91, 92, 93, 94, 95, 96, 97, 98, 99, 100,
          101, 102, 103, 104, 105, 106, 107, 108, 109, 110, 111, 112, 113,
          114, 115, 116, 117, 118, 119, 120, 121, 122, 123, 124, 125, 126],
        "speed":.4
      }
    }
}
```

Notice how the data actually references *two* sprite sheet images. This is because the amount of frames didn't fit on one sheet, so Zoe created two. It's a good idea to keep your sprite sheet images as small as possible so you can be assured that they will bypass any image limitations from various browsers and devices. Figure 6-13 shows all of the pig frames generated for the pig animation.

▨ **Note**   A typical animation for games are significantly shorter in frames. This demonstration should show you the level of complexity you can achieve in your animations with EaselJS.

Next, a list of all rectangle areas is declared for each frame. I've truncated this array in the listing quite a bit in an effort to save space. If following along with this pig animation, this array would consist of 127 indices.

There is a single animation named `all` and it contains every frame, 0 through 126. Within this animation object, the speed property is adjusted so it will play closer to your original speed in a 60 FPS environment. You can adjust this speed property in the Animations tab within Zoe.

Let's put this sprite sheet data into a working example. Listing 6-7 adds the pig sprite to the stage, and combines its animation frames with your Ticker updates to slowly glide your pig down from the sky.

Listing 6-7. Adding and Moving an Animated Sprite

```
var stage, spritesheet, pig;

// body onload
function init() {
    stage = new createjs.Stage(document.getElementById('canvas'));
    createjs.Ticker.addEventListener("tick", runGame);
    createjs.Ticker.setFPS(60);
    addPig();
}
function addPig() {
    var data = {.....} // data from Zoe
    spritesheet = new createjs.SpriteSheet(data);
    pig = new createjs.Sprite(ss, 'all');
    stage.addChild(pig);
}
function runGame(e) {
    pig.y += 1;
    pig.x += 1;
    stage.update();
    if (pig.y > stage.canvas.height) {
        pig.x = pig.y = 0;
    }
}
```

This example demonstrates how easy it is to add animation sprites to the stage once the data and images have been created in Zoe. As the pig sprite plays, you can continue to move it along the screen and manipulate it in the same ways you have with other display objects.

Zoe is a fantastic tool for working with EaselJS. Next, let's look at more ways you can create sprite sheets.. You will be returning to Flash for the next animation, but this time you'll export directly to EaselJS from the Flash IDE.

Animations with Flash CC

Exporting to EaselJS directly from Flash has a few extra features that are not easily achievable when working out of Zoe. With Flash, you can scale and apply filters to movieclips directly on the stage, which will then be applied to the sprite sheet frames. You can also easily export multiple animations into one sheet. Let's take a look at a coin animation laid out in a movieclip inside of Flash (see Figure 6-14).

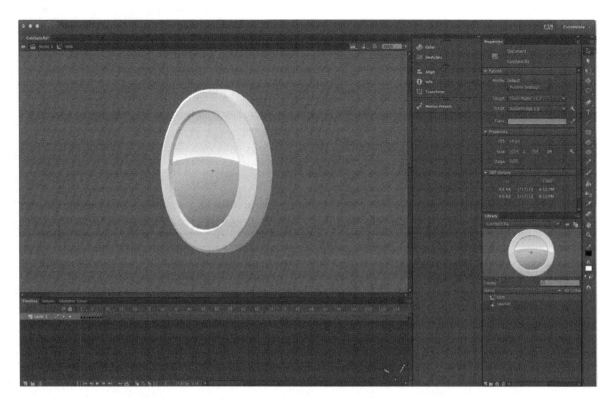

Figure 6-14. *Coin animation in Flash Movieclip*

The coin simply spins and consists of eight frames. Unlike your pig animation, the coin is inside its own movieclip, named *coin*. Because you won't be exporting a .swf file to be used in Zoe, you can organize your animations inside of movieclips. This also allows you to add filters to it from the main stage, which will result in multiple colored coin animations using the same clip.

The goal here is to have a few more colors for your coins before exporting the sprite sheet assets. By dragging three instances of the coin to the main stage, some filters can be applied directly on the movieclips. Figure 6-15 shows two of the coins tinted.

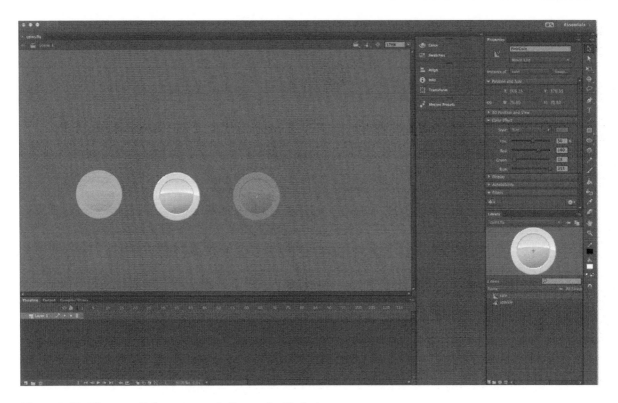

Figure 6-15. *Filters applied to coin movieclips on the Flash stage*

The sprite sheets generated will honor any scaling or filtering that is applied to these movieclip animations. Doing this, as opposed to doing them in the EaselJS code, you can greatly improve your game's performance. Figure 6-16 shows the export screen after selecting all coin instances on the stage, right-clicking on them, and choosing *Generate Sprite Sheet.*

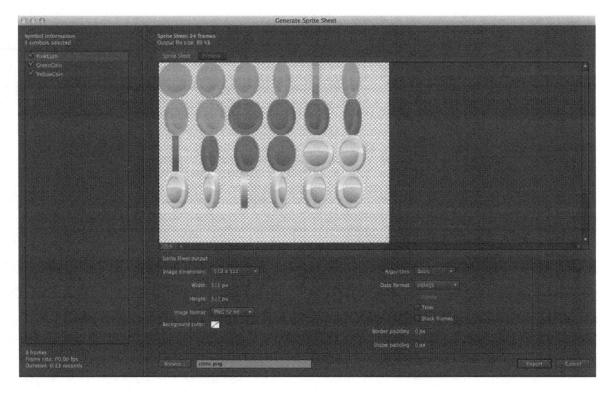

Figure 6-16. *Sprite sheet export screen in Flash CC*

As you can now see, you can export multiple animations into a single sprite sheet by exporting directly out of the Flash IDE. As convenient as this is, it's even more convenient that the data exported for the sprite sheets will also create the necessary SpriteSheet and Sprite objects for you. Because of this, you want to make sure that you give each movieclip an instance name that will make sense in your game. In this case, the coin instances are named GreenCoin, YellowCoin, and PinkCoin.

Let's take a look at the data exported from Flash in Listing 6-8, which is written to the generated coins.js file.

Listing 6-8. Objects Extending Sprite Class, Generated from Flash CC

```
(function (window) {
    GreenCoin = function () {
        this.initialize();
    }
    GreenCoin._SpriteSheet = new createjs.SpriteSheet({images:["coins.png"],
        frames:[
            [0, 0, 78, 78, 0, 38.4, 38.5],
            [78, 0, 78, 78, 0, 38.4, 38.5],
            [156, 0, 78, 78, 0, 38.4, 38.5],
            [234, 0, 78, 78, 0, 38.4, 38.5],
            [312, 0, 78, 78, 0, 38.4, 38.5],
            [390, 0, 78, 78, 0, 38.4, 38.5],
            [468, 0, 78, 78, 0, 38.4, 38.5],
            [546, 0, 78, 78, 0, 38.4, 38.5]
    ]});
```

```
        var GreenCoin_p = GreenCoin.prototype = new createjs.Sprite();
        GreenCoin_p.Sprite_initialize = GreenCoin_p.initialize;
        GreenCoin_p.initialize = function () {
            this.Sprite_initialize(GreenCoin._SpriteSheet);
            this.paused = false;
        }
        window.GreenCoin = GreenCoin;

        PinkCoin = function () {
            this.initialize();
        }
        PinkCoin._SpriteSheet = new createjs.SpriteSheet({images:["coins.png"],
            frames:[
                [624, 0, 78, 78, 0, 38.4, 38.5],
                [702, 0, 78, 78, 0, 38.4, 38.5],
                [780, 0, 78, 78, 0, 38.4, 38.5],
                [858, 0, 78, 78, 0, 38.4, 38.5],
                [936, 0, 78, 78, 0, 38.4, 38.5],
                [0, 78, 78, 78, 0, 38.4, 38.5],
                [78, 78, 78, 78, 0, 38.4, 38.5],
                [156, 78, 78, 78, 0, 38.4, 38.5]
        ]});
        var PinkCoin_p = PinkCoin.prototype = new createjs.Sprite();
        PinkCoin_p.Sprite_initialize = PinkCoin_p.initialize;
        PinkCoin_p.initialize = function () {
            this.Sprite_initialize(PinkCoin._SpriteSheet);
            this.paused = false;
        }
        window.PinkCoin = PinkCoin;

        YellowCoin = function () {
            this.initialize();
        }
        YellowCoin._SpriteSheet = new createjs.SpriteSheet({images:["coins.png"],
            frames:[
                [234, 78, 77, 78, 0, 38.4, 38.5],
                [311, 78, 77, 78, 0, 38.4, 38.5],
                [388, 78, 77, 78, 0, 38.4, 38.5],
                [465, 78, 77, 78, 0, 38.4, 38.5],
                [542, 78, 77, 78, 0, 38.4, 38.5],
                [619, 78, 77, 78, 0, 38.4, 38.5],
                [696, 78, 77, 78, 0, 38.4, 38.5],
                [773, 78, 77, 78, 0, 38.4, 38.5]
        ]});
        var YellowCoin_p = YellowCoin.prototype = new createjs.Sprite();
        YellowCoin_p.Sprite_initialize = YellowCoin_p.initialize;
        YellowCoin_p.initialize = function () {
            this.Sprite_initialize(YellowCoin._SpriteSheet);
            this.paused = false;
        }
        window.YellowCoin = YellowCoin;
}(window));
```

There appears to be a lot going on here, and it most likely looks pretty confusing if you are not familiar with *inheritance* in JavaScript. This is the code generated in the coins.js file. What it is doing is simply creating three sprite objects, along with their corresponding SpriteSheet data, and adding them to the global scope of window. The good news is that you really don't have to understand this code to use it. You can simply create new instances of each coin by using the instance name assigned to each movieclip in Flash. By including the coins.js in your document, these sprite objects are instantly at your disposal without any sprite sheet setup. The following is an example of using the pink coin:

```
var coin = new PinkCoin();
stage.addChild(coin);
```

▨ **Note**   Depending on the version of Flash you are using, the generated code might be utilizing EaselJS' now deprecated BitmapAnimation class instead of Sprite. This name refactoring was primarily due to the confusion some developers were having on how the class was used for single-frame sprites. The functionality is exactly the same, but BitmapAnimation will no longer work in EaselJS versions after 0.7. If this is the case for you, simply do a *Replace All* in your text editor and replace BitmapAnimation with Sprite in the code generated by Flash.

You can now repeatedly return to Flash to add or tweak existing animations, and re-export your sprite sheet. Everything will remain in place in your game. Any new animation will be available, and any animation that has been tweaked will be instantly updated. As long as you don't change the names given to each clip in Flash, you can develop a nice workflow by using this approach. This can be extremely convenient, however, use caution when allowing flash to create and store your sprites in the global scope of your application. Let's put these coins into a working example. Listing 6-9 shows the Flash created sprite sheets in action.

Listing 6-9. Using the Sprite Sheet Assets Generated from Flash CC

```
var stage;
function init() {
    stage = new createjs.Stage(document.getElementById('canvas'));
    createjs.Ticker.setFPS(60);
    createjs.Ticker.addEventListener("tick", stage);
    addCoins();
}
function addCoins() {
    var coin = new YellowCoin();
    var coin2 = new GreenCoin();
    var coin3 = new PinkCoin();
    coin.y = coin2.y = coin3.y = 100;
    coin.x = 100;
    coin2.x = 200;
    coin3.x = 300;
    stage.addChild(coin, coin2, coin3);
}
```

Listing 6-9 demonstrates the amount of code you are able to extract from the game logic when your sprites and their data are written by Flash and included into your document. The inheritance process that was used in the generated code is an important technique in game development, and we'll dive into it deeper in Chapter 8. Figure 6-17 shows the three colored coins spinning on the stage.

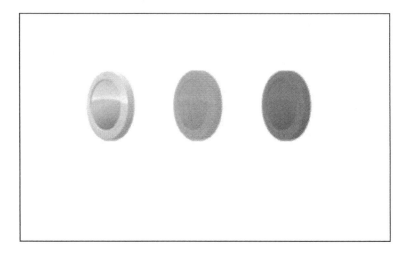

Figure 6-17. *Three animated sprites generated by Flash for EaselJS*

These coin animations were exported for EaselJS from instances on the main stage. Alternatively, you can export sprite sheets directly from the library, as shown in Figure 6-18. This can be convenient if you have no need to alter the movieclips for exporting.

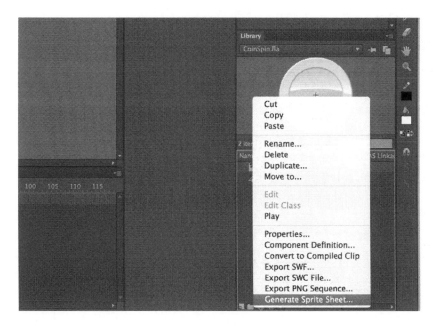

Figure 6-18. *Exporting sprite sheet from Flash library*

■ **Note**   When exporting from the library, the name of your movieclip will be used to name your sprite objects, as opposed to the instance name on the stage. An added benefit to this is that you can use periods in your movieclip names, which will create namespaces for your generated sprite objects—for example, `sprites.RedCoin`.

Summary

In this chapter, you learned the process of packing your graphics into a single file, and how you can use sprite sheet data to extract the desired frames for your game's visuals. The concept of *bitmap fonts* was also introduced, and you learned how to accomplish this technique by using various approaches and software. Animations were also introduced by using sprite sheets, and you saw the various tools you can use to create them and export them for EaselJS.

You've come a long way since the Break-It game that was built in Chapter 4. With the knowledge of bitmaps, sprite sheets, and containers, the next chapter will utilize these new skills to create a well-polished game.

CHAPTER 7

■ ■ ■

Game Project: Fakezee

With sprite sheets and containers now in your toolset, let's put them into action by building another complete game. In this chapter, you'll be writing quite a bit of code to accompany your newly learned skills, which will result in a game that is not only fun, but looks good.

Fakezee

Fakezee is based on the widely popular game Yahtzee. Although its name is different, the rules are pretty much the same. This version will be similar, but a solitary version. Listed below are the technical procedures needed to complete the game.

- Preload all game graphics.
- Put the game background graphic under the stage, keeping it out of the drawing cycle.
- Use animated sprites to add cool effects for the scorecard buttons.
- Use containers to group similar elements into separate, manageable objects.
- Reveal all groups when a new game begins in a fancy, animated manner.
- Write a separate class to handle all scoring calculations.
- Allow the player to easily play again when the game is complete.
- Display a simple scoreboard for all section scores.

Figure 7-1 shows the game being played in its complete state.

Figure 7-1. *The complete game of Fakezee*

Before diving into the development of the game, let's take a moment to go over the rules of Yahtzee.

Yahtzee Rules

As previously mentioned, Fakezee in a clone of the game Yahtzee, so the original rules will apply. The idea is to get as many points as you can by using the combination of five dice to fill in the 13 categories available on your scorecard. These categories and their score values are as follows:

- Ones: The sum of all dice with a value of 1.

- Twos: The sum of all dice with a value of 2.

- Threes: The sum of all dice with a value of 3.

- Fours: The sum of all dice with a value of 4.

- Fives: The sum of all dice with a value of 5.

- Sixes: The sum of all dice with a value of 6.

- Three of a Kind: The sum of all dice if three are alike.

- Four of a Kind: The sum of all dice if four are alike.

- Small Straight: 30 points if any four dice form a sequence.

- Large Straight: 40 points if all five dice form a sequence.

- Full House: 25 points if dice show two of one kind and three of another.

- Chance: The sum of all dice.

- Yahtzee: 50 points if all dice are of the same value.

- Bonus Yahtzee: 100 extra points for all subsequent Yahtzees.

The player gets three rolls during their turn. They may hold dice between rolls, and if they wish, can mark their score in the appropriate category before all three rolls are used up. The game continues until all 13 categories are scored.

These rules will be periodically reiterated as the development evolves throughout the chapter. Let's start by setting up the project files.

Setting Up the Project Files

With an understanding of the game that will be built, start by creating your project directory, and adding an index.html file that includes the appropriate CreateJS library files (see Listing 7-1). You'll also be writing code in three separate JavaScript files. Create these files in a new directory named js, and name these files ssData.js, Scoring.js, and fakezee.js.

Listing 7-1. index.html for the Fakezee Game

```
<!DOCTYPE html>
<html>
<head>
    <title>Fakezee</title>
    <script src="lib/easeljs-0.7.1.min.js"></script>
    <script src="lib/tweenjs-0.5.1.min.js"></script>
    <script src="lib/soundjs-0.5.2.min.js"></script>
    <script src="lib/preloadjs-0.4.1.min.js"></script>
    <script src="js/ssData.js"></script>
    <script src="js/Scoring.js"></script>
    <script src="js/fakezee.js"></script>
</head>

<body onload="init()">

    <div style="width:550px;margin: 40px auto">
        <img src="img/bg.jpg" style="position: absolute;">
        <canvas id="canvas" width="550" height="500" style="position: absolute"></canvas>
</div>

</body>

</html>
```

Reviewing the Sprite Sheet Files

The sprite sheet files for this chapter are available with the book's source code download. The animation frames for this sprite sheet were created in FlashCC and imported into TexturePacker using the same procedures learned in Chapter 6. Start by opening up the sprite sheet image, fakezee.png.

Reviewing the Sprite Sheet Image

The fakezee.png sprite sheet file contains all graphics needed for the game, with the exception of the background image, which was added to the DOM under the canvas element. Figure 7-2 shows the amount of graphics needed for the animations and static sprites.

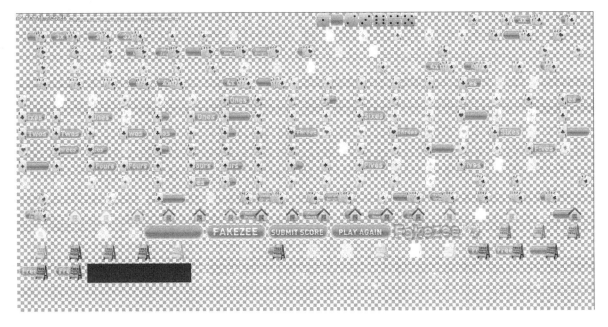

Figure 7-2. *The full sprite sheet image for all graphics and animations in Fakezee*

Setting Up the Sprite Sheet Data

As you can imagine from the size of the image, there is quite a bit of data that corresponds with it. As your games increase in graphical size, the data object will likely be large as well. Polluting the game logic code with giant data objects will quickly become messy, so it's a good idea to simply load in the data as JSON files within PreloadJS.

The sprite sheet data object generated by most sprite sheet tools will be saved as a JSON file in JSON format when exporting for EaselJS. Accessing this data for your sprite sheet will be done in the following way, after loaded in with PreloadJS:

```
var spritesheet = new createjs.Sprite(queue.getResult('manifestID'));
```

The Fakezee sprite sheet data object has nearly 300 frames and over 35 sprites, both animated and static. This will be loaded in the preload process, but take a look at the data to get an idea of how it is formatted, and the amount of sprites you'll be using in the game (see Listing 7-2).

Listing 7-2. The Sprite Sheet Data for All Sprites in Fakezee

```
{
        "images":["img/fakezee.png"],
        "frames":[...],
        "animations":{
                "diceHold":[63],
                "diceTray":{frames:[64]},
                "die":{frames:[65, 66, 67, 68, 69, 70]},
                "fakezee":{frames:[71]},
                "fakezee_score":{frames:[72]},
                "logoSmall":{frames:[157]},
                "ones":{frames:[158, 159, 160 ... 177] },
```

```
        "ones_score":{frames:[178] },
        "twos":{frames:[275, 276, 277 ... 294] },
        "twos_score":{frames:[295] },
        "threes":{frames:[253, 254, 255 ... 272] },
        "threes_score":{frames:[273] },
        "fours":{frames:[94, 95, 96 ... 113] },
        "fours_score":{frames:[114] },
        "fives":{frames:[73, 74, 75 ... 92] },
        "fives_score":{frames:[93] },
        "sixes":{frames:[184, 185, 186 ... 203] },
        "sixes_score":{frames:[204] },
        "threeKind":{frames:[0, 1, 2, 3 ... 19] },
        "threeKind_score":{frames:[20] },
        "fourKind":{frames:[21, 22, 23 ... 40] },
        "fourKind_score":{frames:[41] },
        "small":{frames:[205, 206, 207 ... 224] },
        "small_score":{frames:[225] },
        "large":{frames:[136, 137, 138 ... 155] },
        "large_score":{frames:[156] },
        "fullHouse":{frames:[115, 116, 117 ... 134] },
        "fullHouse_score":{frames:[135] },
        "chance":{frames:[42, 43, 44 ... 61] },
        "chance_score":{frames:[62] },
        "playAgain":[179],
        "playGame":[180],
        "rollButton":[181],
        "rollMessage":[182],
        "scoreBar":[183],
        "totalScoreLabel":[274]
}
```

With the sprite sheet data set up and ready to load, the game programming can begin.

Beginning the Game Code

As usual, the game code begins by declaring a series of constants and variables, the preloading of assets, and the initializing functions that will begin building the elements that make up your game. The fakezee.js file will be used to program the game logic.

Declaring the Game Constants and Variables

The constants in Fakezee are used to position the main containers and store values needed to make up the game. Listing 7-3 shows these constants.

Listing 7-3. Constants Used in fakezee.js for Counts and Positioning

```
const TITLE_YPOS = 15;
const DICE_TRAY_POSITION = {x:78, y:78};
const SCORE_CARD_POSITION = {x:20, y:155};
const SCOREBOARD_POSITION = {x:75, y:460};
```

```
const NUM_DICE = 5;
const NUM_SCORES = 13;
const NUM_ROLLS = 3;
```

Next is a group of variables that hold various CreateJS objects, and a list of EaselJS display objects that will make up the main groups of game elements (see Listing 7-4).

Listing 7-4. First Set of Variables in fakezee.js, Used to Hold the CreateJS objects for the Game

```
// createjs
var canvas, stage, queue, spritesheet;

// display objects
var title, diceTray, scoreboard, scoreCard;
```

Lastly, a few groups of variables are set with initial values (see Listing 7-5).

Listing 7-5. Arrays for Building Scorecard Buttons and Variables for Storing Game Progress

```
// scorecard buttons
var scorecardButtons = ['ones', 'twos', 'threes', 'fours', 'fives', 'sixes', 'threeKind',
    'fourKind', 'small', 'large', 'fullHouse', 'chance'];
var scorecardButtonKeys = [1, 2, 3, 4, 5, 6, 2, 3, 3, 4, 0, 0];

// game values to reset
var section1Score = 0;
var section2Score = 0;
var bonusScore = 0;
var totalScore = 0;
var rollsLeft = 3;
var numScored = 0;
var diceValues = [];
var scoredFakezee = false;
```

The first group of variables is used to build the category buttons in the scorecard. These buttons will be used when the player is ready to submit the score after their turn is complete. The scorecardButtons array is used for the loop when creating the buttons. These values are the strings used to name each button and they are needed in a few scenarios. Each string dictates what animation to use from the sprite sheet, and is also used to decide how to evaluate the dice when calculating the category's score.

The scorecardButtonKeys array holds numbers that will be injected into each button and is used to further help the score calculating process. For example, a single function is used to score all of the categories, *ones* through *sixes*. This value is used to decide what dice values should be added to the score returned. This process will be covered in much more depth in the "Calculating the Scores" section.

The last series of values are the set of game variables that will be adjusted as the game is played. This is also the set of values that needs to be reset when restarting the game. These values include scores, how many rolls the player has left during their turn, the number of scores taken all together, and the value of each die after every roll. The last variable, scoredFakezee, is used to determine bonus Fakezee points.

When the body is loaded, the init function is called, which sets up the stage.

Setting Up the Stage and Preloader

The `init` function is used to set up the stage. Unlike other examples, you won't be initializing the game itself at this point. The game initialization will begin after a few setup functions are first complete, and are kicked off by the `init` function (see Listing 7-6).

Listing 7-6. Stage and Preload Setup

```
function init() {
    canvas = document.getElementById('canvas');
    stage = new createjs.Stage(canvas);
    createjs.Ticker.setFPS(60);
    createjs.Ticker.on('tick', stage);
    preload();
}

function preload() {
    queue = new createjs.LoadQueue();
    queue.addEventListener('complete', setupSpritesheet);
    queue.loadManifest([
        {id:"fakezeeSpritesheet", src:"img/fakezee.png"},
        {id:"fakezeeSpritesheetData", src:"js/fakezee.json "}
    ]);
}
```

The `canvas` element is stored away so you can access the stage's size when positioning game elements. The stage is then created using this value, and the ticker is set up to run 60 frames per second.

The nature of Fakezee is low action and turn-based, so there is no need to set up an update/render cycle. Because of this, the shortcut for the ticker can be used to update the stage.

```
createjs.Ticker.on('tick', stage);
```

Finally, the `preload` function is called. Once all files are loaded the `SpriteSheet` object is set up in the `setUpSpritesheet` function.

Setting Up the Sprite Sheet

As you saw earlier, there are quite a few sprites contained in the sprite sheet that was created for Fakezee. This one and only `SpriteSheet` object will be used for all graphics, and is created next in the `setUpSpritesheet` function, shown in Listing 7-7.

Listing 7-7. The Game's Single Sprite Sheet Created from Loaded Data

```
function setupSpritesheet() {
    spritesheet = new createjs.SpriteSheetqueue.getResult('fakezeeSpritesheetData');
    initGame();
}
```

The `spritesheet` game variable is created and will be available for creating all sprites throughout the game. Finally, the `initGame` function is called and will initialize the game.

Initializing the Game

Initializing the game consists primarily of building the elements that will make the game. The game is split up into four major areas, most being containers that hold several display objects. The initGame function calls each of these game-building functions (see Listing 7-8).

Listing 7-8. The initGame Function Kicks Off a Series of Game-Building Functions

```
function initGame() {
    buildTitle();
    buildDiceTray();
    buildScoreCard();
    buildScoreboard();
}
```

Each function will create each of the four areas of the game, which include the *game title*, the *dice tray* where the player will roll and hold dice, the *scorecard* where the player will choose categories to score in, and finally, the *scoreboard* that displays the section scores.

Building the Game Title

The game title is a simple sprite that sits on top of the screen. This sprite is created in the buildTitle function, shown in Listing 7-9.

Listing 7-9. The Fakezee Title Sprite

```
function buildTitle() {
    title = new createjs.Sprite(spritesheet, 'logoSmall');
    title.regX = title.getBounds().width / 2;
    title.x = canvas.width / 2;
    title.y = TITLE_YPOS;
    //title.alpha = 0;
    stage.addChild(title);
}
```

After the title is created, the getBounds method is used to retrieve the width of the sprite and is used to set its registration point and centered on the stage. The title's alpha is set to 0 before added to the stage.

■ **Note** Visibility and alpha values for various objects will be set to hidden, but commented out as you build the game elements. These will eventually be uncommented when it comes time to write their *reveal* animations.

Figure 7-3 shows the Fakezee title screen on the stage.

Figure 7-3. *The title sprite sdded to the stage*

Building the Dice Tray

The dice tray holds all five dice, the button to trigger the roll, and a few other graphical elements. These will all be contained within the diceTray container and are all built in the buildDiceTray function. Listing 7-10 shows the first third of this function, which declares some variables and creates the tray container and graphics.

Listing 7-10. The buildDiceTray Function Creates the Dice Tray Container

```
function buildDiceTray() {
    var trayBG, rollMsg, rollBtn, rollBG, rollsTxt, i, die;
    var rollBtnOffset = -27;
    var hGap = 60;
    var xPos = 37;
    var yPos = 37;
    //dice tray container
    diceTray = new createjs.Container();
    diceTray.x = DICE_TRAY_POSITION.x;
    diceTray.y = DICE_TRAY_POSITION.y;
    //diceTray.alpha = 0;
    //tray bg
    trayBG = new createjs.Sprite(spritesheet, 'diceTray');
    diceTray.addChild(trayBG);
    rollMsg = new createjs.Sprite(spritesheet, 'rollMessage');
    rollMsg.x = trayBG.getBounds().width;
    rollMsg.y = rollBtnOffset;
    rollMsg.name = 'rollMsg';
    //rollMsg.visible = false;
    diceTray.addChild(rollMsg);
    ...
```

Some variables that will be used for display objects and loops are first created. Then some position values are set that will be used for various placements during the function. The dice tray container is then created, set to the game variable diceTray, and positioned using some of the game constants that were declared earlier.

The background image for the tray is created as a sprite and added as the tray container's first child. A simple "roll" message graphic is also added and positioned to the container. Next, the dice are created (see Listing 7-11).

Listing 7-11. The buildDiceTray Function Continued: Creating the Dice

```
...
//dice
for (i = 0; i < NUM_DICE; i++) {
    die = new createjs.Sprite(spritesheet, 'die');
    die.name = 'die' + i;
    die.paused = true;
    // die.visible = false;
    die.mouseEnabled = false;
    die.regX = die.getBounds().width / 2;
    die.regY = die.getBounds().height / 2;
    die.x = xPos;
    die.y = yPos;
    die.hold = false;
    die.on('click', holdDie);
    xPos += hGap;
    diceTray.addChild(die);
}
...
```

With a loop, the dice are each created using the animation die that is declared in the sprite sheet data. Figure 7-4 shows the six frames used for this sprite.

Figure 7-4. *The six frames that make up a die sprite*

Each die is given a sequential name so it can be easily accessed later when evaluating their values. The dice are also set to paused so they don't start spinning as soon as they are created. Each die will also be initially hidden by setting its visible property to false. For now, this line will be commented out so the dice can be seen while positioning. Their mouseEnabled property is set to false to prevent them from being interactive before a player makes an actual roll.

The registration points for the dice sprites are set to the center. This is so you can create an interesting bounce effect when you initially reveal them at the start of a game. Using xPos and yPos values, they are placed horizontally across the tray (see Figure 7-5).

Figure 7-5. *Five die sprites added to the dice tray container*

When the player rolls the dice, they are allowed to hold dice before making another roll. To hold this value, you assign the sprite the custom property, hold, and default it to false. This will be used to determine if you should spin the die when making a roll. This property will be toggled using the function holdDie when the player clicks the die. This function will be written in the "Holding Dice" section later in this chapter.

▥ **Note**   The on method is used in this project as a shortcut to addEventListener. This method is jam-packed with useful parameters, including scope control. Since you are still working in the global space, only the event type and listener are needed when using this method. However, its power will be reviewed in-depth in the upcoming chapters and used almost exclusively when adding event listeners.

Finally, the xPos value is increased and the die is added to the tray container. There's one more thing needed for the dice tray, the Roll button, which triggers the roll of the dice (see Listing 7-12).

Listing 7-12. The buildDiceTray Function Continued: Creating the Roll Button That Will Roll the Dice

```
...
//roll button
rollBtn = new createjs.Container();
rollBtn.name = 'rollBtn';
//rollBtn.visible = false;
rollBtn.x = xPos;
rollBtn.y = yPos;
rollBG = new createjs.Sprite(spritesheet, 'rollButton');
rollBtn.addChild(rollBG);
//roll text
rollsTxt = new createjs.Text(rollsLeft, '27px Calibri', '#FFF');
rollsTxt.name = 'rollsTxt';
rollsTxt.textAlign = 'center';
rollsTxt.textBaseline = 'middle';
rollsTxt.x = rollBtn.getBounds().width / 2;
rollsTxt.y = rollBtn.getBounds().height / 2;
//add roll button
rollBtn.regX = rollBtn.getBounds().width / 2;
rollBtn.regY = rollBtn.getBounds().height / 2;
rollBtn.addChild(rollsTxt);
rollBtn.on('click', rollDice);
diceTray.addChild(rollBtn);
stage.addChild(diceTray);
}
```

The Roll button is a container, and it is set to the game variable rollBtn. It's named and positioned using the values from the previous loop so it falls in line with the five dice.

This container will hold two display objects: a graphic for its background, and a text object to display the number of rolls left in the player's current turn. The background is a sprite and it is added to the container. Next, a text object is created to display the current value of rollsLeft, which was initially declared as 3. The text is given a name and some styles, and is then positioned using the bounds of the background sprite. The rollButton container's registration points are set to the center before adding the text object as its second child.

An event listener is set to the Roll button and assigned the handler rollDice, which will be covered in the "Rolling the Dice" section. Finally, the button is added to the diceTray container. Figure 7-6 shows the complete dice tray added to the game.

Figure 7-6. *The complete dice tray container added to the stage*

Building the Scorecard

Next up is the scorecard, which takes up most of the screen in Fakezee. It contains all of the category options, the total score, and eventually the Play Again button, which will start a brand new game. The buildScoreCard function creates all of these assets and places them into a single container. Listing 7-13 kicks off this function with several variables for display objects and positioning.

Listing 7-13. The buildScoreCard Function Builds the Scoreboard Container

```
function buildScoreCard() {
    var i, btn, scoreMsg, scoreTxt;
    var xPos = 0;
    var yPos = 0;
    var row = 0;
    var hGap = 49;
    var vGap = 390;
    var btnsPerRow = 6;
    var fakezeeBtnYPos = 75;
    var scoreMsgYPos = 150;
    var section = 1;
    scoreCard = new createjs.Container();
    scoreCard.mouseEnabled = false;
    scoreCard.x = SCORE_CARD_POSITION.x;
    scoreCard.y = SCORE_CARD_POSITION.y;
    ...
```

After the long set of local variables, the scorecard container is created and set to the game variable scoreCard. The scorecard's buttons won't always be enabled during gameplay so you can quickly disable them by setting mouseEnabled to false for entire container. It's then positioned using some game constants declared earlier. Next, the score buttons are added to the container (see Listing 7-14).

Listing 7-14. The buildScoreCard Function Continued: Creating the Category Buttons

```
...
// score buttons
for (i = 0; i < scorecardButtons.length; i++) {
    btn = new createjs.Sprite(spritesheet, scorecardButtons[i]);
    //btn.paused = true;
    btn.name = scorecardButtons[i];
    btn.key = scorecardButtonKeys[i];
    btn.section = section;
    btn.y = yPos;
    btn.x = xPos;
    btn.framerate = 30;
    btn.on('animationend', function (e) {
        this.stop();
    });
    btn.on('click', onScoreCardBtnClick);
    scoreCard.addChild(btn);
    yPos += hGap;
    row++;
    if (row === btnsPerRow) {
        section++;
        row = 0;
        yPos = 0;
        xPos += vGap;
    }
}
...
```

Each score button is a sprite with multiple frames for its revealing animation. As mentioned earlier, the scorecardButtons game array will dictate what animation object to use for each sprite. The loop is used to access those values. Figure 7-7 shows the frames in one of the scorecard category buttons.

Figure 7-7. *The frames for the large straight category sprite*

Each category button will start paused so you can dictate when you want to actually reveal each one. This is now commented out in the same manner as many other visual properties to help position each element as you create them.

The buttons are given a name and the two custom properties, key and section. Their keys come from the scorebuttonKeys game array, and are helpers to decide how to evaluate the dice when calculating the category score.

149

Its section value does a few things. In traditional Yahtzee, the categories are split up into two sections, *upper score* and *lower score*. The upper section (in this case, section *one*) consists of the categories, *ones* through *sixes*. The rest falls into section two. This section property tells you which section to append the given score to. It's also used for positioning, since the score buttons will be displayed in two columns, one on each side of the stage.

The buttons are positioned using the typical, incremented xPos and yPos values. Their frame rate is also explicitly set to control the speed in which their revealing animations are played.

A few event listeners are set next. By default, the animation will loop forever, but it needs to stop on its last frame. You can prevent an animation from looping by using the animation object's next property in the sprite sheet data. This property can be set using Zoe when building your sprite sheets. However, sometimes it's easier to simply listen for it to end and force it to stop in code, like so:

```
btn.on('animationend', function (e) {
    this.stop();
});
```

The next listener is for the *click*, and will fire the onScoreCardBtnClick handler function, which will be covered in the section "Scoring on Categories." Finally, each button is added to the container. Some positioning calculations are then executed, which also determines if a new row should be started.

Along with some messaging, there is one more button to be added, the Fakezee score button (See Listing 7-15).

Listing 7-15. The buildScoreCard Function Continued: the Fakezee Category Button and Score Messaging

```
...
// fakezee button
btn = new createjs.Sprite(spritesheet, 'fakezee');
btn.paused = true;
btn.name = btn.key = 'fakezee';
btn.section = 2;
btn.regX = btn.getBounds().width / 2;
btn.regY = btn.getBounds().height / 2;
btn.x = scoreCard.getBounds().width / 2;
btn.y = 75;
//  btn.alpha = 0;
btn.on('click', onScoreCardBtnClick);
scoreCard.addChild(btn);
//score message
scoreMsg = new createjs.Sprite(spritesheet, 'totalScoreLabel');
scoreMsg.name = 'scoreMsg';
scoreMsg.regX = scoreMsg.getBounds().width / 2;
scoreMsg.x = scoreCard.getBounds().width / 2;
scoreMsg.y = scoreMsgYPos;
// scoreMsg.alpha = 0;
scoreCard.addChild(scoreMsg);
// score
scoreTxt = new createjs.Text('0', '50px Calibri', '#FFF');
scoreTxt.name = 'scoreTxt';
scoreTxt.textAlign = 'center';
scoreTxt.x = scoreCard.getBounds().width / 2;
scoreTxt.y = scoreMsg.y + 30;
// scoreTxt.alpha = 0;
scoreCard.addChild(scoreTxt);
stage.addChild(scoreCard);
}
```

The Fakezee button is for the best score you can get, so it's large and placed in the center of the two columns of buttons. It's positioned and given the same custom properties as the rest of the score buttons, and it will be used in the same ways. Its score will be added to section two, and clicking it will also call the onScoreCardBtnClick function.

The scoreMsg sprite is simply a graphical message that will sit on top of the text object scoreTxt, which will hold the total score. Both are positioned and added to the stage. Figure 7-8 shows the stage with the scorecard added.

Figure 7-8. *The complete scorecard container added to the stage*

Building the Scoreboard

The scoreboard is the final group needed for the game. It will also be a container and will hold the scores for both sections and bonus points scored when scoring multiple Fakezees (see Listing 7-16).

Listing 7-16. The buildScoreBoard Function Builds the Container to Hold the Game Scores

```
function buildScoreboard() {
    var scoreBar, txt, xPos;
    var padding = 5;
    var sec1XPos = 12;
    var sec2XPos = 145;
    var bonusXPos = 280;
    scoreboard = new createjs.Container();
    scoreboard.x = SCOREBOARD_POSITION.x;
    scoreboard.y = SCOREBOARD_POSITION.y;
    //scoreboard.alpha = 0;
    scoreBar = new createjs.Sprite(spritesheet, 'scoreBar');
    scoreBar.name = 'scoreBar';
    scoreboard.addChild(scoreBar);
```

```
    //section 1
    txt = createScoreboardText('Section 1 Score:', sec1XPos, padding)
    scoreboard.addChild(txt);
    xPos = txt.getMeasuredWidth() + txt.x + padding;
    txt = createScoreboardText(section1Score, xPos, padding,
        'section1Txt');
    scoreboard.addChild(txt);
    //section 2
    txt = createScoreboardText('Section 2 Score:', sec2XPos, padding);
    scoreboard.addChild(txt);
    xPos = txt.getMeasuredWidth() + txt.x + padding;
    txt = createScoreboardText(section2Score, xPos, padding,
        'section2Txt');
    scoreboard.addChild(txt);
    //bonus
    txt = createScoreboardText('Bonus Score:', bonusXPos, padding);
    scoreboard.addChild(txt);
    xPos = txt.getMeasuredWidth() + txt.x + padding;
    txt = createScoreboardText(bonusScore, xPos, padding, 'bonusTxt');
    scoreboard.addChild(txt);
    stage.addChild(scoreboard);
}
function createScoreboardText(label, x, y, name) {
    var txt = new createjs.Text(label, '16px Calibri', '#FFF');
    txt.x = x;
    txt.y = y;
    txt.name = name;
    return txt;
}
```

The scoreboard game variable is used to create the scoreboard container. It contains one background sprite and six text objects. Three of the text objects are labels, and the other three will be updated with scores after each turn.

This function builds and places each text object horizontally across the board. The text objects that need to be updated are given names so they are easily accessible when updating them. The actual creation of each text object is built and returned in a separate function named createScoreboardText. All text uses the same styling, so this function is used to split up the code and make things a little easier to read. The text-creating function is passed the necessary values to create the text, and passes back the new text object. Figure 7-9 shows the scoreboard added to the stage.

Figure 7-9. *The scoreboard container completes the graphical elements needed for the game*

A lot of sprites, containers, and text were just created to make up the necessary elements of Fakezee. With each asset in place, let's backtrack a bit to hide the containers and sprites so you can give them all a fancy entrance.

Revealing the Game Elements

As the game elements were being built, several display objects were set to be initially hidden, either by given an alpha value of 0, a visibility of false, or set as paused when first created. These lines of code were all commented out so you could see what was being created and where things were being placed. In this section, each element will be revealed, either by fading, sliding, or bouncing.

Hiding the Game Elements

Go back and uncomment the necessary lines of code so the game will start with an empty stage. The lines of code and their functions are as follows:

1. Under the buildTitle function, uncomment

    - title.alpha = 0;

2. Under the buildDiceTray function, uncomment

    - diceTray.alpha = 0;

    - rollMsg.alpha = 0;

    - die.visible = false; (in dice creating loop)

    - rollBtn.visible = false;

3. Under the buildScoreCard function, uncomment

    - btn.paused = true; (in button creating loop)

    - btn.alpha = 0; (fakezee button)

    - scoreMsg.alpha = 0;

    - scoreTxt.alpha = 0;

4. Under the buildScoreboard function, uncomment

    - scoreboard.alpha = 0;

Now when you run your game, you should get an empty stage, showing nothing but the background image in the DOM element behind it (see Figure 7-10).

Figure 7-10. *The game's sprites and containers are initially hidden and ready for a grand entrance*

Now that everything is hidden, the revealGame function needs to be called to fire each revealing animation. A series of timeouts are chained together by utilizing TweenJS. This will create a short delay before each section starts their animations (see Listing 7-17).

Listing 7-17. Each Section Holds its Own Revealing Function

```
function revealGame() {
    createjs.Tween.get(this)
        .wait(100).call(revealTitle)
        .wait(400).call(revealDiceTray)
        .wait(1400).call(revealScoreCard)
        .wait(2000).call(revealScoreboard);
}
```

For this function to work, it needs to be called. Revisit the initGame function and one final function call at the end.

```
function initGame() {
    buildTitle();
    buildDiceTray();
    buildScoreCard();
    buildScoreboard();
    revealGame();
}
```

Revealing the Title and Dice Tray

The first areas of the game that are animated in are the title and dice tray. Listing 7-18 shows this being accomplished with two functions, one for each section.

Listing 7-18. The revealTitle and revealDiceTray Functions

```
function revealTitle() {
    createjs.Tween.get(title).to({alpha:1}, 400);
}
function revealDiceTray() {
    var i, die, delay, btn, rollMessage;
    createjs.Tween.get(diceTray).to({alpha:1}, 500);
    for (i = 0; i < NUM_DICE; i++) {
        die = diceTray.getChildByName('die' + i);
        die.scaleX = die.scaleY = 0;
        die.visible = true;
        delay = (i * 150) + 500;
        createjs.Tween.get(die).wait(delay)
            .to({scaleX:1, scaleY:1}, 1000, createjs.Ease.elasticOut);
    }
    btn = diceTray.getChildByName('rollBtn');
    btn.scaleX = btn.scaleY = 0;
    btn.visible = true;
    delay += 150;
    createjs.Tween.get(btn).wait(delay)
        .to({scaleX:1, scaleY:1}, 1000, createjs.Ease.elasticOut);
    rollMsg = diceTray.getChildByName('rollMsg');
    createjs.Tween.get(rollMsg).wait(delay).to({alpha:1},1000);
}
```

The title shouldn't need much explanation. A simple fade is accomplished using a tween. Revealing the dice tray is a bit more exciting. At first, only the tray's background is revealed as the entire container is faded in using a tween. Next, each die is handled.

A loop is created to access each die in the tray. Using getChildByName and the loop iterator value, each die is found. The scaleX and scaleY of each die is set to 0, which will essentially give it a size of nothing, and the visibility is then turned back on. By gradually incrementing the delay local variable, an offset to each die animation is accomplished. This value is used in the tween call, which scales each die back up with a bounce effect. Using the same approach, the roll button follows suit, and bounces in line with the dice. Finally, the roll message sprite is faded in, and the dice tray is then fully revealed. Figure 7-11 shows the dice tray revealing, mid animation.

Figure 7-11. *The dice animating in sequentially with a bounce effect*

Revealing the Scorecard

The scorecard is revealed in a similar fashion as the dice tray. The scorecard container holds several animated sprites that will play their frames to reveal themselves, each starting their animation with a slight offset from the proceeding one. In this case, an interval is set to play each sprite (see Listing 7-19).

Listing 7-19. The scoreCard Function Plays all Category Button Sprites

```
function revealScoreCard() {
    var btn, timer;
    var len = scorecardButtons.length;
    var i = 0;
    timer = setInterval(function () {
        btn = scoreCard.getChildAt(i);
        btn.play();
        i++;
        if (i === len) {
            clearInterval(timer);
            btn = scoreCard.getChildByName('fakezee');
            btn.y -= 10;
            createjs.Tween.get(btn).to({alpha:1, y:btn.y + 10}, 500);
        }
    }, 100);
}
```

During each interval, the appropriate sprite animation is played by using getChildAt and the incremented variable i. These buttons were the first things to be added to the container, so this method will work fine. The interval should stop when the interval counter i has reached the length of the scorecardButtons array. The interval is then cleared, and a simple fade-in-and-slide-down effect is applied to the large Fakezee button in the middle.

Revealing the Scoreboard

The scoreboard is simply revealed by fading up. The scorecard's total score sprite and its corresponding text object are handled in this function as well (see Listing 7-20).

Listing 7-20. All Scores' Messages Are Revealed with the revealScoreBoard Function

```
function revealScoreboard() {
    var totalScoreMsg = scoreCard.getChildByName('scoreMsg');
    var totalScoreTxt = scoreCard.getChildByName('scoreTxt');
    createjs.Tween.get(totalScoreTxt).to({alpha:1}, 500);
```

```
createjs.Tween.get(totalScoreMsg).to({alpha:1}, 500);
createjs.Tween.get(scoreboard).to({alpha:1}, 500);
}
```

All objects are simultaneously faded in, and the entire game is now visible and ready to play.

Playing the Rounds

It's now time to program the game logic for Fakezee. There were a few listeners that were set on display objects as as they were built, which will roll and hold the dice, and choose sections to score on. Each round starts with rolling and holding dice, which will be covered in this section.

Rolling the Dice

Rolling the dice is triggered by clicking on the rollBtn container. This container holds a text object that displays the number of rolls available, which will be three at the beginning of each round. Listing 7-21 shows the handler function that is called when clicking the Roll button.

Listing 7-21. The rollDice Function Rolls the Dice by Playing the Dice Sprites

```
function rollDice(e) {
    var i, die;
    var rollBtn = e.currentTarget;
    var rollsTxt = rollBtn.getChildByName('rollsTxt');
    enableDice(false);
    scoreCard.mouseEnabled = false;
    rollBtn.mouseEnabled = false;
    rollBtn.alpha = .7;
    rollsLeft -= 1;
    rollsTxt.text = rollsLeft;
    for (i = 0; i < NUM_DICE; i++) {
        die = diceTray.getChildByName('die' + i);
        if (die.hold) {
            continue;
        }
        die.framerate = Math.floor(Math.random() * 10) + 20;
        die.play();
    }
    setTimeout(stopDice, 1000);
}
```

A reference to the roll button is stored by accessing the currentTarget property of the event passed into the function.

```
var rollBtn = e.currentTarget;
```

■ **Note** You should always use `currentTarget` as opposed to `target` when accessing a container that triggered the event. The `target` property will usually refer to the child inside of the container that was clicked, as opposed to the actual container object itself.

The text object inside the roll button is also stored away so you can update it later in the function. A function named `enableDice` is then called and passed a value of false. This will disable all dice while they are spinning. This function will be covered in the next section, "Holding Dice." The scorecard and the Roll button both need to be disabled during a roll as well, which is done by disabling mouse events on each of them.

When the Roll button is hit, its disabled state is visually represented by setting its `alpha` to 0.7. The `rollsLeft` game variable is decreased by 1, and the text object inside the Roll button is immediately updated to display this. Next, a loop is set to roll each die.

The die sprites are created with a custom property called `hold`, which is set to false. When these values get updated during the holding process, they will be skipped and not set to roll in the loop. If they are not held, each die is given a random frame rate value and then played. After one second, the `stopDice` function is called, which will stop each die from playing its frames. The random frame rates result in the random frame each die lands on.

Holding Dice

After the dice are rolled, the next step in the round is to select or deselect the dice you wish to hold during your next roll. Before you can choose these dice, the spinning needs to stop, and several objects need to become active and clickable. This is all handled in the `stopDice` function, shown in Listing 7-22.

Listing 7-22. The stopDice Stops the Dice on Random Frames, Based on Their Frame Rate

```
function stopDice() {
    var i, die;
    diceValues = [];
    for (i = 0; i < NUM_DICE; i++) {
        die = diceTray.getChildByName('die' + i);
        die.stop();
        diceValues[i] = Math.floor(die.currentAnimationFrame) + 1;
    }
    if (rollsLeft > 0) {
        enableDice(true);
        var rollBtn = diceTray.getChildByName('rollBtn');
        rollBtn.alpha = 1;
        rollBtn.mouseEnabled = true;
    }
    scoreCard.mouseEnabled = true;
}
```

The game variable `diceValues` is used to store the current values of all dice after each roll. This array is emptied before setting up the dice loop. Each die is accessed via its name and stopped by calling `stop()`. The value of each die is pushed to `diceValues` and is determined by the frame it stopped on. You can access this by the `currentAnimationFrame` on a sprite. This value is not a whole number, so you need to floor it. These animation frame numbers start at 0, so adding a 1 will give you the values that match the dice graphics. Figure 7-12 shows the dice stopped after the first roll.

Figure 7-12. *The state of the dice tray after a player roll*

Next, the number of rolls left in the current round is checked. If the number is greater than 0, the dice and roll button are enabled so both dice holding and dice rolling can continue.

One more thing needs to happen when the dice stop. A player can choose a category in the middle of a round, so the scorecard needs to become enabled every time the dice stop, regardless of how many rolls are left.

You've seen the enableDice and holdDie functions called on in a few different cases so far in the code. You most likely have a pretty good idea of what these functions are doing. Listing 7-23 shows how these functions are written.

Listing 7-23. The holdDie Function Toggles the Hold Value on the Die Clicked

```
function enableDice(enable) {
   var die, i;
   for (i = 0; i < NUM_DICE; i++) {
      die = diceTray.getChildByName('die' + i);
      die.mouseEnabled = enable;
   }
}
function holdDie(e) {
   var die = e.target;
   if (!die.hold) {
      die.hold = true;
      die.alpha = .7;
   }
   else {
      die.hold = false;
      die.alpha = 1;
   }
}
```

The enableDice function accepts one parameter, which is a Boolean and will be used to set the mouseEnabled of each die. This allows you to write one function for handling both the enabling and disabling of the dice.

The dice are held by calling the holdDie function, which is the click handler set on each die sprite. A simple conditional is written to toggle its hold value, as well as its alpha value to visually represent its state.

Scoring on Categories

When a player is out of rolls, or is happy with the current roll they are on, the next step in a round is to choose a category to apply a score to. This section will cover score messaging for the category buttons, as well as the scoreboard section scores and total score message, respectively.

Choosing a Category

A player chooses a category to score on by clicking an available category button in the scorecard container. These event listeners are already set on each button, and their handler function is shown in Listing 7-24.

Listing 7-24. The onScoreCardBtnClick Marks the Score in the Appropriate Category

```
function onScoreCardBtnClick(e) {
    var btn = e.target;
    btn.mouseEnabled = false;
    scoreCard.mouseEnabled = false;
    var score = 100;
    btn.gotoAndStop(btn.name + '_score');
    updateScore(btn, score);
    updateScoreboard();
    evalGame();
}
```

The category clicked is first referenced and set to btn. It is immediately disabled to prevent it from being clicked on for the remainder of the game. The scorecard itself is then disabled to prevent any other category from also being pressed.

This next line is temporary. Every score will be set to 100 for the time being. There is quite a bit of scoring logic to determine the category score, but you can hold off on that now and finish the game logic first. This score will be accessed by calling on a Scoring object, or *class,* that will be built during the "Calculating the Scores" section later in this chapter.

With the score statically set, the value needs to be displayed in the category to which it belongs. As you know, each category button is a sprite with multiple frames. In the sprite sheet object, each animation has a corresponding frame that uses its same name with an appended _score at the end.

```
"ones":{frames:[158, 159, 160, 161, ...177] },
"ones_score":{frames:[178] }
```

This extra frame is a clone of the animation's last frame, only without the text in the graphic. This leaves room to place a text object on top with the score value. Figure 7-13 shows this frame.

Figure 7-13. *The frame used for the fours category button when chosen to score on*

A series of functions are next called, which will add text objects to each category, update the scoreboard, and evaluate the game.

Updating the Score

When a score is determined, the category needs to display it, and the score messaging inside the scoreboard and scorecard should be updated. The sprite frame for the selected category is now updated to make room for text and is added using the udpateScore function, shown in Listing 7-25.

Listing 7-25. The udpateScore Function Creates a Text Object and Places It Above the Chosen Category

```
function updateScore(btn, score) {
    var label = new createjs.Text(score, '27px Calibri', '#FFF');
    var labelXOffset;
    var labelYOffset;
    switch (btn.section) {
        case 1:
            section1Score += score;
            labelXOffset = 70;
            labelYOffset = 11;
            break;
        case 2:
            section2Score += score;
            if (btn.name == 'fakezee') {
                labelXOffset = 0;
                labelYOffset = -15;

            }
            else {
                labelXOffset = 35;
                labelYOffset = 10;
            }
            break;
    }
    label.name = 'label';
    label.textAlign = 'center';
    label.x = btn.x + labelXOffset;
    label.y = btn.y + labelYOffset;
    scoreCard.addChild(label);
}
```

A text object is created and given a value of the score passed into the function. A few positioning variables are then declared and will be given values based on the section of the category button selected. The appropriate score is also updated using this same section value.

Because the buttons in section one are graphically different than those in section two, the text offset position needs to be different. Using the section value of the button passed into the function, the offset values are set. The giant Fakezee button in the middle has its own layout as well, and is considered in the case of section two.

```
        case 2:
            section2Score += score;
            if (btn.name == 'fakezee') {
                labelXOffset = 0;
                labelYOffset = -15;

            }
```

```
        else {
            labelXOffset = 35;
            labelYOffset = 10;
        }
        break;
```

The text is then appropriately positioned above its corresponding section and added to the scorecard container. Figure 7-14 demonstrates the *ones* and *threes* sections updated after being clicking.

Figure 7-14. *The category buttons when scores are applied*

After a category is scored, the rest of the scoring messages need to update as well. The updateScoreboard function updates the appropriate text objects (see Listing 7-26).

Listing 7-26. All Score Messaging is Updated in the updateScoreboard Function

```
function updateScoreboard() {
    var section1Txt = scoreboard.getChildByName('section1Txt');
    var section2Txt = scoreboard.getChildByName('section2Txt');
    var bonusTxt = scoreboard.getChildByName('bonusTxt');
    var totalScoreTxt = scoreCard.getChildByName('scoreTxt');
    section1Txt.text = section1Score;
    section2Txt.text = section2Score;
    bonusTxt.text = bonusScore;
    totalScoreTxt.text = totalScore =  (section1Score + section2Score + bonusScore);
}
```

Each text object is referenced by its name and accessed via the container to which it belongs. The game variables that hold the scores were updated in the previous function, so their values are simply assigned to their corresponding text object. The total score message is then updated to be the sum of all scores.

Evaluating the Game

When a score is made, the game will either carry on or end. This section will cover both scenarios, which are determined by the function evalGame (see Listing 7-27).

Listing 7-27. The evalGame Function Determines if the Game Should End

```
function evalGame() {
    numScored++;
    if (numScored == NUM_SCORES) {
        setTimeout(gameOver, 1500);
    }
    else {
        resetDiceTray();
    }
}
```

The numScored game variable is increased and then evaluated to see if it has reached the predetermined number of scores per game. The gameOver function is called if the player has scored on all categories, or the resetDiceTray function is called to resume the game.

Resetting the Dice Tray

For the game to continue, the dice and roll button need to be reset to their appropriate states to start a new round. Listing 7-28 shows the process of preparing a new round.

Listing 7-28. Resetting the Dice Tray so the Player Can Start a New Round

```
function resetDiceTray() {
    var die, i;
    var rollBtn = diceTray.getChildByName('rollBtn');
    var rollsTxt = rollBtn.getChildByName('rollsTxt');
    for (i = 0; i < NUM_DICE; i++) {
        die = diceTray.getChildByName('die' + i);
        die.alpha = 1;
        die.mouseEnabled = false;
        die.hold = false;
    }
    rollBtn.alpha = 1;
    rollBtn.mouseEnabled = true;
    rollsLeft = rollsTxt.text = NUM_ROLLS;
}
```

The Roll button and its text is first accessed and set to local variables. Next, a loop is set up to access each of the dice. The alpha of each die is restored, mouse interaction is disabled, and their hold properties are all reset to false. Lastly, the Roll button is enabled, the rollsLeft game variable is reset to 3, and the Roll button's text object is updated to match.

Ending and Replaying the Game

The final game logic is to end the game and restart it. The game over state will simply add a Play Again button, which is done in the function gameOver, shown in Listing 7-29.

Listing 7-29. The gameOver Function Creates a Play Again Button and Puts It in Place of the Fakezee Category Button

```
function gameOver() {
    var playAgainBtn = new createjs.Sprite(spritesheet, 'playAgain');
    var fakezeeBtn = scoreCard.getChildByName('fakezee');
    playAgainBtn.regX = fakezeeBtn.regX;
    playAgainBtn.regY = fakezeeBtn.regY;
    playAgainBtn.x = fakezeeBtn.x;
    playAgainBtn.y = fakezeeBtn.y;
    playAgainBtn.on('click', replayGame);
    scoreCard.addChild(playAgainBtn);
    scoreCard.removeChild(fakezeeBtn);
    scoreCard.mouseEnabled = true;
}
```

The Play Again button is a sprite and will completely replace the Fakezee button (see Figure 7-15).

Figure 7-15. *The game Fakezee when all scores are counted and the game is complete*

Its click handler is the function replayGame, shown in Listing 7-30.

Listing 7-30. Game Variables Are Reset and All Display Objects Are Removed from the Stage

```
function replayGame() {
    section1Score = section2Score = bonusScore = numScored = 0;
    rollsLeft = NUM_ROLLS;
    stage.removeAllChildren();
    initGame();
}
```

To reset the game, a list of game variables is reset to 0 and `rollsLeft` is set back to 3. Next, all four display objects on the stage are completely removed, and `initGame` is called, which will start the whole process over and make a new game.

The game should be completely playable at this point, minus the actual score calculations. After confirming that you can get to the end of the game and restart it, the `Scoring` class will be built next.

Calculating the Scores

The scoring functions will be built in a separate object in a separate JavaScript file. Moving functionality into self-contained objects is a common practice in JavaScript, and makes larger games much more manageable. Building more complex JavaScript objects as *classes* will be discussed further in Chapter 8.

To get started with scoring, open the `Scoring.js` file that was created and added to the document at the beginning of the chapter. This file will contain only the `Scoring` object.

Setting Up the Scoring Class

Objects in JavaScript can be set up in several ways and can very much act as working classes. In the case of scoring, the class will be called statically. In other words, instances of the object will not be created. An example of this would be the `Math` object that is built into JavaScript.

```
var num = Math.floor(123.45);
```

The object `Math` has a method named `floor` that takes one parameter and returns a result. The `Scoring` class will be utilized in the same way. Listing 7-31 shows how the object is set up.

Listing 7-31. Settng Up the Scoring Class

```
var Scoring = {
    dice:[],
    btnKey:null
};

Scoring.getScore = function (type, dice, key) {
    dice.sort();
    this.dice = dice;
    this.btnKey = key;
}
```

The object is set up similar to your typical JavaScript object literal and contains two properties, `dice` and `btnKey`. The methods to this object are added directly on the object after it has been declared.

The getScore method is the only method called from within the game. It needs three values, the first being the type of category, such as *ones* or *fullHouse*. This determines what scoring function to call. The second is an array of the dice values, and lastly is the button key, which is a number used in certain types of calculations.

To make things easier in certain scoring functions, the dice array is sorted so the dice are in order sequentially. Next, the dice and btnKey properties are set so you can access them in each function.

■ **Note**   Since you are in the scope of Scoring, this can be used to access all properties and methods that belong to it.

Next, the type parameter is used to find the appropriate function to execute. A switch statement is added to the end the getScore function (see Listing 7-32).

Listing 7-32. A Switch Statement Is Added to Determine the Scoring Function to Run

```
Scoring.getScore = function (type, dice, key) {
    dice.sort();
    this.dice = dice;
    this. btnKey = key;
    switch (type) {
        case 'ones':
        case 'twos':
        case 'threes':
        case 'fours':
        case 'fives':
        case 'sixes':
            return this.getNumberScore();
            break;
        case 'threeKind':
        case 'fourKind':
            return this.getKinds();
            break;
        case 'small':
        case 'large':
            this.dice = this.uniqueArray(this.dice);
            return this.getStraights();
            break;
        case 'fullHouse':
            return this.getFullHouse();
            break;
        case 'chance':
            return this.getChance();
            break;
        case 'fakezee':
            return this.getFakezee();
            break;
        case 'bonus':
            return this.getFakezee() * 2;
            break;
    }
}
```

Each scoring calculation function returns the score, which is then immediately returned back to the game, where the method was called.

```
// from game with static values
var score = Scoring.getScore('sixes',[2,4,6,6,1],6);   // returns 12
```

You can see how only one line of code is needed within your game logic to retrieve each score. You'll see next, in the "Scoring for Number Categories" section, where the button key 6 came into play in the previous example.

Scoring for Number Categories

All six categories in section one use this next function. The scoring for this category works by adding the total of all dice with the number that the category represents. For instance, if the category type is *threes,* the sum of all dice with the value of 3 is returned (see Listing 7-33).

Listing 7-33. The Ones Through Sixes Categories Used the getNumberScore

```
Scoring.getNumberScore = function () {
    var i, value;
    var score = 0;
    var len = this.dice.length;
    for (i = 0; i < len; i++) {
        if (this.dice[i] == this.btnKey) {
            score += this.dice[i];
        }
    }
    return score;
}
```

In this function, you loop through each die value and append its value to the score variable, but only if its value is equal to btnKey. In this case, this is how the button key is used. Finally, the score is returned.

Scoring for Kinds

Two categories use this next function. For a three of a kind, a score is rewarded if three of the dice have equal values. The awarded score is the sum all dice. The same scoring is used for four-of-a-kinds as well (see Listing 7-34).

Listing 7-34. Scoring for Three- and Four-of-a-kinds

```
Scoring.getKinds = function () {
    var i;
    var match = 0;
    var score = 0;
    var pass = false;
    var matchesNeeded = this.btnKey;
    var len = this.dice.length;
    for (i = 0; i < len; i++) {
        score += this.dice[i];
        if (this.dice[i] == this.dice[i + 1]) {
            if (i != this.dice.length) {
                match++;
```

```
            if (match >= matchesNeeded) {
                pass = true;
            }
        }
    }
    else {
        match = 0;
    }
}
score = pass ? score : 0;
return score;
}
```

Scoring for kinds is one of the functions that take advantage of the dice being sorted. Looping through the dice, each die is compared to the die in front of it. When matches are found, the local variable match is incremented.

Along with match being declared as 0, a few more variables are set. The score variable starts at 0 and is incremented with each iteration of the loop by the value of each die. At the end of the loop, the score variable will contain the sum of all dice. The pass value is set to true as soon as the appropriate consecutive matches are found. This pass variable is determined by comparing matches against the button key and will be used to determine if the player is awarded the score or not.

Scoring for Straights

Two categories use this next function. Thirty points are awarded for four dice that form a sequence. Forty points are given if all dice form a sequence (see Listing 7-35).

Listing 7-35. Small and Large Straight Scores

```
Scoring.getStraights = function () {
    var i;
    var match = 0;
    var score = this.btnValue == 4 ? 30 : 40;
    var matchesNeeded = this.btnValue;
    var pass = false;
    var len = this.dice.length - 1;
    for (i = 0; i < len ; i++) {
        if (this.dice[i] == (this.dice[i + 1] - 1)) {
            match++;
            if (match >= matchesNeeded) {
                pass = true;
                break;
            }
        }
        else {
            match = 0;
        }
    }
    score = pass ? score : 0;
    return score;
}
```

This function basically works the same way as the getKinds; however, when comparing two dice for equal values in the loop, the *next* die value is subtracted by one. If they match in value, then you know that they are in sequence. This continues on and either increments matches or resets it back to 0. The button key is also used in this function as the necessary goal for matches.

Before running this function, a function was called to extract any duplicate values in the dice values array. Since it is quite possible for two dice to be of the same value and still achieve a small straight, this could break the match count in the middle of a run. Consider the following dice values:

```
[1,2,3,3,4];
```

During the loop, the third and fourth dice will not pass the conditional, and this will result in a reset of the match count. Therefore it is necessary to make this array a *unique* array.

```
[1,2,3,4];
```

This procedure is accomplished by adding the utility function, uniqueArray to the Scoring object (see Listing 7-36).

Listing 7-36. The uniqueArray Utility Function Removes All Duplicates in an Array

```
Scoring.uniqueArray = function (a) {
    var temp = {};
    for (var i = 0; i < a.length; i++) {
        temp[a[i]] = true;
    }
    var r = [];
    for (var k in temp) {
        r.push(k / 1);
    }
    return r;
}
```

This simple utility function loops through the dice values and assigns each as a property name in a temporary, local object. When coming across a value that has already been added to the object, it simply overrides it. You would end up with this object, using the previous example array:

```
{1:true,2:true,3:true,4:true}
```

This object can now be used in a loop to create and return a unique array.

Scoring for a Full House

A full house is used for only one category, so the button's key is not needed. Listing 7-37 shows how to check the dice for a full house.

Listing 7-37. Scoring for the Full House Category

```
Scoring.getFullHouse = function () {
    var pass = false;
    var score = 0;
    if (this.dice[0] == this.dice[1] && this.dice[1] != this.dice[2] &&
            this.dice[2] == this.dice[3] && this.dice[3] == this.dice[4]) {
        pass = true;
    }
```

```
    else if (this.dice[0] == this.dice[1] && this.dice[1] == this.dice[2] &&
        this.dice[2] != this.dice[3] && this.dice[3] == this.dice[4]) {
      pass = true;
    }
    score = (pass ? 25 : 0);
    return score;
}
```

A full house is awarded if one of two possible scenarios occurs. If the first two dice are of equal value, and the last three are equal of a different value, 25 points are awarded. The only other possible scenario is checked in a similar way, only the first three are evaluated, and then the last two. If neither of these is true, a score of 0 is returned.

Scoring for Chance

Chance is usually chosen when your dice won't give you a particularly good score, given the available choices. The getChance function is shown in Listing 7-38.

Listing 7-38. The Sum of All Dice for the Chance Category

```
Scoring.getChance = function () {
    var score = 0;
    var len = this.dice.length;
    for (var i = 0; i < len; i++) {
       score += this.dice[i];
    }
    return score;
}
```

Chance is simply the sum of all dice. A loop is created to increment the score variable, which is then returned at the end of the function.

Scoring for Fakezee and Bonus Fakezee

A Fakezee is a five of a kind. Listing 7-39 loops through all dice to check for a valid Fakezee.

Listing 7-39. The getFakezee Function Checks if All Dice Are of the Same Value

```
Scoring.getFakezee = function () {
    var pass = false;
    var score = 0;
    if (this.dice[0] == this.dice[1] && this.dice[1] == this.dice[2] &&
        this.dice[2] == this.dice[3] && this.dice[3] == this.dice[4]) {
      pass = true;
    }
    score = (pass ? 50 : 0);
    return score;
}
```

Fifty points are rewarded for a Fakezee. This same function is used to check for bonus Fakezees. To receive a bonus Fakezee, the player must have previously rolled a Fakezee and scored on the Fakezee category, respectively. In the getScore function, a case for the type *bonus* calls on this same function to check the dice. The result is multiplied by 2 and returned back to the game. This gives a score of either 100 or 0. Later, in the section "Using the Scoring Class," this bonus check will be added to the game logic.

The Complete Scoring Class

The Scoring class is now complete and ready to be used in the game. Listing 7-40 shows the entire Scoring object, which resides in the file Scoring.js.

Listing 7-40. Scoring.js, the Complete Scoring Class

```
var Scoring = {
    dice:[],
    btnKey:null
};

Scoring.getScore = function (type, dice, key) {
    dice.sort();
    this.dice = dice;
    this.btnKey = key;
    switch (type) {
        case 'ones':
        case 'twos':
        case 'threes':
        case 'fours':
        case 'fives':
        case 'sixes':
            return this.getNumberScore();
            break;
        case 'threeKind':
        case 'fourKind':
            return this.getKinds();
            break;
        case 'small':
        case 'large':
            this.dice = this.uniqueArray(this.dice);
            return this.getStraights();
            break;
        case 'fullHouse':
            return this.getFullHouse();
            break;
        case 'chance':
            return this.getChance();
            break;
        case 'fakezee':
            return this.getFakezee();
            break;
```

```
            case 'bonus':
                return this.getFakezee() * 2;
                break;
        }
    }
    Scoring.getNumberScore = function () {
        var i, value;
        var score = 0;
        var len = this.dice.length;
        for (i = 0; i < len; i++) {
            if (this.dice[i] == this.btnKey) {
                score += this.dice[i];
            }
        }
        return score;
    }
    Scoring.getKinds = function () {
        var i;
        var match = 0;
        var score = 0;
        var pass = false;
        var matchesNeeded = this.btnKey;
        var len = this.dice.length;
        for (i = 0; i < len; i++) {
            score += this.dice[i];
            if (this.dice[i] == this.dice[i + 1]) {
                if (i != this.dice.length) {
                    match++;
                    if (match >= matchesNeeded) {
                        pass = true;
                    }
                }
            }
            else {
                match = 0;
            }
        }
        score = (pass ? score : 0);
        return score;
    }
    Scoring.getStraights = function () {
        var i;
        var match = 0;
        var score = this.btnKey == 3 ? 30 : 40;
        var matchesNeeded = this.btnKey;
        var pass = false;
        var len = this.dice.length;
        for (i = 0; i < len - 1; i++) {
            if (this.dice[i] == (this.dice[i + 1] - 1)) {
                match++;
```

```
            if (match >= matchesNeeded) {
                pass = true;
                break;
            }
        }
        else {
            match = 0;
        }
    }
    score = pass ? score : 0;
    return score;
}
Scoring.getFullHouse = function () {
    var pass = false;
    var score = 0;
    if (this.dice[0] == this.dice[1] && this.dice[1] != this.dice[2] &&
            this.dice[2] == this.dice[3] && this.dice[3] == this.dice[4]) {
        pass = true;
    }
    else if (this.dice[0] == this.dice[1] && this.dice[1] == this.dice[2] &&
            this.dice[2] != this.dice[3] && this.dice[3] == this.dice[4]) {
        pass = true;
    }
    score = pass ? 25 : 0;
    return score;
}
Scoring.getChance = function () {
    var score = 0;
    for (var i = 0; i < this.dice.length; i++) {
        score += this.dice[i];
    }
    return score;
}
Scoring.getFakezee = function () {
    var pass = false;
    var score = 0;
    if (this.dice[0] == this.dice[1] && this.dice[1] == this.dice[2] &&
            this.dice[2] == this.dice[3] && this.dice[3] == this.dice[4]) {
        pass = true;
    }
    score = (pass ? 50 : 0);
    return score;
}
//UTIL
Scoring.uniqueArray = function (a) {
    var temp = {};
    for (var i = 0; i < a.length; i++) {
        temp[a[i]] = true;
    }
```

```
    var r = [];
    for (var k in temp) {
        r.push(k / 1);
    }
    return r;
}
```

Using the Scoring Class

A temporary value of 100 is currently used when scoring on categories. Now that the Scoring class is complete, it can be used in the game logic. Moving back into fakezee.js, a few additions are needed for the onScoreCardBtnClick function (see Listing 7-41).

Listing 7-41. Using the Scoring Class in the Game

```
function onScoreCardBtnClick(e) {
    var btn = e.target;
    btn.mouseEnabled = false;
    scoreCard.mouseEnabled = false;
    var score = Scoring.getScore(btn.name, diceValues, btn.key);
    if (scoredFakezee) {
        bonusScore += Scoring.getScore('bonus', diceValues, null);
    }
    if (btn.name == 'fakezee' && score == 50) {
        scoredFakezee = true;
    }
    btn.gotoAndStop(btn.name + '_score');
    updateScore(btn, score);
    updateScoreboard();
    evalGame();
}
```

First, delete the temporary line that sets the score to 100 and replace it with the following code that utilizes the new scoring class:

```
var score = Scoring.getScore(btn.name, diceValues, btn.key);
```

The name of the clicked category button is used for the *type* parameter, the diceValues game variable is used for *dice,* and the button's key is used for *key.* Now the scoring is fully functional, but there is one more topic to cover: bonus Fakezee.

The scoredFakezee game variable is used to determine if a Fakezee roll has been scored. If so, *bonus* is passed into a quick call on the getScore function, which will return 100 or 0, which will be added to the game variable bonusScore.

```
if (scoredFakezee) {
    bonusScore += Scoring.getScore('bonus', diceValues, null);
}
```

After this bonus code, a check is used to see if bonusScore should be set to true for future scoring. The result will be true in only one scenario, when the current category button's name is "fakezee" and it resulted in a score of 50.

This brings us to the end of the code for Fakezee. For your convenience, the entire game logic is available in the fakezee.js file available with the other source code from the Source Code/Downloads tab on this book's Apress product page (www.apress.com/9781430263401).

Summary

With the power of CreateJS, a fully enjoyable game, complete with polished graphics and animations was built with a fairly small amount of code. By using a sprite sheet, several graphics, including animated ones, were added to the game, each with only a single line of code. This sprite sheet's large, corresponding object was tucked away into its own JSON file and loaded in to keep from polluting the game logic code. The extensive scoring logic was also written separately in a highly organized, self-contained manner by encapsulating it into a class-like object.

At this point in the book, a major portion of the EaselJS API and how it pertains to games has been covered. For the second half of the book, we'll be taking this further with better programming techniques, performance optimizations, and the extra polish that will take your games to the next level. In the next chapter, you'll learn to further organize your game by creating custom containers and sprites that contain custom behaviors.

CHAPTER 8

Extending EaselJS Display Objects

So far, you've used EaselJS display objects to add graphical game elements to the stage. You've seen situations where you have needed to add some custom properties and methods to these display objects to help program the game logic around them. So far, the process of *dynamic injection* has been used to accomplish this. With this approach, you are essentially extending the functionality of these objects, but when doing this *on-the-fly* approach, your game can quickly become messy and hard to manage. In this chapter, you'll learn how to build and organize new, custom objects that inherit from EaselJS display objects.

Inheritance

Inheritance is a term used in object-oriented programming that refers to the process of creating an object or class that inherits the behavior and attributes from a pre-existing class. The class you inherit from is typically referred to as the *super class,* or *base class.* This lets you create new classes that will carry their own, unique behavior, but also use common functionality that has been already written.

EaselJS and Inheritance

Classical Inheritance is not the only way to accomplish this type of behavior in JavaScript. Many developers prefer other types of *extending* objects, but we'll be focusing on classical inheritance because the EaselJS library itself uses this method.

■ **Note**   Technically, there are no *classes* in JavaScript. However, when referring to reusable objects that contain class-like behavior, this term is often used to describe them.

When we speak of display objects, we are actually referring to the base class that all visual objects inherit from. This base class is the DisplayObject class. The DisplayObject class defines properties such as alpha and x, methods like draw and hitTest, and all mouse handlers. Another behavior of a display object is that it is allowed to be added to the stage or any other container.

Sprite, for instance, is a *subclass* of DisplayObject. It carries all of its behaviors, but needs more of its own unique attributes, such as the play method and the currentFrame property. We won't be diving into the source code for EaselJS in this book, although it is open and perfectly acceptable to do so. However, you can easily see what classes extend what, if any, by viewing the online documentation. Figure 8-1 demonstrates how you can refer to the documentation to easily see that the Sprite class extends DisplayObect.

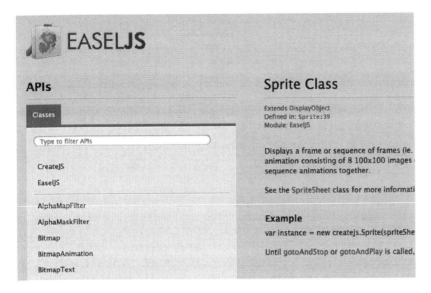

Figure 8-1. *EaselJS online documentation for class inheritance*

You'll also notice that that the properties, methods, and events that these classes have are neatly listed after its definition. These attributes will be listed in bold if they are new and unique to that particular class, as opposed to being inherited from its super class. Figure 8-2 shows the bold, unique attributes for Sprite. All other properties and methods are inherited from DisplayObject.

Methods

addEventListener	getMatrix	localToGlobal	setTransform
advance	getStage	localToLocal	**stop**
cache	getTransformedBounds	off	toString
clone	globalToLocal	on	uncache
dispatchEvent	**gotoAndPlay**	**play**	updateCache
draw	**gotoAndStop**	removeAllEventListeners	updateContext
getBounds	hasEventListener	removeEventListener	
getCacheDataURL	hitTest	set	
getConcatenatedMatrix	isVisible	setBounds	

Properties

alpha	filters	parent	skewX
cacheCanvas	**framerate**	**paused**	skewY
cacheID	hitArea	regX	snapToPixel
compositeOperation	id	regY	**spriteSheet**
currentAnimation	mask	rotation	visible
currentAnimationFrame	mouseEnabled	scaleX	x
currentFrame	name	scaleY	y
cursor	onTick	shadow	

Events

animationend	mousedown	pressmove	rollover
click	mouseout	pressup	tick
dblclick	mouseover	rollout	

Figure 8-2. EaselJS online documentation with uninherited attributes listed in bold

You can further extend EaselJS classes yourself by using inheritance. As previously mentioned, you've come close to this already by injecting custom attributes to display objects as you instantiate them. The following is a reminder of how you've done this so far:

```
var orb = new createjs.Shape();
orb.graphics.beginFill('blue').drawCircle(0,0,20);
orb.points = 4;
orb.die = function(){
   createjs.Tween.get(this).to({alpha:0},100).call(function(e){
      stage.removeChild(this);
   });
}
stage.addChild(orb);
```

This example creates a shape object named orb. It then proceeds to add extra behavior to the object that will pertain to the game play. The points property and die method are not part of the Shape class, but by dynamically injecting them into the instance, they are now accessible through the orb object.

```
someScore += orb.points;
orb.die();
```

This will work fine but it's not ideal in larger games. For one, you are simply adding this behavior to each instance of the shape object. If you decide you need more orbs in the future, you will need to repeat the process of adding the new properties and methods. Granted, you could probably build some sort of *spawn* function to handle this, but diving into a function to further build onto these new attributes is not a very elegant way to program. Ideally, you can build an entirely new custom Orb object that can be instantiated and added to your game.

Extending EaselJS

By creating new objects that extend EaselJS display objects, you can carry on using them as you have on the stage in your game, plus give them new, unique properties. These objects will contain encapsulated logic that is completely unique and extracted from your game code.

Using the proceeding orb example, let's look at how you could add new orbs to your game. The following example demonstrates the use of a custom Orb class:

```
var orb = new Orb();
stage.addChild(orb);
```

An instance of the class Orb is created and added to the stage. Its properties and methods are created within its declaration, which can be located in a separate file, which makes it much more manageable. No longer do you need to pollute your game logic space by creating dynamic attributes.

So how is this accomplished? Take a look at Listing 8-1, which shows the template code, which will be used for extending all EaselJS classes in this book.

Listing 8-1. Code Template for Extending Shape

```
(function() {

    var Orb = function() {
        this.initialize();
    }
    Orb.prototype = new createjs.Shape();

    Orb.prototype.Shape_initialize = Orb.prototype.initialize;

    Orb.prototype.initialize = function() {
        this.Shape_initialize();
    }

    window.Orb = Orb;

}());
```

Before diving into the code for Orb, take a look at what it is surrounded in. The code is within an immediate function, which is a function that executes only once, and immediately. This assures you that you are out of the global space when writing the logic to create the new class. A function named Orb is then created, which is the actual object you are writing. This function is known as the object's *constructor* function and is called immediately when you make a new instance of Orb. This function calls its initialize method, which we will go over shortly.

After the constructor function, which is what declares the Orb class, its prototype is set to a new Shape. This is how you inherit all of the shape's properties and methods. At this point, Orb is essentially a carbon copy of Shape. Next, the initialize method on Shape needs to be overridden so the new, custom shape will be called on instantiation. This is done by assigning it to a property on Orb so you can access it later during your own initialize function.

```
Orb.prototype.Shape_initialize = Orb.prototype.initialize;
```

The orb's initialize function is then created. At the very least, this function needs to fire its super class's initialize function, which is absolutely essential in order to fully extend all of the behavior of the class you are extending. In other languages, this is equivalent to calling a super method inside a constructor function.

```
this.Shape_initialize();
```

Finally, the Orb class gets added to window so it is accessible throughout your application. Again, at this point this Orb is nothing more than a Shape object. To make it unique, some custom properties and methods need to be added to it. This was already done with the initialize function. This is done by using prototype.

```
Orb.prototype.initialize = function(){

};
```

You can similarly add properties to your custom class.

```
Orb.prototype.points = 4;
```

Let's put this all together to see the Orb class in completion, with the option to pass in a different color to each orb (see Listing 8-2).

Listing 8-2. Sample Orb Class that Extends Shape

```
(function() {

    var Orb = function(color) {
        this.initialize(color);
    }
    Orb.prototype = new createjs.Shape();

    Orb.prototype.Shape_initialize = Orb.prototype.initialize;

    Orb.prototype.points = 4;

    Orb.prototype.initialize = function(color) {
        this.Shape_initialize();
        this.graphics.beginFill(color).drawCircle(0,0,20);
    }

    Orb.prototype.die = function(){
        createjs.Tween.get(this).to({alpha:0},100).call(function(e){
            this.parent.removeChild(this);
        });
    }

    window.Orb = Orb;

}());
```

The following example shows this in use in an application. Notice how much easier it is to use when its functionality is *black boxed* into a reusable object.

```
// new orb
var orb = new Orb('#0F0');
stage.addChild(orb);

// using orb
score += orb.points;
orb.die();
```

Let's make a simple application using these new procedures.

Pulsing Orbs

Pulsing Orbs is an application where the user can click around the screen to add colorful, pulsing orbs to create an artful image.

- Allow user to click anywhere on the stage to create a new pulsing orb.

- The orbs should be custom objects that extend the EaselJS Shape class.

- Orbs should be both random in color and size.

- User can export a snapshot image of their art by pressing *Enter* on the keyboard.

- This feature will turn the canvas into an image and open it in a new window, where the user can copy or save their image.

Set up the HTML document that includes a canvas element and the necessary CreateJS file includes. You'll also create two JavaScript files: one for the application (pulsingOrbs.js) and another for the orb class (PulsingOrb.js), as shown in Listing 8-3.

Listing 8-3. HTML File for Pulsing Orbs

```
<!DOCTYPE html>
<html>
<head>
    <title></title>
    <script src="lib/easeljs-0.7.1.min.js"></script>
    <script src="PulsingOrb.js"></script>
    <script src="pulsingOrbs.js"></script>
</head>

<body onload="init()">

<canvas id="canvas" width="800" height="600" style="border: black solid 1px"></canvas>

</body>

</html>
```

Let's start with the PulsingOrb class. This object will be written its own file, PulsingOrb.js (see Listing 8-4).

Listing 8-4. PulsingOrb.js , The PulsingOrb Class

```
(function () {

    var PulsingOrb = function (color,size) {
        this.initialize(color,size);
    }

    var p = PulsingOrb.prototype = new createjs.Shape();

    p.count = 0;

    p.Shape_initialize = p.initialize;

    p.initialize = function (color,size) {
        this.Shape_initialize();
        size = size != undefined ? size : 20;
        color = color != undefined ? color : '#F00';
        this.alpha = Math.random();
        this.graphics.beginFill(color).drawCircle(0, 0, size);
        this.on('tick', this.pulse);
    }

    p.pulse = function () {
        this.alpha = Math.cos(this.count++ * 0.1) * 0.4 + 0.6;
    }

    window.PulsingOrb = PulsingOrb;

}());
```

This class is constructed similar to the Orb object you built earlier, only with a few different behaviors. You can optionally pass in a color and size into each orb instance, and it begins to animate after it's been created. Note that the object's prototype was set to the variable p. This is done to prevent you from having to write out PulsingOrb.prototype every time you want to create new properties. This makes it a lot easier to read as well. We will be using this approach throughout the rest of the book.

If no size or color is passed into the instance, some default values are set before drawing the orb. Lastly, a listener is set on *tick* to create the pulsing animation. The orb is now ready to use in the application, which is implemented in the pulsingOrbs script (see Listing 8-5).

Listing 8-5. pulsingOrbs.js

```
var stage;

function init() {
    stage = new createjs.Stage(document.getElementById('canvas'));
    createjs.Ticker.addEventListener("tick", stage);
    drawBackground();
    setListeners();
}
```

```
function drawBackground() {
    var bg = new createjs.Shape();
    bg.graphics.beginFill('#A9BBC9').drawRect(0, 0, stage.canvas.width,
        stage.canvas.height);
    stage.addChild(bg);
}

function setListeners() {
    stage.on('stagemousedown', drawOrb);
    window.onkeyup = takeSnapShot;
}

function drawOrb(e) {
    var randomColor = '#' + Math.floor(Math.random() * 16777215).toString(16);
    var randomSize = Math.floor(Math.random() * 100) + 20;
    var orb = new PulsingOrb(randomColor, randomSize);
    orb.x = e.stageX;
    orb.y = e.stageY;
    stage.addChild(orb);
}

function takeSnapShot(e) {
    if (e.keyCode === 13) {
        var img = stage.canvas.toDataURL("image/png");
        window.open(img);
    }
}
```

All of the orb's functionality was built within the class, which drastically cuts down the code in your logic. The first set of functions draws a colored background on the stage and adds the listeners for the applications. When a user clicks on the stage, a new orb will be created and positioned at the coordinates of the mouse click. A random color and size are generated and passed into the constructor of the new orb. Finally, the orb is added to the stage.

A keyboard listener was also set, which will first check the key code for the *Enter* key. If *Enter* was pressed, the dataToURL method is called on the stage's canvas, passing in the type of file you wish to create. This is set to an img variable, which is finally opened in a new window (see Figure 8-3).

Figure 8-3. *Pulsing Orbs canvas exported to PNG*

This should give you an idea of the benefits with writing reusable classes. Next, we'll look at some practical uses of extending EaselJS by creating some UI components.

Creating Reusable UI Components

You'll often need UI elements in your games for user interaction between game play, such as buttons in menu screens and load indicators. In this section, you'll create a highly extendable button that can be used throughout this book. You'll also revisit the preloader that was started in Chapter 2.

Creating Buttons

Creating reusable buttons is easy to do in EaselJS by extending `Container`. These containers will contain a border, background, and text object. Colors and sizes should also be adjustable. Start by extending `Container` in a file called `SimpleButton.js` (see Listing 8-6).

Listing 8-6. SimpleButton.js, SimpleButton Class Declaration

```
(function () {

    window.ui = window.ui || {};

    var SimpleButton = function (label) {
        this.label = label;
        this.initialize();
    }
```

```
    var p = SimpleButton.prototype = new createjs.Container();

    p.label;

    p.Container_initialize = p.initialize;

    p.initialize = function () {
        this.Container_initialize();
    }

    window.ui.SimpleButton = SimpleButton;

}());
```

Before the constructor function for SimpleButton, a ui namespace is declared, but only if it has not yet been created. Doing this allows you to tack onto an existing ui object if it already exists. You set up the rest of the class in the same way you did with Shape, but of course this time, you extend Container instead.

The constructor takes one parameter, label. This is the text that will be drawn on the button. This value is immediately set to the button's label property so you can set it when you first draw or redraw the button.

This button needs to be customizable, so some more properties are needed. Below the label property, several more are added. Listing 8-7 lists these button properties.

Listing 8-7. SimpleButton Properties

```
p.label;
p.width;
p.height;
p.background;
p.labelTxt;
p.fontSize = 24;
p.borderColor = '#000';
p.buttonColor = '#ccc';
p.upColor = '#ccc';
p.overColor = '#aaa';
```

These values will be used when drawing the button. The background property will hold your shape object that will draw the stroke and background color for the button. The width and height of the button is driven by the size and length of the label, and won't be set until you create the text object labelTxt.

The initialize function will call a few functions to draw the button and set its listeners (see Listing 8-8).

Listing 8-8. SimpleButton Initialization Method Draws Button and Sets Up Mouse Events

```
p.initialize = function () {
    this.Container_initialize();
    this.drawButton();
    this.setButtonListeners();
}
p.drawButton = function(){
    this.removeAllChildren();
    this.labelTxt = new createjs.Text(this.label,this.fontSize + 'px
        Arial',this.color);
    this.labelTxt.textAlign = 'center';
```

```
        this.labelTxt.textBaseline = 'top';
        this.width = this.labelTxt.getMeasuredWidth() + 30;
        this.height = this.labelTxt.getMeasuredHeight() + 20;
        this.labelTxt.x = this.width / 2;
        this.labelTxt.y = 10;
        this.background = new createjs.Shape();
        this.background.graphics.beginStroke(this.borderColor)
            .beginFill(this.buttonColor)
            .drawRect(0,0,this.width,this.height);
        this.addChild(this.background,this.labelTxt);
}

p.setButtonListeners = function (){
    this.cursor = 'pointer';
    this.on('rollover',this.onButtonOver);
    this.on('rollout',this.onButtonOut);
}
p.onButtonOver = function(){
    this.buttonColor = this.overColor;
    this.drawButton();
}
p.onButtonOut = function(){
    this.buttonColor = this.upColor;
    this.drawButton();
}
```

All children are removed from the container when the drawButton method is called. This is to clear any old graphics when needing to change or update the current state. The text object is created so you can set the width and height of the button. The getMeasuredWidth and getMeasuredHeight methods are called on the text field to get the size properties, which are then set to the instance variables with a bit of padding. The text is positioned in the center before drawing the button's shape. Lastly, the background and text object are added to the container.

The setButtonListener method sets the event listeners for when the mouse rolls on and off the button. The color of the button shape always takes the value of buttonColor, so each handler sets this to the appropriate value before calling on drawButton to redraw the button.

The following is an example of how you can use this button:

```
var btn = ui.SimpleButton('button 1');
var btn2 = ui.SimpleButton('button 2');
stage.addChild(btn);
btn2.y = btn.y + btn.height + 20;
stage.addChild(btn2);
```

Figure 8-4 demonstrates the button in both its up and over state.

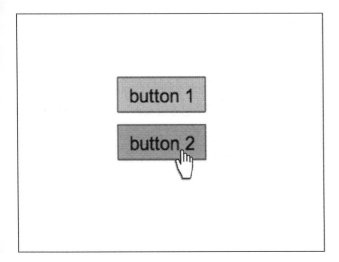

Figure 8-4. *Two instances of the SimpleButton class in its default appearance*

This would make for a decent, reusable button, but you can do better by allowing more functionality to change its appearance. You can create a method for every attribute of the button you wish to make unique with each button instance. We'll cover a few here, shown in Listing 8-9.

Listing 8-9. SimpleButton Set Methods to Customize Appearance

```
p.setUpColor = function(color){
    this.upColor = color;
    this.buttonColor = color;
    this.drawButton();
}
p.setOverColor = function(color){
    this.overColor = color;
}
p.setColor = function(color){
    this.color = this.labelTxt.color = color;
}
p.setFontSize = function(size){
    this.fontSize = size;
    this.drawButton();
}
```

Each method can be called on any instance of `SimpleButton`. Each method simply changes the appropriate property, and with the exception of the `setOverColor`, the button is then immediately redrawn. Listing 8-10 demonstrates how you can now change these properties to make unique buttons in your application.

Listing 8-10. SimpleButton Objects Created and Customized

```
var stage;

// onload
function init() {
    stage = new createjs.Stage(document.getElementById('canvas'));
```

```
        stage.enableMouseOver();
        createjs.Ticker.addEventListener("tick", stage);
        addButtons();
}

function addButtons() {
        var btn = new ui.SimpleButton('button 1');
        var btn2 = new ui.SimpleButton('button 2');
        var btn3 = new ui.SimpleButton('button 3');
        btn.setColor('#FFF');
        btn.setUpColor('#000');
        btn2.setFontSize(40);
        btn2.setUpColor('#A9BBC9');
        btn3.setOverColor('#EEE');
        btn.x = btn2.x = btn3.x = 130;
        btn.y = 20;
        btn2.y = btn.y + btn.height + 20;
        btn3.y = btn2.y + btn2.height + 20;
        stage.addChild(btn,btn2,btn3);
}
```

You can add many more methods to this button to make it even more extensible. Figure 8-5 shows these new buttons in action.

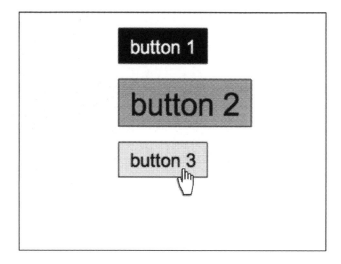

Figure 8-5. *Three instances of SimpleButton class with custom appearance*

Let's add one more addition to SimpleButton before moving on to the preloader component. Every EaselJS display object comes with a handy method called set. To use this method, you pass in a generic object that contains the properties and values you wish to set on the instance of the display object. You can tack onto this functionality to create a shortcut method for creating custom buttons using SimpleButton. Add one more method after your final method in the class (see Listing 8-11).

Listing 8-11. SimpleButton Shortcut Method to Update Multiple Properties

```
p.setButton = function(obj){
   this.set(obj);
   this.buttonColor = obj.upColor != undefined ? obj.upColor :
      this.buttonColor;
   this.drawButton();
}
```

The set method is contained in Container, so you have access to it. The set method updates all properties on SimpleButton that were included in the object passed into it. One thing to notice is that whenever upColor is set, the buttonColor needs to be immediately set to match it, since that is the property used to draw the button. Finally, the button is redrawn. The following is an example of how to change multiple attributes on buttons using only one line of code:

```
btn.setButton({color:'white', fontSize:50, upColor:'green',
   overColor:'#ff69b4'});
```

Now that you've gotten a good look at how to build reusable components, let's revisit the preloader idea that you used in Chapter 2. This time, you'll also utilize Container and inheritance to make it reusable in your games.

Creating a Preloader

You created a prototype of this component when you were learning how to draw graphics in Chapter 2. That prototype was meant to give you an idea of how you can use vector graphics to create dynamic components for visual feedback. It's time to extend on that a bit, and create it as a custom class.

This component is actually quite a bit easier than the SimpleButton class. By now, the extending process should be familiar. Take a look at the complete class Preloader, shown in Listing 8-12.

Listing 8-12. Preloader.js, The Complete Preloader Class

```
(function () {

   window.ui = window.ui || {};

   var Preloader = function (fill, stroke) {
      this.fillColor = fill;
      this.strokeColor = stroke;
      this.initialize();
   }
   var p = Preloader.prototype = new createjs.Container();

   p.width = 400;
   p.height = 40;
   p.fillColor;
   p.strokeColor;
   p.bar;

   p.Container_initialize = p.initialize;
```

```
p.initialize = function () {
    this.Container_initialize();
    this.drawPreloader();
}

p.drawPreloader = function () {
    var outline = new createjs.Shape();
    outline.graphics.beginStroke(this.strokeColor);
    outline.graphics.drawRect(0, 0, this.width, this.height);
    this.bar = new createjs.Shape();
    this.bar.graphics.beginFill(this.fillColor);
    this.bar.graphics.drawRect(0, 0, this.width, this.height);
    this.bar.scaleX = 0;
    this.addChild(this.bar, outline);
}

p.update = function (perc) {
    perc = perc > 1 ? 1 : perc;
    this.bar.scaleX = perc;
}

window.ui.Preloader = Preloader;

}());
```

Some values are sent into the constructor for coloring the stroke and bar for the loader. The graphics are then drawn in the drawPreloader function. We've come a long way since the preloader prototype, so a few things are built differently. Shapes are still used to draw the graphics, but the stroke and fill are now separate objects, so simply changing the x scale of the fill shape will work nicer than redrawing everything on each update. The update function takes a percentage and updates the bar. You'll be using this in conjunction with PreloadJS, so you will typically be pushing in values received from the PreloadJS events to update the preloader.

This class is finished and ready to use in your next project. Listing 8-13 shows a static example of how you can use it in your application.

Listing 8-13. Example of Preloader Class in Use

```
var stage, preloader;

// onload
function init() {
    stage = new createjs.Stage(document.getElementById('canvas'));
    createjs.Ticker.addEventListener("tick", stage);
    addPreloader();
}

function addPreloader() {
    preloader = ui.new Preloader('#34FABC', '#000');
    preloader.x = (stage.canvas.width / 2) - (preloader.width / 2);
    preloader.y = (stage.canvas.height / 2) - (preloader.height / 2);
    stage.addChild(preloader);
    preloader.update(.6);
}
```

This example simply creates a new `Preloader` instance and calls on its update method with a value of 60 percent. This should give you an idea of how to use it with future games. Figure 8-6 demonstrates the loader object at 60 percent complete.

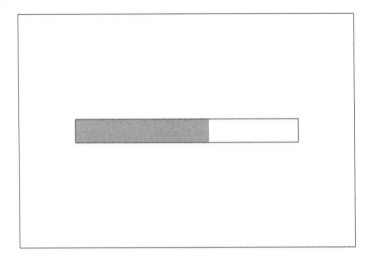

Figure 8-6. *Preload class showing a loader at 60 percent*

With a reusable button and a preloader nicely built and packaged into custom display objects, you now have a simple UI component set. These components will be used in several examples throughout the remainder of this book. However, extending EaselJS for UI is only a small example of the power of inheritance in your games. You can use this same approach to extend `Sprite`, which will make creating your game sprites much more manageable.

Creating Custom Sprites

The `Sprite` class will most likely be the EaselJS class you extend the most when building your games. As you know, the `Sprite` class handles all of the heavy lifting of drawing and cycling through your sprite sheet frames. In games, these sprites have much more responsibility than to just look good. They need to attack, move around, jump, dodge, and die. They need special properties such as health, power, and point values.

Extending the Sprite Class

So far, you've extended Shape and `Container`. `Sprite` is pretty much the same with the exception that it needs `SpriteSheet` data passed into its constructor to work properly. This shouldn't be a surprise to you since this is how you've built sprites so far. Listing 8-14 demonstrates the template code for extending `Sprite`.

Listing 8-14. Code Template for Extending Sprite

```
(function () {

  window.sprites = window.sprites || {};

  var Ship = function (spritesheet) {
     this.initialize(spritesheet);
  }
```

```
    var p = Ship.prototype = new createjs.Sprite();

    p.Sprite_initialize = p.initialize;

    p.initialize = function (spritesheet) {
        this.Sprite_initialize(spritesheet);
    }

    window.sprites.Ship = Ship;
}());
```

The sprite sheet object is passed into the instance of the sprite and is passed along to the `initialize` function so it can be used when calling the super's initializing function. Note that your namespacing code is not necessary to extend `Sprite`, but you will be using it here as you did with the UI elements to keep them out of the global space.

```
window.sprites = window.sprites || {};
```

Using Custom Sprites

As you would expect, using custom sprites in your application is as easy as using one out of the box. Your custom sprite will need a sprite sheet, so be sure you have one ready before trying to add your new sprites to the stage. The following is an example of a custom sprite being instantiated by passing it an existing sprite sheet:

```
var ship = new sprites.Ship(shipSpriteSheet);
addChild(ship);
```

Your custom sprites will often contain methods to act or animate in certain ways, depending on the situation in your game. Listing 8-15 shows a custom property and some methods that might be added to a `Ship` class.

Listing 8-15. Example of Extending Sprite for a Ship Class

```
p.points = 10;

p.die = function(){
    this.gotoAndPlay('explode');
    this.on('animationend',this.destroy);
}
p.destroy = function(){
    this.parent.removeChild(this);
    this = null;
}
```

You can then use this ship in the following way:

```
score += ship.points;
ship.die();
```

This will increment a `score` variable by the value of the `points` property on the `ship` instance. The ship will clean itself up by playing an *explode* sequence, then removing itself from the container it's in when the animation has ended.

Let's combine your new inheritance skills in the final project for this chapter. The SimpleButton class will be used to create a series of buttons to control a custom, animated sprite. The Preloader class will also be used to load in the sprite sheet image.

Running Man

As you know, Grant Skinner is the creator of CreateJS, and we will be using an illustrated version of him in this project. Running Man is a simple application that will utilize the inheritance techniques that you've learned in this chapter. The SimpleButton class will be used to create some buttons that will call on methods in a custom sprite named Runner. The following is a list of the features and procedures needed for this exercise.

- Create a custom sprite named Runner.

- Use PreloadJS and the Preloader class to load in the assets needed for the sprite sheet used in the Runner sprite.

- Give the sprite a series of functions that will play various animations declared in its sprite sheet's data.

- Use the SimpleButton class to create buttons that will fire these methods on the instance of Runner.

Setting Up the Game Files

Set up the HTML document that includes a canvas element and the necessary CreateJS file includes. You'll also create a few JavaScript files: one for the application (runningMan.js) and another for the sprite class (Runner.js). Be sure to also include the UI components you built earlier in this section (see Listing 8-16).

Listing 8-16. HTML File for Running Man

```
<!DOCTYPE html>
<html>
<head>
    <title></title>
    <script src="lib/easeljs-0.7.1.min.js"></script>
    <script src="lib/preloadjs-NEXT.min.js"></script>
    <script src="Runner.js"></script>
    <script src="SimpleButton.js"></script>
    <script src="Preloader.js"></script>
    <script src="runningMan.js"></script>
</head>

<body onload="preload()">

<canvas id="canvas" width="800" height="600" style="border: black solid 1px;background-color:
    #add8e6"></canvas>

</body>

</html>
```

Creating the Runner Sprite

The Runner sprite will be created first. Start with the template code you've used to start your other custom classes in this chapter (see Listing 8-17).

Listing 8-17. Runner Class Declaration

```
(function () {

    window.sprites = window.sprites || {};

    var Runner = function (spritesheet) {
        this.initialize(spritesheet);
    }

    var p = Runner.prototype = new createjs.Sprite();

    p.Sprite_initialize = p.initialize;

    p.initialize = function (spritesheet) {
        this.Sprite_initialize(spritesheet, 'idle');
    }

    window.sprites.Runner = Runner;

}());
```

Only one property will be needed in this sprite. Create a property named speed before the initialize function.

```
p.speed = 0;
```

Moving back into the initialize function, add a tick listener that will move the sprite's x position.

```
p.initialize = function (spritesheet) {
    this.Sprite_initialize(spritesheet, 'idle');
    this.on('tick',function(e){
        this.x += this.speed;
        if(this.x > stage.canvas.width){
            this.x = -this.getBounds().width;
        }
    });
}
```

Since speed is set to 0 and the initial animation set to idle, the instance of this sprite will simply sit on the stage with no movement when created. Add the remainder of the methods now, directly following initialize, as shown in Listing 8-18.

Listing 8-18. Runner Methods Used to Animate

```
p.run = function () {
    if (this.currentAnimation === 'idle') {
        this.gotoAndPlay('run');
        this.speed = 10;
    }
}
p.jump = function () {
    if (this.currentAnimation != 'jump') {
        this.gotoAndPlay('jump');
        this.on('animationend',function(e){
            if(this.speed > 0){
                this.gotoAndPlay('run');
            }
        })
    }
}
p.stand = function () {
    if (this.currentAnimation === 'run') {
        this.gotoAndStop('idle');
        this.speed = 0;
    }
}
```

Each method is fairly similar and straightforward. First, each checks against current animations to prevent unwanted results. For example, having the sprite jump when it is already jumping is not what you want. Each method plays the appropriate animation when allowed to do so. The run and stand methods both change the speed property so it will stop or move across the screen accordingly.

The jump animation in the sprite sheet data is set to immediately play the idle animation when complete. You want this to be the case when jumping in place, but if the sprite is running (i.e. the speed property is greater than 0), the next animation should be run. You use the animationend event to check this when the sprite is finished jumping. Listing 8-19 shows the complete Grant class.

Listing 8-19. Runner Class in Completion

```
(function () {

    window.sprites = window.sprites || {};

    var Runner = function (spritesheet) {
        this.initialize(spritesheet);
    }
    var p = Runner.prototype = new createjs.Sprite();

    p.Sprite_initialize = p.initialize;

    p.speed = 0;

    p.initialize = function (spritesheet) {
        this.Sprite_initialize(spritesheet, 'idle');
        this.on('tick',function(e){
```

```
                this.x += this.speed;
                if(this.x > stage.canvas.width){
                    this.x = -this.getBounds().width;
                }
            })
        }
    p.run = function () {
        if (this.currentAnimation === 'idle') {
            this.gotoAndPlay('run');
            this.speed = 10;
        }
    }
    p.jump = function () {
        if (this.currentAnimation != 'jump') {
            this.gotoAndPlay('jump');
            this.on('animationend',function(e){
                if(this.speed > 0){
                    this.gotoAndPlay('run');
                }
            })
        }
    }
    p.stand = function () {
        if (this.currentAnimation === 'run') {
            this.gotoAndStop('idle');
            this.speed = 0;
        }
    }

    window.sprites. Runner = Runner;
}());
```

Preloading and Initializing the Application

With The Runner class now complete, jump into the runningMan.js file (see Listing 8-20). The application code will begin with some declared variables and the preload function, which is called when the body is loaded.

Listing 8-20. runningMan.js, Variables and preload Function

```
var stage, queue, preloader, spritesheet, runner;

function preload() {
    queue = new createjs.LoadQueue();
    queue.loadManifest([
        {id:"runner", src:"img/runningMan.png"}
    ],false);
    init();
}
```

You've seen this setup before; however, notice that `false` is passed in as the second parameter for `loadManifest`. This is done so it will not immediately start loading. The `init` method is then called to set up the stage and start the load (see Listing 8-21).

Listing 8-21. init Function Creates Preloader and Sets Up Stage

```
function init(){
    stage = new createjs.Stage(document.getElementById('canvas'));
    createjs.Ticker.on('tick', stage);
    stage.enableMouseOver();
    preloader = new ui.Preloader('#FFF','#000');
    preloader.x = (stage.canvas.width / 2) - (preloader.width / 2);
    preloader.y = (stage.canvas.height / 2) - (preloader.height / 2);
    stage.addChild(preloader);
    queue.addEventListener("complete", initGame);
    queue.addEventListener('fileprogress', onFileProgress);
    queue.load();
}
function onFileProgress(e) {
    preloader.update(e.progress);
}
```

The stage is created and an instance of `Preloader` is added to it and positioned. With the stage and preloader ready, the load is started by calling `load` on queue, and will call `onFileProgress` when the overall load progress changes. This method will update the preloader display object. When all files are loaded, `initGame` is called (see Listing 8-22).

Listing 8-22. initGame Function Sets Up Sprite Sheet

```
function initGame() {
    stage.removeChild(preloader);
    preloader = null;
    spritesheet = new createjs.SpriteSheet({
        "images":[queue.getResult("runner")],
        "frames":{"regX":0, "height":292, "count":64, "regY":0,
            "width":165},
        "animations":{"idle":[60], "run":[0, 25], "jump":[31, 60, 'idle']}
    });
    buildRunner();
    buildButtons();
}
```

Setting Up the Sprite Sheet and Buttons

In `initGame`, the preloader is removed from the stage and set to null. Next, the sprite sheet object is built. All of the frames in the sprite sheet image are the same size, so you can take advantage of some of the shortcuts available when creating your data. The data will be built using the `runningMan.png` file, located in your Chapter 8 exercise files. Figure 8-7 displays this sprite sheet image file.

Figure 8-7. *runningMan.png*

Two functions are then called to create an instance of Runner and the buttons to control him (see Listing 8-23).

Listing 8-23. Using the Runner Class and Setting the Button Listeners

```
function buildRunner() {
    runner = new sprites.Runner(spritesheet);
    runner.y = 100;
    stage.addChild(runner);
}
function buildButtons() {
    var jumpBtn = new ui.SimpleButton("JUMP");
    var runBtn = new ui.SimpleButton("RUN");
    var idleBtn = new ui.SimpleButton("IDLE");
    jumpBtn.on('click', function (e) {
        runner.jump();
    });
    runBtn.on('click', function (e) {
        runner.run();
    });
    runBtn.x = jumpBtn.width + 10;
    idleBtn.on('click', function (e) {
        runner.stand();
    });
```

```
        idleBtn.x = runBtn.x + runBtn.width + 10;
        stage.addChild(jumpBtn, runBtn, idleBtn);
}
```

The Runner sprite is positioned and added to the stage; same goes for the three buttons. Figure 8-8 demonstrates all custom display objects added to the stage.

Figure 8-8. *Custom sprite called Runner on stage with three simple buttons*

The Complete Code for Running Man

The entire runningMan.js code for the Running Man application is shown in Listing 8-24.

Listing 8-24. Complete Running Man Application Code

```
var stage, queue, preloader, spritesheet, runner;

function preload() {
    queue = new createjs.LoadQueue();
    queue.loadManifest([
        {id:"runner", src:"img/runningMan.png"}
    ],false);
    init();
}
function init(){
    stage = new createjs.Stage(document.getElementById('canvas'));
    createjs.Ticker.on('tick', stage);
    stage.enableMouseOver();
    preloader = new ui.Preloader('#FFF','#000');
```

```
    preloader.x = (stage.canvas.width / 2) - (preloader.width / 2);
    preloader.y = (stage.canvas.height / 2) - (preloader.height / 2);
    stage.addChild(preloader);
    queue.addEventListener("complete", initGame);
    queue.addEventListener('progress', onFileProgress);
    queue.load();
}
function onFileProgress(e) {
    preloader.update(e.progress);
}
function initGame() {
    stage.removeChild(preloader);
    preloader = null;
    spritesheet = new createjs.SpriteSheet({
        "images":[queue.getResult("runner")],
        "frames":{"regX":0, "height":292, "count":64, "regY":0, "width":165},
        "animations":{"idle":[60], "run":[0, 25], "jump":[31, 60, 'idle']}
    });
    buildRunner();
    buildButtons();
}
function buildRunner() {
    runner = new sprites.Runner(spritesheet);
    runner.y = 100;
    stage.addChild(runner);
}
function buildButtons() {
    var jumpBtn = new ui.SimpleButton("JUMP");
    var runBtn = new ui.SimpleButton("RUN");
    var idleBtn = new ui.SimpleButton("IDLE");
    jumpBtn.on('click', function (e) {
        runner.jump();
    });
    runBtn.on('click', function (e) {
        runner.run();
    });
    runBtn.x = jumpBtn.width + 10;
    idleBtn.on('click', function (e) {
        runner.stand();
    });
    idleBtn.x = runBtn.x + runBtn.width + 10;
    stage.addChild(jumpBtn, runBtn, idleBtn);
}
```

When running this application, it is likely that you won't even see the preloader in action. This is because only one file is being loaded. If you would like to see it animate, try running the application on a server, or include some extra, larger files in the manifest.

Click the buttons to make the runner run, jump, or stop entirely. Figure 8-9 shows the runner in full stride, after the Jump button has been clicked while running.

Figure 8-9. *Runner sprite after running and jumping*

Summary

The lessons learned in this chapter will greatly improve the way you build and manage your games. Building custom display objects that inherit from EaselJS classes gives you the power to write your custom logic inside new and reusable sprites and containers. A set of UI components was built in this chapter and will be used often in the remaining exercises in this book; also, extending `Sprite` will be heavily used from now on.

In the next chapter, you'll look deeper into the `SoundJS` library in order to play sounds in your games. An asset manager class will also be built to manage the loading and access of the files needed for sound, graphics, and data.

■ ■ ■

CHAPTER 9

Sounds and Asset Management

Sound effects and music are a crucial part of your games. Adding background music and audible feedback will instantly increase its polish and overall entertainment value tremendously. This chapter will cover how SoundJS is used in game development, and how sound restrictions on mobile can be avoided.

Along with playing and controlling sounds, you'll take a deep look at how asset management can help organize your games to make them easier to update and read. With the inclusion of sound files into your applications, a self-contained class to handle the ids, loading, and organizing of these sound files, along with other assets, becomes essential. To handle this, an asset manager class will be built in this chapter and will be used to create a simple game.

SoundJS

SoundJS is extremely easy to use. In fact, it's so easy to use that the brief intro in Chapter 1 covers quite a lot. In this section, a quick review of SoundJS will be covered, and some more techniques will be introduced, including loading and mobile considerations.

Using the Sound Class

The **Sound** class is the API for creating and controlling sounds. A sound can be played directly on the Sound class by passing in either an id or the full path to the sound file.

```
createjs.Sound.play("soundID",createjs.Sound.INTERRUPT_NONE,0,0,10,.5,0);
```

The additional, optional parameters passed into the play method are as follows:

- interrupt: How to handle other sounds of the same source currently playing.
- delay: The delay in milliseconds before the sound starts.
- offset: How far into the sound to begin playback, in milliseconds.
- loop: Number of times to loop the audio, -1 for infinite.
- volume: The volume of the sound.
- pan: The pan of the sound between -1 (left) and 1 (right)

The play method returns an instance of the class, SoundInstance, which can give you more control over when and what to do with the sound. You can alternatively create an instance without first playing it by using the createInstance method. Listing 9-1 shows this procedure, along with a few of the methods you can call on a SoundInstance object.

Listing 9-1. Creating a Sound Instance Using createInstance

```
var mySound = createjs.Sound.createInstance("myID");
mySound.setVolume(.5);
mySound.addEventListener("fileload", handleComplete);

function handleComplete(e){
    mySound.play();
}
```

In Listing 9-1, methods were assigned directly to the sound instance, as opposed to passing them into the constructor.

Registering Sounds

Before playing sounds, you must register them. This was covered in Chapter 1 when introducing SoundJS. As a recap, the following is an example of how a sound is registered:

```
createjs.Sound.registerSound("path/sound.mp3", "soundId", 4);
```

The first parameter is the path to the sound file, and the second is the id, which will be used when accessing it later for playback. The third parameter is one that was not previously covered, and it dictates the number of concurrent sounds that should be allowed to play.

It's unlikely that you will only play one sound in your game, so registering multiple files is a must. You can handle this by building a manifest, similar to when using PreloadJS. Listing 9-2 shows a series of sounds being registered.

Listing 9-2. Registering Multiple Sound Files

```
var manifest = [
    {src:"boom.mp3", id:"boom"},
    {src:"snap.mp3 ", id:"snap", data:6},
    {src:"crack.mp3 ", id:"crack"}
];
createjs.Sound.alternateExtensions = ["ogg"];

createjs.Sound.registerManifest(manifest, "sounds/");
```

If you want to load in multiple file types for each sound, you'll need to set the `alternateExtensions` property on Sound. In this example, an ogg file will load, if needed, for each sound object in the manifest. You want to include at least these two file types, mp3 and ogg, so you can be assured your sound will play across all browsers and devices.

The second object in the previous manifest example includes a third property, data. This value is used to set the number of allowed concurrent sounds to play, similar to the third parameter that is used in the `registerSound` method.

```
createjs.Sound.registerSound("boom.mp3", "snap", 6);
```

Preloading Sounds with PreloadJS

Because you will be preloading several assets, along with registering multiple sounds, it would be convenient to handle the entire process with one manifest using PreloadJS. Luckily, this can be achieved by tacking on the sound assets to the load queue's manifest. PreloadJS will handle and register the sound files appropriately as the files are loaded into your application by installing the plug-in *createjs.Sound*. Listing 9-3 shows how you can mix file types, including sounds, into one manifest for preloading.

Listing 9-3. Preloading Sounds with PreloadJS

```
var manifest = [
    {src:"boom.mp3", id:"boom"},
    {src:"crack.mp3", id:"crack"},
    {src:"spritesheet.png", id:"ss"},
    {src:"ssData.json", id:"ssData"},
];
queue = new createjs.LoadQueue();
queue.installPlugin(createjs.Sound);
createjs.Sound.alternateExtensions = ["ogg"];
queue.loadManifest(queue);
```

Considering Mobile

Sound on mobile is the one of the major issues game developers have today when targeting devices. There are many issues with mobile and audio, one of the larger ones is the restriction from playing sound without a user initiating an event, such as a tap or click event.

This doesn't have to be a deal-breaker in many cases. For example, a *play game* button will initiate this event, which can start some background music when your game level begins. Many other game interactivity events and sounds will work fine as well since mobile games tend to be more *touch-centric.*

SoundJS takes care of this all as much as possible behind the scenes, depending on the device and browser. However, the appropriate plug-in must first be installed. To do this, use this convenient method, which will install the needed plug-in for mobile optimization:

```
createjs.Sound.initializeDefaultPlugins();
```

This method prevents the need to set up plug-ins manually. The default plug-ins used are WebAudioPlugin, followed by HTMLAudioPlugin.

Many more methods and properties can be used with SoundJS, and can give you the power to create amazing applications. We'll stick with the needs for most games, which have been explored in this chapter. For more information on the SoundInstance class, as well as current support and limitations on mobile, visit the extensive documentation at www.createjs.com/Docs/SoundJS/modules/SoundJS.html.

Before moving on to using sound in a real world example, some organization is needed to properly load and access all game assets, including sound files within your applications.

Creating an Asset Manager Class

Adding sounds to your games means loading even more assets. Because of this, proper management of these assets is important. Creating a class to store the ids for these files as properties makes it much easier to access them throughout the game code. In this section, all asset references, including sounds, will be declared and stored in one class. This class will also handle the loading and event dispatching of their progress and completion.

Extending the EventDispatcher Class

Because preloading files is a functionality needed in this class, the ability to dispatch events is necessary. The class will handle the preloading work using PreloadJS, but will not handle any actual messaging to the stage, nor will it reference properties or call methods from the application that is using it. It merely needs to send messages when progress on a load has changed and when the load is complete. In order to achieve this, the class will extend from CreateJS's EventDispatcher class.

The EventDispatcher class is used throughout the entire CreateJS suite. If you recall, all EaselJS display objects extend DisplayObject, which itself inherits from EventDispatcher. This is how you can set event listeners on shapes, sprites, and containers. You can also create your own events on these objects and dispatch them. This will be done in the "Creating and Dispatching Events" section when handling the preloading of assets in the AssetManager class.

To extend EventDispatcher, set up an object the same as you would when extending display objects (see Listing 9-4).

Listing 9-4. Extending the EventDispatcher Class

```
(function () {

    var AssetManager = function () {
        this.initialize();
    }

    var p = AssetManager.prototype = new createjs.EventDispatcher();

    p.EventDispatcher_initialize = p.initialize;

    p.initialize = function () {
        this.EventDispatcher_initialize();
    }

    window.AssetManager = AssetManager;

}());
```

This should look familiar to you already as it uses the exact same structure you used when extending display objects in Chapter 8. To use this class, simply instantiate it like you did with your custom display objects.

```
var assets = new AssetManager();
```

This class will be meant to handle assets, so naturally you are going to need to reference the actual assets.

Declaring the Assets and Events

For each asset needed in the application, a string constant should be made. This will be a property that will hold the string used when identifying the file in the load manifest. Listing 9-5 shows an example of some assets being declared.

Listing 9-5. Constants Used for File Ids

```
//sounds
p.EXPLOSION = 'explosion';
p.SHIP_FIRE = 'ship fire';
p.POWER_UP = 'power up';
p.SOUNDTRACK = 'soundtrack';

//graphics
p.GAME_SPRITES = 'game sprites';
p.UI_SPRITES = 'ui sprites';

//data
p.GAME_SPRITES_DATA = 'game sprites data';
p.UI_SPRITES_DATA = 'ui game sprites data';
```

These values will be used when building the manifest for the load queue. You'll also need to declare a property for this queue, along with a few others, shown in Listing 9-6.

Listing 9-6. Properties for the AssetManager Class

```
p.queue = null;
p.assetsPath = 'assets/';
p.loadManifest = null;
p.loadProgress = 0;
```

Along with the queue, the assets path is created for use when building the manifest, which will also be stored as a property named loadManifest. Lastly, a loadProgress property is made so the progress can be easily accessed from outside the class. Next, a few event strings are declared in Listing 9-7.

Listing 9-7. Events Used in AssetManager

```
//events
p.ASSETS_PROGRESS = 'assets progress';
p.ASSETS_COMPLETE = 'assets complete';
```

These strings will be the names of the events that are dispatched from the class. As with manifest ids, events are created using simple strings, so setting them to the value of a property makes it much easier to access in the future.

Now that the properties are set, the manifest needs to be built so it can be loaded into PreloadJS.

Preloading in the AssetManager Class

The manifest will be built directly in the initialize method, which assures you that all property values have been set and ready to use. Listing 9-8 extends on to the initialize method.

Listing 9-8. Creating a Load Manifest

```
p.initialize = function () {
 this.EventDispatcher_initialize();
 this.loadManifest = [
   {id:this.EXPLOSION, src:this.assetsPath + 'explosion.mp3'},

   {id:this.SHIP_FIRE, src:this.assetsPath + 'fire.mp3'},

   {id:this.POWER_UP, src:this.assetsPath + 'powerup.mp3'},

   {id:this.SOUNDTRACK, src:this.assetsPath + 'dreamRaid1.mp3'},

   {id:this.GAME_SPRITES_DATA, src:this.assetsPath +
      'gameSpritesData.json'},

   {id:this.UI_SPRITES_DATA, src:this.assetsPath +
      'uiSpritesData.json'},
   {id:this.GAME_SPRITES, src:this.assetsPath + 'gameSprites.png'},

   {id:this.UI_SPRITES, src:this.assetsPath + 'uiSprites.png'}
 ];
}
```

By the time the AssetManager class completely instantiates, the manifest will be ready to use. The next method, preloadAssets, will be called on the instance of the class and will trigger the loading process (see Listing 9-9).

Listing 9-9. The preloadAssets Method Is Called from the Game to Load all Assets

```
p.preloadAssets = function () {
    createjs.Sound.initializeDefaultPlugins();
    this.queue = new createjs.LoadQueue();
    this.queue.installPlugin(createjs.Sound);
    this.queue.on('progress',this.assetsProgress,this);
    this.queue.on('complete',this.assetsLoaded,this);
    createjs.Sound.alternateExtensions = ["ogg"];
    this.queue.loadManifest(this.loadManifest);
}
```

The necessary plug-ins are used to properly handle sounds in the preload and to take care of mobile situations before loading the manifest. Next, the on method is used to listen for events that are dispatched when the load progress has changed and when it is complete. This addEventListener shortcut was used in Chapters 7 and 8, but its other useful features have not been examined yet. One of those features is its ability to manage scope.

Managing Scope with the on Method

In Chapter 1, the issue of *scope* was briefly discussed when we were going over the call function in TweenJS. The issue is that in JavaScript, it's easy to lose scope of objects within callback functions. In the case of the AssetManager class that we are currently outlining, the progress and complete event handlers on the load queue will not be in scope of AssetManager. Instead, the scope will actually be in Window by default. This is a problem because you need to dispatch events during those updates within the class.

This is where the on method helps. The first two parameters in the on method are identical to addEventListener, the type of event to listen for and the callback function to handle it. The third parameter allows you to declare the scope of the event handler function.

```
this.queue.on('progress',this.assetsProgress,this);
```

Now within the assetsProgress function, you will be in scope of this, or in this case, the AssetManager class. This is set up for the queue's complete event as well. Now you can be assured that when these event handlers fire, you will still be in scope of the class you are building, and can safely access its instance variables and call on its methods.

Creating and Dispatching Events

With scope under control, the handler functions are created next and are used to dispatch events back to the application (see Listing 9-10).

Listing 9-10. Dispatching the AssetManager Events

```
p.assetsProgress = function (e) {
    this.loadProgress = e.progress;
    this.dispatchEvent(this.ASSETS_PROGRESS);
}
p.assetsLoaded = function (e) {
    this.dispatchEvent(this.ASSETS_COMPLETE);
}
```

The assetsProgress and assetsLoaded methods dispatch the appropriate events by using the two constant strings that were declared earlier. Now the application that instantiates this object can listen for these events. In the "Exploding Asteroids" section, you'll see this being applied in a full working example that uses this class. But first, there is one more method that needs to be created.

Accessing Assets from the AssetManager Class

The assets are all preloaded and ready to use. Next, the getAsset method is created to help access these assets (see Listing 9-11).

Listing 9-11. The getAsset Function Returns Results from the Load Queue

```
p.getAsset = function (asset) {
   return this.queue.getResult(asset);
}
```

This method takes a string and returns the result from the load queue. Of course, this queue could be accessed from the instance of this object, but this makes it a little less verbose when accessing assets. Listing 9-12 shows how the AssetManager class can be used to access assets for both data and sound.

Listing 9-12. Example of AssetManager in Use

```
assets = new AssetManager();
assets.on(assets.ASSETS_COMPLETE, assetsComplete);

function assetsComplete(e){
   var data = assets.getAsset(assets.GAME_SPRITES_DATA);
   spritesheet = new createjs.SpriteSheet(data);
   createjs.Sound.play(assets.EXPLODE);
}
```

A similar, fully working class will be built in the next section, "Exploding Asteroids," where you will get a chance to see the full benefits to creating this functionality.

Exploding Asteroids

Exploding Asteroids is a simple game created to put sound effects and music into a working example. The point of this exercise is to access sounds and other assets using a fully working asset manager class. The same techniques learned in this chapter will be applied.

Asteroids will eternally fall down the screen at various speeds. The player must destroy them by clicking them, where they will explode into oblivion. The following is a list of features you wish to accomplish:

- Create a class to handle all loading and accessing of assets, including sprite sheet data, the sprite sheet image, and sounds.

- Use the preloader and button components built in Chapter 8.

- Create an asteroid sprite class that can play sounds and dispatch an event when it is destroyed.

- Click on asteroids to play their explosion animation and explosion sound.

- Play background music when the game starts.

- No ending or scoring is needed in this exercise.

Setting Up the Game Files

In this section, you will set up the HTML document that includes a canvas element and the necessary CreateJS file includes. A few JavaScript files will also be needed in this exercise: one for the application named exploadingAsteroids.js, one for the asteroid sprite named Asteroid.js, and another for the asset manager named AssetManager.js. Be sure to also include the UI components Preloader.js and SimpleButton.js that were built in Chapter 8 (see Listing 9-13).

Listing 9-13. index.html for Exploding Asteroids

```html
<!DOCTYPE html>
<html>
<head>
    <title>Exploding Asteroids</title>
    <script src="lib/easeljs-0.7.1.min.js"></script>
    <script src="lib/soundjs-0.5.2.min.js"></script>
    <script src="lib/preloadjs-0.4.1.min.js"></script>
    <script src="js/AssetManager.js"></script>
    <script src="js/Preloader.js"></script>
    <script src="js/SimpleButton.js"></script>
    <script src="js/Asteroid.js"></script>
    <script src="js/exploadingAsteroids.js"></script>
</head>

<body onload="init()">

<canvas id="canvas" width="800" height="600" style="background-color:
    #000"></canvas>

</body>

</html>
```

The Complete AssetManager for Exploding Asteroids

The first thing that should be created is the AssetManager class. The procedures for building this class were fully examined earlier in the "Creating an Asset Manager Class" section, so the code in this class should be easy to follow. The complete code for AssetManager.js is shown in Listing 9-14.

Listing 9-14. The AssetManager class – AssetManager.js

```javascript
(function () {

    window.game = window.game || {};

    var AssetManager = function () {
        this.initialize();
    }
    var p = AssetManager.prototype = new createjs.EventDispatcher();

    p.EventDispatcher_initialize = p.initialize;

    //sounds
    p.EXPLOSION = 'explosion';
    p.SOUNDTRACK = 'soundtrack';
```

```
        //graphics
        p.GAME_SPRITES = 'game sprites';

        //data
        p.GAME_SPRITES_DATA = 'game sprites data';

        //events
        p.ASSETS_PROGRESS = 'assets progress';
        p.ASSETS_COMPLETE = 'assets complete';

        p.assetsPath = 'assets/';

        p.loadManifest = null;
        p.queue = null;
        p.loadProgress = 0;

        p.initialize = function () {
            this.EventDispatcher_initialize();
            this.loadManifest = [
                {id: this.EXPLOSION, src: this.assetsPath + 'explosion.mp3'},
                {id: this.SOUNDTRACK, src: this.assetsPath + 'dreamRaid1.mp3'},
                {id:this.GAME_SPRITES_DATA, src:this.assetsPath +
                    'gameSpritesData.json'},
                {id:this.GAME_SPRITES, src:this.assetsPath +
                    'gameSprites.png'}
            ];
        }
        p.preloadAssets = function () {
            createjs.Sound.initializeDefaultPlugins();
            this.queue = new createjs.LoadQueue();
            this.queue.installPlugin(createjs.Sound);
            this.queue.on('progress',this.assetsProgress,this);
            this.queue.on('complete',this.assetsLoaded,this);
            createjs.Sound.alternateExtensions = ["ogg"];
            this.queue.loadManifest(this.loadManifest);
        }
        p.assetsProgress = function (e) {
            this.loadProgress = e.progress;
            this.dispatchEvent(this.ASSETS_PROGRESS);
        }
        p.assetsLoaded = function (e) {
            this.dispatchEvent(this.ASSETS_COMPLETE);
        }
        p.getAsset = function (asset) {
            return this.queue.getResult(asset);
        }

        window.game.AssetManager = AssetManager;

}());
```

Creating the Asteroid Class

Next, the asteroid sprite will be created. The Asteroid.js file contains the entire Asteroid class (see Listing 9-15).

Listing 9-15. The Asteroid Class – Asteroid.js

```
(function () {

    window.game = window.game || {};

    var Asteroid = function (spritesheet) {
        this.initialize(spritesheet);
    }
    var p = Asteroid.prototype = new createjs.Sprite();

    p.Sprite_initialize = p.initialize;

    p.EXPLOSION_COMPLETE = 'explosion complete';

    p.bounds = null;
    p.speed = null;

    p.initialize = function (spritesheet) {
        this.Sprite_initialize(spritesheet);
        var frame = this.speed = Math.floor(Math.random() * 4) + 1;
        this.gotoAndStop('asteroid' + this.frame);
        this.bounds = this.getBounds();
        this.regX = this.bounds.width / 2;
        this.regY = this.bounds.height / 2;
        this.on('tick', this.move);
    }
    p.move = function (e) {
        this.rotation += this.speed;
        this.y += this.speed * 2;
        if (this.y > canvas.height + this.bounds.height) {
            this.y = -this.bounds.height;
        }
    }
    p.explode = function () {
        this.speed /= 2;
        this.on('animationend', this.explosionComplete);
        this.gotoAndPlay('explosion');
        createjs.Sound.play(game.assets.EXPLOSION);
    }
    p.explosionComplete = function (e) {
        this.stop();
        this.dispatchEvent(this.EXPLOSION_COMPLETE);
    }

    window.game.Asteroid = Asteroid;

}());
```

The `Asteroid` class has a few properties for speed and to store the bounds of the sprite. There is also a string that will be used for the event that will be dispatched when destroyed. The asteroid has four possible frames to randomly pick from, which are shown in the sprite sheet image in Figure 9-1.

Figure 9-1. *Exploding Asteroids sprite sheet – gameSprites.png*

The sprite sheet also includes an explosion animation that will play when the asteroid is clicked and destroyed. The registration point is centered so the rock can spin as it moves down the screen in the move method, which runs on the *tick*. If the asteroid makes it past the bottom of the stage without being destroyed, it is recycled by resetting its y position back at the top.

Next are the methods that handle its explosion. The `explode` method will be called from the game when the asteroid is clicked. The speed is slowed down for effect, and an event listener is set for when the explosion animation has ended. Next, the animation is played, and the explosion sound is referenced from the `AssetsManager` instance that will be created in the game code. Using `SoundJS`, the sound is played.

When the animation is complete, the `explosionComplete` handler is called, which stops the animation and dispatches the *explosion complete* event, which is set to the property `EXPLOSION_COMPLETE`.

With the `AssetManager` and `Asteroid` classes complete, it's time to create the game.

Creating the Exploding Asteroids Game

The game code will be written in the `explodingAsteroids.js` file. Open the file and start by declaring the game variables and writing the `init` function, shown in Listing 9-16.

Listing 9-16. Game Variables and init Function

```
window.game = window.game || {};

var canvas, stage, assets, preloader, spritesheet;

var spawnDelay = 40;
var count = 0;

function init() {
    canvas = document.getElementById('canvas');
    stage = new createjs.Stage(canvas);
    createjs.Ticker.setFPS(30);
    game.assets = new game.AssetManager();
    preloadAssets();
}
```

The `spawnDelay` value will be the count at which another asteroid will be spawned, which is determined by the incrementing `count` variable. The `init` function, which is called when the body loads, sets up the `stage` and `Ticker`. An instance of `AssetManager` is created and set to the game namespace, which will be accessible throughout the game. Next, the assets are loaded using the functions shown in Listing 9-17.

Listing 9-17. Using the Preloader Component with AssetManager Events

```
function preloadAssets() {
    preloader = new ui.Preloader('#0F0', '#FFF');
    preloader.x = (stage.canvas.width / 2) - (preloader.width / 2);
    preloader.y = (stage.canvas.height / 2) - (preloader.height / 2);
    stage.addChild(preloader);
    game.assets.on(game.assets.ASSETS_PROGRESS, assetsProgress);
    game.assets.on(game.assets.ASSETS_COMPLETE, assetsComplete);
    game.assets.preloadAssets();
}
function assetsProgress(e) {
    preloader.update(e.target.loadProgress);
    stage.update();
}
function assetsComplete(e) {
    stage.removeChild(preloader);
    createSpriteSheet();
    buildStartMenu();
}
```

The preloader component is first positioned and added to the stage. Next, some listeners are set on the AssetManager instance to handle the load progress and completion. Finally, the preloadAssets method is called, which will kick start the loading of the assets.

When the load progress has updated, the preloader component is updated by accessing the loadProgress property from the assets object that fired the handler function. Figure 9-2 demonstrates the preloader component displaying the load progress.

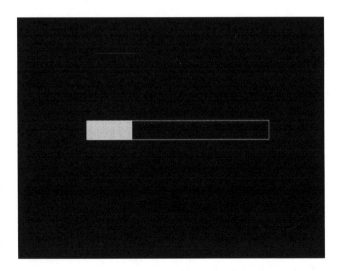

Figure 9-2. *Preloader component displapying loading progress*

When all files are loaded, the assetsComplete function removes the preloader container, and calls on the functions to create the sprite sheet and create the start menu (see Listing 9-18).

Listing 9-18. Sprite Sheet Creation and a Simple Start Menu

```
function createSpriteSheet() {
    var assets = game.assets;
    spritesheet = new
        createjs.SpriteSheet(assets.getAsset(assets.GAME_SPRITES_DATA));
}
function buildStartMenu() {
    var button = new ui.SimpleButton('PLAY GAME');
    button.regX = button.width / 2;
    button.regY = button.height / 2;
    button.x = canvas.width / 2;
    button.y = canvas.height / 2;
    button.on('click', startGame);
    stage.addChild(button);
    stage.update();
}
```

The spritesheet object is created and stored away. Notice how the sprite sheet data is utilizing the assets class to retrieve the preloaded JSON file. Next, in buildStartMenu, a simple button is created that will start the game ticker by calling the startGame function (see Figure 9-3).

Figure 9-3. *Start menu using the SimpleButton component*

When the play game button is clicked, **startGame** is called (see Listing 9-19).

Listing 9-19. Starting the Game with Some Sounds and a Simple Game Loop

```
function startGame() {
    var assets = game.assets;
    stage.removeAllChildren();
    createjs.Sound.play(assets.EXPLOSION)
    createjs.Sound.play(assets.SOUNDTRACK,0,0,0,10,.5);
    createjs.Ticker.on('tick', onTick);
}
function onTick(e) {
    count++;
    checkForSpawn();
    stage.update();
}
```

An explosion is first played as an effect for the button click. Then some background music is started, which will loop 10 times and play at a volume of .5. Finally, the ticker is set to fire the onTick function. This function increments the count variable, checks if a new asteroid should be created, and finally updates the stage. The asteroid functions are written next (see Listing 9-20).

Listing 9-20. The Game Functions That Create and Destory Asteroids

```
function checkForSpawn() {
    if (count == spawnDelay) {
        spawnAsteroid();
        count = 0;
    }
}
function spawnAsteroid() {
    var a = new game.Asteroid(spritesheet);
    a.x = Math.random() * canvas.width;
    a.on('click', onAsteroidClick);
    a.on(a.EXPLOSION_COMPLETE, destroyAsteroid);
    stage.addChild(a);
}
function onAsteroidClick(e) {
    var asteroid = e.target;
    asteroid.explode();
}
function destroyAsteroid(e) {
    var asteroid = e.target;
    stage.removeChild(asteroid);
    asteroid = null;
}
```

An asteroid is created when the count has reached the predetermined value by calling the spawnAsteroid function, which will then reset the counter back to 0. Each asteroid is an instance of the Asteroid class and given a random x value. Two listeners are then set on the sprite, one for a click and another for the event you created inside of the sprite that dispatches after its explosion animation.

The click event will fire the function to explode the asteroid instance. This is done by calling on its explode function, which will play the explosion animation, play a sound, and dispatch the EXPLOSION_COMPLETE event, which will remove it from the stage. Figure 9-4 shows an asteroid exploding during gameplay.

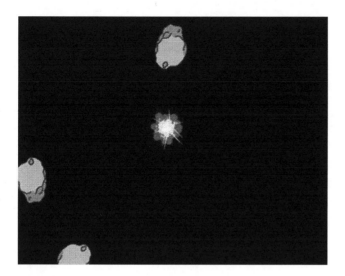

Figure 9-4. *Mid-game asteroid explosion*

The Complete Exploding Asteroids Game Code

The complete game code for Exploding Asteroids is shown in Listing 9-21.

Listing 9-21. Exploding Asteroids - explodingAsteroids.js

```
window.game = window.game || {};

var canvas, stage, assets, preloader, spritesheet;

var spawnDelay = 40;
var count = 0;

function init() {
    canvas = document.getElementById('canvas');
    stage = new createjs.Stage(canvas);
    createjs.Ticker.setFPS(30);
    game.assets = new game.AssetManager();
    preloadAssets();
}
```

```
function preloadAssets() {
   preloader = new ui.Preloader('#0F0', '#FFF');
   preloader.x = (stage.canvas.width / 2) - (preloader.width / 2);
   preloader.y = (stage.canvas.height / 2) - (preloader.height / 2);
   stage.addChild(preloader);
   game.assets.on(game.assets.ASSETS_PROGRESS, assetsProgress);
   game.assets.on(game.assets.ASSETS_COMPLETE, assetsComplete);
   game.assets.preloadAssets();
}
function assetsProgress(e) {
   preloader.update(e.target.loadProgress);
   stage.update();
}
function assetsComplete(e) {
   stage.removeChild(preloader);
   createSpriteSheet();
   buildStartMenu();
}
function createSpriteSheet() {
   spritesheet = new
      createjs.SpriteSheet(game.assets.getAsset(game.assets.GAME_SPRITES_DATA));
}
function buildStartMenu() {
   var button = new ui.SimpleButton('PLAY GAME');
   button.regX = button.width / 2;
   button.regY = button.height / 2;
   button.x = canvas.width / 2;
   button.y = canvas.height / 2;
   button.on('click', startGame);
   stage.addChild(button);
   stage.update();
}
function startGame() {
   var assets = game.assets;
   stage.removeAllChildren();
   createjs.Sound.play(assets.EXPLOSION)
   createjs.Sound.play(assets.SOUNDTRACK,0,0,0,10,.5);
   createjs.Ticker.on('tick', onTick);
}
function spawnAsteroid() {
   var a = new game.Asteroid(spritesheet);
   a.x = Math.random() * canvas.width;
   a.on('click', onAsteroidClick);
   a.on(a.EXPLOSION_COMPLETE, destroyAsteroid);
   stage.addChild(a);
}
function onAsteroidClick(e) {
   var asteroid = e.target;
   asteroid.explode();
}
```

```
function destroyAsteroid(e) {
    var asteroid = e.target;
    stage.removeChild(asteroid);
    asteroid = null;
}
function checkForSpawn() {
    if (count == spawnDelay) {
        spawnAsteroid();
        count = 0;
    }
}
function onTick(e) {
    count++;
    checkForSpawn();
    stage.update();
}
```

Summary

In this chapter, you learned how to use SoundJS to add sounds and music to your games. The robust and easy-to-use Sound class makes adding sound a breeze, and by installing plug-ins you were able to preload sounds and even play them on a mobile platform. Asset management was also introduced by creating an asset management class to handle the loading and accessing of loaded files. In the next chapter, code management and organization will be extended even further by building a state machine to run your game.

■ ■ ■

CHAPTER 10

The State Machine and Scenes

A typical game will include multiple states during its existence. A state can be one of many different *scenes* in a game, including a home screen, a leaderboard, a settings menu, the game itself, and many others. A game can consist of a few or many states, and the management system to assure that only one state is running at a time is an important technique in game development. The collective components that make up this management system are referred to as a *state machine*.

This chapter will take a close look at each area that makes up a state machine, and then you'll put your new knowledge into practice by creating a simple game that will implement one. This game will consist of a title screen, the game level, and a game over screen. These scenes will all be written outside of the global scope, which will provide better code structure, but will introduce more of those pesky scope issues. I will further address those issues in this chapter.

Deconstructing a State Machine

So far, the games in this book have all been built within one screen. In other words, they have had only one *state* during the entire game. The Break-It game in Chapter 4 used a Boolean variable to determine if the game was in play; if not, it fell into a waiting state for the user to take action. This approach is a simple technique to manage state, but it's not practical once you start tacking on more states and scenes to your game. This section will break down the process of building a state machine to properly run and manage your game scenes.

Declaring States

States are typically stored in constants that can easily be accessed and readable within the code of your game. This approach was used in Chapter 9 when declaring assets in an asset manager. These values will be used to determine what state the game should switch to or continue to run in. Listing 10-1 shows an example of a few states being declared and stored inside an object.

Listing 10-1. Example of State Ids Being Declared

```
var GameStates = {
    MAIN_MENU:0,
    RUN_SCENE:10,
    GAME:20,
    GAME_OVER:30
}
```

The states listed in this object can now be access in following way:

```
currentGameState = GameStates.MAIN_MENU;
```

The state machine will most often run within the main class of your application, and will be used to load and unload scenes. The current state of the application will be held in a variable so it can be accessed at any time.

Setting the Game State

The game state is typically set within a function that is called when the state should change. It should accept a parameter, which will be used to set the new game state. This function will also contain a switch statement to evaluate the current state and appropriately change the game's behavior.

The behavior of the game is determined by the function that will run on each tick of the game loop. This function should also be stored in a variable so it can be continuously called while the game is running. Listing 10-2 demonstrates an example of this important function.

Listing 10-2. A State Machine Function, Used for Changing Game State

```
function changeState (state) {
    currentGameState = state;
    switch (currentGameState) {
        case GameStates.MAIN_MENU:
            currentGameStateFunction = gameStateMainMenu;
            break;
        case GameStates.GAME:
            currentGameStateFunction = gameStateGame;
            break;
        case GameStates.RUN_SCENE:
            currentGameStateFunction = gameStateRunScene;
            break;
        case GameStates.GAME_OVER:
            currentGameStateFunction = gameStateGameOver;
            break;
    }
}

//change game state
changeState(GameStates.GAME_OVER);
```

Running the Game

When the game state and game state functions have been set, the game loop will react by firing the current game state function. Listing 10-3 creates the ticker handler, which will call the current game state function before updating the stage.

Listing 10-3. The Current Game State Function Is Called Within Each tick Event

```
createjs.Ticker.on('tick', onTick);

function onTick(e){
    currentGameStateFunction(e);
    stage.update();
}
```

There are various patterns when it comes to setting up a state machine, all slightly different, but all should accomplish the same goal in managing state. In the approach I've decided to use in this book, these game functions will typically do one of two actions. When the state changes, a new scene should be initiated, while disposing of the previous one. A scene is a collection of both code and visuals that should take over the screen when called upon to do so. In EaselJS, this will most often be done within a custom container class.

The second type of action used in game state functions is to simply update the current scene. In the approach used in this book, the same function will be used for every scene that has been initiated, and will try to call a run method on the current scene (see Listing 10-4). The tick event from the game loop is also passed into this run method. The tick event carries useful properties that might be used within the game scene, such as delta and time. You will be using these properties for the Space Hero game in Chapter 11.

Listing 10-4. *A Run Scene State Will Run the Current Scene if Needed*

```
function gameStateRunScene (tickEvent) {
    if (currentScene.run) {
        currentScene.run(tickEvent);
    }
}
```

Not all scenes will need this type of constant updating, nor will it have a run method to execute, so this call will be wrapped in a conditional. This RUN_SCENE state will be immediately set after a new scene has been created. Listing 10-5 shows an example of a game state function that is called on to start a new game.

Listing 10-5. *An Example of a State Function Creating a New Scene*

```
function gameStateGame () {
    var scene = new game.Game();
    stage.addChild(scene);
    stage.removeChild(currentScene);
    currentScene = scene;
    changeState(game.GameStates.RUN_SCENE);
}
```

Notice that this state only exists for a single tick, and is used to simply change the current scene before changing to the RUN_SCENE state.

Setting Up Game State Events

The changing of a state will most often be decided within the current running scene. This might happen from the click of a button or the destruction of all lives in a game level. Similar to declaring game states, the game state events are declared in the same fashion (see Listing 10-6).

Listing 10-6. *Game State Event Ids Declared in an Object*

```
var GameStateEvents = {
    MAIN_MENU:'main-menu-event',
    GAME_OVER:'game-over-event',
    MAIN_MENU_SELECT:'game-menu-select-event',
    GAME:'game-event',
    SCORE_SCREEN:'score-screen-event'
}
```

Because the base of each scene will most likely extend a display object, dispatching events is a great way to communicate back to the main application that something needs to happen. Listing 10-7 shows an example of this being done within a game menu screen.

Listing 10-7. A Button that Dispatches a State Event

```
function onStartButton(e){
    dispatchEvent(GameStateEvents.GAME);
}
```

This example demonstrates the action that happens when a player clicks a button to play the game. Because this menu resides in a container class, dispatching this event is possible. Back in the state function that added this menu screen is where the listener is set up (see Listing 10-8).

Listing 10-8. Setting a State Event Listener on a New Scene

```
p.gameStateMainMenu = function () {
    var scene = new game.GameMenu();
    scene.on(game.GameStateEvents.GAME, this.onStateEvent, this, false,
        {state:game.GameStates.GAME});
    stage.addChild(scene);
    stage.removeChild(currentScene);
    this.currentScene = scene;
    this.changeState(game.GameStates.RUN_SCENE);
}
```

The changeState function is written to be called from anywhere by passing it the state you wish to change to. In the case of an event, a handler function needs to be set up as an intermediate step in the state changing process. By utilizing the on method to listen for these events, an object can be passed into the handler. You'll also notice the use of the third parameter, which is used to keep the scope to **this** within the handler function. You used this same approach with PreloadJS when building the asset manager in Chapter 9.

▨ **Note**   In order to reach the fifth parameter in the on method, you need to fill out all proceeding options, even if you don't need them. This is done in most cases by simply assigning the default value for all properties you need to bypass.

A generic object is created as the data you wish to pass into the onStateEvent function. The object will contain one property, state, and will hold the value of the state you wish to change to. Listing 10-9 shows this intermediate function for state changing.

Listing 10-9. The Handler Function for All State Events

```
function onStateEvent (e, data) {
    this.changeState(data.state);
}
```

The first parameter of any event handler will be the event object that invoked it. This object is not needed in this case, but must be entered so the second parameter can be declared and accessed.

This concludes the major components of a working state machine. The next exercise, Orb Destroyer, will fully utilize these procedures to build a state machine for a simple game.

Orb Destroyer

Orb Destroyer is a very simple game, but it will be used to put the state machine pattern into practice. You will complete the following procedures in this exercise:

- Create an application that consists of two menus and a game level.

- Use a state machine to control the state of the application.

- Create and dispatch events within the scenes to communicate back to the main application, which will change states.

- Keep the entire application out of global scope by utilizing the on method to control scope and pass values.

Setting Up the Game Files

Set up the HTML document that includes a canvas element, the necessary CreateJS files, the PulsingOrb class, and the SimpleButton component. You'll also create the following JavaScript files:

- state.js

- GameMenu.js

- Game.js

- GameOver.js

- OrbDestroyer.js

Listing 10-10 shows the inclusion of all JavaScript files and their locations, as well as the HTML and init function that fires when the body has loaded.

Listing 10-10. The index.html for Orb Destroyer Includes All JavaScript Files and Initializes the Application

```
<!DOCTYPE html>
<html>
<head>
    <title></title>
    <script src="js/lib/easeljs-0.7.1.min.js"></script>
    <script src="js/lib/soundjs-0.5.2.min.js"></script>
    <script src="js/lib/preloadjs-0.4.1.min.js"></script>
    <script src="js/state.js"></script>
    <script src="js/SimpleButton.js"></script>
    <script src="js/PulsingOrb.js"></script>
    <script src="js/scenes/GameMenu.js"></script>
    <script src="js/scenes/Game.js"></script>
    <script src="js/scenes/GameOver.js"></script>
    <script src="js/OrbDestroyer.js"></script>
</head>

<body onload="init();">

<canvas id="canvas" width="800" height="600" style="border: black solid
    1px"></canvas>

</body>
```

```
<script>
    var stage;
    var canvas;

    function init() {
        window.game = window.game || {};
        game.main = new game.OrbDestroyer();
    }
</script>
</html>
```

Building the States and State Events

The states and state events will be declared in a separate JavaScript file, which will hold both objects to hold these properties. Listing 10-11 shows these two objects, written in state.js.

Listing 10-11. The State and State Event Ids Both Declared in state.js

```
(function () {

    window.game = window.game || {};

    var GameStates = {
        MAIN_MENU:0,
        RUN_SCENE:1,
        GAME:10,
        GAME_OVER:20
    }

    var GameStateEvents = {
        MAIN_MENU:'main-menu-event',
        GAME_OVER:'game-over-event',
        GAME:'game-event',
    }

    window.game.GameStates = GameStates;
    window.game.GameStateEvents = GameStateEvents;

}());
```

As you can see, you can easily declare and organize crucial objects within one separate file. For smaller, related objects such as these, combining them into a single script is often a good approach.

■ **Note**   Because this JavaScript file contains more than one object, I've opted to not use the uppercase naming convention for its file name, which derives from other class-based programming languages. This uppercase naming convention should be used only when creating single complex classes. Remember, JavaScript does not technically have classes, but following these classic conventions helps keep your code organized and easy to follow.

Building the Game Menu

The menu screen will be the first scene loaded into the application. It will extend Container; it also will contain a simple play button, which will call back to the application and change the state. Listing 10-12 shows the entire GameMenu class.

Listing 10-12. GameMenu.js - The Main Game Menu Class

```
(function (window) {

    window.game = window.game || {}

    function GameMenu() {
        this.initialize();
    }

    var p = GameMenu.prototype = new createjs.Container();

    p.Container_initialize = p.initialize;

    p.titleTxt = null;
    p.count = 0;

    p.initialize = function () {
        this.Container_initialize();
        this.addBG();
        this.addTitle();
        this.addOrbs();
        this.addButton();
    }
    p.addBG = function () {
        var bg = new createjs.Shape();
        bg.graphics.beginFill('0').drawRect(0, 0, canvas.width, canvas.height);
        this.addChild(bg);
    }
    p.addTitle = function () {
        this.titleTxt = new createjs.Text("ORB DESTROYER!", '40px Arial',
            '#FFF');
        this.titleTxt.x = canvas.width / 2;
        this.titleTxt.y = 200;
        this.titleTxt.textAlign = 'center';
        this.addChild(this.titleTxt);
    }
    p.addOrbs = function () {
        var i, orb;
        var orbContainer = new createjs.Container();
        var numOrbs = 5;
        var orbSize = 20;
        var orbPadding = 10;
        var orbsPosition = 300;
        for (i = 0; i < numOrbs; i++) {
```

```
            orb = new PulsingOrb('#FFF', orbSize);
            orb.x = i * ((orbSize * 2) + orbPadding);
            orbContainer.addChild(orb);
        }
        orbContainer.x = orbContainer.y = orbsPosition;
        this.addChild(orbContainer);
    }
    p.addButton = function () {
        var btn, event;
        btn = new ui.SimpleButton('Play Game');
        btn.on('click',this.playGame,this);
        btn.regX = btn.width / 2;
        btn.x = canvas.width / 2;
        btn.y = 400;
        btn.setButton({upColor:'#FF0000', color:'#FFF', borderColor:'#FFF',
            overColor:'#900'});
        this.addChild(btn);
    }
    p.playGame = function (e) {
        this.dispatchEvent(game.GameStateEvents.GAME);
    }
    p.run = function (tickEvent) {
        this.titleTxt.alpha = Math.cos(this.count++ * 0.1) * 0.4 + 0.6;
    }
    window.game.GameMenu = GameMenu;

}(window));
```

This menu contains a simple text object, which is the title to the game. Under that are five small `PulsingOrb` objects that are created to add some visuals to the screen. Finally, a button, using the `SimpleButton` component, is added below. The important thing to notice in this class is the button `click` handler, which dispatches the `GameStateEvents.GAME` event. When this menu is added to the application, a listener will be set on it for this event, which will take the appropriate action when it is dispatched. The main game menu is shown in Figure 10-1.

Figure 10-1. *The main game menu includes the title, graphics, and a play button*

Building the Game

The game in this exercise really isn't much of a game, but it will demonstrate a working example of a state machine and how the game will communicate back to the main application. The key concept to take from the game in this exercise is that it is encapsulated within a class. This drastically alters the approach that is taken when handling scope.

The games written in this book so far have been written in the global scope of window, meaning the functions and variables were accessible from anywhere. This prevented us from running into scope issues when writing the game logic, but working directly within window is widely frowned upon for a variety of reasons. It becomes extremely easy to override properties and functionality throughout your application, and your code will quickly becomes messy and hard to debug.

The game class will simply be named Game and will extend Container (see Listing 10-13).

Listing 10-13. Game.js – The Game Scene

```
(function (window) {

    window.game = window.game || {}

    function Game() {
       this.initialize();
    }

    var p = Game.prototype = new createjs.Container();

    p.Container_initialize = p.initialize;
```

```
    p.msgTxt = null;
    p.orbContainer = null;

    p.initialize = function () {
        this.Container_initialize();
        this.addBG();
        this.addMessages();
        this.createOrbContainer();
        this.createOrbs();
    }
    p.addBG = function () {
        var bg = new createjs.Shape();
        bg.graphics.beginFill('#92CBD6').drawRect(0, 0, canvas.width,
            canvas.height);
        this.addChild(bg);
    }
    p.addMessages = function () {
        this.msgTxt = new createjs.Text("", '24px Arial', '#FFF');
        this.addChild(this.msgTxt);
    }
    p.createOrbContainer = function () {
        this.orbContainer = new createjs.Container();
        this.addChild(this.orbContainer);
    }
    p.createOrbs = function () {
        var i, orb, color;
        var orbs = this.orbContainer;
        var numOrbs = 12;
        var orbSize = 25;
        for (i = 0; i < numOrbs; i++) {
            color = '#' + Math.floor(Math.random() * 16777215).toString(16)
            orb = new PulsingOrb(color, orbSize);
            orb.speed = Math.random() * 4;
            orb.size = orbSize;
            orb.x = orbSize;
            orb.y = orbSize + (i * orbSize * 2);
            orb.on('click',this.onOrbClick,this);
            orbs.addChild(orb);
        }
    }
    p.onOrbClick = function (e) {
        this.orbContainer.removeChild(e.target);
    }
    p.update = function () {
        var i, orb, nextX;
        var len = this.orbContainer.getNumChildren();
        for (i = 0; i < len; i++) {
            orb = this.orbContainer.getChildAt(i);
            nextX = orb.x + orb.speed;
```

```
            if (nextX + orb.size > canvas.width) {
                nextX = canvas.width - orb.size;
                orb.speed *= -1;
            }
            else if (nextX - orb.size < 0) {
                nextX = orb.size;
                orb.speed *= -1;
            }
            orb.nextX = nextX;
        }
    }
    p.render = function () {
        var i, orb;
        var len = this.orbContainer.getNumChildren();
        for (i = 0; i < len; i++) {
            orb = this.orbContainer.getChildAt(i);
            orb.x = orb.nextX;
        }
        this.msgTxt.text = "ORBS LEFT: " +
            this.orbContainer.getNumChildren();
    }
    p.checkGame = function () {
        if (!this.orbContainer.getNumChildren()) {
            this.dispatchEvent(game.GameStateEvents.GAME_OVER);
        }
    }
    p.run = function (tickEvent) {
        this.update();
        this.render();
        this.checkGame();
    }

    window.game.Game = Game;
}(window));
```

You'll notice that like the game menu, the game class utilizes the run function, which is called from the game loop in the main application. This is used to constantly animate all orbs in the container. The msgTxt text object is updated within the render function, and will reflect the number of remaining children in orbContainer. Figure 10-2 shows the game in action.

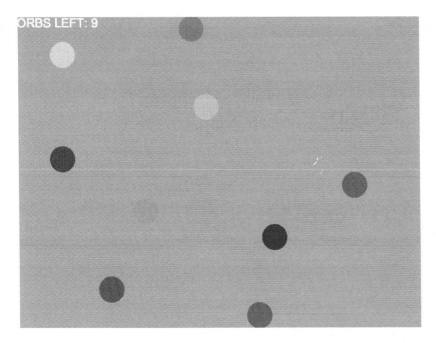

ORBS LEFT: 9

Figure 10-2. *Orb Destroyer game in action*

The final function in the run method is used to check on the progress of the game. When all orbs have been destroyed, the GameStateEvents.GAME_OVER event is dispatched.

Building the Orb Sprite

The PulsingOrb sprite from Chapter 8 will be reused for the orbs in the game class. For the purposes of this game, one more property needs to be added to hold the speed of each orb (see Listing 10-14).

Listing 10-14. PulsingOrb.js – The Orb for Orb Destroyer Uses the PulsingOrb Class (Built in Chapter 8)

```
(function () {

    var PulsingOrb = function (color, size) {
        this.initialize(color, size);
    }

    var p = PulsingOrb.prototype = new createjs.Shape();

    p.count = 0;
    p.speed = 0;
    p.size = 0;

    p.Shape_initialize = p.initialize;
```

```
    PulsingOrb.prototype.initialize = function (color, size) {
        size = size != undefined ? size : 20;
        color = color != undefined ? color : '#F00';
        this.size = size;
        this.Shape_initialize();
        this.alpha = Math.random();
        this.graphics.beginFill(color).drawCircle(0, 0, size);
        this.on('tick', this.pulse);
    }
    PulsingOrb.prototype.pulse = function () {
        this.alpha = Math.cos(this.count++ * 0.1) * 0.4 + 0.6;
    }
    window.PulsingOrb = PulsingOrb;
}());
```

Building the Game Over Screen

One more scene is needed before getting into the main application code. When the game is over, a game over screen should appear, with an option to replay the game or go back to the main menu screen. The GameOver container class is shown in Listing 10-15.

Listing 10-15. GameOver.js – The Game Over Scene

```
(function (window) {

    window.game = window.game || {}

    function GameOver() {
        this.initialize();
    }

    var p = GameOver.prototype = new createjs.Container();

    p.Container_initialize = p.initialize;

    p.initialize = function () {
        this.Container_initialize();
        this.addBG();
        this.addMessage();
        this.addButton();
    }
    p.addBG = function () {
        var bg = new createjs.Shape();
        bg.graphics.beginFill('#09E').drawRect(0, 0, canvas.width,
            canvas.height);
        this.addChild(bg);
    }
```

```
    p.addMessage = function () {
        this.titleTxt = new createjs.Text("YOU DESTROYED THE ORBS!", '40px
            Arial','#FFF');
        this.titleTxt.x = canvas.width / 2;
        this.titleTxt.y = 200;
        this.titleTxt.textAlign = 'center';
        this.addChild(this.titleTxt);
    }
    p.addButton = function () {
        var btn;
        btn = new ui.SimpleButton('Main Menu');
        btn.regX = btn.width / 2;
        btn.x = canvas.width / 2;
        btn.y = 280;
        btn.on('click',this.mainMenu, this);
        this.addChild(btn);
        btn = new ui.SimpleButton('Play Again');
        btn.regX = btn.width / 2;
        btn.x = canvas.width / 2;
        btn.y = 350;
        btn.on('click',this.playGame, this);
        this.addChild(btn);
    }
    p.mainMenu = function (e) {
        this.dispatchEvent(game.GameStateEvents.MAIN_MENU);
    }
    p.playGame = function (e) {
        this.dispatchEvent(game.GameStateEvents.GAME);
    }

    window.game.GameOver = GameOver;

}(window));
```

The GameOver screen is similar to the main menu, except it has two buttons instead of one and does not utilize a run method. Each button will dispatch the events GameStateEvents.MAIN_MENU and GameStateEvents.GAME, respectively. Figure 10-3 demonstrates the game over screen.

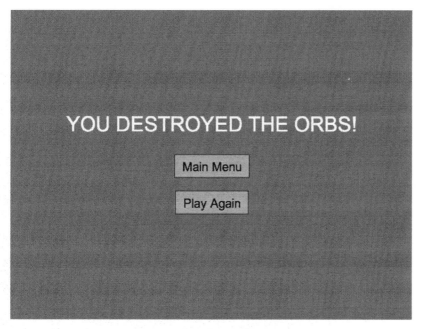

Figure 10-3. *The game over screen lets players play again or go to the main menu*

With all scenes created and ready to use, the main application class will next be created.

Building the Main Application with State Machine

The main application code for the Orb Destroyer game will be encapsulated into a class, but does not need to extend anything from EaselJS. It will handle the stage setup and the state machine itself. All scene instantiations will be added directly to the main stage, which will be one of the few properties that will actually be left in global space. A reference to the canvas will also remain global for easy access across the game scenes. Listing 10-16 shows the initial setup of the main application.

Listing 10-16. OrbDestroyer.js – The Main Application Class That Runs the State Machine

```
(function (window) {

    window.game = window.game || {}

    function OrbDestroyer() {
        this.initialize();
    }

    var p = OrbDestroyer.prototype;
```

```
    p.initialize = function () {
        canvas = document.getElementById('canvas');
        stage = new createjs.Stage(canvas);
        createjs.Ticker.setFPS(60);
        createjs.Ticker.on('tick', this.onTick, this);
        this.changeState(game.GameStates.MAIN_MENU);
    }

    window.game.OrbDestroyer = OrbDestroyer;

}(window));
```

The initialize method also sets up the ticker, and starts the game with the state MAIN_MENU, which will create the main menu. Next, the state machine to make this work will be set up with a few functions, which will be used to change the current state in the game (see Listing 10-17).

Listing 10-17. OrbDestroyer.js – The Functions Used for Changing States

```
    p.changeState = function (state) {
        this.currentGameState = state;
        switch (this.currentGameState) {
            case game.GameStates.MAIN_MENU:
                this.currentGameStateFunction = this.gameStateMainMenu;
                break;
            case game.GameStates.GAME:
                this.currentGameStateFunction = this.gameStateGame;
                break;
            case game.GameStates.RUN_SCENE:
                this.currentGameStateFunction = this.gameStateRunScene;
                break;
            case game.GameStates.GAME_OVER:
                this.currentGameStateFunction = this.gameStateGameOver;
                break;
        }
    }
    p.onStateEvent = function (e, data) {
        this.changeState(data.state);
    }
```

There are four states in this exercise: two for the menu scenes, one for the game, and finally the RUN_SCENE state, which will continuously run the current scene. All state functions are seen in Listing 10-18.

Listing 10-18. OrbDestroyer.js – The State Functions that Run According to the Current Game State

```
p.gameStateMainMenu = function () {
    var scene = new game.GameMenu();
    scene.on(game.GameStateEvents.GAME, this.onStateEvent, this,
        false, {state:game.GameStates.GAME});
    stage.addChild(scene);
    stage.removeChild(this.currentScene);
    this.currentScene = scene;
    this.changeState(game.GameStates.RUN_SCENE);
}
```

```
p.gameStateGame = function () {
    var scene = new game.Game();
    scene.on(game.GameStateEvents.GAME_OVER, this.onStateEvent, this,
        false, {state:game.GameStates.GAME_OVER});
    stage.addChild(scene);
    stage.removeChild(this.currentScene);
    this.currentScene = scene;
    this.changeState(game.GameStates.RUN_SCENE);
}
p.gameStateGameOver = function () {
    var scene = new game.GameOver();
    stage.addChild(scene);
    scene.on(game.GameStateEvents.MAIN_MENU, this.onStateEvent, this,
        false, {state:game.GameStates.MAIN_MENU});
    scene.on(game.GameStateEvents.GAME, this.onStateEvent, this,
        false, {state:game.GameStates.GAME});
    stage.removeChild(this.currentScene);
    this.currentScene = scene;
    this.changeState(game.GameStates.RUN_SCENE);
}
p.gameStateRunScene = function (tickEvent) {
    if (this.currentScene.run) {
        this.currentScene.run(tickEvent);
    }
}
```

Most of these functions share a pretty common pattern. For this exercise, with the exception of gameStateRunScene, the major task of each state function is to create new scenes and dispose of the old. After creating each new scene, a listener is set on them to notify the application that the current state should change. Each of these functions ultimately changes the state to RUN_SCENE when it's finished with its scene management tasks. This state will run the newly created scene on each subsequent game tick.

You will notice that the majority of these game state functions only last for one tick, so why bother making them states at all? In this exercise, the state machine is pretty simple, so a simple, repeating pattern is recognized. However, as your games start to grow and involve more states, these state functions will likely have a much larger responsibility.

Finally, the heartbeat of the game, and the state machine itself, is run from each game tick in the onTick handler that is set up on the Ticker, seen in Listing 10-19.

Listing 10-19. OrbDestroyer.js – The Tick Handler Runs the State Machine

```
p.onTick = function (e) {
    if (this.currentGameStateFunction != null) {
        this.currentGameStateFunction(e);
    }
    stage.update();
}
```

Although the game itself is extremely simple, this exercise outlines the state machine template that will be used for the remaining games in this book. You should have a good understanding of how more states could easily be added by adjusting the parts that make up the state machine.

Summary

In this chapter, a crucial procedure in game development was introduced. Centralizing the logic that creates and removes scenes assures that the game will only run in one state at a time, and allows the addition of new states to be easily accomplished. As you build more games, the patterns I introduced for state machines might change to fit your personal needs or preferences, but the underlying goal to manage game state will remain the same.

The last three chapters introduced three major development techniques. Extending EaselJS to create custom classes, the management of assets, and the utilization of a state machine will make your next game project a well-oiled machine. In the next chapter, these techniques will be used to create a high-action space shooter game.

CHAPTER 11

■ ■ ■

Game Project: Space Hero

In this chapter, a high action, space shooter game will be built by using the same state machine built in Chapter 10. A few new game development techniques will be introduced as well, including object pooling, time-based animation, and pixel-perfect collision detection.

Space Hero

Space Hero is a space shooter game where the enemy ships fly down from the top of the screen and fires bullets at you, the hero. The hero ship also fires bullets, and it can maneuver around the screen using all direction keys on the keyboard. The features we want to accomplish in the development of Space Hero include the following:

- Use the asset management approach learned in Chapter 9.
- Use the same application class, and its corresponding state machine, that was built in Chapter 10.
- Use sounds for ship explosions and background music.
- Create three scenes: the main game menu, the game level, and a game over screen.
- Use the UI components built in Chapter 8.
- Create an object pool to store sprites for reuse in the game.
- Use a third party library to handle pixel-perfect collision detection for the bullets and ships.
- Use bitmap fonts for the scoreboard.
- Use the keyboard for controlling the ship's movement and the firing of its bullets.

Figure 11-1 shows the game being played in its complete state.

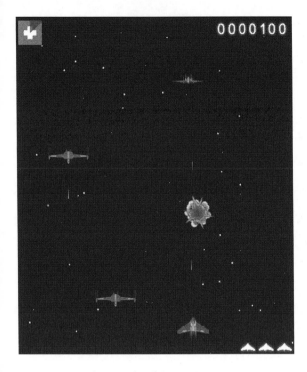

Figure 11-1. *The completed Space Hero game*

Before getting into the game code that drives the Space Hero game, let's take a look at the files you will be using and *reusing* to build the application.

Preparing for the Project

Several files and procedures need to be set up for the creation of this game project. This section will walk you through the necessary steps to prepare for the Space Hero game.

Setting Up the HTML

The HTML file used for this game will include several JavaScript files. It will also create an instance of the application and fire its `init` function, which will initialize the application. The index file will also be used to declare a handful of global variables for use throughout the application. Listing 11-1 shows the entire `index.html` file.

Listing 11-1. The index.html File for Space Hero

```
<!DOCTYPE html>
<html>
<head>
    <title>SPACE HERE</title>

    <!--CREATEJS-->
    <script src="js/lib/easeljs-0.7.1.min.js"></script>
```

```html
<script src="js/lib/soundjs-0.5.2.min.js"></script>
<script src="js/lib/preloadjs-0.4.1.min.js"></script>
<script src="js/lib/tweenjs-0.5.1.min.js"></script>
<script src="js/lib/BitmapText.js"></script>

<!--NDGMR-->
<script src="js/lib/ndgmr.Collision.sprite.js"></script>

<!--GAME CLASSES-->
<script src="js/state.js"></script>
<script src="js/utils/Utils.js"></script>

<!--COMPONENTS-->
<script src="js/classes/components/Preloader.js"></script>
<script src="js/classes/components/SimpleButton.js"></script>

<!--SCENES-->
<script src="js/scenes/GameMenu.js"></script>
<script src="js/scenes/Game.js"></script>
<script src="js/scenes/GameOver.js"></script>

<!--MANAGERS-->
<script src="js/classes/managers/AssetManager.js"></script>
<script src="js/classes/managers/SpritePool.js"></script>

<!--SPRITES-->
<script src="js/classes/sprites/Explosion.js"></script>
<script src="js/classes/sprites/HealthMeter.js"></script>
<script src="js/classes/sprites/LifeBox.js"></script>
<script src="js/classes/sprites/Scoreboard.js"></script>
<script src="js/classes/sprites/EnemyShip.js"></script>
<script src="js/classes/sprites/HeroShip.js"></script>
<script src="js/classes/sprites/Bullet.js"></script>

<!--APPLICATION-->
<script src="js/SpaceHero.js"></script>

</head>

<body onload="init();">
    <img src="img/bg.png" style="position: absolute">
    <canvas id="canvas" width="600" height="700" style="position:
      absolute"></canvas>
</body>

<script>
    var ARROW_KEY_SPACE = 32;
    var ARROW_KEY_UP = 38;
    var ARROW_KEY_DOWN = 40;
    var ARROW_KEY_LEFT = 37;
    var ARROW_KEY_RIGHT = 39;
```

```
    var stage;
    var canvas;
    var spritesheet;
    var screen_width;
    var screen_height;

    function init() {
        window.game = window.game || {};
        game.main = new game.SpaceHero();
    }
</script>
</html>
```

As you can see, there are quite a bit of JavaScript files in this application. We will be covering each of these new scripts, as well as the reuse of old ones, in depth in this chapter.

Reviewing the Sprite Sheet Files

The sprite sheet files for this chapter are available with the book's source code download. The animation frames for this sprite sheet were created in Flash CC and imported into Zoe using the same procedures learned in Chapter 6. Start by opening up the sprite sheet image `sprites.png`.

The `sprites.png` sprite sheet file contains all graphics needed for the game, with the exception of the background image, which was added to the DOM under the `canvas` element. Figure 11-2 shows the amount of graphics needed for the animations and static sprites.

Figure 11-2. *The full sprite sheet image for all graphics and animations in Space Hero*

The sprite sheet for Space Hero contains mostly animation frames for various elements in this high action game. It also includes some bonus power ups and other sprites that can be used to further enhance the gameplay when you complete this game project.

The Space Hero sprite sheet JSON object, created with Zoe, will be loaded in the preload process. Take a look at the data now to get an idea how it is formatted and the amount of animations you'll be using in the game (see Listing 11-2).

Listing 11-2. The Sprite Sheet Data `sprites.json`, Used For All Sprites in Space Hero

```json
{
    "framerate":24,
    "images":["assets/sprites.png"],
    "frames":[...],
    "animations":{
        "1": {"frames": [138], "speed": 1},
        "2": {"frames": [139], "speed": 1},
        "4": {"frames": [141], "speed": 1},
        "5": {"frames": [142], "speed": 1},
        "6": {"frames": [143], "speed": 1},
        "7": {"frames": [144], "speed": 1},
        "0": {"frames": [137], "speed": 1},
        "8": {"frames": [145], "speed": 1},
        "3": {"frames": [140], "speed": 1},
        "9": {"frames": [146], "speed": 1},
        "asteroid3": {"frames": [37], "speed": 1},
        "enemy2Hit": {
            "frames": [21, 22, 23, 24, 25, 26],
            "next": "enemy2Idle",
            "speed": 1
        },
        "powerup": {
            "frames": [39, 40, 41, ... 67],
            "speed": 1
        },
        "asteroid4": {"frames": [38], "speed": 1},
        "shield": {
            "frames": [68, 69, 70, ... 96],
            "speed": 1
        },
        "life": {
            "frames": [147, 148, 149, ... 154, 155, 98],
            "speed": 0.4
        },
        "shieldHUD": {"frames": [97], "speed": 1},
        "heroPrize": {
            "frames": [1, 2, 3, ... 13],
            "speed": 1
        },
        "progessHUD": {
            "frames": [98, 99, 100, ... 133],
            "speed": 1
        },
        "powerHUD": {"frames": [134], "speed": 1},
        "enemy1Hit": {
            "frames": [28, 29, 30, 31, 32, 33],
            "next": "enemy1Idle",
            "speed": 1
        },
        "asteroid2": {"frames": [36], "speed": 1},
```

```
        "enemy1Idle": {"frames": [27], "speed": 1},
        "healthHUD": {"frames": [34], "speed": 1},
        "star1": {"frames": [98], "speed": 1},
        "explosion": {
          "frames": [
              156,
              157,
              158,
              159,
              160,
              161,
              162,
              163,
              164,
              165,
              166,
              167,
              168,
              169,
              170,
              171,
              172,
              172,
              173
          ],
            "speed": 0.4
        },
        "star2": {"frames": [174], "speed": 1},
        "star3": {"frames": [175], "speed": 1},
        "heroIdle": {"frames": [0], "speed": 1},
        "enemy2Idle": {"frames": [20], "speed": 1},
        "gameOver": {"frames": [177], "speed": 1},
        "asteroid1": {"frames": [35], "speed": 1},
        "bullet": {"frames": [135, 136], "speed": 1},
        "heroHit": {
            "frames": [0, 14, 15, 16, 17, 18, 19],
            "next": "heroIdle",
            "speed": 0.4
        },
        "title": {"frames": [176], "speed": 1}
    }
}
```

As you can see in the animation objects, the speed and next properties are included. The Zoe interface gives you the ability to adjust these properties on each animation so you can control their speed and dictate what frame should load when an animation is complete. This is a great feature of Zoe; it allows you to command each ship to sit back at its idle frame when various in-game animations are complete.

Preparing the Asset Manager

The AssetManager class is nearly identical to the one built in Chapter 9. The functionality is the same, but the actual assets will be different. Similar to application class, the AssetManager.js file can be reused, only this time, the code that lists and loads the assets should be changed to fit the application. Listing 11-3 shows the list of assets being declared and loaded in the initialize function.

Listing 11-3. The Assets Added and Loaded in the AssetManager Class

```
//sounds
p.EXPLOSION = 'explosion';
p.SOUNDTRACK = 'soundtrack';

//graphics
p.GAME_SPRITES = 'game sprites';

//data
p.GAME_SPRITES_DATA = 'game sprites data'

//events
p.ASSETS_PROGRESS = 'assets progress';
p.ASSETS_COMPLETE = 'assets complete';

p.assetsPath = 'assets/';

p.loadManifest = null;
p.queue = null;
p.loadProgress = 0;


p.initialize = function () {
   this.EventDispatcher_initialize();
   this.loadManifest = [
      {id:this.EXPLOSION, src:this.assetsPath + 'explosion.mp3|' +
         this.assetsPath + 'explosion.ogg'},
      {id:this.SOUNDTRACK, src:this.assetsPath + 'dreamRaid1.mp3|' +
         this.assetsPath + 'dreamRaid1.ogg'},
      {id:this.GAME_SPRITES_DATA, src:this.assetsPath + 'sprites.json'},
      {id:this.GAME_SPRITES, src:this.assetsPath + 'sprites.png'}
   ];
}
```

Creating the Application Class

The ExplodingAsteroids.js class was the main application script used in the Exploding Asteroids exercise built in Chapter 10. The state machine that will run the game in this chapter uses the same scene names, and the state events used will be identical. This class can be used to fit the needs for Space Hero. Create a copy and change the name of the file to SpaceHero.js.

■ **Note**   As you build more games and applications, it might be a good idea to give this class a generic name, such as `App.js` or `Main.js`. This can make it easier to copy over to new applications.

Creating the Sprites

The action sprites that make up the Space Hero gameplay are one hero ship, two enemy ships, bullets, and explosions. In this section, you will prepare each sprite for the game.

Creating the Hero Ship

The hero ship is the ship that is controlled by the player. The object of the game is to steer this ship away from danger while destroying as many enemy ships as you can. The frames that make up the hero ship are demonstrated in Figure 11-3.

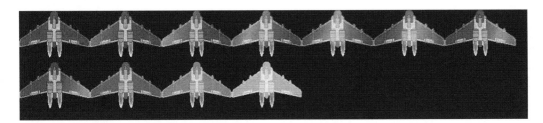

Figure 11-3.   *The sprite frames for the hero ship*

There are three animations that make up the hero ship. The two used in this exercise are its *idle* frame and its *damage* sequence, which plays a white glow animation to indicate damage being taken from an enemy bullet. The third sequence can be used to indicate power ups that can be used if you wish to extend the game after this chapter.

You'll notice that there are only 11 frames that make up the hero ship. This is because Zoe was smart enough to find similar frames and reused them in the animation objects that make its sequences. This technique of reusing, or *stacking* frames, can drastically reduce the size of your sprite sheets.

Among other things, the class for the hero ship handles the state of the ship for idle and damage animations. Listing 11-4 shows the entire HeroShip class.

Listing 11-4.   The HeroShip Class , Declared in HeroClass.js

```
(function (window) {

    window.game = window.game || {}

    function HeroShip() {
        this.initialize();
    }

    var p = HeroShip.prototype = new createjs.Sprite();
```

```
    p.Sprite_initialize = p.initialize;

    p.EXPLOSION_COMPLETE = 'explosion complete';
    p.EXPLOSION_OFFSET = 55;
    p.INVINCIBLE_TIME = 1500;

    p.invincible = false;
    p.shouldDie = false;
    p.speed = 500;
    p.nextX = null;
    p.nextY = null;

    p.initialize = function () {
        this.Sprite_initialize(spritesheet, "heroIdle");
        this.regX = this.getBounds().width / 2;
        this.regY = this.getBounds().height / 2;
    }
    p.takeDamage = function () {
        this.gotoAndPlay("heroHit");
    }
    p.explode = function () {
        this.gotoAndPlay('explosion');
        this.regX = this.regY = this.EXPLOSION_OFFSET;
        this.on('animationend', this.explosionComplete, this, true);
        createjs.Sound.play(game.assets.EXPLOSION);
    }
    p.explosionComplete = function (e) {
        this.stop();
        this.dispatchEvent(this.EXPLOSION_COMPLETE);
    }
    p.reset = function () {
        this.shouldDie = false;
        this.gotoAndStop('heroIdle');
        this.regX = this.getBounds().width / 2;
        this.regY = this.getBounds().height / 2;
    }
    p.makeInvincible = function () {
        this.invincible = true;
        this.alpha = .4;
        setTimeout(this.removeInvincible.bind(this), this.INVINCIBLE_TIME);
    }
    p.removeInvincible = function () {
        this.invincible = false;
        this.alpha = 1;
    }

    window.game.HeroShip = HeroShip;

}(window));
```

The class starts with some constants for an explosion event, the offset for the explosion sequence, and the time the ship should be invincible after a new life starts. They are followed by some Boolean variables that determine if the ship is invincible or if it should die in the next render cycle. Some speed and position values are also declared.

The takeDamage method is called when a bullet collides with it. This will play the sequence "heroHit", which will cause a white, glowing shimmer. The explode method will be called from the game in the render cycle, which will play the explosion frames and an explosion sound. The registration points are adjusted so that the explosion will be properly placed. A listener is set on this animation, which will fire explosionComplete to stop the animation and dispatch the EXPLOSION_COMPLETE event.

The reset method resets shouldDie to false, puts the frame back on idle, and resets its registration points. Lastly, the makeInvincible method prevents damage from being inflicted on the ship by setting isInvincible to true and setting its alpha value to .4. The invincibility is reset with a setTimeout method using the INVINCIBLE_TIME constant.

Creating the Enemy Ships

There are two enemies in the game, each with their own damage animation frames. These ships will periodically move down the screen and fire bullets that the hero must dodge. The frames that make up the enemy ships are demonstrated in Figure 11-4.

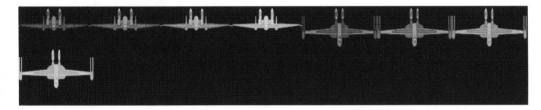

Figure 11-4. *The sprite frames for the enemy ships*

Although there are two enemy ships, only one sprite class will be created. This class will randomly decide what the ship's type should be, 1 or 2, and display the appropriate frame. The type property will also dictate the amount of hit points it should have and the total points it will give when destroyed. The complete EnemyShip class is shown in Listing 11-5.

Listing 11-5. The EnemyShip Class, Declared in EnemyShip.js

```
(function (window) {
    window.game = window.game || {}

    function EnemyShip(startX) {
        this.initialize(startX);
    }

    var p = EnemyShip.prototype = new createjs.Sprite();

    p.Sprite_initialize = p.initialize;

    p.type = null;
    p.HP = null;
    p.points = null;
```

```
        p.lastFired = 0;
        p.fireDelay = 2000;

        p.speed = 150;
        p.nextY = 0;
        p.shouldDie = false;

        p.initialize = function (startX) {
            this.type = Utils.getRandomNumber(0, 2) + 1;
            this.HP = this.type * 3;
            this.points = this.type * 100;
            this.Sprite_initialize(spritesheet, "enemy" + this.type + "Idle");
            this.regX = this.getBounds().width / 2;
            this.regY = this.getBounds().height / 2;

        }
        p.takeDamage = function () {
            this.gotoAndPlay("enemy" + this.type + "Hit");
            this.HP--;
            if (this.HP <= 0) {
                this.shouldDie = true;
            }
        }
        p.reset = function () {
            this.type = Utils.getRandomNumber(0, 2) + 1;
            this.shouldDie = false;
            this.HP = this.type * 3;
            this.points = this.type * 100;
            this.gotoAndPlay("enemy" + this.type + "Idle");
        }

        window.game.EnemyShip = EnemyShip;

}(window));
```

The type, HP, and points properties are crucial variables for the behavior of each ship. The type, which will be randomly assigned in the initialize function, will decide the frame, hit points, and worth of each ship sprite. The next set is used for firing bullets. The lastFired variable holds the time when the last enemy bullet was fired, and fireDelay is the time that should pass before the next attack. The speed variable is used to determine how fast it should move down the stage, and nextY is set and used in the update/render cycle during the game loop. Finally, shouldDie is used to determine if the ship should blow up during the next render cycle.

Next is a small series of methods. The initialize function randomly determines what type of ship the enemy should be and adjusts the appropriate properties. When the ship is hit, its takeDamage function will immediately play either the enemy1Hit or enemy2Hit animations, depending on the ship's type. Its HP value is decreased by one and is followed by a conditional to check if the ship should die. If so, the shouldDie property is set to true. This property will be examined during the render cycle in the game loop.

The final function, reset, will reset its properties by choosing a new type. This might seem strange now, but these ship sprites will be recycled and served up from an *object pool*. This technique will be looked at in detail in the upcoming "Using Object Pools" section.

Creating the Bullets and Explosions

Bullets are shot from both the enemy and hero ship, and travel at a velocity that is faster and in the opposite direction of the ship that fired it. When a bullet hits a ship, an explosion animation will take the ship's place. Figure 11-5 demonstrates the frames used for both the bullet and explosion sprites.

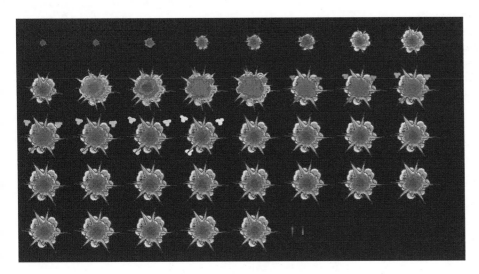

Figure 11-5. *The sprite frames for the explosion and bullets*

There are two bullet frames, one green and one red. The red bullets are fired from the hero and the green from the enemies. The Bullet class renders the appropriate frame (see Listing 11-6).

Listing 11-6. The Bullet Class, Declared in Bullet.js

```
(function (window) {

    window.game = window.game || {}

    function Bullet() {
        this.initialize();
    }

    var p = Bullet.prototype = new createjs.Sprite();

    p.Sprite_initialize = p.initialize;

    p.speed = 500;
    p.nextY = null;
    p.shouldDie = false;

    p.initialize = function () {
        this.Sprite_initialize(spritesheet, "bullet");
        this.paused = true;
    }
```

```
    p.reset = function () {
        this.shouldDie = false;
    }

    window.game.Bullet = Bullet;

}(window));
```

Similarly to the EnemyShip class, the bullet sprite has properties for speed and its next position, plus a Boolean value to determine its fate in the next render cycle. The sprite consists of two frames, so it is initially paused on frame one, which is the red bullet for the hero. This will be advanced to frame 2 for enemies from within the game code. An object pool will also be created for the bullets, so a reset function is needed to reset the object for later use. The Explosion class will be recycled in a similar way, as shown in Listing 11-7.

Listing 11-7. The Explosion Class, Declared in Explosion.js

```
(function (window) {

    window.game = window.game || {}

    function Explosion() {
        this.initialize();
    }

    var p = Explosion.prototype = new createjs.Sprite();

    p.Sprite_initialize = p.initialize;

    p.initialize = function () {
        this.Sprite_initialize(spritesheet, 'explosion');
        this.paused = true;
    }
    p.reset = function(){
        this.gotoAndStop('explosion');
    }

    window.game.Explosion = Explosion;

}(window));
```

Creating the HUD

The acronym HUD stands for *heads-up display*. These are typically the messaging elements that are persistent during a game level. In Space Hero, three HUD elements are needed. The health meter, score, and life indicators are all sprites that make up the HUD in the game.

Reviewing the HUD Sprite Frames

There are a few animations and static frames that make up the graphics for the HUD game elements. The frames used for these HUD sprites are shown in Figure 11-6.

Figure 11-6. The sprite frames for the HUD elements

The first large set of frames might look a little odd. This is the health meter animation that will increase in a clockwise animation as the hero takes damage. It will be placed over the health icon, shown in the bottom right corner of Figure 11-6. These items are separated so the sequence can be used above the other bonus HUD elements provided in the sprite sheet.

The ship icon indicates a life in the life box, and will represent one life in the number of lives left in the game. It includes a series of frames to show an animation of the ship icon blurring out when the hero ship explodes. Lastly, the numbers 0 through 9 are used for the bitmap font that will be used for the score.

Creating the Health Meter

The health meter represents the amount of health left in the current life of the ship. It consists of an animated sprite that gradually covers a static sprite underneath. The health meter is shown in action in Figure 11-7.

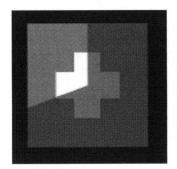

Figure 11-7. The HealthMeter sprite diplaying damage

The HealthMeter class extends Container and controls the behavior of the health meter (see Listing 11-8).

Listing 11-8. The HealthMeter Class, Declared in HeroMeter.js

```
(function (window) {

    window.game = window.game || {}

    function HealthMeter() {
        this.initialize();
    }

    var p = HealthMeter.prototype = new createjs.Container();
```

```
        p.meter = null;
        p.maxDamage = null;
        p.damage = 0;
        p.empty = false;

        p.Container_initialize = p.initialize;

        p.initialize = function () {
            this.Container_initialize();
            this.x = this.y = 5;
            this.buildMeter();
        }
        p.buildMeter = function () {
            var health = new createjs.Sprite(spritesheet, 'healthHUD');
            this.meter = new createjs.Sprite(spritesheet, 'progessHUD');
            this.maxDamage = this.meter.spriteSheet
                .getAnimation(this.meter.currentAnimation)
                .frames.length - 1;
            this.meter.paused = true;
            this.addChild(health, this.meter);
        }
        p.takeDamage = function (damage) {
            this.damage += damage;
            var perc = this.damage / this.maxDamage > 1 ? 1 : this.damage /
                this.maxDamage;
            var frame = (this.maxDamage * perc);
            createjs.Tween.get(this.meter)
                .to({currentAnimationFrame:frame}, 100)
                .call(this.checkHealth, null, this);
        }
        p.checkHealth = function (e) {
            if (this.meter.currentAnimationFrame == this.maxDamage) {
                this.empty = true;
            }
        }
        p.reset = function (e) {
            this.damage = 0;
            this.empty = false;
            this.meter.currentAnimationFrame = 0;
        }

        window.game.HealthMeter = HealthMeter;

}(window));
```

The meter property holds the meter animation, which will be updated when the hero ship takes damage. The maxDamage property will be set in the buildMeter method and will match the total frames of the meter animation. The damage value will be incremented on hero hits and will be used to determine what frame in the meter sequence the animation should advance to. The empty property will be set to true when the final frame in the sequence is reached and will be used to tell the game that the ship should explode. How this works will be closely looked at next in the buildMeter method. Lastly, the meter animation is paused, and both sprites are added to the container and positioned.

The `buildMeter` function creates two sprites, one for the health icon and another for the meter. The `maxDamage` value is set to the number of frames in the meter animation. At the time of writing this book, there is no method in the API to access the number of frames in a sprite's current animation. You can still access this by chaining a few methods and properties that are available.

```
this.maxDamage = this.meter.spriteSheet
        .getAnimation(this.meter.currentAnimation)
        .frames.length - 1;
```

You can access the sprite's `SpriteSheet` object by referencing its `spriteSheet` property. You can use then use the `getAnimation` method to access any animation object in the sprite sheet object. To get this animation, you need to pass in the string that defined the animation object. You could easily hard-code this value to suit your needs here, but the string can also be retrieved by accessing the sprite's current animation. This is a better approach in case the animation name changes in the future. Finally, with the animation object referenced, the length of its `frames` array is set to the `maxDamage` property.

The `takeDamage` method will be called when a bullet hits the hero ship. It's written so it can take variable damage and is instantly used to tack on to the `damage` property. Next, the new `damage` value needs to be used to determine the percentage of total damage allotted to the ship. Remember, total damage is tied to the number of frames in the `meter` animation, so this percentage can be used to find the appropriate frame in the sprite. If the last strike caused enough damage to exceed its animation frames, it's set to the value of `maxDamage`, its last frame. Finally, the target frame number on `meter` is tweened to using TweenJS.

```
createjs.Tween.get(this.meter)
        .to({currentAnimationFrame:frame}, 100)
        .call(this.checkHealth, null, this);
```

This demonstrates how dynamic TweenJS can be. Instead of simply tweening a display object's position or visual property, you can tween an animation to a specific frame. When the tween is complete, the `checkHealth` function is called, which will set the `empty` property to `true` if all of the meter's frames have been used up and the static health sprite is completely covered by it.

Lastly, the `reset` function will reset the meter when a player starts a new life in the game.

Creating the Scoreboard

The scoreboard will use bitmap fonts to display the current score in the game. The `Scoreboard` class (see Listing 11-9) will be a container that will create and add a `BitmapText` object when the score has been updated.

Listing 11-9. The Scoreboard Class, Declared in Scoreboard.js

```
(function (window) {

    window.game = window.game || {}

    function Scoreboard() {
        this.initialize();
    }

    var p = Scoreboard.prototype = new createjs.Container();

    p.scoreTxt;
    p.score = 0;
```

```
    p.Container_initialize = p.initialize;

    p.initialize = function () {
        this.Container_initialize();
        this.x = screen_width - 165;
        this.y = 5;
        this.updateScore(0);
    }
    p.updateScore = function(points){
        var formattedScore;
        this.removeAllChildren();
        this.score += points;
        formattedScore = this.addLeadingZeros(this.score, 7);
        this.scoreTxt = new createjs.BitmapText(formattedScore, spritesheet);
        this.addChild(this.scoreTxt);
    }
    p.addLeadingZeros = function (score, width) {
        score = score + '';
        return score.length >= width ? score : new Array(width -
            score.length + 1).join(0) + score;
    }
    p.getScore = function () {
        return this.addLeadingZeros(this.score, 7);
    }
    window.game.Scoreboard = Scoreboard;
```

```
}(window));
```

The Scoreboard class holds two properties, the score and the score BitmapText display object. When the scoreboard should be updated, the updateScore method is called, which accepts the number of points that the score should be increased by. Since a new bitmap text object needs to be created to update the message, the old one is removed by removing all of the children in the container. The new score is then updated and passed through the addLeadingZeros method. This function takes the new score and adds the appropriate number of leading zeros so that the total length of the score text is always 7. This method takes two parameters, the score and the number of characters the returned string should be. For example, if the current score were 1600, the returned value from the addLeadingZeros method would be 0001600. This is primarily for effect and to mimic the look of a classic score board (see Figure 11-8).

Figure 11-8. *The Scoreboard HUD element*

A simple method is then added to the class to get the current score. This is used later in the game when the score needs to be accessed for messaging in the game over screen.

Creating the Life Box

The life box is the area designated to display the number of lives the player currently has. It will contain a sprite for each life and is located in the lower right corner of the game board. The complete LifeBox class is seen in Listing 11-10.

Listing 11-10. The LifeBox Class, Declared in LifeBox.js

```javascript
(function (window) {

    window.game = window.game || {}

    function LifeBox(numLives) {
        this.numLives = numLives;
        this.initialize();
    }

    var p = LifeBox.prototype = new createjs.Container();

    p.numLives = null;

    p.Container_initialize = p.initialize;

    p.initialize = function () {
        this.Container_initialize();
        this.buildSprites();
        this.positionBox();
    }
    p.buildSprites = function () {
        var i, life;
        var xPos = 0;
        for (i = 0; i < this.numLives; i++) {
            life = new createjs.Sprite(spritesheet, 'life');
            life.paused = true;
            life.x = xPos;
            this.addChild(life);
            xPos += life.getBounds().width;
        }
    }
    p.positionBox = function () {
        this.x = screen_width - this.getBounds().width;
        this.y = screen_height - this.getBounds().height;
    }
    p.removeLife = function () {
        var life = this.getChildAt(0);
        life.on('animationend', function (e) {
            e.target.stop();
            this.removeChild(e.target);
        }, this)
        life.play();
    }

    window.game.LifeBox = LifeBox;

}(window));
```

This class is a container that will hold a sprite for every life the player currently has. It accepts one parameter in its constructor, numLives, which is assigned to the one and only property on the class. The initialize method then calls on two functions, the first creates the sprites for the container and the second positions it.

A loop is created based on the number of lives that the game will give the player at the start of the game. During the loop, a life sprite is created, paused, added to the container, and then positioned accordingly in a horizontal fashion. The container itself is then positioned at the bottom right corner of the game in the positionBox function.

When a player loses a life, the removeLife method is called. The first child, which will always be the left-most sprite, is referenced and its animation frames are played. A listener is set on this animation, which will stop when complete, and then it is removed from the container. Figure 11-9 shows three lives in the LifeBox container.

Figure 11-9. *The LifeBox HUD element*

Using Object Pools

The technique of using object pools is common among game developers. The concept is simple. Instead of creating a new instance of something every time you need one, you create several of them right away and stick them into an array. When you need the object, you grab it from this array. When you are finished with it, you put it back. To build the game's object pools, you will be using a custom class that will create these pools (see Listing 11-11).

Listing 11-11. The SpritePool Class, Declared in SpritePool.js

```
(function () {

    var SpritePool = function (type, length) {
        this.pool = [];
        var i = length;
        while (--i > -1) {
            this.pool[i] = new type();
        }
    }
    SpritePool.prototype.getSprite = function () {
        if (this.pool.length > 0) {
            return this.pool.pop();
        }
        else {
            throw new Error("You ran out of sprites!");
        }
    }
    SpritePool.prototype.returnSprite = function (sprite) {
        this.pool.push(sprite);
    }

    window.game.SpritePool = SpritePool;

}());
```

The constructor of the SpritePool class takes two parameters. The first is the type of object that should be created and pooled. This allows you to use this class to pool any type of object you wish. The second is the number of instances that should be created. Be sure that this number is high enough to handle enough concurrent instances that will be needed in your game. This process usually takes a few guesses, but ultimately should be low enough to be efficient but high enough to support your needs.

To create an object pool, simply create an instance of the SpritePool class.

```
var bullets = new game.SpritePool(game.Bullet, 20);
```

Now when you need an instance from the pool, you can call on the getSprite method.

```
var bullet = bullets.getSprite();
stage.addChild(bullet)
```

When you are finished, be sure to send it back so that it can be reused in the game by using the returnSprite method.

```
bullets.returnSprite(bullet);
stage.removeChild(bullet);
```

You will be using this convenient class to create several object pools in Space Hero. Let's now move on to the scene container classes that will be used in the game.

Creating the Scenes

There are three scenes in Space Hero. This section will go over each scene in detail, starting with the main menu.

Creating the Game Menu Scene

The main menu will start out with a dramatic, slow moving title that creeps down the screen from the top and rests in the center of the screen. This is followed by revealing a play button, which should switch to the game state when clicked. The entire GameMenu class is seen in Listing 11-12.

Listing 11-12. The GameMenu Scene Class, Delcared in GameMenu.js

```
(function (window) {

    window.game = window.game || {}

    function GameMenu() {
        this.initialize();
    }

    var p = GameMenu.prototype = new createjs.Container();

    p.playBtn = null;

    p.Container_initialize = p.initialize;

    p.initialize = function () {
```

```
        this.Container_initialize();
        this.addTitle();
        this.addButton();
    }
    p.addTitle = function () {
        var titleYPos = 200;
        var title = new createjs.Sprite(spritesheet, 'title');
        title.regX = title.getBounds().width / 2;
        title.x = screen_width / 2;
        title.y = -50;
        createjs.Tween.get(title).to({y:titleYPos}, 5000)
            .call(this.bringTitle, null, this);
        this.addChild(title);
    }
    p.addButton = function () {
        this.playBtn = new ui.SimpleButton('Play Game');
        this.playBtn.on('click', this.playGame, this);
        this.playBtn.regX = this.playBtn.width / 2;
        this.playBtn.x = canvas.width / 2;
        this.playBtn.y = 400;
        this.playBtn.alpha = 0;
        this.playBtn.setButton({upColor:'#d2354c', color:'#FFF',
            borderColor:'#FFF', overColor:'#900'});
        this.addChild(this.playBtn);
    }
    p.bringTitle = function (e) {
        createjs.Tween.get(this.playBtn).to({alpha:1}, 1000);
    }
    p.playGame = function (e) {
        createjs.Sound.play(game.assets.EXPLOSION);
        this.dispatchEvent(game.GameStateEvents.GAME);
    }
    window.game.GameMenu = GameMenu;

}(window));
```

The title is a sprite and uses TweenJS to crawl down the screen. The play button, which uses the SimpleButton component is styled, added to the container, and then faded up with the bringTitle function. The button will call playGame to play an explosion sound and dispatch the appropriate game event to start the game. The menu screen is shown in Figure 11-10.

Figure 11-10. *The main menu scene with crawling title and play button*

Creating the Game Scene

The game scene is where all of the game-playing magic takes place. There is quite a bit of code that will go into it, so a template for the class is temporarily made so you can finish up the application classes before diving into game code. The start of the Game class is shown in Listing 11-13.

Listing 11-13. The Game Scene Class Template, Declared in Game.js

```
(function (window) {

    window.game = window.game || {}

    function Game() {
        this.initialize();
    }

    var p = Game.prototype = new createjs.Container();

    p.Container_initialize = p.initialize;

    p.initialize = function () {
        this.Container_initialize();
        var me = this;
```

```
            setTimeout(function(){
                me.dispatchEvent(game.GameStateEvents.GAME_OVER);
            },3000)
    }

    window.game.Game = Game;

}(window));
```

When the game initializes, a simple setTimeout method is used, which will dispatch the game event to move on to the game over scene. This is temporary. Meanwhile, there is one more scene container class to set up.

Creating the Game Over Scene

The game over scene is the final screen in the game, and it should appear when the player loses all of their lives. A *Game Over* title, which is another sprite from the sprite sheet, will scale up while rotating in a full circle. The score is also displayed to show the player how well they did in the game. Below that are two buttons that play the game again or return the player to the main menu. The entire GameOver class is show in Listing 11-14.

Listing 11-14. The GameOver Scene Class, Declared in GameOver.js

```
(function (window) {

    window.game = window.game || {}

    function GameOver() {
        this.initialize();
    }

    var p = GameOver.prototype = new createjs.Container();

    p.Container_initialize = p.initialize;

    p.initialize = function () {
        this.Container_initialize();
        createjs.Sound.stop();
        this.addMessage();
        this.addScore();
        this.addButton();
    }
    p.addMessage = function () {
        var msg = new createjs.Sprite(spritesheet, 'gameOver');
        msg.regX = msg.getBounds().width / 2;
        msg.regY = msg.getBounds().height / 2;
        msg.x = screen_width / 2;
        msg.y = 250;
        msg.scaleX = msg.scaleY = 0;
        createjs.Tween.get(msg).to({scaleX:1, scaleY:1, rotation:360}, 500);
        this.addChild(msg);
    }
```

```
    p.addScore = function () {
        var scorePoint = {x:220, y:310};
        var scoreTxt = new createjs.BitmapText(game.score, spritesheet);
        scoreTxt.x = scorePoint.x;
        scoreTxt.y = scorePoint.y;
        this.addChild(scoreTxt);
    }
    p.addButton = function () {
        var playBtn, menuBtn;
        var playBtnPoint = {x:140, y:380};
        var menuBtnPoint = {x:310, y:380};
        var me = this;
        playBtn = new ui.SimpleButton('Play Again');
        playBtn.on('click', this.playAgain, this);
        playBtn.setButton({upColor:'#d2354c', color:'#FFF',
            borderColor:'#FFF', overColor:'#900'});
        playBtn.x = playBtnPoint.x;
        playBtn.y = playBtnPoint.y;
        this.addChild(playBtn);
        menuBtn = new ui.SimpleButton('Main Menu');
        menuBtn.on('click', this.mainMenu, this);
        menuBtn.setButton({upColor:'#d2354c', color:'#FFF',
            borderColor:'#FFF', overColor:'#900'});
        menuBtn.x = menuBtnPoint.x;
        menuBtn.y = menuBtnPoint.y;
        this.addChild(menuBtn);
    }
    p.playAgain = function (e) {
        this.dispatchEvent(game.GameStateEvents.GAME);
    }
    p.mainMenu = function (e) {
        this.dispatchEvent(game.GameStateEvents.MAIN_MENU);
    }

    window.game.GameOver = GameOver;

}(window));
```

In this scene, a series of methods add, position, and animate the elements on the screen. The game over screen is shown in Figure 11-11.

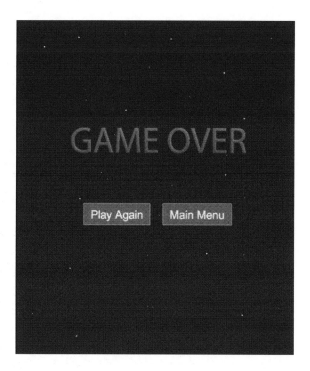

Figure 11-11. *The game over screen with option to replay or return to main menu*

You now have all assets loading in, the state manager in place, and all sprites and game scenes written. At this point, make sure you can cycle through each state by clicking on the buttons in the menu screens. When you play the game, you should see nothing but a star field for three seconds before switching to the game over screen. With everything working correctly, it's time to add action to this empty space.

Creating the Game

The application files are now completely set up; the only thing left is to program the game. The Game class was set up in the "Creating the Game Scene" section. Remove the temporary setTimeout function that was set up to automatically move on to the game over screen. Your initialize method should now simply look like the following:

```
p.initialize = function () {
    this.Container_initialize();
}
```

Declaring the Game Variables

The game takes many variables, which are declared at the top of the class (see Listing 11-15). The variables are grouped into categories that are labeled by comments. Many of these variables may look new to you but will be explained in full throughout following sections.

Listing 11-15. The Properties Declared for the Game Class

```
// Hero
p.heroShip = null;
p.heroBulletPool = null;
p.heroBullets = null;

// Enemies
p.enemyPool = null;
p.enemies = null;
p.enemyBulletPool = null;
p.enemyBullets = null;
p.enemyLastSpawnTime = null;
p.enemySpawnWaiter = 2000;

// SPRITES
p.stars = null;
p.explosionPool = null;
p.healthMeter = null;
p.lifeBox = null;
p.scoreboard = null;

// GAME VARIABLES
p.leftWall = null;
p.rightWall = null;
p.ceiling = null;
p.floor = null;
p.betweenLevels = true;
p.numLives = 3;
p.delta = null;

// Controls
p.leftKeyDown = false;
p.rightKeyDown = false;
p.upKeyDown = false;
p.downKeyDown = false;
```

A series of variables are first set up for the hero and enemies. These properties hold the instances of each ship, all bullets in play, and a few values to determine the speed at which the enemies will attack. The next series declares a group of properties that will hold references to all other sprites and HUD elements in the game.

Next up are some values that will be used during gameplay to evaluate scenarios and sprite positions. The walls create the bounds that the hero ship is allowed to move in. The betweenLevels Boolean property decides if the game loop should continue or wait a moment while the hero ship explodes and resets. The numLives variable is used to determine if the player should continue playing after exploding. Finally, the delta property is set from the ticker that runs the game and is used to calculate the positions of the moving sprites. This will be explained in the upcoming "Using Delta for Time Based Movement" section.

Initializing the Game

As usual, the `initialize` method calls a list of methods that set up a new game. The first method is used to initialize the game arrays and set a few properties (see Listing 11-16). The other initializing methods create the game sprites, hero ship boundaries, and set the controls. Lastly, the background music is started.

Listing 11-16. The Initializing Methods for the Game

```
p.initialize = function () {
    this.Container_initialize();
    this.setProperties();
    this.buildStarField();
    this.buildSprites();
    this.setWalls();
    this.setControls();
    createjs.Sound.play(game.assets.SOUNDTRACK);
}
p.setProperties = function () {
    this.heroBulletPool = [];
    this.heroBullets = [];
    this.enemyPool = [];
    this.enemies = [];
    this.enemyBulletPool = [];
    this.enemyBullets = [];
    this.stars = [];
    this.explosionPool = [];
    this.betweenLevels = false;
    this.enemyLastSpawnTime = 0;
}
```

The `setProperties` method initializes the arrays in the game. It is imperative that you **not** initialize array properties when declaring them in your classes. Doing so will cause these arrays to be shared among all instances of the class. For example, you will be adding bullet objects to the `heroBullets` array during gameplay. When you are finished with the `Game` instance, the final value of `heroBullets` will carry over to a new instance of the game. This can easily be avoided by creating a function when initializing the game to initialize all of the class's arrays.

Creating the Game Sprites

Several sprite objects are initialized at the beginning of the game. A function is created for creating all stars in the star field and another to create the hero ship, the object pools, and the HUD elements. These two functions are shown in Listing 11-17.

Listing 11-17. Creating the Stars and Game Sprite Object Pools

```
p.buildStarField = function () {
    var star;
    var numStars = 20;
    for (i = 0; i < numStars; i++) {
        star = new createjs.Sprite(spritesheet, 'star3');
        star.speed = Utils.getRandomNumber(100, 200);
        star.x = Math.random() * screen_width;
        star.y = Math.random() * screen_height;
```

```
        this.addChild(star);
        this.stars.push(star);
    }
}
p.buildSprites = function () {
    this.heroShip = new game.HeroShip();
    this.heroShip.on(this.heroShip.EXPLOSION_COMPLETE, this.checkGame,
        this);
    this.heroShip.x = screen_width / 2;
    this.heroShip.y = screen_height - this.heroShip.getBounds().height;
    this.heroBulletPool = new game.SpritePool(game.Bullet, 20);
    this.enemyBulletPool = new game.SpritePool(game.Bullet, 20);
    this.enemyPool = new game.SpritePool(game.EnemyShip, 10);
    this.explosionPool = new game.SpritePool(game.Explosion, 10);
    this.healthMeter = new game.HealthMeter();
    this.scoreboard = new game.Scoreboard();
    this.lifeBox = new game.LifeBox(this.numLives);
    this.addChild(this.heroShip, this.healthMeter, this.scoreboard,
        this.lifeBox);
}
```

The stars created in buildStars are randomly positioned in the container and added to the stars array. These are stored in an array so they can be accessed and moved during the game loop.

Several elements are created in the buildSprites method. First, the hero ship is created and positioned at the bottom of the screen. A listener is set on the sprite for when the ship has finished exploding. When this event occurs, the check game is called to evaluate what should happen next. This will be covered in the "Building the Check Functions" section.

Next, the enemy ships, bullets, and explosions are created by using the SpritePool class. These pools are set to the appropriate game properties and will be used to add and recycle sprite objects during the game. Finally, the HUD elements are instantiated and added to the container.

Setting Up the Controls

The controls are set up similarly to the paddle controls in Break-It. However, this time you have the ability to move up and down and fire bullets. The bounds for the hero ship are first created in setWalls. Next, the controls are set by adding keyboard listeners to the document, which will fire the appropriate handlers. These methods are shown in Listing 11-18.

Listing 11-18. Setting Up the Walls and Keyboard Controls

```
p.setWalls = function () {
    this.leftWall = this.heroShip.getBounds().width / 2;
    this.rightWall = screen_width - this.heroShip.getBounds().width / 2;
    this.floor = screen_height - this.heroShip.getBounds().height;
    this.ceiling = screen_height - (this.heroShip.getBounds().height *
        3);
}
p.setControls = function () {
    document.onkeydown = this.handleKeyDown.bind(this);
    document.onkeyup = this.handleKeyUp.bind(this);
}
```

```
p.handleKeyDown = function (e) {
    e = !e ? window.event : e;
    switch (e.keyCode) {
        case ARROW_KEY_LEFT:
            this.leftKeyDown = true;
            break;
        case ARROW_KEY_RIGHT:
            this.rightKeyDown = true;
            break;
        case ARROW_KEY_UP:
            this.upKeyDown = true;
            break;
        case ARROW_KEY_DOWN:
            this.downKeyDown = true;
            break;
    }
}
p.handleKeyUp = function (e) {
    e = !e ? window.event : e;
    switch (e.keyCode) {
        case ARROW_KEY_LEFT:
            this.leftKeyDown = false;
            break;
        case ARROW_KEY_RIGHT:
            this.rightKeyDown = false;
            break;
        case ARROW_KEY_SPACE:
            this.spawnHeroBullet();
            break;
        case ARROW_KEY_UP:
            this.upKeyDown = false;
            break;
        case ARROW_KEY_DOWN:
            this.downKeyDown = false;
            break;
    }
}
```

Notice the use of the native JavaScript method bind. This is used to set the event handler's scope. These event handlers should look very familiar. The global constants for the key codes are used to detect the key pressed. The arrow keys will set the proper game properties to true when the key is pressed down and back to false when they are released. These values are evaluated during the update cycle to determine if and where the hero should be placed in the next render cycle. The space bar, which will fire a bullet, is only evaluated in the handleKeyUp handler. This is done so the player needs to release the key to fire, instead of a constant rapid fire that would occur when holding down the spacebar.

Creating the Game Loop

The game is now initialized. It is time now for the action. Remember that the state machine will fire a run method on the current scene with every tick, if it has one to call. This game does have a run method, and it is used to create the game loop in the game. The run method is shown in Listing 11-19.

Listing 11-19. The run Function Runs the Game Loop

```
p.run = function (tickEvent) {
    this.delta = tickEvent.delta;
    if (!this.betweenLevels) {
        this.update();
        this.render();
        this.checkForEnemySpawn(tickEvent.time);
        this.checkForEnemyFire(tickEvent.time);
        this.checkHeroBullets();
        if (!this.heroShip.invincible) {
            this.checkEnemyBullets();
            this.checkShips();
        }
        this.checkHealth();
        this.checkHero();
    }
}
```

The run method does quite a few things. Remember that the state machine passes the tick event into the game scene's run method. This is done because there are a few properties on the tick event that will help you in the game. The first property used is the delta property, which is assigned to the game property delta. This property is used to determine the next position for each moving sprite when updating. This technique is referred to as *time-based animation,* as opposed to *frame-based animation,* which has been used in all previous game loop exercises. The delta property tells you the difference in time since the last tick and can be used to determine how far the sprite should move, based on a predetermined speed value. This allows you to get smoother, more consistent sprite animations over varying framerates due to inconsistent processor speeds. This technique will be used when updating all sprites in this game.

After storing away the current delta value, a quick check is run to determine if the game is between levels. If the game is not currently between levels (i.e. the hero is not currently exploding), a series of game loop functions are called. Each of these functions will run the game and check for scenarios that call for further action. The first two functions are the update and render functions, which are seen in Listing 11-20.

Listing 11-20. The update and render Functions

```
p.update = function () {
    this.updateStars();
    this.updateHeroShip()
    this.updateEnemies();
    this.updateHeroBullets();
    this.updateEnemyBullets();
}
p.render = function () {
    this.renderStars();
    this.renderHeroShip();
    this.renderEnemies();
    this.renderHeroBullets();
    this.renderEnemyBullets();
}
```

The update and render functions calculate and move the sprite positions during the game loop. This technique was used in Break-It, and it works the same here in Space Hero. The updating and rendering of the game sprites will be closely looked at in the upcoming sections.

Building the Update Functions

The update functions calculate the current positions and states of all active sprites and determine where they should be rendered next. All update functions will be examined in detail next.

Updating the Star Field

All stars in the game should move in a constant manner down the screen. This gives the illusion of the ships traveling through space. Listing 11-21 shows the update function for the stars.

Listing 11-21. The udpateStars Method Moves All Stars Down the Screen

```
p.updateStars = function () {
   var i, star, velY, speed, nextY;
   var len = this.stars.length;
   for (i = 0; i < len; i++) {
      star = this.stars[i];
      velY = star.speed * this.delta / 1000;
      nextY = star.y + velY;
      if (nextY > screen_height) {
         nextY = -10
      }
      star.nextY = nextY;
   }
}
```

The stars array is looped through to access each star in the game. The star's next position is calculated and dynamically assigned to each star as nextY. If the star's next y position puts it below the height of the screen, it is recycled by placing it above the stage. Since the star sprites are so minimal, the need to make a class specifically for them was bypassed.

Updating the Hero and Enemy Ships

The ships in the game are updated similarly to the stars in that their nextY and/or nextX properties are updated for the next render cycle. Both update functions are seen in Listing 11-22.

Listing 11-22. Updating the Hero and Enemy Ships

```
p.updateHeroShip = function () {
   var velocity = this.heroShip.speed * this.delta / 1000;
   var nextX = this.heroShip.x;
   var nextY = this.heroShip.y;
   if (this.leftKeyDown) {
      nextX -= velocity;
      if (nextX < this.leftWall) {
```

```
            nextX = this.leftWall;
        }
    }
    else if (this.rightKeyDown) {
        nextX += velocity;
        if (nextX > this.rightWall) {
            nextX = this.rightWall;
        }
    }
    else if (this.downKeyDown) {
        nextY += velocity;
        if (nextY > this.floor) {
            nextY = this.floor;
        }
    }
    else if (this.upKeyDown) {
        nextY -= velocity;
        if (nextY < this.ceiling) {
            nextY = this.ceiling;
        }
    }
    this.heroShip.nextX = nextX;
    this.heroShip.nextY = nextY;
}
p.updateEnemies = function () {
    var enemy, i, velY;
    var len = this.enemies.length - 1;
    for (i = len; i >= 0; i--) {
        enemy = this.enemies[i];
        velY = enemy.speed * this.delta / 1000;
        enemy.nextY = enemy.y + velY;
        if (enemy.nextY > screen_height) {
            enemy.reset();
            this.enemyPool.returnSprite(enemy);
            this.removeChild(enemy);
            this.enemies.splice(i, 1);
        }
    }
}
```

The hero ship's next position is factored by calculating its velocity. Its velocity is calculated by comparing its speed against the current delta value. The keys currently being pressed on the keyboard determine what direction the ship should travel; if the new position should put the ship out of bounds, the values are adjusted accordingly to keep it in.

The enemy ships are animated automatically, and their positions are also calculated by using the delta technique used with the stars and hero ship. Much like the stars, when an enemy travels past the screen, it needs to be reset. In the case of an enemy, which was spawned from an object pool, its reset process is a little more detailed. First, the reset method is called on it. If you recall, this function creates a new random type and updates its properties accordingly. Next, it is returned back to the object pool from where it was spawned and removed from the display list. When the enemy was spawned, a reference to it was pushed into the enemyShips array for updating, so it needs to be removed from it to prevent further updates.

```
this.enemies.splice(i, 1);
```

This is done in the same way that the bricks were removed in Break-It, and is the reason for backwards looping through the enemyShips array. Updating the bullets is done in a similar fashion.

Updating the Hero and Enemy Bullets

The bullets act very similar to the enemy ships. The only real difference is that hero bullets travel up instead of down. Listing 11-23 shows these two bullet updating methods.

Listing 11-23. Updating the Hero and Enemy Bullets

```
p.updateHeroBullets = function () {
    var bullet, i, velY;
    var len = this.heroBullets.length - 1;
    for (i = len; i >= 0; i--) {
        bullet = this.heroBullets[i];
        velY = bullet.speed * this.delta / 1000;
        bullet.nextY = bullet.y - velY;
        if (bullet.nextY < 0) {
            this.heroBulletPool.returnSprite(bullet);
            this.removeChild(bullet);
            this.heroBullets.splice(i, 1);
        }
    }
}
p.updateEnemyBullets = function () {
    var bullet, i, velY;
    var len = this.enemyBullets.length - 1;
    for (i = len; i >= 0; i--) {
        bullet = this.enemyBullets[i];
        velY = bullet.speed * this.delta / 1000;
        bullet.nextY = bullet.y + velY;
        if (bullet.nextY > screen_height) {
            this.enemyBulletPool.returnSprite(bullet);
            this.removeChild(bullet);
            this.enemyBullets.splice(i, 1);
        }
    }
}
```

Building the Render Functions

Rendering the sprites is pretty straightforward. All of the calculations were handled in the updating process. Other than a few checks that are first needed for the bullets and enemies, the render process simply *puts* the sprites in their new position. These render functions are shown in Listing 11-24.

Listing 11-24. The render Functions Put the Game Sprites in their New Positions

```
p.renderStars = function () {
    var i, star;
    for (i = 0; i < this.stars.length; i++) {
        star = this.stars[i];
        star.y = star.nextY;
    }
}
p.renderHeroShip = function () {
    this.heroShip.x = this.heroShip.nextX;
    this.heroShip.y = this.heroShip.nextY;
}
p.renderHeroBullets = function () {
    var bullet, i;
    var len = this.heroBullets.length - 1;
    for (i = len; i >= 0; i--) {
        bullet = this.heroBullets[i];
        if (bullet.shouldDie) {
            this.removeChild(bullet);
            bullet.reset();
            this.heroBulletPool.returnSprite(bullet);
            this.heroBullets.splice(i, 1);
        }
        else {
            bullet.y = bullet.nextY;
        }
    }
}
p.renderEnemyBullets = function () {
    var bullet, i;
    var len = this.enemyBullets.length - 1;
    for (i = len; i >= 0; i--) {
        bullet = this.enemyBullets[i];
        if (bullet.shouldDie) {
            this.removeChild(bullet);
            bullet.reset();
            this.enemyBulletPool.returnSprite(bullet);
            this.enemyBullets.splice(i, 1);
        }
        else {
            bullet.y = bullet.nextY;
        }
    }
}
p.renderEnemies = function () {
    var enemy, i;
    var len = this.enemies.length - 1;
    for (i = len; i >= 0; i--) {
        enemy = this.enemies[i];
        if (enemy.shouldDie) {
            this.scoreboard.updateScore(enemy.points);
```

```
            this.enemies.splice(i, 1);
            this.removeChild(enemy);
            this.spawnEnemyExplosion(enemy.x, enemy.y);
            enemy.reset();
            this.enemyPool.returnSprite(enemy);
        }
        else {
            enemy.y = enemy.nextY;
        }
    }
}
```

Before the bullets and enemies are ultimately placed in their new positions, you need to check if they were deemed dead during the update process. In the case of a bullet, it is reset in the same way it is when passing below the screen. With the enemies, a few more things need to done. Other than its reset actions, the scoreboard should be updated, and an explosion should be spawned in its place.

A few things were *spawned* in the update/render process. These sprites were spawned in a series of spawning functions that will be covered next.

Building the Spawn Functions

When a bullet is fired, an explosion occurs, or a new enemy ship should appear, they are *spawned*. The functions that were called to create these new spawns are shown in Listing 11-25.

Listing 11-25. The Spawn Functions Create New Enemy Ships, Bullets, and Explosions

```
p.spawnEnemyShip = function () {
    var enemy = this.enemyPool.getSprite();
    enemy.y = -enemy.getBounds().height;
    enemy.x = Utils.getRandomNumber(enemy.getBounds().width,
        screen_width - enemy.getBounds().width);
    this.addChild(enemy);
    this.enemies.push(enemy);
}
p.spawnEnemyBullet = function (enemy) {
    var bullet = this.enemyBulletPool.getSprite();
    bullet.currentAnimationFrame = 1;
    bullet.y = enemy.y;
    bullet.x = enemy.x;
    this.addChildAt(bullet,0);
    this.enemyBullets.push(bullet);
}
p.spawnHeroBullet = function () {
    var bullet = this.heroBulletPool.getSprite();
    bullet.x = this.heroShip.x;
    bullet.y = this.heroShip.y - this.heroShip.getBounds().height / 2;
    this.addChildAt(bullet, 0);
    this.heroBullets.push(bullet)
}
p.spawnEnemyExplosion = function (x, y) {
    var explosion = this.explosionPool.getSprite();
```

```
    explosion.x = x - 45;
    explosion.y = y - 30;
    this.addChild(explosion);
    explosion.on('animationend', this.explosionComplete, this, true);
    explosion.play();
    createjs.Sound.play(game.assets.EXPLOSION);
}
p.explosionComplete = function (e) {
    var explosion = e.target;
    this.removeChild(explosion);
    this.explosionPool.returnSprite(explosion);
}
```

The single, most important feature that all of these functions share is the utilization of an object pool. When a bullet, ship, or explosion is needed, it is pulled from the object pool it was pushed into when it was created. When an enemy is spawned, it is placed at a random horizontal position, slightly above the screen. With the bullets, they are placed in the center and under the ship that shot it.

When an enemy explosion is spawned during the render process, the coordinates of the ship that caused it were passed into spawnEnemyExplosion. This is because that ship should be replaced with an explosion sprite in the exact same position. A little position adjusting is needed because the ship and explosion bounds and shapes are different. A listener is set on the sprite for when its animation is complete. It is then played, along with an explosion sound. When the animation is finished, the explosionComplete function is called, which will remove it from the display list and return it back to the object pool from which it came.

The final process of the game loop is to run some check functions. Among these checks is the evaluation of collisions. You will be using a third party library for these collision detections. Let's look at this library, and how to obtain it, before moving into the check functions.

Detecting Pixel-Perfect Collision

Because we are not dealing with simple rectangle shapes in this game, merely checking the rectangle bounds of each sprite will not do. Because of the complexity that goes into this type of detection, a third party library will be used to handle the heavy lifting of pixel-perfect collision detection.

A great collision detection library has been written by Olaf Horstmann to work with EaselJS. It's extremely easy to use once included in your application. To use it, first go to the web site and download it from github.com at https://github.com/olsn/Collision-Detection-for-EaselJS. Once included in your application, it is used as follows:

```
var collision = ndgmr.checkPixelCollision(sprite1, sprite2);
```

The method will either return an object or the value of false. Checking for collision is as simple as follows:

```
if(collision){
    //collision detected
}
```

Now that the library is obtained and included in the game, let's move back into the game code and examine the check functions.

Building the Check Functions

The final phase of the game loop is the check functions. These functions check on a variety of situations and determine if things should happen. These functions check if something should explode, if the game or level should be over, or if an enemy should fire a bullet.

Checking Time for Enemy Spawns and Attacks

When an enemy should be spawned, or when it should fire a bullet, are both determined by time. The two functions that decide these actions are shown in Listing 11-26.

Listing 11-26. Checking Time to Determine If New Enemies or Enemy Bullets Should be Created

```
p.checkForEnemySpawn = function (time) {
    if (time - this.enemyLastSpawnTime > this.enemySpawnWaiter) {
        this.spawnEnemyShip();
        this.enemyLastSpawnTime = time;
    }
}
p.checkForEnemyFire = function (time) {
    var enemy, i;
    var len = this.enemies.length - 1;
    for (i = len; i >= 0; i--) {
        enemy = this.enemies[i];
        if (time - enemy.lastFired > enemy.fireDelay) {
            this.spawnEnemyBullet(enemy);
            enemy.lastFired = time;
        }
    }
}
```

When these two functions are called, a reference to the `time` property on the tick event was passed into them. This `time` property holds the time that has elapsed since `Ticker` was initialized.

```
this.checkForEnemySpawn(tickEvent.time);
```

This time value can be used to detect the time that has passed since the last bullet was fired for each enemy. If it's time to fire a bullet, a new bullet is spawned, and the `lastFired` property on the enemy is reset back to 0. The spawning of an enemy is done the same way by comparing the time to `enemyLastSpawnTime`.

Checking for Collisions

A collision can happen between bullets and ships, and between enemy ships with the hero. Listing 11-27 shows these collision detection functions.

Listing 11-27. Checking for Collisions with Bullets Against Ships and Ships Against Ships

```
p.checkHeroBullets = function () {
    var i, b, bullet, enemy, collision;
    for (i in this.enemies) {
        enemy = this.enemies[i];
```

```
        for (b in this.heroBullets) {
            bullet = this.heroBullets[b];
            collision = ndgmr.checkPixelCollision(enemy, bullet);
            if (collision) {
                enemy.takeDamage();
                bullet.shouldDie = true;
            }
        }
    }
}
p.checkEnemyBullets = function () {
    var b, bullet, collision;
    for (b in this.enemyBullets) {
        bullet = this.enemyBullets[b];
        collision = ndgmr.checkPixelCollision(this.heroShip, bullet);
        if (collision) {
            bullet.shouldDie = true;
            this.heroShip.takeDamage();
            this.healthMeter.takeDamage(10);
        }
    }
}
p.checkShips = function () {
    var enemy, i;
    var len = this.enemies.length - 1;
    for (i = len; i >= 0; i--) {
        enemy = this.enemies[i];
        if (enemy.y > screen_height / 2) {
            collision = ndgmr.checkPixelCollision(this.heroShip, enemy);
            if (collision) {
                this.removeChild(enemy);
                this.enemies.splice(i, 1);
                this.spawnEnemyExplosion(enemy.x, enemy.y);
                this.heroShip.shouldDie = true;
                break;
            }
        }
    }
}
```

All hero bullets are checked to see if they collide with any enemy ship. If a bullet collision is detected on an enemy ship, its takeDamage method is invoked, and the bullet's shouldDie is set to true so it can be disposed of in the next cycle. The same approach is used to check enemy bullets against the hero. A collision there will cause damage to the ship and update the health meter as well.

When detecting ship-on-ship collisions, the check on each enemy's position is first run to determine if the enemy is anywhere near the ship. This is simply done by using the middle of the screen. If the enemy is not passed this point, then you know the check would be wasteful. With a ship-on-ship collision, the enemy should explode instantly. In other words, you shouldn't wait till the next tick to determine if the enemy should die, and the destruction process should happen now. This is done because the hero's death will temporarily stop the update/render cycle. The hero's fate is determined by its own upcoming check function, so its shouldDie property is simply set to true.

Checking If the Hero Should Die

When it's time for the hero to die, the appropriate actions are taken in checkHero, which checks on the hero's shouldDie property. So far, the only death deciding factor on the hero has been a ship-on-ship collision. A quick check on the hero's health is first run to also determine if the hero should explode (see Listing 11-28).

Listing 11-28. Checking If the Hero Should Die

```
p.checkHealth = function (e) {
   if (this.healthMeter.empty) {
      this.heroShip.shouldDie = true;
   }
}
p.checkHero = function () {
   if (this.heroShip.shouldDie) {
      this.numLives--;
      this.heroShip.explode();
      this.lifeBox.removeLife();
      this.betweenLevels = true;
   }
}
```

Checking the empty status of the health bar is done in the checkHealth method. If it is empty, the hero ship should be set to die. Finally, the checkHero method is run to check the hero's status.

If the hero should die, the number of lives is decreased by one. Next, the explode method is fired on the hero, which will play the explosion within itself by playing the explosion sequence. A life is removed from the life box and the betweenLevels Boolean is set to true, which will temporarily stop all action. Whether the game should continue is factored next in the final check function.

Checking the Game

If you recall, you set a listener on the hero ship instance for when the explosion animation is complete. This is how the checkGame function is called (see Listing 11-29).

Listing 11-29. Checking if the Game Should Continue or End After a Hero Explosion

```
p.checkGame = function (e) {
   if (this.numLives > 0) {
      this.heroShip.reset();
      this.heroShip.makeInvincible(true);
      this.healthMeter.reset();
      this.betweenLevels = false;
   }
   else {
      game.score = this.scoreboard.getScore();
      this.dispose();
      this.dispatchEvent(game.GameStateEvents.GAME_OVER);
   }
}
```

```
p.dispose = function () {
    document.onkeydown = null;
    document.onkeyup = null;
}
```

If there are more lives to spare, the hero ship is reset. It is then set to be invincible by invoking its makeInvincible method. This is so the player has a few seconds to dodge oncoming danger after the game is set back into action. The health meter is reset and the betweenLevels game property is set back to false, which will resume the action.

If the player is out of lives, the game should end. First, the current score is retrieved and stored in the global game namespace. Remember, you referenced this value when adding the score to the game over screen. Next, the dispose method is called and the game event GAME_OVER is dispatched.

The dispose method is created for cleanup before the game scene is removed in the state machine. In this case, the listeners are removed from the keyboard since they are no longer needed in the application. This also prevents unwanted results with the keyboard the next time a game instance is created.

That concludes the game code for Space Hero. A lot of code was introduced, which was broken into smaller sections to help you understand the structure of a high action game. You can find the complete game code in the Game.js file along with the other source code. You can download the code from the Source Code/Downloads tab on this book's Apress product page (www.apress.com/9781430263401). You should be able to follow it from beginning to end, but if you find yourself stuck on any section of the code, stop and refer back to the section in this chapter that examined it.

Summary

The game created in this chapter demonstrates how you can organize your loaded assets and game code into several manageable classes. The concept of object pooling was introduced to enhance the performance in your games, and the use of the delta property in Ticker can further assure fluid movements when dropping frames. Precise, pixel-perfect collision detection was also accomplished by taking advantage of an open source, third party library that was built specifically to work with EaselJS.

In the next chapter, you'll take a look at how a game created with CreateJS can be optimized for mobile browsers. You'll enhance touch responsiveness and look at ways to scale your games to fit different screen sizes.

CHAPTER 12

■ ■ ■

Building for Mobile Browsers

One of the greatest advantages of using HTML5 for your games is that you can target mobile browsers. When considering mobile, many factors come into play. One of the biggest challenges you'll face with mobile is preparing for the vast variety of screen sizes across devices.

In this chapter, you'll learn how to prepare your canvas game to scale and fill as much screen as possible on handheld devices and even desktop displays. You'll also learn how you can distribute your game over the Web by using the *Add to Home Screen* option in iOS Safari. To put this into practice, you will be adding code to Fakezee (see Chapter 7) so it will fit on mobile screens and will also be optimized for touch events.

Enabling Touch Events

To begin the mobile optimization of Fakezee, the init function will be updated to run a new function (see Listing 12-1). The optimizeForTouchAndScreens function will handle optimization for touch events on mobile devices. More code will be added later to handle screen sizes and orientations.

Listing 12-1. Updated init Function in index.html

```
function init() {
    canvas = document.getElementById('canvas');
    stage = new createjs.Stage(canvas);
    createjs.Ticker.setFPS(60);
    createjs.Ticker.on('tick', stage);
    optimizeForTouchAndScreens ();
    preload();
}
function optimizeForTouchAndScreens () {
    if (createjs.Touch.isSupported()) {
        createjs.Touch.enable(stage);
    }
}
```

The Touch class has a method named enable, which will enable touch interaction with the stage passed into it. This will also allow for multi-touch modes to work in your application. At the time of writing this book, Touch supports iOS, modern mobile browsers, and IE10. Although we will not be utilizing multi-touch with the mobile games in this book, enabling touch is still essential to gain full responsiveness for touch events. Not doing so will cause noticeable delays on various devices.

Before enabling touch, you should check if the browser running your application is a touchscreen device. There's no need to add features where they are not needed or supported, so wrapping a simple conditional around the touch-enabling code should be done. The isSupported method on Touch will return true if touch events are supported.

Setting the Viewport

The viewport meta tag informs the browser how to behave when it renders your web page. It represents the viewable area, and is what is zoomed, scaled, and rotated. The default behavior of the viewport lends itself nicely to most web sites, and gives the user a lot of control over how they can view the page. However, in a gaming environment it's best to tweak these values to better suit the needs of your game. Listing 12-2 displays the viewport meta tag that is added to the head of index.html in the Fakezee game.

Listing 12-2. The Viewport Meta Tag Is Used to Control How the Screen is Rendered

```
<meta name="viewport" content="user-scalable=no,width=device-width,initial-
    scale=1 maximum-scale=1.0"/>
```

The content property for viewport can be set to customize the way the screen renders and reacts to user touches. Preventing the user from scaling will essentially lock the assets in place and prevent default mobile browser behaviors. You'll typically want to prevent your game from dragging around or zooming while the player is interacting with it. Disabling user scaling on the viewport's content will prevent this from happening. The last three properties set in this example assure you that your application will initially load at full scale and will take advantage of the entire available screen real estate.

■ **Note** Preventing users from scaling your content will lock your assets in place and prevent pinching or scrolling. However, there is currently no way to prevent the browser from reacting to device orientation changes.

Scaling Fakezee for Multiple Screen Size

It's extremely difficult to predict how your game will appear on all of the phone, tablet, and computer screens it might come across. When it comes to handheld devices, your biggest challenge will be the limited space provided to you for your content. This precious space is often cluttered with navigation bars and other browser UI that can't be avoided.

Before getting into the JavaScript code, some extra styles are needed. Place these styles in either a style block or separate style sheet. Strip out the inline styles that are currently in the img and canvas elements in the index.html file for Fakezee. Listing 12-3 shows the new styles and updated HTML elements.

Listing 12-3. The Updated Styles and HTML Elements for Fakezee

```
//updated styles
body{
    background-color: #8b0000;
    margin: 0;
}
#gameWrapper{
    position: absolute;
}
canvas, img{
    -webkit-transform-origin:0px 0px;
    transform-orgin: 0 0;
    position: absolute;
}
```

```
//updated HTML elements
<div id="gameWrapper">
    <img id="bg" src="img/bg.jpg">
    <canvas id="canvas" width="550" height="500"></canvas>
</div>
```

There are a several approaches when it comes to preparing for screen sizes, but we'll be looking at just one. The technique I prefer is to scale the canvas to adjust to screen sizes and to adjust upon orientation changes. Listing 12-4 adds the code that listens for orientation and screen resizing events.

Listing 12-4. Checking For Devices and Desktop to Set the Appropriate Event Listeners

```
function optimizeForTouchAndScreens () {
    if (typeof window.orientation !== 'undefined') {
        window.onorientationchange = onOrientationChange;
        if (createjs.Touch.isSupported()) {
            createjs.Touch.enable(stage);
        }
        onOrientationChange();
    }
    else {
        window.onresize = resizeGame;
        resizeGame();
    }
}
```

This function is updated to check if the user is on a desktop or a device. First, if it's a device, the onorientationchange event is set on window, which will trigger when the user moves from portrait to landscape, or vice versa. The function onOrientationChange function is called, which will handle this event. You'll want to manually call this function as well because you won't get the change event when the page is first loaded, which is needed to trigger the initial scaling and positioning of the canvas.

In the case of a desktop, there will never be an orientation change. However, you still want the game to respond to window resizing. The resizeGame function is called on this event, and it is also initially called when the page is loaded to properly adjust the canvas.

The onOrientationChange and resizeGame functions are shown in Listing 12-5.

Listing 12-5. The onOrientation and resizeGame Functions Adjust the Size of the Game to Fit the Screen

```
function onOrientationChange() {
    setTimeout(resizeGame, 100);
}
function resizeGame() {
    var nTop, nLeft, scale;
    var gameWrapper = document.getElementById('gameWrapper');
    var bg = document.getElementById('bg');
    var w = window.innerWidth;
    var h = window.innerHeight;
    var nWidth = window.innerWidth;
    var nHeight = window.innerHeight;
    var widthToHeight = canvas.width / canvas.height;
    var nWidthToHeight = nWidth / nHeight;
```

```
    if (nWidthToHeight > widthToHeight) {
        nWidth = nHeight * widthToHeight;
        scale = nWidth / canvas.width;
        nLeft = (w / 2) - (nWidth / 2);
        gameWrapper.style.left = (nLeft) + "px";
        gameWrapper.style.top = "0px";
    }
    else {
        nHeight = nWidth / widthToHeight;
        scale = nHeight / canvas.height;
        nTop= (h / 2) - (nHeight / 2);
        gameWrapper.style.top = (nTop) + "px";
        gameWrapper.style.left = "0px";
    }
    canvas.setAttribute("style", "-webkit-transform:scale(" + scale +
        ")");
    bg.setAttribute("style", "-webkit-transform:scale(" + scale + ")");
    window.scrollTo(0, 0);
}
```

When the user rotates their device, or resizes their browser window on desktop, the resizeGame function is ultimately called. The reason for the intermediate onOrientationChange function is because you'll need a short timeout set after the onorientationchange event is handled. This is because some device browsers will run the event handler code before the window actually rotates and resizes. This is problem because you need the new window sizes to properly resize the canvas.

A series of variables are first set at the top of the function (see Listing 12-6).

Listing 12-6. The resizeGame Function's Local Variables

```
var nTop, nLeft, scale;
var gameWrapper = document.getElementById('gameWrapper');
var bg = document.getElementById('bg');
var w = window.innerWidth;
var h = window.innerHeight;
var nWidth = window.innerWidth;
var nHeight = window.innerHeight;
var widthToHeight = canvas.width / canvas.height;
var nWidthToHeight = nWidth / nHeight;
```

A reference to the div that the holds the game elements is first referenced. You will need this to reposition the game after its resized. In this particular game, an image was created in the DOM as the background for the game. This image will also need to be resized to match the new size of the canvas.

The current width and height of the window is set to the variables w, nWidth, h, and nHeight. Next, the widthToHeight variable is set to the ratio of the game, which can be retrieved by referencing the width and height of the canvas. Finally, nWidthToHeight is set the current ratio of the window.

In a nutshell, the desired game ratio is being set along with the current window ratio. These values will determine how the canvas should be scaled and placed in the screen. With the appropriate values set, a conditional is written to determine how the scaling should be handled (see Listing 12-7).

Listing 12-7. Factoring the Direction in Which to Scale and Position the Game

```
if (nWidthToHeight > widthToHeight) {
    nWidth = nHeight * widthToHeight;
    scale = nWidth / canvas.width;
    nLeft = (w / 2) - (nWidth / 2);
    gameWrapper.style.left = (nLeft) + "px";
    gameWrapper.style.top = "0px";
}
else {
    nHeight = nWidth / widthToHeight;
    scale = nHeight / canvas.height;
    nTop = (h / 2) - (nHeight / 2);
    gameWrapper.style.top = (nTop) + "px";
    gameWrapper.style.left = "0px";
}
```

If the nWidthToHeight value (the current width-to-height ratio of the window) is greater than widthToHeight (the desired width-to-height ratio of your game), then you know that the window is too wide to attempt to scale the canvas to the sides of the window. You then calculate nWidth by using the *height* of the window. Now that you know what the new width of the game should be, scale is calculated by dividing it by the canvas width. This scale value is the ultimate goal here, and will be used to scale the canvas.

▨ **Note** Although the canvas will be scaling on window resizing and orientation changes, the original width and the height *properties* on your canvas will always remain the same.

Now that the scale has been calculated, the game's positioning needs to be adjusted. In this first case, where the canvas will be hugging the top and bottom of the window, its left position needs to be updated so it sits perfectly in the middle. This is set to nLeft by finding the middle of the window and subtracting half of the canvas' new width. You've done this often when centering display objects on the stage. Figure 12-1 shows the results on an Android Nexus device and an iPhone 5. Note that in the case of the iPhone running iOS7 (the bottom image), full screen is launched automatically when rotated to landscape orientation.

Figure 12-1. *Fakzee scaled to fit in landscape orientation for Android (top) and iOS (bottom)*

Similar techniques are used in the case where the screen is tall, or in *portrait* mode, and the results are shown in Figure 12-2.

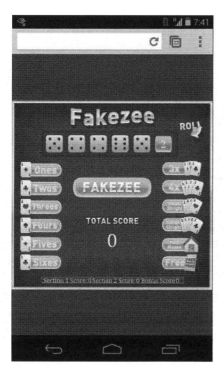
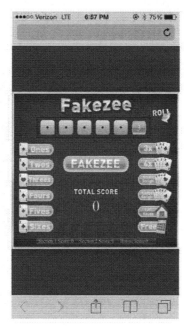

Figure 12-2. *Fakzee scaled to fit in portrait orientation for Android (left) and iOS (right)*

Although you've seen these results in the above figures, the function is not quite complete. With the new scale property acquired, it needs to be applied to the canvas (see Listing 12-8).

Listing 12-8. Updating the Styles to Scale the Canvas and Background Image

```
canvas.setAttribute("style", "-webkit-transform:scale(" + scale + ")");
bg.setAttribute("style", "-webkit-transform:scale(" + scale + ")");
window.scrollTo(0, 0);
```

The scaling is accomplished via transform styles on the canvas and background image, which are set with JavaScript. Lastly, the window scroll is set to 0, which can help remove unwanted address bars on mobile devices.

Optimizing Fakezee for iOS Home Pages

A really cool feature of iOS is the ability to save a bookmark to a site on your home page. However, this feature goes beyond being a simple bookmark. Using the appropriate meta tags and image preparation, you can get your game to appear and behave much like a native application.

Adding the Web App Meta Tags

Two more meta tags are needed to optimize Fakezee to behave the way you want it to when being launched from the home screen. These two meta tags are shown in Listing 12-9.

Listing 12-9. The Meta Tags Used To Optimize iOS Home Screen Apps

```
<meta name="apple-mobile-web-app-capable" content="yes"/>
<meta name="apple-mobile-web-app-status-bar-style" content="black"/>
```

The first tag, `apple-mobile-web-app-capable`, will display your app in full screen when launched from the home screen. Not supplying this tag will result in your app simply launching in the Safari browser. The second tag, `apple-mobile-web-app-status-bar-style`, specifies the style that the status bar will be displayed in. In this example, the background color will be black.

Creating a Home Screen App Icon

The icon on the home screen will, by default, be a screenshot of the web page. However, you can specify the icon that will be used. Listing 12-10 shows a series of `link` tags that are used to specify the icon image.

Listing 12-10. The link Tags to Set the Fakezee Icons

```
<!-- iOS 7 iPad (retina) -->
<link href="webapp/apple-touch-icon-152x152.png"
    sizes="152x152"
    rel="apple-touch-icon">

<!-- iOS 6 iPad (retina) -->
<link href="webapp/apple-touch-icon-144x144.png"
    sizes="144x144"
    rel="apple-touch-icon">

<!-- iOS 7 iPhone (retina) -->
<link href="webapp/apple-touch-icon-120x120.png"
    sizes="120x120"
    rel="apple-touch-icon">

<!-- iOS 6 iPhone (retina) -->
<link href="webapp/apple-touch-icon-114x114.png"
    sizes="114x114"
    rel="apple-touch-icon">

<!-- iOS 7 iPad -->
<link href="webapp/apple-touch-icon-76x76.png"
    sizes="76x76"
    rel="apple-touch-icon">

<!-- iOS 6 iPad -->
<link href="webapp/apple-touch-icon-72x72.png"
    sizes="72x72"
    rel="apple-touch-icon">

<!-- iOS 6 iPhone -->
<link href="webapp/apple-touch-icon-57x57.png"
    sizes="57x57"
    rel="apple-touch-icon">
```

As you can see, there are several images prepared for the icon. These tags are commented appropriately and represent the many possible iOS devices that could be running your application. When preparing an icon, it's best to design it large, and then save it in the appropriate sizes that are listed above. Figure 12-3 shows the icon that was prepped in a variety of sizes for the Fakezee home screen app.

Figure 12-3. *The Fakezee icon used for the iOS home screen app*

The icon will appear in a few locations. The first is in the modal screen that appears when the user selects the *Add to Home Screen* option in the mobile Safari menu. Figure 12-4 shows this being done on an iPad.

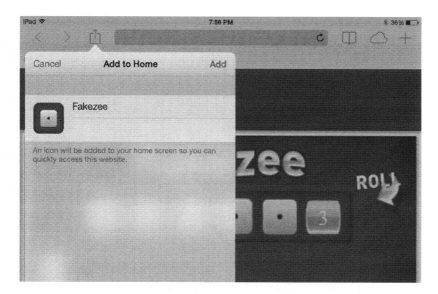

Figure 12-4. *The Fakezee icon in the Add to Home modal screen in iOS*

The other location where the icon is used is on the home screen where it will represent the application itself and launch the app. Figure 12-5 shows the Fakezee icon on the home screen of an iPad.

Figure 12-5. *The Fakezee iOS home screen app icon on an iPad*

Creating the Startup Image

The startup image is the splash screen image that will appear as your application is loading. If you are familiar with native iOS development, this is equivalent to the Default.png file that is required for your application. Listing 12-11 shows the list of link tags needed for the startup image on various iOS devices.

Listing 12-11. The link Tags Used to Set the Startup Image for Fakezee

```
<!-- iOS 6 & 7 iPad (retina, portrait) -->
<link href="webapp/apple-touch-startup-image-1536x2008.png"
    media="(device-width: 768px) and (device-height: 1024px)
        and (orientation: portrait)
        and (-webkit-device-pixel-ratio: 2)"
    rel="apple-touch-startup-image">

<!-- iOS 6 & 7 iPad (retina, landscape) -->
<link href="webapp/apple-touch-startup-image-1496x2048.png"
    media="(device-width: 768px) and (device-height: 1024px)
        and (orientation: landscape)
        and (-webkit-device-pixel-ratio: 2)"
    rel="apple-touch-startup-image">

<!-- iOS 6 iPad (portrait) -->
<link href="webapp/apple-touch-startup-image-768x1004.png"
    media="(device-width: 768px) and (device-height: 1024px)
        and (orientation: portrait)
        and (-webkit-device-pixel-ratio: 1)"
    rel="apple-touch-startup-image">

<!-- iOS 6 iPad (landscape) -->
<link href="webapp/apple-touch-startup-image-748x1024.png"
    media="(device-width: 768px) and (device-height: 1024px)
```

```
        and (orientation: landscape)
        and (-webkit-device-pixel-ratio: 1)"
    rel="apple-touch-startup-image">

<!-- iOS 6 & 7 iPhone 5 -->
<link href="webapp/apple-touch-startup-image-640x1096.png"
    media="(device-width: 320px) and (device-height: 568px)
        and (-webkit-device-pixel-ratio: 2)"
    rel="apple-touch-startup-image">

<!-- iOS 6 & 7 iPhone (retina) -->
<link href="webapp/apple-touch-startup-image-640x920.png"
    media="(device-width: 320px) and (device-height: 480px)
        and (-webkit-device-pixel-ratio: 2)"
    rel="apple-touch-startup-image">

<!-- iOS 6 iPhone -->
<link href="webapp/apple-touch-startup-image-320x460.png"
    media="(device-width: 320px) and (device-height: 480px)
        and (-webkit-device-pixel-ratio: 1)"
    rel="apple-touch-startup-image">
```

Much like the icon, several variations of the startup image must be created. Because of the variety of resolutions and ratios on iOS screens, the startup image cannot simply be created large and scaled down for each case. Another important thing you'll notice is that landscape startup images do not have landscape resolutions. This is because iOS will simply rotate your image in the case of a device in landscape mode; therefore you should prep your images at landscape, but rotate 90 degrees when saving for production. Figure 12-6 shows the startup image prepped for the retina iPad.

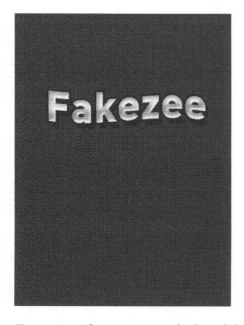

Figure 12-6. *The startup image displays while the app is loading*

Now your web app is fully optimized to launch full-screen from the home screen of an iOS device. There are more features you may wish to look into when creating these types of applications, including caching, which will download all of the files to the user's device and allow for offline use. The mobile Safari API includes even more functionality that might suit your needs when developing iOS web apps, so I encourage you to dig in and see what might make your game or application even more enjoyable. Figure 12-7 shows the final, full screen Fakezee game being launched on an iPad.

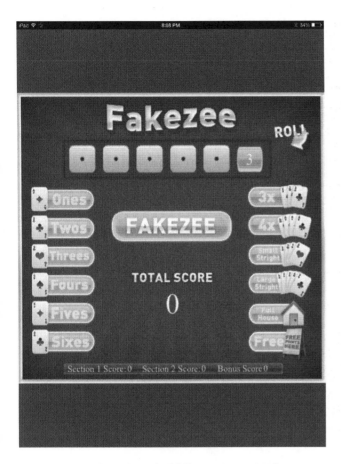

Figure 12-7. *Fakezee launched full-screen as an iOS home screen app*

Summary

In this chapter, CSS scaling techniques were introduced to enhance the Fakezee game to fit on the various screen sizes of tablets, handhelds, and desktops. Further enhancements were implemented to optimize the game for being added to iOS home screens, which can allow for the native-like, full-screen appearance of your applications.

This chapter focused heavily on mobile browsers and the optimizations that can be considered to best distribute your canvas games for the Web. However, this is only half the fun when it comes to mobile game development. In the next chapter, you'll learn how to package and publish your HTML5 games for mobile app stores.

■ ■ ■

CHAPTER 13

Packaging and Compiling with PhoneGap Build

With HTML5, it's possible to easily distribute your games over the Web, which can help you reach a wide range of browsers and devices. You've seen how adding web applications to the iOS home screen can mimic a native, installed application. An alternative to these web and browser distribution approaches is to use tools such as PhoneGap to package and compile your applications to be installed on devices. They can then be distributed to mobile application stores, such as Apple App Store and Google Play.

In this chapter, you will learn how to use PhoneGap Build to compile and install your applications to a variety of devices. The techniques learned in this chapter will help you develop and prepare your applications for app store distribution, and a few gotchas will be introduced that you'll run into when using CreateJS applications with PhoneGap.

Introducing PhoneGap Build

PhoneGap is a tool that is used to wrap web applications, built with web standards, into applications that can be installed on devices. There are a few ways to use PhoneGap, and it is loaded with features and compiling options. For the purposes of this book, we will be focusing on one approach, PhoneGap Build. To get started, visit `http://build.phonegap.com` (see Figure 13-1).

Figure 13-1. *The PhoneGap Build web site*

If you currently are a member of the Adobe Creative Cloud service, you can have up to 25 active applications free with your account. Each application can be compiled as many times as you like. If you are not currently a member, you can have 1 free application. In any case, you should have no trouble setting up an application to follow along in this chapter.

The benefit in using PhoneGap Build is that it is extremely easy to use. You only need to send up a ZIP file of your application, and PhoneGap Build will take care of the rest. PhoneGap Build supports several platforms, including iOS, Android, and Windows Phone. For the purposes of this chapter, we will be focusing on deploying to iOS and Android.

Acquiring Developer Accounts For iOS and Android

The process of packaging your application and installing on your device for development will be covered in this chapter. Everything from configuring your application files, uploading to PhoneGap Build, and installing on your devices will be reviewed. However, the necessary steps needed to sign up for the various vendor developer accounts will not be covered. Help on acquiring an iOS developer account, as well as obtaining the necessary certificate files needed to package your app, can be found at https://developer.apple.com/ (see Figure 13-2).

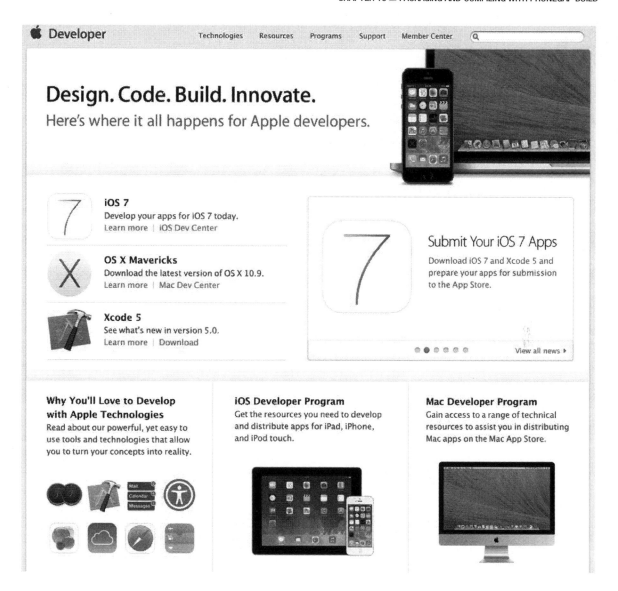

Figure 13-2. *The iOS Developer web site*

When it comes Android development, there are far less restrictions. You can instantly start testing on Android devices built by PhoneGap Build. You can then begin sharing with testers and even start self-distributing. As previously mentioned, application submissions to app stores won't be covered in this book, but you will need similar developer credentials if you plan on packaging and distributing in Google's Play Store. For more information, visit https://play.google.com/apps/publish. Figure 13-3 shows the dashboard after logging in with your Google account.

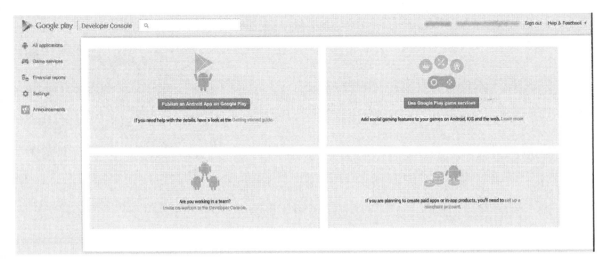

Figure 13-3. *The Google Play Developer Console*

Updating the Fakezee Game For Packaging

A few things need to be done to the current Fakezee game to prepare it for packaging as an application. First, it will be reformatted visually to better suit portrait orientations on devices. The same assets are used, but various positioning values are updated to lay out the sprites and containers into new positions. We won't be covering the code for this layout, but you can review it in the source code provided for this chapter. The second adjustment needed for the game to properly be compiled with PhoneGap is the refactoring of asset-loading code. Because PhoneGap uses JSONP to load in data, some code updates will be needed for preloading assets. This code will be covered later in this section.

Adjusting the Visual Layout for Fakezee

The scaling code built in the Chapter 12 will still be used in this application. Because of the various screen sizes on devices between iOS and Android, you'll still want the game to utilize this logic so it will adjust accordingly. The game will be packaged and configured to stay locked on portrait mode, so some slight adjustments will be made to fill up the screen (see Figure 13-4).

Figure 13-4. *Fakezee game elements, adjusted for mobile applications*

The background image and canvas sizes were changed accordingly to fit the height of device screens in portrait mode. Some code was also altered to move the game elements to better fit in the new screen format. The game logic and application code has remained the same.

Preloading JSONP for PhoneGap

As mentioned earlier, there are currently some show-stopping conflicts between PhoneGap and PreloadJS. This can cause issues in your application, primarily when it comes to loading data text files. In the case of Fakezee, PreloadJS is being used to load and parse a JSON data file so it can be used in the application. This will not properly work in the PhoneGap environment because the two use different approaches to loading data.

PhoneGap requires JSONP to be used when loading JSON data. In order to get JSONP to properly work with PreloadJS, you must define a callback in the object you are building for the manifest.

```
{id:"sheetData", src:"js/fakezee.json",callback: setupSpritesheet}
```

With JSONP, the file is loaded in as JavaScript and auto exectutes. In your `fakezee.json` file, simply wrap a function call around your sprite sheet JSON data. Now this function will fire, which is the same method declared in the manifest object, and will pass along the JSON as it's first parameter. Listing 13-1 demonstrates this function call in `fakezee.json`.

Listing 13-1. Updated fakezee.json File Passes Sprite Sheet JSON Data to a Global Function

```
setupSpritesheet ({
    "images":["img/fakezee.png"],
    "frames":[
        [702, 1806, 113, 50],
        [817, 1787, 113, 50],
        ...
    ],
    "animations":{
        "diceHold":[63],
        "diceTray":{
            "frames":[64]
        },
        "die":{
            "frames":[65, 66, 67, 68, 69, 70]
        },
        ...
    }
});
```

This JSON data is now passed into the setupSpritesheet function back in the game. In this function, you can safely use the passed-in data parameter to create your sprite sheet. Listing 13-2 shows the updated preload and setupSpritesheet functions for Fakezee.

Listing 13-2. Updated fakezee.json File Passes Sprite Sheet JSON Data to a Global Function

```
function preload() {
    queue = new createjs.LoadQueue();
    queue.loadManifest([
        {id:"sheetData", src:"js/fakezee.json",callback: setupSpritesheet}
    ]);
}
function setupSpritesheet (data){
    spritesheet = new createjs.SpriteSheet(data);
    initGame();
}
```

You'll also notice that you are not declaring the sprite sheet image in the load manifest. This is because the sprite sheet data object contains this reference and will handle the preload for you. This is the case whether you are using JSON or JSONP.

You can continue to use PreloadJS to load your other assets for PhoneGap applications, such as images and sounds as you normally would. However, be sure to include a separate listener for the completion of all files to init your application. The callbacks declared for JSONP should only be used for setting up sprite sheets if other assets are being preloaded in the queue.

■ **Note**   When using PhoneGap, you may need to reference assets by using their full location path, as opposed to using the *id* that you assigned it in the load manifest. The asset will be successfully loaded and available, but might not be available via the preload queue object's getResult method. I've found this to be the case in iOS, but not in Android.

Preparing Assets for PhoneGap

Similar to the iOS home screen app that was built in Chapter 12, icons and splash screens are needed for packaging your apps. These assets will be referenced in the `config.xml` file that is needed for PhoneGap to properly build your application.

These graphics are built similarly to how they were prepared for the Fakezee web app, and the icons can be reused for this project. The main difference is in the splash images: in the PhoneGap app they need to be a bit bigger. This is because you no longer need to compensate for the status bar, like you are forced to in a web app environment. Another key difference is that the landscape images should actually be landscape in ratio, as opposed to rotated, like is needed with web apps.

The icons and splash images for Android are prepared similarly, but will need their own set of properties to work across devices. Using the same design files for iOS, these assets can be prepared accordingly to match the required sizes. Using the configuration file for a reference, you will find the list of necessary assets and sizes. Let's get into this configuration file now.

Preparing the PhoneGap Configuration File

The configuration file holds many configuration properties for your PhoneGap application. It holds version numbers, asset locations, permissions, plug-ins, and more. For the purposes of this project, you don't need to configure much more than the locations to the graphical assets and a few platform settings and preferences.

The configuration file for PhoneGap is written in XML, and must be included at the root of your application when packaging for PhoneGap Build. The configuration file is used to apply settings and features to your application that would otherwise be set within files or the IDEs used to build native apps.

Listing 13-3 shows the beginning of the `config.xml` file. You will be adding more nodes to this file throughout this chapter.

Listing 13-3. config.xml – The Outline XML Structure

```
<?xml version="1.0" encoding="UTF-8" ?>
<widget xmlns="http://www.w3.org/ns/widgets"
        xmlns:gap="http://phonegap.com/ns/1.0"
        id="com.games.fakezee"
        version="1.0.0">

    <name>Fakezee</name>

    <description>
        Fakezee is a dice game that is fun for everyone!
    </description>

    <author href="" email="">
        Fun Times Games
    </author>

</widget>
```

A unique id is needed for your application and is set to the `id` attribute in the main `widget` node. This unique id is crucial when it comes time to package your application for distribution. It is less important during the development phase, which this chapter will cover, but just remember that this id must match certain provisioning files when publishing to app stores.

The current application version can also be set in this main node. This can be useful, especially when collaborating with other developers. This version number will be displayed within the application listing on the PhoneGap Build web site (see Figure 13-5).

Figure 13-5. *Application build properties, seen in the application page*

The name of your application is also declared here in the configuration file within the element name. The `description` and `author` elements specify metadata and contact information that may appear within app store listings.

Next, the platforms that you want PhoneGap to build for are listed (see Listing 13-4).

Listing 13-4. config.xml – Specifying Target Platforms

```
<gap:platform name="ios"/>
<gap:platform name="android"/>
```

In recent past, PhoneGap Build would automatically begin a build for all available platforms when uploading your content. This welcomed feature allows you to specify only the platforms you are currently developing for. Next is a set of preference and access elements (see Listing 13-5).

Listing 13-5. config.xml – Preference and Access Elements

```
<preference name="orientation" value="portrait"/>
<preference name="fullscreen" value="true"/>

<access origin="*" />
```

Here you can specify the preferred orientation for your application. Unlike web apps, you can lock the orientation here if you prefer to do so. In the Fakezee game, it will be locked in portrait orientation. It will also launch in full screen, which is also listed here.

You can use `access` elements to create a *whitelist* of domains that your application is allowed to load data and assets from. In this project, a wildcard is used to indicate that the application is fine to load from anywhere.

The icon and splash image elements, as prepared for iOS, are listed in Listing 13-6.

Listing 13-6. config.xml – Icon and Splash Screen Assets for iOS

```
<icon src="icons/apple-touch-icon-57x57.png" gap:platform="ios"
    width="57" height="57" />
<icon src="icons/apple-touch-icon-72x72.png" gap:platform="ios"
    width="72" height="72" />
```

```
<icon src="icons/apple-touch-icon-114x114.png" gap:platform="ios"
    width="114" height="114" />
<icon src="icons/apple-touch-icon-144x144.png" gap:platform="ios"
    width="144" height="144" />

<gap:splash src="splash/apple-touch-startup-image-320x480.png"
    gap:platform="ios" width="320" height="480" />
<gap:splash src="splash/apple-touch-startup-image-640x960.png"
    gap:platform="ios" width="640" height="960" />
<gap:splash src="splash/apple-touch-startup-image-640x1136.png"
    gap:platform="ios" width="640" height="1136" />
<gap:splash src="splash/apple-touch-startup-image-1024x748.png"
    gap:platform="ios" width="1024" height="748" />
<gap:splash src="splash/apple-touch-startup-image-768x1004.png"
    gap:platform="ios" width="768" height="1004" />

<!-- retina iPad support: PhoneGap 2.5.0+ only -->

<gap:splash src="splash/apple-touch-startup-image-2048x1496.png"
    gap:platform="ios" width="2048" height="1496" />
<gap:splash src="splash/apple-touch-startup-image-1536x2008.png"
    gap:platform="ios" width="1536" height="2008" />
```

As you can see, the icons prepped for the Fakezee web app can be used here as well. As mentioned earlier, the splash images are slightly different and should be prepped accordingly for use in your PhoneGap application.

Listing 13-7 lists these same assets and how they should be prepared for Android.

Listing 13-7. config.xml – Icon and Splash Screen Assets for Android

```
<icon src="icons/android/ldpi.png" gap:platform="android"
    gap:density="ldpi" width="36" height="36"/>
<icon src="icons/android/mdpi.png" gap:platform="android"
    gap:density="mdpi" width="48" height="48"/>
<icon src="icons/android/hdpi.png" gap:platform="android"
    gap:density="hdpi" width="72" height="72"/>
<icon src="icons/android/xdpi.png" gap:platform="android"
    gap:density="xhdpi" width="96" height="96"/>

<gap:splash src="splash/android/ldpi.png" gap:platform="android"
    gap:density="ldpi" />
<gap:splash src="splash/android/mdpi.png" gap:platform="android"
    gap:density="mdpi" />
<gap:splash src="splash/android/hdpi.png" gap:platform="android"
    gap:density="hdpi" />
<gap:splash src="splash/android/xhdpi.png" gap:platform="android"
    gap:density="xhdpi" />
```

With all assets prepped and placed in the directories that the configuration elements dictate, the config.xml file is ready.

The Complete Configuration File for Fakezee

We have only scratched the surface of the features available within PhoneGap, and the available elements for your configuration files extend much further than what is needed for the Fakezee game. As your games and applications progress in size and complexity, you'll need more elements so that your PhoneGap application properly builds and runs.

Listing 13-8 shows the entire config.xml file.

Listing 13-8. config.xml – The Complete Configuration XML File

```xml
<?xml version="1.0" encoding="UTF-8" ?>
<widget xmlns="http://www.w3.org/ns/widgets"
     xmlns:gap="http://phonegap.com/ns/1.0"
     id="com.games.fakezee"
     version="1.0.0">

  <name>Fakezee</name>

  <description>
     Fakezee is a dice game that is fun for everyone!
  </description>

  <author href="{insert your url here}" email="{insert your support email
        here}">
     Fun Times Games
  </author>

  <gap:platform name="ios"/>
  <gap:platform name="android"/>

  <!--IOS-->

  <icon src="icons/apple-touch-icon-57x57.png" gap:platform="ios"
     width="57" height="57" />
  <icon src="icons/apple-touch-icon-72x72.png" gap:platform="ios"
     width="72" height="72" />
  <icon src="icons/apple-touch-icon-114x114.png" gap:platform="ios"
     width="114" height="114" />
  <icon src="icons/apple-touch-icon-144x144.png" gap:platform="ios"
     width="144" height="144" />

  <gap:splash src="splash/apple-touch-startup-image-320x480.png"
     gap:platform="ios" width="320" height="480" />
  <gap:splash src="splash/apple-touch-startup-image-640x960.png"
     gap:platform="ios" width="640" height="960" />
  <gap:splash src="splash/apple-touch-startup-image-640x1136.png"
     gap:platform="ios" width="640" height="1136" />
  <gap:splash src="splash/apple-touch-startup-image-1024x748.png"
     gap:platform="ios" width="1024" height="748" />
  <gap:splash src="splash/apple-touch-startup-image-768x1004.png"
     gap:platform="ios" width="768" height="1004" />
```

```
<!-- retina iPad support: PhoneGap 2.5.0+ only -->
<gap:splash src="splash/apple-touch-startup-image-2048x1496.png"
    gap:platform="ios" width="2048" height="1496" />
<gap:splash src="splash/apple-touch-startup-image-1536x2008.png"
    gap:platform="ios" width="1536" height="2008" />

<!--ANDROID-->
<icon src="icons/android/ldpi.png" gap:platform="android"
    gap:density="ldpi" width="36" height="36"/>
<icon src="icons/android/mdpi.png" gap:platform="android"
    gap:density="mdpi" width="48" height="48"/>
<icon src="icons/android/hdpi.png" gap:platform="android"
    gap:density="hdpi" width="72" height="72"/>
<icon src="icons/android/xdpi.png" gap:platform="android"
    gap:density="xhdpi" width="96" height="96"/>

<gap:splash src="splash/android/ldpi.png" gap:platform="android"
    gap:density="ldpi" />
<gap:splash src="splash/android/mdpi.png" gap:platform="android"
    gap:density="mdpi" />
<gap:splash src="splash/android/hdpi.png" gap:platform="android"
    gap:density="hdpi" />
<gap:splash src="splash/android/xhdpi.png" gap:platform="android"
    gap:density="xhdpi" />

<preference name="orientation" value="portrait"/>
<preference name="fullscreen" value="true"/>

<access origin="*" />

</widget>
```

Submitting your Application to PhoneGap Build

With your configuration file complete, zip up your application directory. This ZIP file is what is uploaded to PhoneGap Build. Be sure that your index.html and config.xml file are at the root of the zipped directory. Head back over to the PhoneGap Build site so you can submit your application. Under the *Apps* tab, press the *+new app* button. Figure 13-6 shows the new app page.

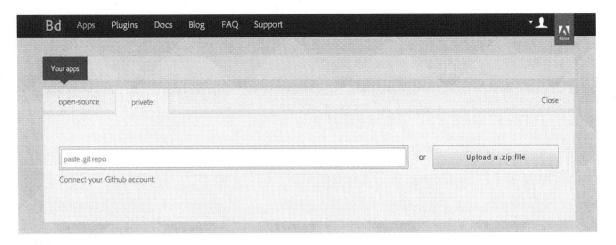

Figure 13-6. New app screen on the PhoneGap Build web site

As you can see in Figure 13-6, you can browse for the ZIP file to upload. If you are Git-savvy, you can alternatively point to a Git repository, which will be used to build your application.

Once your new project is successfully uploaded, your application will be ready to build. With iOS, you need to supply a certificate and provisioning file, which can be acquired with an Apple developer account. You need to provide these files before PhoneGap will build your application, even if it's just for development. Figure 13-7 shows the message you will receive when attempting to build for iOS without your Apple certificate files entered into the system.

Figure 13-7. iOS error message indicates that an action is required to build

When your applications successfully compile, the app screen will provide links for the install files to download. In this case of Fakezee, you will be offered both an `.ipa` file and an `.apk` file. These links can also be shared for installation on other devices. When accessed from a device, the installation process with begin immediately when the link is vistited.

You can alternatively use the QR code by using a QR reader app on your device. This will allow you to download and install the application without having to connect or sync your device to a computer. Figure 13-8 shows the application screen in PhoneGap Build with an application that has been built and ready to install.

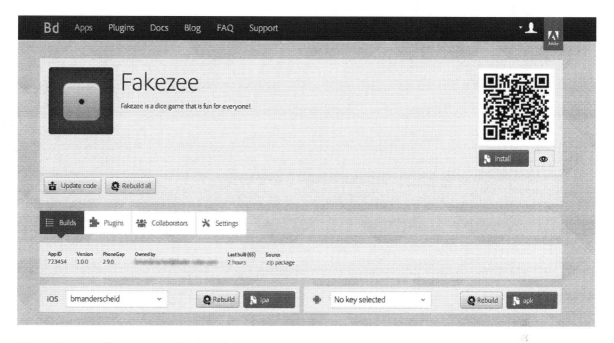

Figure 13-8. *Application screen for the Fakezee game in PhoneGap Build*

For iOS applications, the device that is installing your application needs to be included in the provisioning file that you uploaded to PhoneGap Build and used to compile the app. With Android, no special signing is needed for simply testing your application across all devices.

As previously mentioned, we've only scratched the surface of what can be done with PhoneGap. Using PhoneGap Build, you can quickly get your web application compiled into multiple platforms by simply uploading a zip file of your web files. You can alternatively install PhoneGap via the command line and compile locally. This option gives you template projects that can be opened in applications such as XCode, where you can fine tune your iOS application from within its native environment before deploying.

For more information on what you can do with this powerful tool and how you can use it, visit the online documentation at `http://docs.phonegap.com/en/edge/index.html`.

Summary

In this chapter, you used PhoneGap Build to compile a game, built with CreateJS, into an application that can ultimately be distributed through app stores and installed onto devices. A few caveats were introduced that can prevent your sprite sheet data from loading appropriately within your application when compiled with PhoneGap.

The configuration file and the XML elements needed to compile your applications with PhoneGap Build were reviewed, and the necessary graphical assets for both iOS and Android were covered.

In the next and final chapter, you will use all of the skills learned in this book to create an RPG battle game. The next chapter also contains an introduction to local storage for saving the player's progress. The state machine code, asset manager class, and scaling techniques will be used to prepare the game to be easily distributed over the Web.

CHAPTER 14

■ ■ ■

Game Project: The Villager RPG

In this chapter, a turn-based RPG game will be built using the lessons learned in this book. The goal for this game is to use RPG-like battle patterns to create a level-based game that can be deployed and scaled across multiple devices. The skills you have already acquired from earlier in this book will be used throughout this chapter, and a few new techniques will be introduced including creating custom events and saving the player's progress using local storage.

There is quite a bit of code in this project, so before getting into it, a quick review of the game you will be building is necessary.

The Villager RPG

The Villager RPG is a nine-level game; each level is a battle that contains enemies that the player must defeat. The battle will be a turn-based battle system that involves a classic style wait bar, and a variety of attack and magic items can be used to attack the enemy. A potion is also available to replenish hit points during a battle. This battle system will be covered in detail in the "Reviewing the RPG Battle System" section.

The following items are the technical achievements and features you want to achieve in the game:

- Build a nine-level game, in which all progress is saved to local storage when each level is complete.

- Each level will use a reusable game class that is a turn-based system where the player attacks enemies by choosing from available attacks and items.

- Each level will be formed by a single data object which will build the enemy grid, provide attributes for level difficulty, and determine the rewards given when the level is beaten.

- Create a single Enemy class that can appear and behave based on data provided to it.

- Create effects on the enemies to indicate the types of attacks that were thrown at it.

- Extend the Event class to create a custom event that stores extra properties.

- Build a shop where the player can purchase items to be used in battle. These items can be purchased using the coins earned in battle.

- The last level should be a single boss enemy.

Figure 14-1 shows the game being played in its complete state.

Figure 14-1. *The Villager RPG in game battle*

Before getting into the game code, let's prepare the project by taking a look at the files that make up the foundation of the application.

Preparing for the Project

Several files and classes need to be set up for the creation of this game project. This section will walk you through the necessary steps to prepare for the game, starting with the single HTML file, index.html.

Setting Up the HTML

The HTML file used for this game will include several JavaScript files. It will also create an instance of the application and fire its init function, which will initialize the application. Saved data will be retrieved and loaded into the game from local storage, and a handful of global variables are declared for use throughout the application. Listing 14-1 shows the entire index.html file.

Listing 14-1. The index.html File for The Village RPG

```
<!DOCTYPE html>
<html>
<head>
    <title>Meynard RPG</title>

    <link href="css/styles.css" rel="stylesheet" type="text/css"/>

    <!--CREATEJS-->
    <script src="js/lib/easeljs-0.7.1.min.js"></script>
    <script src="js/lib/soundjs-0.5.2.min.js"></script>
    <script src="js/lib/preloadjs-0.4.1.min.js"></script>
    <script src="js/lib/tweenjs-0.5.1.min.js"></script>
    <script src="js/lib/BitmapText.js"></script>

    <!--DATA-->
    <script src="js/data/data.js"></script>

    <!--GAME CLASSES-->
    <script src="js/state.js"></script>
    <script src="js/events.js"></script>
    <script src="js/classes/Hero.js"></script>

    <!--COMPONENTS-->
    <script src="js/classes/components/Preloader.js"></script>

    <!--SCENES-->
    <script src="js/scenes/GameMenu.js"></script>
    <script src="js/scenes/LevelSelect.js"></script>
    <script src="js/scenes/Game.js"></script>
    <script src="js/scenes/LevelComplete.js"></script>

    <!--MANAGERS-->
    <script src="js/classes/managers/AssetManager.js"></script>

    <!--SPRITES-->
    <script src="js/classes/sprites/BattlePanel.js"></script>
    <script src="js/classes/sprites/BattleButton.js"></script>
```

```html
    <script src="js/classes/sprites/Enemy.js"></script>
    <script src="js/classes/sprites/EnemyHealthBar.js"></script>
    <script src="js/classes/sprites/MagicShop.js"></script>

    <!--APPLICATION-->
    <script src="js/device.js"></script>
    <script src="js/Villager.js"></script>

</head>

<body onload="init();">

<div id="gameWrapper">
    <canvas id="canvas" width="640" height="1136"></canvas>
</div>

</body>

<script>

    var stage;
    var canvas;
    var spritesheet;
    var fontsheet;
    var screen_width;
    var screen_height;

    function init() {
        window.game = window.game || {};
        data.PlayerData.getData();
        game.main = new game.Villager();
    }

</script>

</html>
```

As you can see, there are quite a few JavaScript files in this application, and the init function is utilizing a few objects that are declared in these scripts. I will be covering each of these files in depth, but first, take a look at the sprite sheet images to get an idea of the sprites that will be used in the game.

Reviewing the Sprite Sheet Images

The sprite sheet files for this chapter are available with the book's source code download. Most animations will be done via TweenJS, with the exception of the block dissolve effect on enemies, which was done in Adobe After Effects and exported as png files for Texture Packer. Another sprite sheet will also be used for the bitmap font that is used heavily in the game. Figure 14-2 and Figure 14-3 shows the sprite sheets that will be used for The Villager RPG.

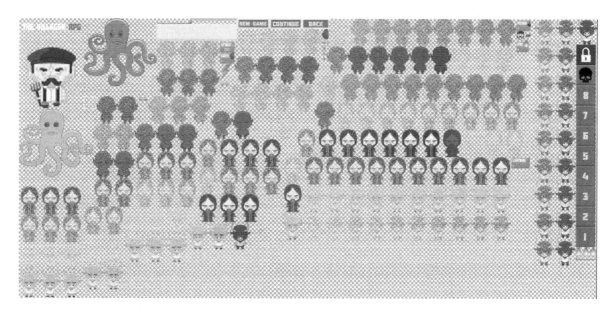

Figure 14-2. *The full sprite sheet image for all sprites in The Villager RPG*

Figure 14-3. *The sprite sheet image for bitmap fonts*

Preparing the Asset Manager

For this game, you'll be using the same `AssetManager` class that was used in Space Hero in Chapter 11, updated appropriately for this game. Listing 14-2 shows the full class, with the necessary assets needed for this application in bold.

Listing 14-2. AssetManager.js - The Complete Asset Mangager Class

```
(function () {

    window.game = window.game || {};

    var AssetManager = function () {
        this.initialize();
    }
    var p = AssetManager.prototype = new createjs.EventDispatcher();

    p.EventDispatcher_initialize = p.initialize;

    //sounds

    //graphics
    p.GAME_SPRITES = 'game sprites';
    p.FONT_SPRITES = 'font sprites';
    p.BATTLE_BG = 'game bg';
    p.MENU_BG = 'menu bg';

    //data
    p.GAME_SPRITES_DATA = 'game sprites data';
    p.FONT_SHEET_DATA = 'font sheet data';

    //events
    p.ASSETS_PROGRESS = 'assets progress';
    p.ASSETS_COMPLETE = 'assets complete';

    p.assetsPath = 'assets/';

    p.loadManifest = null;
    p.queue = null;
    p.loadProgress = 0;

    p.initialize = function () {
        this.EventDispatcher_initialize();
        this.loadManifest = [
            {id:this.GAME_SPRITES_DATA, src:this.assetsPath +
                'spritesheet.json'},
            {id:this.GAME_SPRITES, src:this.assetsPath + 'spritesheet.png'},

            {id:this.FONT_SHEET_DATA, src:this.assetsPath + 'abc.json'},
            {id:this.FONT_SPRITES, src:this.assetsPath + 'abc.png'},
```

```
            {id:this.BATTLE_BG, src:this.assetsPath + 'battleBG.png'},
            {id:this.MENU_BG, src:this.assetsPath + 'menuBG.png'}
        ];
    }
    p.preloadAssets = function () {
        createjs.Sound.initializeDefaultPlugins();
        this.queue = new createjs.LoadQueue();
        this.queue.installPlugin(createjs.Sound);
        this.queue.on('progress',this.assetsProgress,this);
        this.queue.on('complete',this.assetsLoaded,this);
        this.queue.loadManifest(this.loadManifest);
    }
    p.assetsProgress = function (e) {
        this.loadProgress = e.progress;
        var event = new createjs.Event(this.ASSETS_PROGRESS);
        this.dispatchEvent(event);
    }
    p.assetsLoaded = function (e) {
        var event = new createjs.Event(this.ASSETS_COMPLETE);
        this.dispatchEvent(event);
    }
    p.getAsset = function (asset) {
        return this.queue.getResult(asset);
    }

    window.game.AssetManager = AssetManager;

}());
```

Creating the Device Class

The scaling and device orientation code that was learned in Chapter 12 will be used to create a reusable object that can be used for this and future games. The purpose of this code will be to extract the screen detection and functionality from the main application (see Listing 14-3).

Listing 14-3. Device.js - The Device Class Handles Screen Scaling

```
(function () {

    window.game = window.game || {};

    var Device = {}

    Device.prepare = function () {
        if (typeof window.orientation !== 'undefined') {
            window.onorientationchange = this.onOrientationChange;
            if (createjs.Touch.isSupported()) {
                createjs.Touch.enable(stage);
            }
```

```
            this.onOrientationChange();
        } else {
            window.onresize = this.resizeGame;
            this.resizeGame();
        }
    }
}
Device.onOrientationChange = function () {
    var me = this;
    setTimeout(me.resizeGame, 100);
}
Device.resizeGame = function () {
    var nTop, nLeft, scale;
    var gameWrapper = document.getElementById('gameWrapper');
    var w = window.innerWidth;
    var h = window.innerHeight;
    var nWidth = window.innerWidth;
    var nHeight = window.innerHeight;
    var widthToHeight = canvas.width / canvas.height;
    var nWidthToHeight = nWidth / nHeight;
    if (nWidthToHeight > widthToHeight) {
        nWidth = nHeight * widthToHeight;
        scale = nWidth / canvas.width;
        nLeft = (w / 2) - (nWidth / 2);
        gameWrapper.style.left = (nLeft) + "px";
        gameWrapper.style.top = "0px";
    }
    else {
        nHeight = nWidth / widthToHeight;
        scale = nHeight / canvas.height;
        nTop= (h / 2) - (nHeight / 2);
        gameWrapper.style.top = (nTop) + "px";
        gameWrapper.style.left = "0px";
    }
    canvas.setAttribute("style", "-webkit-transform:scale(" + scale +
        ")");
    window.scrollTo(0, 0);
}
    window.game.Device = Device;

}());
```

This code should all look very familiar to you. The only difference here is that it is all wrapped up in an object that can be called upon when initializing your application. The prepare function is called after all necessary values have been set—primarily the references to the canvas element and its size.

Creating the Application Class

The application class, Villager, is used to manage state by loading, running, and unloading game scenes. Again, this should be review to you at this point. Looking at the code, a few new states are introduced to adhere to this application, including a level select and a level complete scene. Listing 14-4 shows the Village.js file in its entirety.

Listing 14-4. Villager.js - The Complete Application Class with State Machine

```javascript
(function (window) {

   window.game = window.game || {}

   function Villager() {
      this.initialize();
   }

   var p = Villager.prototype = new createjs.Container();

   p.Container_initialize = p.initialize;

   p.initialize = function () {
      this.Container_initialize();
      canvas = document.getElementById('canvas');
      screen_width = canvas.width;
      screen_height = canvas.height;
      stage = new createjs.Stage(canvas);
      game.Device.prepare();
      this.preloadAssets();
   }
   p.preloadAssets = function () {
      game.assets = new game.AssetManager();
      this.preloader = new ui.Preloader('#d2354c', '#FFF');
      this.preloader.x = (canvas.width / 2) - (this.preloader.width / 2);
      this.preloader.y = (canvas.height / 2) - (this.preloader.height /
         2);
      stage.addChild(this.preloader);
      game.assets.on(game.assets.ASSETS_PROGRESS, this.onAssetsProgress,
         this);
      game.assets.on(game.assets.ASSETS_COMPLETE, this.assetsReady, this);
      game.assets.preloadAssets();
   }
   p.onAssetsProgress = function () {
      this.preloader.update(game.assets.loadProgress);
      stage.update();
   }
   p.assetsReady = function () {
      stage.removeChild(this.preloader);
      this.createSpriteSheet();
      this.gameReady();
   }
   p.createSpriteSheet = function () {
      var assets = game.assets;
      spritesheet = new
         createjs.SpriteSheet(assets.getAsset(assets.GAME_SPRITES_DATA));
      fontsheet = new
         createjs.SpriteSheet(assets.getAsset(assets.FONT_SHEET_DATA));
   }
```

```
p.gameReady = function () {
    createjs.Ticker.setFPS(60);
    createjs.Ticker.on("tick", this.onTick, this);
    this.changeState(game.GameStates.MAIN_MENU);
}
p.changeState = function (state) {
    switch (state) {
        case game.GameStates.MAIN_MENU:
            this.currentGameStateFunction = this.gameStateMainMenu;
            break;
        case game.GameStates.LEVEL_SELECT:
            this.currentGameStateFunction = this.gameStateLevelSelect;
            break;
        case game.GameStates.GAME:
            this.currentGameStateFunction = this.gameStateGame;
            break;
        case game.GameStates.LEVEL_COMPLETE:
            this.currentGameStateFunction = this.gameStateLevelComplete;
            break;
        case game.GameStates.RUN_SCENE:
            this.currentGameStateFunction = this.gameStateRunScene;
            break;
    }
}
p.onStateEvent = function (e, obj) {
    this.changeState(obj.state);
}
p.disposeCurrentScene = function () {
  if (this.currentScene != null) {
     stage.removeChild(this.currentScene);
     if (this.currentScene.dispose) {
        this.currentScene.dispose();
     }
     this.currentScene = null;
  }
}
p.gameStateMainMenu = function () {
     var scene = new game.GameMenu();
     scene.on(game.GameStateEvents.GAME, this.onStateEvent, this, true,
        {state:game.GameStates.GAME});
     scene.on(game.GameStateEvents.LEVEL_SELECT, this.onStateEvent, this,
        true, {state:game.GameStates.LEVEL_SELECT});
     stage.addChild(scene);
     this.disposeCurrentScene();
     this.currentScene = scene;
     this.changeState(game.GameStates.RUN_SCENE);
   }
```

```
        p.gameStateLevelSelect = function () {
            var scene = new game.LevelSelect()
            scene.on(game.GameStateEvents.GAME, this.onStateEvent, this, true,
                {state:game.GameStates.GAME});
            scene.on(game.GameStateEvents.MAIN_MENU, this.onStateEvent, this,
                true, {state:game.GameStates.MAIN_MENU});
            stage.addChild(scene);
            this.disposeCurrentScene();
            this.currentScene = scene;
            this.changeState(game.GameStates.RUN_SCENE);
        }
        p.gameStateGame = function (tickEvent) {
            var gameData = data.GameData.levelData[data.GameData.currentLevel -
                1];
            var scene = new game.Game(gameData, tickEvent.time);
            scene.on(game.GameStateEvents.LEVEL_COMPLETE, this.onStateEvent,
                this, true, {state:game.GameStates.LEVEL_COMPLETE});
            scene.on(game.GameStateEvents.MAIN_MENU, this.onStateEvent, this,
                true, {state:game.GameStates.MAIN_MENU});
            stage.addChild(scene);
            this.disposeCurrentScene()
            this.currentScene = scene;
            this.changeState(game.GameStates.RUN_SCENE);
        }
        p.gameStateLevelComplete = function () {
            var scene = new game.LevelComplete();
            scene.on(game.GameStateEvents.LEVEL_SELECT, this.onStateEvent, this,
                true, {state:game.GameStates.LEVEL_SELECT});
            stage.addChild(scene);
            this.disposeCurrentScene();
            this.currentScene = scene;
            this.changeState(game.GameStates.RUN_SCENE);
        }
        p.gameStateRunScene = function (tickEvent) {
            if (this.currentScene.run) {
                this.currentScene.run(tickEvent);
            }
        }
        p.onTick = function (e) {
            if (this.currentGameStateFunction != null) {
                this.currentGameStateFunction(e);
            }
            stage.update();
        }

        window.game.Villager = Villager;

    }(window));
```

The application class is responsible for not only managing state, but for setting the global variables that were declared in the HTML file. The global references are used to access sprite sheets, the stage, the stage dimensions, and its canvas element. This is set up in the same manner as in the Space Hero game in Chapter 11. However, for this application, the `Device` object is used to handle scaling and device orientations. This is accomplished by calling its `prepare` method, like so:

```
game.Device.prepare();
```

You can now be assured that the game will fit in various device resolutions.

Building the Game Data

The Break-It game in Chapter 4 used an array of level objects to set up each new level in the game. This same approach will again be used, only in a much more detailed way. Data will also be built for each type of enemy and the hero stats, which will load from and save to local storage. Starting with the enemy data, let's meet the cast of villains that the villager must defeat in the battle levels.

Meeting the Bad Guys

The bad guys make up the levels in the game. To win a level is to beat all enemies that are present in the field. Each villain, including the boss, has its own set of properties that will be pushed into the `Enemy` class that creates it. Before reviewing these data objects, take a look at the six enemies and the final boss that these data objects will be controlling in Figure 14-4.

Figure 14-4. *All enemies in the game*

As you can see, there are three main types of field villains, each with a duplicate of itself with a **slight appearance** change. This technique was used often in old RPGs to extend the graphics. Because the enemies are built in a modular way, simply altering the graphic, and its data, instantly doubles the available enemies.

Now that you've seen a look at these menaces, it's time to build their data, which will give them battle attributes and will dictate what sprite sheet frames should display.

Creating the Enemy Data

The data that controls each instance of Enemy will be held within an EnemyData object. This object will reside in the same file as the GameData and PlayerData objects. Before getting into the enemy data, create this JavaScript file now and name it data.js. Listing 14-5 starts this code, which declares all data objects.

Listing 14-5. The data.js File Declares All Game Data

```
(function () {

    window.data = window.data || {};

    var EnemyData = {};
    var GameData = {};
    var PlayerData = {};

    //build objects here

    window.data.EnemyData = EnemyData;
    window.data.GameData = GameData;
    window.data.PlayerData = PlayerData;

}());
```

Each enemy object will need a set of attributes, which will be pushed into each Enemy instance. These attributes are as follows:

- **frame**: A string used to draw the correct frame to the enemy sprite.
- **maxHP**: The total hit points the enemy has.
- **weakness**: A string that dictates what magic the enemy is weak against, if any.
- **power**: The power value of the enemy, used when attacking hero.
- **defense**: The defense value of the enemy, used when attacked by the hero.

For example, the data for an enemy might look something like this:

```
EnemyData.badGuy = {
    frame:'badguy',
    maxHP:10,
    weakness:'fire',
    power:2,
    defense:1
}
```

A key string for each enemy is used when building levels, and will be used to access the appropriate data when building levels. This process will be covered in the "Creating the Game and Level Data" section. Listing 14-6 shows the data for all enemies used in this game.

Listing 14-6. The Data Objects For All Enemeies

```
EnemyData.troll1 = {
    frame:'troll1',
    maxHP:10,
    weakness:'',
    power:2,
    defense:0
}
EnemyData.sorcerer1 = {
    frame:'sorcerer1',
    maxHP:12,
    weakness:'earth',
    power:5,
    defense:2
}
EnemyData.troll2 = {
    frame:'troll2',
    maxHP:15,
    weakness:'fire',
    power:8,
    defense:4
}
EnemyData.sorcerer2 = {
    frame:'sorcerer2',
    maxHP:18,
    weakness:'lightning',
    power:12,
    defense:6
}
EnemyData.minotaur1 = {
    frame:'minotaur1',
    maxHP:22,
    weakness:'earth',
    power:15,
    defense:8
}
EnemyData.minotaur2 = {
    frame:'minotaur2',
    maxHP:25,
    weakness:'fire',
    power:20,
    defense:12
}
EnemyData.octopus = {
    frame:'octopus',
    maxHP:100,
    weakness:'lightning',
    power:50,
    defense:20
}
```

Creating the Game and Level Data

The GameData object will hold values that pertain to the game as a whole, including the game's current level, the cost and power of magic items, and most importantly, the level data. This is an array of objects what will be used to build each level. The attributes that make up a level are as follows:

- **type**: Can be 'field' or 'boss'. Used to determine if the battle should load multiple enemies, or one boss.

- **enemies**: An array of string keys. Used to instantiate the enemy objects in a battle.

- **boss**: The string key for the boss enemy.

- **enemyStreak**: The number of consecutive enemy attacks when an enemy attack commences.

- **enemyAttackWait**: The duration between enemy attack streaks.

- **powerIncreaseAwarded**: The amount that the player's power will increase by when beating the level.

- **defenseIncreaseAwarded**: The amount that the player's defense will increase by when beating the level.

- **HPEarned**: The amount that the player's max hit points will increase by when beating the level.

- **coinsAwarded**: The amount of coins the player receives when beating the level.

Listing 14-7 shows this level data within the entire GameData object.

Listing 14-7. data.js - The GameData Object Declares the Level Data

```
GameData = {
    currentLevel:1
}
GameData.levelData = [
    {
        type:'field',
        enemies:['troll1', 'troll1', 'troll1'],
        enemyStreak:1,
        enemyAttackWait:5000,
        powerIncreaseAwarded:1,
        defenseIncreaseAwarded:0,
        coinsAwarded:3,
        HPEarned:1
    },
    {
        type:'field',
        enemies:['troll1', 'sorcerer1', 'troll1', 'troll1',
            'sorcerer1', 'troll1'],
        enemyStreak:2,
        enemyAttackWait:5000,
        powerIncreaseAwarded:2,
        defenseIncreaseAwarded:1,
        coinsAwarded:4,
        HPEarned:3
    },
```

```
{
    type:'field',
    enemies:['troll2', 'sorcerer1', 'troll1', 'troll1',
        'sorcerer1', 'troll1'],
    enemyStreak:2,
    enemyAttackWait:5000,
    powerIncreaseAwarded:4,
    defenseIncreaseAwarded:2,
    coinsAwarded:8,
    HPEarned:5
},
{
    type:'field',
    enemies:['sorcerer1', 'troll2', 'sorcerer1', 'sorcerer1',
        'troll2', 'troll1', 'troll2', 'sorcerer1', 'troll1'],
    enemyStreak:3,
    enemyAttackWait:8000,
    powerIncreaseAwarded:6,
    defenseIncreaseAwarded:4,
    coinsAwarded:12,
    HPEarned:8
},
{
    type:'field',
    enemies:['sorcerer1', 'troll2', 'sorcerer2', 'sorcerer2',
        'sorcerer1', 'troll2', 'troll2', 'sorcerer1',
        'troll1'],
    enemyStreak:3,
    enemyAttackWait:7000,
    powerIncreaseAwarded:10,
    defenseIncreaseAwarded:6,
    coinsAwarded:15,
    HPEarned:12
},
{
    type:'field',
    enemies:['troll1', 'minotaur1', 'sorcerer2', 'sorcerer1',
        'troll2', 'minotaur1', 'sorcerer2', 'troll2',
        'troll1'],
    enemyStreak:3,
    enemyAttackWait:10000,
    powerIncreaseAwarded:1,
    defenseIncreaseAwarded:0,
    coinsAwarded:20,
    HPEarned:15
},
{
    type:'field',
    enemies:['troll1', 'minotaur1', 'minotaur2', 'sorcerer1',
        'troll2', 'minotaur1', 'sorcerer2', 'minotaur2', 'troll1'],
    enemyStreak:2,
```

```
        enemyAttackWait:6000,
        powerIncreaseAwarded:0,
        defenseIncreaseAwarded:0,
        coinsAwarded:0,
        HPEarned:0
    },
    {
        type:'field',
        enemies:['minotaur1', 'minotaur2', 'sorcerer1', 'sorcerer2',
            'minotaur2', 'troll2', 'sorcerer2',
            'minotaur2', 'minotaur2'],
        enemyStreak:3,
        enemyAttackWait:8000,
        powerIncreaseAwarded:1,
        defenseIncreaseAwarded:0,
        coinsAwarded:3,
        HPEarned:0
    },
    {
        type:'boss',
        boss:'octopus',
        enemyStreak:1,
        enemyAttackWait:4000,
        powerIncreaseAwarded:1,
        defenseIncreaseAwarded:0,
        coinsAwarded:3,
        HPEarned:0
    }
];
GameData.attackPower = {
    attack:0,
    fire:4,
    earth:7,
    lightning:10
}
GameData.magicCosts = {
    potion:2,
    fire:5,
    earth:7,
    lightning:10
}
```

After the level data, the last two objects pertain to magic items. The attackPower property lists the extra damage caused from each magic item when cast against an enemy. The last object, magicCosts, is used for building the magic shop after a level is complete. This shop will be covered in the "Creating the Magic Shop" section.

Creating the Player Data

The final data object is PlayerData, which is used to reference the data saved in local storage and is set to the property player. Listing 14-8 shows the entire PlayerData object.

Listing 14-8. data.js - The PlayerData Object Retrieves and Stores Player Data from Local Storage

```
PlayerData = {
        player:null,
        dataTemplate:{
            board:1,
            level:1,
            maxHP:10,
            power:5,
            defense:1,
            coins:3,
            attack:-1,
            fire:1,
            earth:0,
            lightning:0,
            potion:1,
            gameLevel:1
        },
        getData:function () {
            if (localStorage.gameLevel) {
                this.player = localStorage;
            }
            else {
                this.player = this.setLocalStorage();
            }
        },
        setLocalStorage:function () {
            for (var key in this.dataTemplate) {
                localStorage.setItem(key, this.dataTemplate[key]);
            }
            return localStorage;
        }
    }
```

The getData method is called before the main application class is created, within the index.html file. This is to assure that the data from local storage is either loaded or created if the values have not yet been set. This can be done by checking if the gameLevel property has been set in local storage.

```
if (localStorage.gameLevel) {
    this.player = localStorage;
}
```

If this property does exist in local storage, then you know there has been data previously saved, so it is assigned to the player property. This will be the access point to local storage when getting and saving values during gameplay.

```
var coins = data.PlayerData.player.coins; //10
coins += 3; //coins updated to 13 and saved to local storage
```

If local storage has not yet been set for the game, it is created by using the dataTemplate object within the setLocalStorage method and is then set to the player property. Figure 14-5 shows some saved data in local storage by using a Local Storage Manager extension for Chrome.

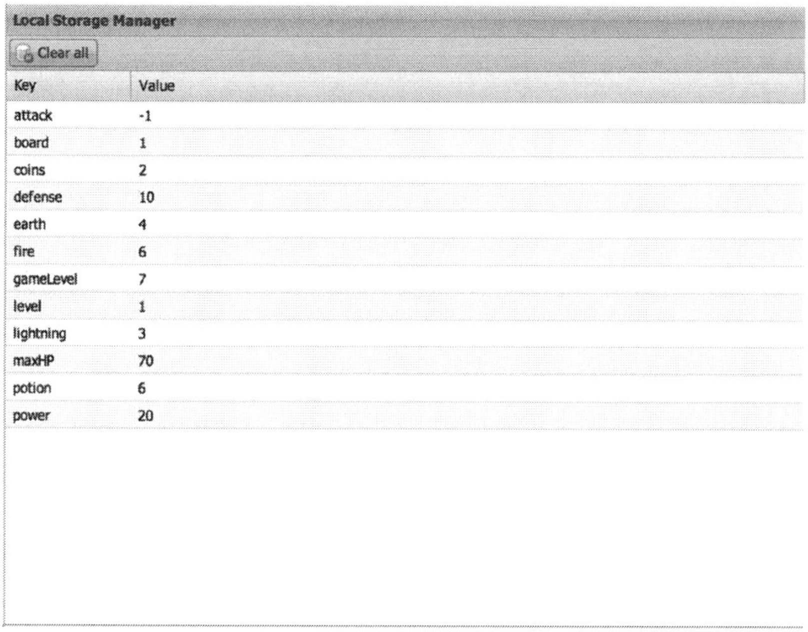

Local Storage Manager	
Key	Value
attack	-1
board	1
coins	2
defense	10
earth	4
fire	6
gameLevel	7
level	1
lightning	3
maxHP	70
potion	6
power	20

Figure 14-5. The player stats stored in local storage

With the data set for the game, player stats, and the enemies, it's time to build the **Enemy** and **Hero** classes.

Building the Enemies and Hero

All enemies will use the same Enemy class. It should simply take a data object, retrieved by the EnemyData object, and appear and function accordingly. The Hero class will simply represent the current stats in PlayerData and will be used to play the level. Both classes will be built in this section.

Creating the Enemy Class

The Enemy class will be a container that holds two consistant display objects. One is a sprite for the enemy sprite sheet frame, and the other is for its health meter, which will be its own container class as well. The Enemy class has a few other elements and a number of things going on so I'll break it down into a few parts, starting with the properties and initialize method (see Listing 14-9).

Listing 14-9. Enemy.js - The Enemy Class's Properties

```
(function () {

    window.game = window.game || {}

    function Enemy(type) {
        this.data = data.EnemyData[type];
        this.initialize();
    }

    var p = Enemy.prototype = new createjs.Container();

    p.data = null;
    p.enemySprite = null;
    p.targetSprite = null;
    p.magicSprite = null;
    p.healthBar = null;

    p.targetTween = null;
    p.targetable = false;

    p.Container_initialize = p.initialize;

    p.initialize = function () {
        this.Container_initialize();
        this.createEnemySprite();
        this.createTargetIndicator();
        this.createHealthBar();
        this.mouseEnabled = false;
    }

    //class methods here

    window.game.Enemy = Enemy;

}());
```

The constructor function takes in one parameter, type, which is a string key from the level data when the level is being built. This string is used to access the appropriate enemy data and set it to the data property. Next is a list of properties used for the display objects in the class. These include the sprite for the enemy graphics, a sprite for a target indicator to imply that the enemy is targetable, a sprite to display magic effects, and finally the health bar that displays the current hit points of the enemy. The final two properties are used for targeting the enemy and will be discussed in detail later in this section.

The initialize function does its typical series of method calls to initialize the class. The mouseEnabled property on the container is initially set to false to prevent any interaction with the enemy. The list of initializing methods is seen in Listing 14-10.

Listing 14-10. Enemy.js - The Display Objects Created for the Enemy Class

```
p.createEnemySprite = function () {
    this.enemySprite = new createjs.Sprite(spritesheet,
        this.data.frame);
    this.addChild(this.enemySprite);
}
p.createTargetIndicator = function () {
    var bounds;
    var targetYPos = 90;
    var tweenSpeed = 700;
    this.targetSprite = new createjs.Sprite(spritesheet, 'target');
    bounds = this.targetSprite.getBounds();
    this.targetSprite.regX = bounds.width / 2;
    this.targetSprite.regY = bounds.height / 2;
    this.targetSprite.y = targetYPos;
    this.targetSprite.x = this.enemySprite.getBounds().width / 2;
    this.targetTween = createjs.Tween
        .get(this.targetSprite, {loop:true})
        .to({alpha:.3}, tweenSpeed)
        .to({alpha:1}, tweenSpeed);
    this.targetTween.setPaused(true);
    this.targetSprite.visible = false;
    this.addChild(this.targetSprite);
}
p.createHealthBar = function () {
    var enemyBounds = this.enemySprite.getBounds();
    this.healthBar = new game.EnemyHealthBar(this.data.maxHP);
    this.healthBar.y = enemyBounds.height + 10;
    this.healthBar.x = (enemyBounds.width / 2) –
        (this.healthBar.getBounds().width / 2);
    this.addChild(this.healthBar);
}
```

The createEnemySprite method creates a new sprite using the appropriate frame by using the frame property in the enemy data. Next, the target indicator sprite is created in the createTargetIndicator function and is centered over the enemy sprite. A pulsing effect is added by creating a looped tween on the target. This tween is set to the class property targetTween so you can start and stop it throughout the game. The tween is paused and its target sprite is set to invisible.

The health bar for the enemy is next created and added to the container in the createHealthBar method. As mentioned earlier, this health bar is another class, and its constructor function take only one parameter, which is the amount of hit points the enemy should have. The bar is positioned and added to the enemy container. This health bar class will be built in the next section, "Creating the Enemy Health Bar." An enemy sprite and health bar are shown in Figure 14-6.

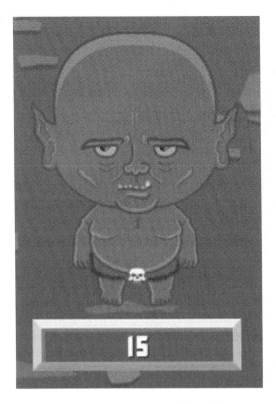

Figure 14-6. *An enemy sprite with health bar*

When an enemy attacks, the only thing the Enemy class actually does is create an animation on the enemy sprite (see Listing 14-11).

Listing 14-11. Enemy.js – The Enemy Sprite Bounces to Indicate it's Attacking

```
p.playAttackAnimation = function () {
   var air = 80;
   createjs.Tween.get(this.enemySprite)
      .to({y:this.enemySprite.y - air}, 500, createjs.Ease.bounceOut)
      .to({y:this.enemySprite.y}, 500, createjs.Ease.bounceOut)
      .call(function () {
         this.dispatchEvent(events.ENEMY_ATTACK_ANIMATION_COMPLETE);
      }, null, this)
}
```

A simple bounce jump is added to enemySprite. When complete, the ENEMY_ATTACK_ANIMATION_COMPLETE event is dispatched, which will carry on the attack logic back in the game. When the hero is the one attacking, the enemy has a lot more responsibility, starting with displaying the target indicator sprite to indicate it to be a valid target (see Listing 14-12).

Listing 14-12. Enemy.js – Enabling and Disabling the Targets on Enemies

```
p.enableTarget = function () {
    this.targetTween.setPaused(false);
    this.targetable = this.targetSprite.visible
        = this.mouseEnabled = true;
}
p.disableTarget = function () {
    this.targetTween.setPaused(true);
    this.targetable = this.targetSprite.visible
        = this.mouseEnabled = false;
}
```

The enableTarget method will start the pulsing effect on the target sprite and show it. It will also set the targetable property to true and enable mouse interaction so that the player can click it. After an attack, the disableTarget method is called and does the exact opposite. An enemy in its targetable state is shown in Figure 14-7.

Figure 14-7. *The target indicator sprite is shown when an enemy can be attacked*

Next, the functionality is written that will react to the enemy being attacked (see Listing 14-13).

Listing 14-13. Enemy.js - The Methods For Attacking the Enemy

```javascript
p.takeDamage = function (power, attackType) {
    var damage = power - this.data.defense;
    this.playAttackedAnimation();
    switch (attackType) {
        case 'fire':
            damage += this.getFireDamage();
            break;
        case 'earth':
            damage += this.getEarthDamage();
            break;
        case 'lightning':
            damage += this.getLightningDamage();
            break;
        default:
            damage += 0;
            break;
    }
    damage = damage > 0 ? damage : 0;
    this.healthBar.updateHP(damage);
}
p.playAttackedAnimation = function () {
    var event;
    var hit = this.enemySprite.clone();
    hit.gotoAndStop(this.data.frame + '_hit');
    this.addChild(hit);
    createjs.Tween.get(hit)
        .to({alpha:.3}, 100, createjs.Ease.bounceInOut)
        .to({alpha:.6}, 100, createjs.Ease.bounceInOut)
        .to({alpha:.2}, 200, createjs.Ease.bounceInOut)
        .to({alpha:.3}, 100, createjs.Ease.bounceInOut)
        .to({alpha:.6}, 100, createjs.Ease.bounceInOut)
        .to({alpha:.2}, 200, createjs.Ease.bounceInOut)
        .call(function (hit) {
            this.removeChild(hit);
            this.removeChild(this.magicSprite);
            this.checkHealth();
        }, [hit], this);
}
```

The total damage on the enemy is factored by a few things. One is the power of the hero that is attacking it, and another is the defense value of the enemy. The last factor is the type of attack given to the enemy. The hero's power and attack type are both passed into the takeDamage method from the game. Before further calculations are taken on damage using the attack type, an animation is first created on the enemy in the playAttackedAnimation method. This simply clones the enemy sprite and loads the red tinted frame of the same enemy from the sprite sheet. This red sprite clone is flickered to indicate being attacked, then removed when the tween is complete. You'll notice that magicSprite is also removed. This sprite is added if a magic attack was used and is used to add extra effects over the attacked enemy sprite. One of three functions might get called, based on the attack used, and is determined in a switch statement.

```
switch (attackType) {
  case 'fire':
    damage += this.getFireDamage();
    break;
  case 'earth':
    damage += this.getEarthDamage();
    break;
  case 'lightning':
    damage += this.getLightningDamage();
    break;
  default:
    damage += 0;
    break;
}
```

Along with creating the extra effects, these functions will also determine the extra damage that should be added. Listing 14-14 shows these three damaging methods.

Listing 14-14. Enemy.js - The Magic Damage Functions Play Animations and Return Damage Values

```
p.getFireDamage = function () {
  var weakness = this.data.weakness == 'fire' ? 5 : 0;
  this.magicSprite = new createjs.Sprite(spritesheet, 'magic_fire');
  this.magicSprite.y = this.enemySprite.y -
    this.magicSprite.getBounds().height +
    this.enemySprite.getBounds().height;
  this.magicSprite.alpha = .3;
  this.addChild(this.magicSprite);
  createjs.Tween.get(this.magicSprite).to({alpha:1}, 100)
    .to({alpha:.3}, 100)
    .to({alpha:.1}, 100)
    .to({alpha:.3}, 100);
  return data.GameData.attackPower.fire + weakness;
}
p.getEarthDamage = function () {
  var weakness = this.data.weakness == 'earth' ? 5 : 0;
  this.magicSprite = new createjs.Sprite(spritesheet, 'magic_rock');
  this.magicSprite.regX = this.magicSprite.getBounds().width / 2;
  this.magicSprite.regY = this.magicSprite.getBounds().height / 2;
  this.magicSprite.x = this.enemySprite.x +
    (this.enemySprite.getBounds().width / 2);
  this.magicSprite.y = -100;
  this.addChild(this.magicSprite);
  createjs.Tween.get(this.magicSprite).to({rotation:720, y:100}, 1000);
  return data.GameData.attackPower.earth + weakness;
}
p.getLightningDamage = function () {
  var weakness = this.data.weakness == 'lightning' ? 5 : 0;
  this.magicSprite = new createjs.Sprite(spritesheet, 'magic_lightning');
  this.magicSprite.regX = this.magicSprite.getBounds().width / 2;
  this.magicSprite.regY = this.magicSprite.getBounds().height / 2;
  this.magicSprite.x = this.enemySprite.x +
```

```
        (this.enemySprite.getBounds().width / 2);
    this.magicSprite.y = 100;
    this.magicSprite.scaleX = this.magicSprite.scaleY = .2;
    this.addChild(this.magicSprite);
    createjs.Tween.get(this.magicSprite).to({scaleX:1, scaleY:1}, 1000,
        createjs.Ease.elasticOut);
    return data.GameData.attackPower.lightning + weakness;
}
```

First, a check on the enemy data's weakness property will determine if the magic used should add any *extra* damage. This value will simply be 5 across all enemies. Next, each function uses the magicSprite property to create that special effect by using the appropriate frame from the sprite sheet. Each magic function uses a chain of tween commands to create something cool over the enemy sprite. Figure 14-8 shows a minotaur being attacked by fire.

Figure 14-8. *An enemy being attacked by fire*

The function will also ultimately return the final damage value caused by the magic. The total magic damage is determined by referencing the attackPower object in GameData and adding it to any weakness that may have been applied. This returned value will be factored at the end of the takeDamage method and passed into the enemy health bar, which is recapped here:

```
damage = damage > 0 ? damage : 0;
this.healthBar.updateHP(damage);
```

After an enemy is attacked, its health is checked in the **checkHealth** method (see Listing 14-15).

Listing 14-15. Enemy.js – Checking Health of the Enemy

```
p.checkHealth = function () {
    var event;
    if (this.healthBar.HP <= 0) {
        this.destroy();
    }
    else {
        event = new createjs.Event(events.ENEMY_ATTACKED_COMPLETE, true);
        this.dispatchEvent(event);
    }
}

p.destroy = function () {
    var event;
    this.enemySprite.on('animationend', function () {
        event = new createjs.Event(events.ENEMY_DESTROYED, true);
        this.dispatchEvent(event);
    }, this);
    this.enemySprite.gotoAndPlay(this.data.frame + '_die');
}
```

If the enemy still has hit points, the ENEMY_ATTACKED_COMPLETE event is dispatched back to the game, where it will resume the battle. If the enemy's health bar is empty, it should die. Each enemy sprite has an animation sequence that will dissolve it away with a pixelated effect. This animation is accessed by appending the string *_die* to the frame data property. Once complete, the ENEMY_DESTROYED event is dispatched, and the current game state will be evaluated.

Listing 14-16 shows the entire Enemy class.

Listing 14-16. Enemy.js – The Complete Enemy Class

```
(function () {

    window.game = window.game || {}

    function Enemy(type) {
        this.data = data.EnemyData[type];
        this.initialize();
    }

    var p = Enemy.prototype = new createjs.Container();

    p.data = null;
    p.enemySprite = null;
    p.targetSprite = null;
    p.magicSprite = null;
    p.healthBar = null;

    p.targetTween = null;
    p.targetable = false;
```

```
p.Container_initialize = p.initialize;

p.initialize = function () {
    this.Container_initialize();
    this.createEnemySprite();
    this.createTargetIndicator();
    this.createHealthBar();
    this.mouseEnabled = false;
}
p.createEnemySprite = function () {
    this.enemySprite = new createjs.Sprite(spritesheet,
        this.data.frame);
    this.addChild(this.enemySprite);
}
p.createTargetIndicator = function () {
    var bounds;
    var targetYPos = 90;
    var tweenSpeed = 700;
    this.targetSprite = new createjs.Sprite(spritesheet, 'target');
    bounds = this.targetSprite.getBounds();
    this.targetSprite.regX = bounds.width / 2;
    this.targetSprite.regY = bounds.height / 2;
    this.targetSprite.y = targetYPos;
    this.targetSprite.x = this.enemySprite.getBounds().width / 2;
    this.targetTween = createjs.Tween.get(this.targetSprite,
        {loop:true}).to({alpha:.3}, tweenSpeed).to({alpha:1},
        tweenSpeed);
    this.targetTween.setPaused(true);
    this.targetSprite.visible = false;
    this.addChild(this.targetSprite);
}
p.createHealthBar = function () {
    var enemyBounds = this.enemySprite.getBounds();
    this.healthBar = new game.EnemyHealthBar(this.data.maxHP);
    this.healthBar.y = enemyBounds.height + 10;
    this.healthBar.x = (enemyBounds.width / 2) -
        (this.healthBar.getBounds().width / 2);
    this.addChild(this.healthBar);
}
//attack hero
p.playAttackAnimation = function () {
    var air = 80;
    createjs.Tween.get(this.enemySprite)
        .to({y:this.enemySprite.y - air}, 500, createjs.Ease.bounceOut)
        .to({y:this.enemySprite.y}, 500, createjs.Ease.bounceOut)
        .call(function () {
            this.dispatchEvent(events.ENEMY_ATTACK_ANIMATION_COMPLETE);
        }, null, this)
}
```

```
//attacked by hero
p.enableTarget = function () {
    this.targetTween.setPaused(false);
    this.targetable = this.targetSprite.visible = this.mouseEnabled =
        true;
}
p.disableTarget = function () {
    this.targetTween.setPaused(true);
    this.targetable = this.targetSprite.visible = this.mouseEnabled =
        false;
}
p.takeDamage = function (power, attackType) {
    var damage = power - this.data.defense;
    this.playAttackedAnimation();
    switch (attackType) {
        case 'fire':
            damage += this.getFireDamage();
            break;
        case 'earth':
            damage += this.getEarthDamage();
            break;
        case 'lightning':
            damage += this.getLightningDamage();
            break;
        default:
            damage += 0;
            break;
    }
    damage = damage > 0 ? damage : 0;
    this.healthBar.updateHP(damage);
}
p.playAttackedAnimation = function () {
    var event;
    var hit = this.enemySprite.clone();
    hit.gotoAndStop(this.data.frame + '_hit');
    this.addChild(hit);
    createjs.Tween.get(hit)
        .to({alpha:.3}, 100, createjs.Ease.bounceInOut)
        .to({alpha:.6}, 100, createjs.Ease.bounceInOut)
        .to({alpha:.2}, 200, createjs.Ease.bounceInOut)
        .to({alpha:.3}, 100, createjs.Ease.bounceInOut)
        .to({alpha:.6}, 100, createjs.Ease.bounceInOut)
        .to({alpha:.2}, 200, createjs.Ease.bounceInOut)
        .call(function (hit) {
            this.removeChild(hit);
            this.removeChild(this.magicSprite);
            this.checkHealth();
        }, [hit], this);
}
```

```
p.getFireDamage = function () {
    var weakness = this.data.weakness == 'fire' ? 5 : 0;
    this.magicSprite = new createjs.Sprite(spritesheet, 'magic_fire');
    this.magicSprite.y = this.enemySprite.y -
        this.magicSprite.getBounds().height +
        this.enemySprite.getBounds().height;
    this.magicSprite.alpha = .3;
    this.addChild(this.magicSprite);
    createjs.Tween.get(this.magicSprite).to({alpha:1}, 100)
        .to({alpha:.3}, 100)
        .to({alpha:.1}, 100)
        .to({alpha:.3}, 100);
    return data.GameData.attackPower.fire + weakness;
}
p.getEarthDamage = function () {
    var weakness = this.data.weakness == 'earth' ? 5 : 0;
    this.magicSprite = new createjs.Sprite(spritesheet, 'magic_rock');
    this.magicSprite.regX = this.magicSprite.getBounds().width / 2;
    this.magicSprite.regY = this.magicSprite.getBounds().height / 2;
    this.magicSprite.x = this.enemySprite.x +
        (this.enemySprite.getBounds().width / 2);
    this.magicSprite.y = -100;
    this.addChild(this.magicSprite);
    createjs.Tween.get(this.magicSprite).to({rotation:720, y:100},
        1000);
    return data.GameData.attackPower.earth + weakness;
}
p.getLightningDamage = function () {
    var weakness = this.data.weakness == 'lightning' ? 5 : 0;
    this.magicSprite = new createjs.Sprite(spritesheet,
        'magic_lightning');
    this.magicSprite.regX = this.magicSprite.getBounds().width / 2;
    this.magicSprite.regY = this.magicSprite.getBounds().height / 2;
    this.magicSprite.x = this.enemySprite.x +
        (this.enemySprite.getBounds().width / 2);
    this.magicSprite.y = 100;
    this.magicSprite.scaleX = this.magicSprite.scaleY = .2;
    this.addChild(this.magicSprite);
    createjs.Tween.get(this.magicSprite).to({scaleX:1, scaleY:1}, 1000,
        createjs.Ease.elasticOut);
    return data.GameData.attackPower.lightning + weakness;
}
p.checkHealth = function () {
    var event;
    if (this.healthBar.HP <= 0) {
        this.destroy();
    }
    else {
        event = new createjs.Event(events.ENEMY_ATTACKED_COMPLETE, true);
        this.dispatchEvent(event);
    }
}
```

```
        p.destroy = function () {
            var event;
            this.enemySprite.on('animationend', function () {
                event = new createjs.Event(events.ENEMY_DESTROYED, true);
                this.dispatchEvent(event);
            }, this);
            this.enemySprite.gotoAndPlay(this.data.frame + '_die');
        }
        window.game.Enemy = Enemy;

}());
```

Creating the Enemy Health Bar

The health of the enemy is displayed as a progress bar, as well as text that shows the amount of hit points left. This works very similarly to the progress bar component that you built in this book, so the code should look pretty familiar. The complete EnemyHealthBar class is shown in Listing 14-17.

Listing 14-17. EnemyHealthBar.js - The EnemyHealthBar Class Displays Enemy Hit Points

```
(function (window) {

    window.game = window.game || {}

    function EnemyHealthBar(maxHP) {
        this.maxHP = this.HP = maxHP;
        this.initialize();
    }

    var p = EnemyHealthBar.prototype = new createjs.Container();

    p.Container_initialize = p.initialize;

    p.progressBar = null;
    p.maxHP = null;
    p.HP = null;
    p.hpTxt = null;

    p.initialize = function () {
        this.Container_initialize();
        this.addHealthBar();
        this.addHP();
    }
    p.addHealthBar = function () {
        var barXOffset = 10;
        var enemyBar = new createjs.Sprite(spritesheet, 'enemyBar');
        var enemyBarBounds = enemyBar.getBounds();
        var barBG = new createjs.Shape();
        barBG.graphics.beginFill('#b6b6b6').drawRect(0, 0,
            enemyBarBounds.width,
            enemyBarBounds.height);
```

```
        this.progressBar = new createjs.Shape();
        this.progressBar.graphics.beginFill('#c14545').drawRect(0, 0,
            enemyBarBounds.width - barXOffset,
            enemyBarBounds.height);
        this.progressBar.x = barXOffset;
        this.addChild(barBG, this.progressBar, enemyBar);
    }
    p.addHP = function () {
        var txtXOffset = 8;
        var yPOs = 13;
        this.hpTxt = new createjs.BitmapText(this.HP.toString(),
            spritesheet);
        this.hpTxt.letterSpacing = 2;
        this.hpTxt.x = this.getBounds().width / 2 - txtXOffset;
        this.hpTxt.y = yPOs;
        this.addChild(this.hpTxt);
    }
    p.updateHP = function (HP) {
        var perc;
        this.HP = this.HP - HP < 0 ? 0 : this.HP - HP;
        perc = this.HP / this.maxHP;
        this.removeChild(this.hpTxt);
        this.addHP();
        createjs.Tween.get(this.progressBar).to({scaleX:perc}, 400);
    }

    window.game.EnemyHealthBar = EnemyHealthBar;

}(window));
```

Some properties are set to reference the hit points and display objects in the class. Moving right into the addHealthBar method, a sprite is created using the graphic created for the outline of the progress bar. Next, a few shapes are created for the actual progress bar: one shape for behind the bar and another for the bar itself. This bar is set to the progressBar property and its scale will be adjusted as the hit points are adjusted. These display objects are positioned accordingly and added to the container in the correct order so that sprite is on top, preserving the inner drop shadow created to overlap the progress bar.

A bitmap font is next created and added to health bar container. Its initial value is set to the HP property and is positioned to the center of the bar. The updateHP method is called from the game when then enemy is attacked, and will update the bar and create a new bitmap text object to represent the new hit point value. A quick check is placed to assure that the text or the scale of the bar will not go below 0. A tween is then applied for effect when updating the scale of the progress bar.

Creating the Hero Class

The Hero class is created to represent the current state of the player. The Hero class does not need to extend a display object. Since the game is played in first person, there is no actual graphical content for the hero attacking or being attacked. Although this is true, you still need to create an instance of something that can represent the player stats during battle. In typical, classic RPG form, losing a battle will simply end the game, as if the losing battle never took place. Because of this, a temporary holder of current player stats is needed during battle. The Hero class is used for exactly that. If the player should win, the values stored in the hero instance will be saved to local storage. Listing 14-18 shows the entire Hero class.

Listing 14-18. Hero.js - The Hero Class is Used in Level Battles

```
(function () {

    window.game = window.game || {}

    function Hero() {
        this.initialize();
    }

    var p = Hero.prototype = new createjs.EventDispatcher();

    p.EventDispatcher_initialize = p.initialize;

    p.HP = null;
    p.maxHP = null;
    p.power = null;
    p.defense = null;
    p.potion = null;
    p.earth = null;
    p.fire = null;
    p.lightning = null;
    p.gameLevel = null;

    p.initialize = function () {
        this.EventDispatcher_initialize();
        this.loadData()
    }
    p.loadData = function () {
        var value;
        var data = window.data.PlayerData.player;
        for (var key in data) {
            value = data[key];
            this[key] = (value * 1);
        }
        this.HP = this.maxHP;
    }
    p.takeDamage = function (damage) {
        var totalDamage = damage - this.defense;
        this.HP -= totalDamage > 0 ? totalDamage : 0;
        this.HP = this.HP >= 0 ? this.HP : 0;
    }
    p.updateInventory = function (item, quantity) {
        this[item] += quantity;
    }
    p.saveStats = function () {
        var value;
        var data = window.data.PlayerData.player;
```

```
      for (var key in data) {
         value = this[key];
         data[key] = (value * 1);
      }
   }
}

   window.game.Hero = Hero;

}());
```

Other than the HP property, all class properties are named identical to data saved to local storage. The loadData method will access the persistent PlayerData object and copy the values over to the instance of the hero. These instance properties will be used during the battle.

The Hero class only has three methods used during a level. The takeDamage method is called when an enemy attacks the hero. The amount of damage is passed into the method, which will be determined by the power value of the attacking enemy. The hero's current defense value will counter against this attack and soften the blow. If this result is below 0, it is forced to be 0 so that a negative value is not added, which would result in added hit points. These situations can happen with high defense stats against weak enemies and is referred to as a *miss*. Finally, another check is needed to prevent negative hit points after the attack.

The updateInventory method will be called when the player uses a magic item during battle. It will take two parameters, the item and the quantity used. Finally, the saveStats method will be called when a level is won and will put all current stats in the hero instance back into local storage.

▨ **Note**   You'll notice that in many situations, values are multiplied by 1. This forces the value to be a number and assures proper calculations throughout the game. Values from local storage can often be evaluated as strings, so this procedure will prevent unwanted results.

Now that all game data is set, and the Enemy and Hero classes are ready to use, let's take a step back and prepare the game menu scenes.

Building the Game Menus

There are only four scenes in The Villager RPG. Two are menu screens for starting the game and selecting the level you wish to play. These two menus will be covered in this section.

Creating the Main Menu Scene

The main title screen is simple. It consists of a background, a title sprite, and two buttons. One button will allow the user to continue with their current progress, and the other is for creating a brand new game. Listing 14-19 shows the entire GameMenu class.

Listing 14-19. GameMenu.js - The GameMenu Class for the Main Title Screen

```
(function () {

    window.game = window.game || {}

    function GameMenu() {
        this.initialize();
    }

    var p = GameMenu.prototype = new createjs.Container();

    p.Container_initialize = p.initialize;

    p.gameBtn = null;
    p.contBtn = null;

    p.initialize = function () {
        this.Container_initialize();
        this.addBG();
        this.addTitle();
        this.addButtons()
    }
    p.addBG = function () {
        var bg = new
            createjs.Bitmap(game.assets.getAsset(game.assets.MENU_BG));
        this.addChild(bg);
    }
    p.addTitle = function () {
        var title = new createjs.Sprite(spritesheet, 'title');
        title.x = 60;
        this.addChild(title);
    }
    p.addButtons = function () {
        var bounds;
        var yPos = 850;
        this.gameBtn = new createjs.Sprite(spritesheet, 'gameBtn');
        bounds = this.gameBtn.getBounds();
        this.gameBtn.regX = bounds.width / 2;
        this.gameBtn.x = screen_width / 2;
        this.gameBtn.y = yPos;
        this.contBtn = this.gameBtn.clone();
        this.contBtn.gotoAndStop('continueBtn');
        this.contBtn.y = (yPos + bounds.height * 1.5);
        this.gameBtn.on('click', this.onButtonClick, this);
        this.contBtn.on('click', this.onButtonClick, this);
        this.addChild(this.gameBtn, this.contBtn);
    }
    p.onButtonClick = function (e) {
        var newGame;
        var btn = e.target
```

```
        if (btn == this.gameBtn) {
            localStorage.clear();
            data.PlayerData.setLocalStorage();
        }
        this.dispatchEvent(game.GameStateEvents.LEVEL_SELECT);
    }
    window.game.GameMenu = GameMenu;

}());
```

This menu is not unlike other menus built in this book so far. A title sprite and button sprites are created and positioned accordingly. Both buttons call the same handler function, which will use the target of the event to determine what to do. In the case that the button clicked was gameBtn, the local storage is cleared and new template data is set. In both cases, the LEVEL_SELECT state event is dispatched, which will bring up the level select scene. Figure 14-9 shows the main menu screen.

Figure 14-9. *The game's main menu screen*

Creating the Level Select Scene

The level select screen displays buttons for all nine levels in the game. With the exception of level 1, each level will initially be locked until the level prior to it is beaten. The player's current level is retrieved from local storage and is called gameLevel. This represents the highest level that the player can enter. Any level that is not playable is represented by a lock graphic. The playable levels are buttons with a text value representing that level number. These graphics are all included as frames in the sprite sheet. The complete LevelSelect class is shown in Listing 14-20.

Listing 14-20. LevelSelect.js - The LevelSelect Class for the Level Select Screen

```
(function (window) {

    window.game = window.game || {}

    function LevelSelect() {
        this.initialize();
    }

    var p = LevelSelect.prototype = new createjs.Container();

    p.Container_initialize = p.initialize;

    p.initialize = function () {
        this.Container_initialize();
        this.addBG();
        this.addBackButton();
        this.addLevelButtons();
    }
    p.addBG = function () {
        var bg = new
            createjs.Bitmap(game.assets.getAsset(game.assets.MENU_BG));
        this.addChild(bg);
    }
    p.addBackButton = function () {
        var btn = new createjs.Sprite(spritesheet, 'backBtn');
        btn.on('click', this.onBackButtonClick, this);
        this.addChild(btn);
    }
    p.addLevelButtons = function () {
        var i, btn, btnBounds, level, frame;
        var numLevels = data.GameData.levelData.length;
        var gameLevel = data.PlayerData.player.gameLevel;
        var col = 0;
        var hGap = 34;
        var vGap = 92;
        var xPos = 50;
        var yPos = 260;
        for (i = 0; i < numLevels; i++) {
            level = i + 1;
            frame = level <= gameLevel ? 'level' + level : 'lock';
            btn = new createjs.Sprite(spritesheet, frame);
            btnBounds = btn.getBounds();
```

```
            btn.level = level;
            btn.x = xPos;
            btn.y = yPos;
            btn.mouseEnabled = level <= gameLevel;
            btn.on('click', this.onLevelButtonClick, this);
            this.addChild(btn);
            xPos += btnBounds.width + hGap;
            col++;
            if (col > 2) {
                col = 0;
                xPos = 50;
                yPos += btn.getBounds().height + vGap;
            }
        }
    }
    p.onBackButtonClick = function(e){
        this.dispatchEvent(game.GameStateEvents.MAIN_MENU);
    }
    p.onLevelButtonClick = function (e) {
        var btn = e.target;
        data.GameData.currentLevel = btn.level;
        this.dispatchEvent(game.GameStateEvents.GAME);
    }
    window.game.LevelSelect = LevelSelect;

}(window));
```

A background graphic and back button are first added to the container. The back button will simply fire the MAIN_MENU state event, which will bring the player back to the main menu. The addLevelButtons method is a bit more detailed. A grid of buttons is made, and the state of each button is determined by the gameLevel property that is stored in local storage. A loop is created to build the grid, and the appropriate frame from the sprite sheet is used to draw each button. As previously mentioned, a level not yet playable is represented by a lock graphic, and its mouseEnabled property is set to false to prevent it from being selected. The level buttons will be selectable and will fire the onButtonClick method when clicked.

A simple number value was dynamically injected into each level button sprite so that it can be retrieved when selected. The onButtonClick method uses this value to set the GameData object's currentLevel property. This value will be used to access the level data needed to build the level. Finally, the GAME state event is dispatched, which will build the level with a new game scene. Figure 14-10 shows this screen with five possible levels to play.

Figure 14-10. *The level select screen unlocks all available levels*

Building the Game Level

The game level is the meat of the game. It is the actual battle between the hero and enemies. The main goal here is to create this game scene to adjust to the level data passed into it. Before getting into the code, here's a quick overview of what the battle will consist of, how it will work, and how to play it.

Reviewing the RPG Battle System

An RPG battle system typically involves some sort of menu for the player to choose from when it's their turn to take action. In a turn-based system, like the one you will be building, there is usually an amount of time that needs to expire before the player can make their next move. A progress bar will be built to display this *wait* time during a battle.

There are several types of these systems, but the one you will be building will allow the enemies to continuously attack, and not *wait* for the player to make an action. The amount of time between enemy attacks is declared in the level data. The player will have a small menu to dictate what action they want to take. An *attack* action is always free, and its strength is determined by the current power status of the player. The other options are one potion, which is taken to replenish hit points, and three magic attacks. These items are not free and must be purchased between levels by using the coins earned when winning battles.

A battle will continue until all enemies are defeated in the level. When a level is complete, the player is rewarded with an increase in power, defense, max hit point count, and coins. These values are declared in the level data. These results will be displayed on a new screen, which will also include a magic shop where the player can purchase items to be used in future battles.

After winning a level, the next concurrent level is then unlocked and ready to play. Each level will increase in difficulty by introducing new, more powerful enemies into the battle. Each level won will reward higher stats, respectively. There are a total of eight field battles and one boss fight. It is very likely that a player will have to repeat levels to gain higher stats before defeating higher levels.

The game data in this type of game will always need to be tested and adjusted accordingly to properly run a successful RPG battle system that is both fun and fair. In the case of this project, the data has been loosely prepared, so it may or may not suit your standards for a well-balanced game. The point of this project is to recognize the data patterns and to see where these values can be adjusted to alter the flow of the game.

With a good understanding of what you will be building, the Game class will now be reviewed in detail, starting with its properties. There is a lot to cover, so let's get started.

Starting the Game Class and its Properties

As in most game scenes, the Game class will be a container that will hold all logic needed to run the level. Listing 14-21 shows the signature and properties for the Game class.

Listing 14-21. Game.js - The Game Class Properties

```
(function () {

    window.game = window.game || {}

    function Game(levelData, startTime) {
        this.levelData = levelData;
        this.lastEnemyAttack = startTime;
        this.initialize();
    }

    var p = Game.prototype = new createjs.Container();

    p.Container_initialize = p.initialize;

    p.ENEMY_ATTACK_DURATION = 2500;

    p.battlePanel = null;
    p.enemyHolder = null;

    p.levelData = null;
    p.hero = null;

    p.enemies = null;
    p.lastEnemyAttack = null;
    p.enemiesAreAttacking = null;
```

```
            p.currentEnemyAttackCount = null;
            p.currentEnemyAttackIndex = null;

            p.attackSelected = null;
            p.levelComplete = null;

        p.gridPos = {x:40, y:60};
        p.grid = [
            {x:10, y:10},
            {x:200, y:10},
            {x:400, y:10},
            {x:10, y:300},
            {x:200, y:300},
            {x:400, y:300},
            {x:10, y:600},
            {x:200, y:600},
            {x:400, y:600}
        ]
        p.bossPos = {x:35, y:60};

        //game logic here


        p.run = function (tickerEvent) {
            if (!this.levelComplete) {
                this.checkBattlePanel();
                this.checkEnemyAttack(tickerEvent.time);
                this.checkHeroHealth();
            }
        }
        window.game.Game = Game;

}());
```

The level data is passed into the constructor function, and it will be used heavily in the game logic. The current time of the ticker when the game was created is also passed into the game so the lastEnemyAttack property can be set to the time at which the level began. This value is what determines when the enemies should start attacking the hero.

The ENEMY_ATTACK_DURATION is the approximate time it takes any given enemy to complete its actions during an attack. This is used along with lastEnemyAttack to properly determine when to attack the hero. This will be discussed in more detail in the "Creating the Check Level Functions" section.

The next two properties are for the two main display objects in the game container. The enemyHolder property is a container that will hold all enemy instances, and battlePanel will be an instance of the BattlePanel class that will hold all action buttons and hero stats. This class will be built and covered in the "Building the Battle Panel" section.

The levelData property is then declared, followed by hero for the Hero instance. The next series of properties pertain to the enemies. The enemies array will hold all enemy instances. These objects will be pushed to this array when building the enemy grid. The lastEnemyAttack property holds the timestamp when the last enemy attack began, and the enemiesAreAttacking will be set to true during the actual enemy attacks. The last two enemy-related values are important for handling the enemy attack sequences. Depending on the level, an enemy attack will consist of one or more sequential enemy attacks. The current streak count is stored in currentEnemyAttackCount, and the current attacking enemy, referenced by index from the enemies array, is stored in currentEnemyAttackIndex. This approach will become clearer during the "Attacking the Hero" section.

When the player selects an attack button, attackSelected is set to true. This will prevent an enemy from attacking in the middle of a hero attack. The levelComplete Boolean is used to determine if game loop should continue or stop completely to let the level finish. Finally, values are set to determine where enemies are placed on the screen when they are created.

This covers all properties in the game. Their purposes will become much clearer as the class is written, and the declared run method will be examined in the "Creating the Check Level Functions" section.

Initializing the Game Level

The initialize method calls a series of methods to build up the level. Listing 14-22 shows the **initialize** method and the first four functions it calls.

Listing 14-22. Game.js - The Game Class Initializing Methods

```
p.initialize = function () {
   this.Container_initialize();
   this.lastEnemyAttack = this.currentEnemyAttackCount =
      this.currentEnemyAttackIndex = 0;
   this.enemiesAreAttacking = this.attackSelected = this.levelComplete = false;
   this.setListeners();
   this.createHero();
   this.addBG();
   this.addEnemies();
   this.addBattlePanel();
}
p.setListeners = function () {
   this.on(events.ENEMY_ATTACKED_COMPLETE, this.onEnemyAttackedComplete,
      this);
   this.on(events.ENEMY_DESTROYED, this.onEnemyDestroyed, this);
}
p.createHero = function () {
   this.hero = new game.Hero();
}
p.addBG = function () {
   var bg = new
      createjs.Bitmap(game.assets.getAsset(game.assets.BATTLE_BG));
   this.addChild(bg);
}
p.addEnemies = function () {
   if (this.levelData.type == 'field') {
      this.populateGrid();
   }
   else {
      this.addBoss();
   }
   this.addChild(this.enemyHolder);
}
```

After setting the intial values of a few instance variables, the setListeners method is called. This method sets up the event listeners for the level, which pertain to the events from each enemy that will bubble up from the enemy grid container. These events will be dispatched after the animations are complete when an enemy is attacked or destroyed. Much more on these events will be covered in the "Attacking the Enemies" section.

The hero instance is created in the createHero method. The class was covered already, so you know that everything that needs to be done with it is handled within its initialization. A background graphic is next added to the container within addBG.

Next, it's time to add the enemies. There are two types of levels. One is *field* and the other is called *boss*. Most of the time it will be a normal field battle, which will call the populateGrid method. If the level should bring a single boss enemy, addBoss is called instead. Both of these methods will add enemy objects to the enemyHolder container, which is added to the game at the end of the addEnemies method. These enemy-creating functions will be covered next.

Populating the Enemies

The enemies are created on a grid. The points on this grid were hard-coded inside of the grid property. The populateGrid will use these points when creating the enemies (see Listing 14-23).

Listing 14-23. Game.js - Adding the Enemies to the Level

```
p.populateGrid = function () {
    var i, startPoint, enemy, point, enemyType;
    var enemies = this.levelData.enemies;
    var len = enemies.length;
    this.enemyHolder = new createjs.Container();
    this.enemyHolder.x = this.gridPos.x;
    this.enemyHolder.y = this.gridPos.y;
    this.enemies = [];
    for (i = 0; i < len; i++) {
        point = this.grid[i];
        enemyType = enemies[i];
        enemy = new game.Enemy(enemyType);
        enemy.x = point.x;
        enemy.y = point.y;
        enemy.on('click', this.attackEnemy, this);
        this.enemyHolder.addChild(enemy);
        this.enemies[i] = enemy;
    }
}
```

The loop runs through the number of enemies assigned to the current level. This array is retrieved from the level data's enemies property. The enemy type, which is the string value from the current array index in the loop, is passed into the enemy object. In the loop, the location point for each enemy is determined by the grid array. A click event listener is then assigned to each enemy, which will fire the attackEnemy event handler. Finally, each enemy instance is added to the enemyHolder container and pushed to the enemies array in the class. Figure 14-11 shows the enemy grid in level 5.

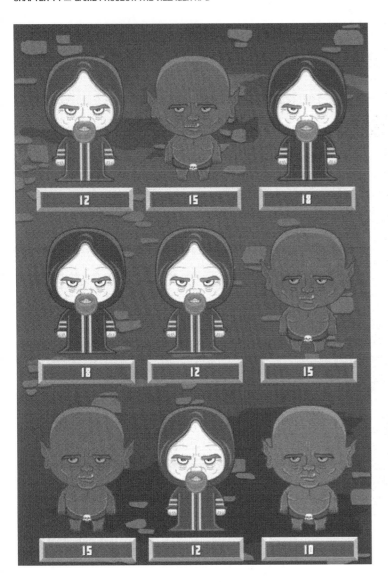

Figure 14-11. *The enemies in a field battle*

When creating a boss, the addBoss method is called, which is shown in Listing 14-24.

Listing 14-24. Game.js - Adding the Boss to the Final Level

```
p.addBoss = function () {
    var boss;
    this.enemies = []
    this.enemyHolder = new createjs.Container();
    this.enemyHolder.x = this.bossPos.x;
    this.enemyHolder.y = this.bossPos.y;
    boss = new game.Enemy(this.levelData.boss);
```

```
    boss.on('click', this.attackEnemy, this);
    this.enemies[0] = boss;
    this.enemyHolder.addChild(boss);
}
```

As you can see, the main difference when creating a boss is that there is only one enemy, so there is no need for a loop, and the key for the enemy type is located in the boss property in the level's data. The boss' location uses the bossPos class property, and the same click event is added as would have been with a regular enemy. It is then pushed to the enemies array and added to enemyContainer. Figure 14-12 shows the boss in battle.

Figure 14-12. The boss level

There is one remaining initializing method, addBattlePanel. The battle panel handles all player actions and is contained within its own class. This class will be built now.

Building the Battle Panel

The battle panel is a container class that sits at the bottom of the screen. It will hold the attack and magic item buttons to use during a battle and will display the current hit points of the hero. These action buttons will be custom classes that will dispatch custom events. The panel will also contain a progress bar that will show the wait time before each player turn. This section will break down all of these components that make up the battle panel.

Creating the BattlePanel Class

The BattlePanel class contains many elements and functionality. It is the control panel for the entire level, and it is started in Listing 14-25.

Listing 14-25. BattlePanel.js - The BattlePanel Class Properties

```javascript
(function () {

    window.game = window.game || {}

    function BattlePanel(hero) {
        this.hero = hero;
        this.initialize();
    }

    var p = BattlePanel.prototype = new createjs.Container();

    p.Container_initialize = p.initialize;

    p.SPEED = 8;

    p.hero = null;
    p.waitBar = null;
    p.buttonHolder = null;
    p.hpTxt = null;

    p.waitingToAttack = null;
    p.currentAttackButton = null;

    p.initialize = function () {
        this.Container_initialize();
        this.addWaitBar();
        this.addBG();
        this.addHeroHP();
        this.addButtons();
        this.disableButtons();
    }

    //class methods here

    window.game.BattlePanel = BattlePanel;

}());
```

The speed constant controls the speed of the wait bar's progress. Next, a reference to the hero instance that was created in the game is passed into the class and set to the hero property. The following three properties are display objects used in the panel. When the progress bar is full, waitingToAttack will be set to true, will enable all available action buttons in the panel, and will stop the bar's progress. Other than the potion, when a button is pressed, the action isn't instantly triggered, but it is stored in the currentAttackButton property so it can be referenced when clicking on an enemy.

The initialize method then calls a list of functions, which will be reviewed now, starting with the creation of the wait bar, the panel's background, and the hero's avatar and stats (see Listing 14-26).

Listing 14-26. BattlePanel.js - Adding Display Objects to the Battle Panel

```
p.addWaitBar = function () {
    var progressWidth = 365;
    var progressBG = new createjs.Shape();
    this.waitingToAttack = false;
    this.waitBar = new createjs.Shape();
    progressBG.graphics.beginFill('#b6b6b6').drawRect(0, 0, progressWidth,
        40);
    this.waitBar.graphics.beginFill('#45c153').drawRect(0, 0,
        progressWidth, 40);
    this.waitBar.scaleX = 0;
    progressBG.x = this.waitBar.x = screen_width - progressWidth;
    this.addChild(progressBG, this.waitBar);
}
p.addBG = function () {
    var bg = new createjs.Sprite(spritesheet, 'battlePanel');
    this.addChild(bg);
}
p.addHeroHP = function () {
    var hero = new createjs.Sprite(spritesheet, 'hero');
    hero.y = -15;
    hero.x = 20;
    this.addChild(hero);
    this.hpTxt = new createjs.BitmapText('', spritesheet);
    this.hpTxt.letterSpacing = 3;
    this.hpTxt.x = 150;
    this.hpTxt.y = 15;
    this.addChild(this.hpTxt);
}
```

The wait bar is a simple progress indicator consisting of two shapes, much like the enemy health meter. One is used for the background and one for the bar. The bar shape is set to the waitBar property so it can be scaled with the panel updates. The background to the entire panel is a sprite and is added to the container on top of the wait bar in the addBG method.

The hero's avatar is a small sprite that is added to the upper left of the panel. Alongside of it is the current hit point status, which is displayed with a bitmap text object. The value of this text will be continuously updated when the panel is updated from the game's ticker.

Now the action buttons need to be placed in the panel. Listing 14-27 shows the next three methods that deal with the action buttons: addButtons, disableButtons, and enableButtons.

Listing 14-27. BattlePanel.js - Adding the Battle Action Buttons

```
p.addButtons = function () {
    var i, btn, btnWidth, prevButton;
    var btns = ['attack', 'potion', 'fire', 'earth', 'lightning' ];
    var player = data.PlayerData.player;
    var xPos = 70;
    var yPos = 140;
    var btnSpacing = 5;
    var len = btns.length;
    this.buttonHolder = new createjs.Container();
    for (i = 0; i < len; i++) {
        btn = new game.BattleButton(btns[i], player[btns[i]]);
        btnWidth = btn.getBounds().width;
        if (prevButton != null) {
            btn.x = ((prevButton.x + (prevButton.getBounds().width / 2)) +
                btnWidth / 2) + btnSpacing;
        }
        else {
            btn.x = xPos;
        }
        btn.y = yPos;
        btn.on('click', this.onAttackButtonSelected, this);
        this.buttonHolder.addChild(btn);
        prevButton = btn;
    }
    this.addChild(this.buttonHolder);
}
p.disableButtons = function () {
    var i, btn;
    var len = this.buttonHolder.getNumChildren();
    for (i = 0; i < len; i++) {
        btn = this.buttonHolder.getChildAt(i);
        btn.disableButton();
    }
}
p.enableButtons = function () {
    var i, btn;
    var len = this.buttonHolder.getNumChildren();
    for (i = 0; i < len; i++) {
        btn = this.buttonHolder.getChildAt(i);
        if (btn.quantity > 0 || btn.quantity < 0) {
            btn.enableButton();
        }
    }
}
```

A local array is built to dictate what buttons and in what order they should be laid out in the panel. A loop runs through this array while making instances of the BattleButton class. These button objects take two parameters: a string value indicating the type of action it should represent, and the quantity of it the player currently has. If you recall, the player has a permanent value of -1 for its attack value. This tells the button that it should not use quantity to determine its enablement and that it should be available forever. This will be covered more when you build this button class in the next section, "Creating the Battle Action Buttons."

Because the buttons vary in width, the local variable prevButton is created to store that last button that was drawn inside of the loop. You do this so you can access its width and properly position the next button in line. Before being added to buttonHolder, a click event listener is attached to each button and will trigger the onAttackButtonSelected method. Figure 14-13 shows the complete visuals for the BattlePanel class.

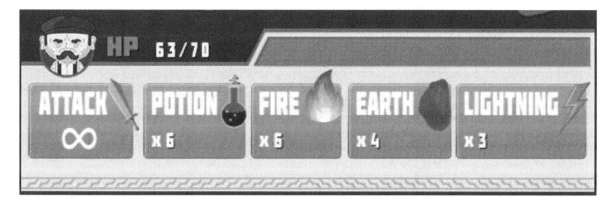

Figure 14-13. *The complete battle panel in the game*

The next two methods are used to enable and disable all buttons in the panel. These methods will be used often during a battle. For instance, when a user attacks an enemy, all buttons should instantly become inactive. The next time the wait bar has reached its end, the player can make another move and the available buttons will again become active.

If you recall, when the button is pressed, it will call the onAttackButtonSelected method. Listing 14-28 shows this function.

Listing 14-28. BattlePanel.js - The Click Event Handler for the Buttons

```
p.onAttackButtonSelected = function (e) {
    if (this.currentAttackButton != null) {
        this.currentAttackButton.enableButton();
    }
    this.currentAttackButton = e.currentTarget;
    this.currentAttackButton.selectButton();
    var event = new events.BattleButtonEvent(events.ATTACK_BUTTON_SELECTED,
        false, false, this.currentAttackButton.type);
    this.dispatchEvent(event);
}
```

Each time a button is clicked in a player's turn, it is stored in the currentAttackButton property. This is for a few reasons, but for now it's used to reset it in the case the user decides to click another. Remember, clicking a button will select it, giving the player the option to then choose their target. If the player selects *fire*, but then decides he just wants to *attack*, he can do so. This would mean that the current button was the fire button, and it should now call its enableButton method. The new attack button is then set to currentAttackButton and its selectButton method is called.

The next thing that happens is new. A custom event is being instantiated and dispatched. You've used plenty of events so far, but this is the first true *custom* event that has been utilized. What this means is that a class called BattleButtonEvent was created that extends Event. Doing this allows you to pass custom parameters into the event, which can then be retrieved by the handler. This class will be built in the "Creating Custom Events" section, but for now, just notice the last parameter. This is the attack type of the button currently in play, which is string, and will be evaluated when the attack finally commences on a target back in the game.

I'm sure you are anxious to get into this custom event, as well as the battle button class, but first let's wrap up the BattlePanel class with the final methods (see Listing 14-29).

Listing 14-29. BattlePanel.js - The Update Functions for the BattlePanel Class

```
p.update = function () {
    if (!this.waitingToAttack) {
        this.updateWaitBar();
    }
    this.updateStats();
}
p.updateWaitBar = function () {
    var scale = this.waitBar.scaleX + (.001 * this.SPEED);
    if (scale > 1) {
        scale = 1;
    }
    this.waitBar.scaleX = scale;
    if (scale == 1) {
        this.waitingToAttack = true;
        this.enableButtons();
    }
}
p.updateStats = function () {
    this.hpTxt.text = this.hero.HP + '_' + this.hero.maxHP;
}
p.resetPanel = function () {
    this.waitingToAttack = false;
    this.waitBar.scaleX = 0;
    this.disableButtons();
    this.mouseEnabled = true;
    this.currentAttackButton = null;
}
```

The next three methods are used to update the battle panel. The update method is continuously called from the game during the game loop. It has two primary purposes: to update the wait bar, and to update the hero's current hit points. If the waitingToAttack property is set to false, which means the wait bar should still be in progress, the updateWaitBar method is called. This will simply update the scale of the bar. When the scale of the bar reaches 1, the available action buttons are then enabled and waitingToAttack is set to true.

The updateStats method is constantly called and updates the hit point text by using the instance of the hero that was passed in from the game. Lastly, resetPanel is used to start the whole process over again after a turn as been successfully executed.

Before stepping back to create the BattleButton and BattleButtonEvent classes, take a look at the BattlePanel class in its entirety, shown in Listing 14-30.

Listing 14-30. BattlePanel.js - The Complete BattlePanel Class

```javascript
(function () {

    window.game = window.game || {}

    function BattlePanel(hero) {
        this.hero = hero;
        this.initialize();
    }

    var p = BattlePanel.prototype = new createjs.Container();

    p.Container_initialize = p.initialize;

    p.SPEED = 8;

    p.hero = null;
    p.waitBar = null;
    p.buttonHolder = null;
    p.hpTxt = null;

    p.waitingToAttack = null;
    p.currentAttackButton = null;

    p.initialize = function () {
        this.Container_initialize();
        this.addWaitBar();
        this.addBG();
        this.addHeroHP();
        this.addButtons();
        this.disableButtons();
    }
    p.addWaitBar = function () {
        var progressWidth = 365;
        var progressBG = new createjs.Shape();
        this.waitingToAttack = false;
        this.waitBar = new createjs.Shape();
        progressBG.graphics.beginFill('#b6b6b6').drawRect(0, 0,
            progressWidth, 40);
        this.waitBar.graphics.beginFill('#45c153').drawRect(0, 0,
            progressWidth, 40);
        this.waitBar.scaleX = 0;
        progressBG.x = this.waitBar.x = screen_width - progressWidth;
        this.addChild(progressBG, this.waitBar);
    }
    p.addBG = function () {
        var bg = new createjs.Sprite(spritesheet, 'battlePanel');
        this.addChild(bg);
    }
```

```
    p.addHeroHP = function () {
        var hero = new createjs.Sprite(spritesheet, 'hero');
        hero.y = -15;
        hero.x = 20;
        this.addChild(hero);
        this.hpTxt = new createjs.BitmapText('', spritesheet);
        this.hpTxt.letterSpacing = 3;
        this.hpTxt.x = 150;
        this.hpTxt.y = 15;
        this.addChild(this.hpTxt);
    }
    p.addButtons = function () {
        var i, btn, btnWidth, prevButton;
        var btns = ['attack', 'potion', 'fire', 'earth', 'lightning' ];
        var player = data.PlayerData.player;
        var xPos = 70;
        var yPos = 140;
        var btnSpacing = 5;
        var len = btns.length;
        this.buttonHolder = new createjs.Container();
        for (i = 0; i < len; i++) {
            btn = new game.BattleButton(btns[i], player[btns[i]]);
            btnWidth = btn.getBounds().width;
            if (prevButton != null) {
                btn.x = ((prevButton.x + (prevButton.getBounds().width /
                    2)) + btnWidth / 2) + btnSpacing;
            }
            else {
                btn.x = xPos;
            }
            btn.y = yPos;
            btn.on('click', this.onAttackButtonSelected, this);
            this.buttonHolder.addChild(btn);
            prevButton = btn;
        }
        this.addChild(this.buttonHolder);
    }
    p.disableButtons = function () {
        var i, btn;
        var len = this.buttonHolder.getNumChildren();
        for (i = 0; i < len; i++) {
            btn = this.buttonHolder.getChildAt(i);
            btn.disableButton();
        }
    }
    p.enableButtons = function () {
        var i, btn;
        var len = this.buttonHolder.getNumChildren();
```

```
            for (i = 0; i < len; i++) {
                btn = this.buttonHolder.getChildAt(i);
                if (btn.quantity > 0 || btn.quantity < 0) {
                    btn.enableButton();
                }
            }
        }
    }
    p.onAttackButtonSelected = function (e) {
        if (this.currentAttackButton != null) {
            this.currentAttackButton.enableButton();
        }
        this.currentAttackButton = e.currentTarget;
        this.currentAttackButton.selectButton();
        var event = new
            events.BattleButtonEvent(events.ATTACK_BUTTON_SELECTED, false,
            false, this.currentAttackButton.type);
        this.dispatchEvent(event);
    }
    p.update = function () {
        if (!this.waitingToAttack) {
            this.updateWaitBar();
        }
        this.updateStats();
    }
    p.updateWaitBar = function () {
        var scale = this.waitBar.scaleX + (.001 * this.SPEED);
        if (scale > 1) {
            scale = 1;
        }
        this.waitBar.scaleX = scale;
        if (scale == 1) {
            this.waitingToAttack = true;
            this.enableButtons();
        }
    }
    p.updateStats = function () {
        this.hpTxt.text = this.hero.HP + '_' + this.hero.maxHP;
    }
    p.resetPanel = function () {
        this.waitingToAttack = false;
        this.waitBar.scaleX = 0;
        this.disableButtons();
        this.mouseEnabled = true;
        this.currentAttackButton = null;
    }

    window.game.BattlePanel = BattlePanel;

}());
```

Creating the Battle Action Buttons

The BattleButton class draws the action button, which properly displays the quantity of the items it represents and enables itself accordingly. At this point in the book, you should be able to understand what is going in the class' code, but I will highlight some of the important areas after you review the entire class (see Listing 14-31).

Listing 14-31. BattleButton.js - The BattleButton Class for Player Actions

```
(function () {

    window.game = window.game || {}

    function BattleButton(frame, quantity) {
        this.initialize(frame, quantity);
    }

    var p = BattleButton.prototype = new createjs.Container();

    p.Container_initialize = p.initialize;

    p.quantityTxt = null;

    p.frame = null;
    p.type = null;
    p.quantity = null;
    p.isDown = null;

    p.initialize = function (frame, quantity) {
        this.Container_initialize();
        this.isDown = false;
        this.frame = this.type = frame;
        this.quantity = (quantity * 1);
        this.addSprite();
        this.setQuantity();
        this.cacheButton();
        this.enableButton();
    }
    p.addSprite = function () {
        var sprite = new createjs.Sprite(spritesheet, this.frame);
        var bounds = sprite.getBounds();
        this.setBounds(0, 0, bounds.width, bounds.height);
        this.regX = bounds.width / 2;
        this.regY = bounds.height;
        this.addChild(sprite);
    }
    p.setQuantity = function () {
        if (this.quantity >= 0) {
            var xPos = 25;
            var yOffset = 28;
            var yPos = this.getBounds().height - yOffset;
```

```
            this.quantityTxt = new
                createjs.BitmapText(this.quantity.toString(), spritesheet);
            this.quantityTxt.x = xPos;
            this.quantityTxt.y = yPos;
            this.addChild(this.quantityTxt);
        }
    }
    p.updateQuantity = function (quantity) {
        this.quantity += quantity;
        this.removeChild(this.quantityTxt);
        this.uncache(0, 0, this.getBounds().width, this.getBounds().height);
        this.setQuantity();
        this.cacheButton();
    }
    p.cacheButton = function () {
        this.cache(0, 0, this.getBounds().width, this.getBounds().height);
    }
    p.enableButton = function () {
        this.mouseEnabled = true;
        this.alpha = 1;
        this.resetButton();
    }
    p.disableButton = function () {
        this.mouseEnabled = false;
        this.alpha = .3;
        this.scaleX = this.scaleY = 1;
    }
    p.selectButton = function () {
        this.scaleX = this.scaleY = .9;
        this.mouseEnabled = false;
    }
    p.resetButton = function () {
        createjs.Tween.get(this).to({scaleX:1, scaleY:1}, 100);
    }
    window.game.BattleButton = BattleButton;

}());
```

The BattleButton class is a container, which holds one sprite and one bitmap text object to display the quantity of the item that the button represents. The button's type, which is a string that also represents the sprite sheet frame, is passed into the constructor along with the quantity.

Once the sprite is added, setBounds is used on the container class so its size can easily be accessed when caching. Caching is a good technique to use on containers when no display objects inside it are changing. However, as you can see in updateQuantity, you need to *uncache* the container so that quantityTxt can be updated. You'll also notice that you check that quantity is above 0 before creating a quantityTxt object at all. Remember that *attack* has an infinite quantity, which is represented with the value -1, and a textual representation of that is not needed. The *potion* action button, with a quantity of 9, is shown in Figure 14-14.

Figure 14-14. *The potion button will replenish hit points*

Creating Custom Events

Custom events can be very handy when you need to easily pass values around in your application. When an instance of your custom event class is created, you can pass in extra parameters into its constructor. This custom class should be written to accept and store those values accordingly. The event is created much like custom display objects are in EaselJS. This class will be written in a file named events.js. This file is set up to write this custom event class, as well as hold the event strings that you've seen throughout the game so far. Listing 14-32 shows the entire events.js file.

Listing 14-32. The events.js File Declares The Game's Event Types and the Custom BattleButtonEvent Event Class

```
window.events = window.events || {};

events.ATTACK_BUTTON_SELECTED = 'attack button selected';
events.ENEMY_ATTACK_ANIMATION_COMPLETE = 'enemy attack animation complete';
events.ENEMY_ATTACKED_COMPLETE = 'enemy attacked complete';
events.ENEMY_DESTROYED = 'enemy destroyed';

(function(){

    function BattleButtonEvent(type,bubbles,cancelable,attackType){
        this.attackType = attackType;
        this.initialize(type,bubbles,cancelable);
    }

    var p = BattleButtonEvent.prototype = new createjs.Event();

    p.attackType = null;

    p.Event_initialize = p.initialize;

    p.initialize = function(type,bubbles,cancelable){
        this.Event_initialize(type,bubbles,cancelable);
    }

    window.events.BattleButtonEvent = BattleButtonEvent;

}());
```

As usual, the custom class is wrapped inside of a closure. Its structure is identical to those classes that extend from other CreateJS classes. Extending Event requires that you accept at least the first type parameter that is used in the Event class that you are extending. You'll need to pass this into the initialize function of Event, much like you need to pass in a sprite sheet object when building a custom sprite.

```
p.initialize = function () {
   this.Sprite_initialize(spritesheet);
}
```

I prefer to pass in all three Event properties, type, bubbles, and cancelable. Any parameters after that are my own custom values that will be assigned to the custom event. Assigning these values to the class will make them accessible in the handler functions that are written to handle this event. The following is an example of how this custom event might be used within an event handler:

```
function onBattleButtonEvent (e){
   console.log(e.attackType); // fire
}
```

You've already seen this custom event dispatched in the "Creating the BattlePanel Class" section, and you'll see it in use when you get back to the game code in the "Handling Battle Button Events" section.

Adding the Battle Panel to the Game

Now that the battle panel, the battle buttons, and even a custom battle button event have been created, it's time to jump back into the game. We last left the game after adding the enemies to the grid. An instance of the BattlePanel class will now be added so you can start attacking bad guys. After the method addBoss, the addBattlePanel function is written (see Listing 14-33).

Listing 14-33. Game.js - Creating and Adding a BattlePanel Instance to the Game Container

```
p.addBattlePanel = function () {
   this.battlePanel = new game.BattlePanel(this.hero);
   this.battlePanel.y = screen_height -
      this.battlePanel.getBounds().height;
   this.battlePanel.on(events.ATTACK_BUTTON_SELECTED,
      this.onAttackButtonSelected, this);
   this.addChild(this.battlePanel);
}
```

This method will simply create the battle panel that was just built and add it to the game. The panel then listens for the ATTACK_BUTTON_SELECTED event, which was used as the type when dispatching the new and custom BattleButtonEvent event. The complete level, with enemies and battle panel, is shown in Figure 14-15.

Figure 14-15. *The battle panel in action*

Handling Battle Button Events

When a battle button is selected, the game should take action. Because a custom event was dispatched when clicked, the event now carries the button's attackType string with it. Listing 14-34 shows how this is accessed in the event handler onAttackButtonSelected and the methods that it fires based on that value.

Listing 14-34. Game.js - Handling the Clicks on Battle Action Buttons

```javascript
p.onAttackButtonSelected = function (e) {
    if (e.attackType == 'potion') {
        this.giveHeroPotion();
    }
    else {
        if (!this.attackSelected) {
            this.enableEnemyTargets();
        }
        this.attackSelected = e.attackType;
    }
}
p.giveHeroPotion = function () {
    var btn = this.battlePanel.currentAttackButton;
    btn.updateQuantity(-1);
    this.hero.HP += 20;
    if (this.hero.HP > this.hero.maxHP) {
        this.hero.HP = this.hero.maxHP;
    }
    this.updateHeroInventory('potion');
    this.onEnemyAttackedComplete();
}
p.enableEnemyTargets = function () {
    var i, enemy;
    var len = this.enemyHolder.getNumChildren();
    for (i = 0; i < len; i++) {
        enemy = this.enemyHolder.getChildAt(i);
        enemy.enableTarget();
    }
}
p.disableEnemyTargets = function () {
    var i, enemy;
    var len = this.enemyHolder.getNumChildren();
    for (i = 0; i < len; i++) {
        enemy = this.enemyHolder.getChildAt(i);
        enemy.disableTarget();
    }
}
```

First off, if the type of button that was pressed is a potion, then the game should immediately fire the giveHeroPotion method. Since the target of a potion button will always be the hero, the action is triggered as soon as it is pressed. If it is another type of action, one that will need an enemy target to commence, then it should show the target animations on each enemy by calling the enableEnemyTargets method. The disableEnemyTargets method is also declared here and does exactly what you would expect. The game holds an attackSelected property that will be used later after selecting an enemy target. This property is set accordingly by accessing the attackType value from the event.

```javascript
this.attackSelected = e.attackType;
```

When taking a potion, the hero gets 20 extra hit points, but cannot exceed the max hit point value. Before doing this, the button needs to be updated to show the new potion quantity. You can access this button via the instance of the battle panel, battlePanel, and by calling on the button's update method by passing in a value of -1. If you recall, the button class will take care of the rest visually. The updateHeroInventory and onEnemyAttackedComplete methods are then called, which will be covered in the "Attacking the Enemies" section. While taking a potion is not attacking an enemy, the next steps to be taken in the game are handled within that function, so it is called here.

■ **Note**   You might be wondering why I went through the hassle of creating a custom event to carry the selected button's type when I could have easily accessed the selected button via the battle panel instance. While this might be true in this case, I find it cleaner to use custom events whenever possible. Though I *am* using both approaches in this book, I encourage you to use custom events if the concept is clear to you, as opposed to digging into an object's properties. After all, that object might not exist anymore in many situations, so the knowledge of custom events should prove beneficial in your future applications.

Attacking the Enemies

Finally the enemies can be attacked! Most of the attack code is within the Enemy class itself; the game just needs to initiate it. Listing 14-35 shows all enemy attacking methods.

Listing 14-35. Game.js - The Game Methods for Attacking Enemies

```
p.attackEnemy = function (e) {
    var enemy = e.currentTarget;
    var player = data.PlayerData.player;
    var btn = this.battlePanel.currentAttackButton;
    btn.updateQuantity(-1);
    this.updateHeroInventory(this.attackSelected);
    this.disableEnemyTargets();
    this.battlePanel.disableButtons();
    enemy.takeDamage(this.hero.power, this.attackSelected);
}
p.onEnemyAttackedComplete = function (e) {
    this.attackSelected = false;
    this.battlePanel.resetPanel();
    this.checkLevel();
}
p.onEnemyDestroyed = function (e) {
    var i, enemy;
    for (i = 0; i < this.enemies.length; i++) {
        enemy = this.enemies[i];
        if (enemy === e.target) {
            this.enemies.splice(i, 1);
            break;
        }
    }
    this.enemyHolder.removeChild(e.target);
    this.onEnemyAttackedComplete(null);
}
p.updateHeroInventory = function (item) {
    this.hero.updateInventory(item, -1);
}
```

After enabling the targets on each enemy, they become click-enabled. Once clicked, the `attackEnemy` method is called. Remember, these `click` event listeners were created on each enemy when creating them. As with a potion action, the current button is retrieved and its quantity is updated. The enemy targets are then disabled by calling the `disableEnemyTargets` method, and the battle panel buttons are also disabled. Finally, the enemy is attacked by calling the `takeDamage` method on the targeted enemy. The method takes the hero's power and the type of attack used. The `Enemy` class takes care of the rest. This might be a good time to revisit that class in the "Creating the Enemy Class" section.

The game sets two listeners on itself at the beginning of the class. As a recap, Listing 14-36 shows these event listeners being added to the game container.

Listing 14-36. Game.js - The Event Listeners Set on the Game

```
p.setListeners = function () {
    this.on(events.ENEMY_ATTACKED_COMPLETE, this.onEnemyAttackedComplete,
        this);
    this.on(events.ENEMY_DESTROYED, this.onEnemyDestroyed, this);
}
```

The enemy will dispatch these events when certain animations are complete. These two events were dispatched with bubbling, which means the event will travel up the entire display list. Because of this, the game is able to listen for these events directly, without having to attach a listener to each enemy object. After an enemy does its animation to show it being attacked, the `onEnemyAttackedComplete` method will be called. This will essentially reset the turn by setting the `attackSelected` property back to false and resetting the battle panel. The `checkLevel` method is then called, which will check the progress of the battle. If the enemy was destroyed, it will also do an animation, after which the `onEnemyDestroyed` method is called. The primary purpose of this function is to remove it from the `enemies` array. This array is what is used to check on the level's progress, so the destroyed enemy needs to go. Since there is no elegant way to find this object in the array, a loop is created to find the appropriate index for splicing. The display object is removed from the stage, and `onEnemyAttackedComplete` is called to wrap up the turn.

One final enemy-attacking method needs to be reviewed. The `updateHeroInventory` method is called after any action has been taken by the player. It takes the attack type that was used and passes it along to the `updateInventory` method on the `hero` instance, along with a value of -1 for quantity. Like the other classes that have been written for the game, the `hero` instance will take care of the rest.

Attacking the Hero

The game would be no fun if all you did was attack and destroy enemies. The enemies will attack in streaks when it is time for an enemy attack to begin. This streak can be a number between 1 and 3, depending on the level difficulty. In a streak, the enemies will attack in sequence along the grid. When this attack should take place is determined in the game loop and the `checkEnemyAttack` method, which will be written in the "Creating the Check Level Functions" section. When the time comes for the enemy to attack, the `beginEnemyAttack` method is executed (see Listing 14-37).

Listing 14-37. Game.js - The Enemy Attack Methods

```
p.beginEnemyAttack = function () {
    var enemy;
    this.enemiesAreAttacking = true;
    this.battlePanel.disableButtons();
    this.currentEnemyAttackIndex = this.currentEnemyAttackIndex >=
        this.enemies.length ?
        this.currentEnemyAttackIndex - 1 : this.currentEnemyAttackIndex;
```

```
        enemy = this.enemies[this.currentEnemyAttackIndex];
        enemy.on(events.ENEMY_ATTACK_ANIMATION_COMPLETE,
            this.onEnemyAttackAnimationComplete, this, true);
        enemy.playAttackAnimation();
    }
    p.onEnemyAttackAnimationComplete = function (e) {
        var enemy = e.target;
        this.hero.takeDamage(enemy.data.power);
        this.battlePanel.updateStats();
        this.heroAttackedEffects();
    }
```

The beginEnemyAttack method will be called to kick off an enemy streak and again for each time the streak advances in attacks. The first thing it does is disable the battle panel so the player cannot attack during this streak. The currentEnemyAttackIndex, which is increased at the end of each attack, is evaluated to make sure it has not exceeded the amount of available enemies. This is needed because the amount of enemies is constantly changing, and this index could be off if the enemy in that slot was killed since the last enemy streak. The next enemy in line is found by using this index value on the enemies array.

An enemy has a bounce effect for when it attacks and will dispatch the event ENEMY_ATTACK_ANIMATION_COMPLETE when it is finished. Notice that the once parameter is set to true in the on method. This is a handy way of removing the listener as soon as it handled. Finally, the enemy plays its attacking animation by calling its playAttackAnimation method.

After this enemy animation, the actual attack should take place. Like the Enemy class, the Hero class also has a takeDamage method, which will take the power value of the enemy attacking. If you recall, this method will update the hit points on the hero instance. Next, the updateStats method is called on the battlePanel object. Since the panel does not update during an enemy attack, this should be called manually after the hero has been attacked so that the HP message can be updated. Lastly, a flashy effect happens on the screen to resemble an attack from the enemy. Listing 14-38 shows how this effect is executed.

Listing 14-38. Game.js - Creating the Effect for Hero Damage

```
p.heroAttackedEffects = function () {
    var flash = new createjs.Shape();
    flash.graphics.beginFill('#900').drawRect(0, 0, screen_width,
        screen_height);
    flash.alpha = 0;
    this.addChild(flash);
    createjs.Tween.get(flash)
        .to({alpha:.6}, 500, createjs.Ease.bounceInOut)
        .to({alpha:0}, 500, createjs.Ease.bounceInOut)
        .call(function (flash) {
            this.removeChild(flash);
            this.evaluateEnemyStreak();
        }, [flash], this);
}
```

A red shape is created and added to the game. A few chained tween commands are applied to give it a flashing effect (see Figure 14-16).

Figure 14-16. *The screen flashes red when the hero is attacked*

This animation will call the `evaluateEnemyStreak` function when complete, which is shown in Listing 14-39.

Listing 14-39. Game.js - Evaluating the Enemy Attacks

```
p.evaluateEnemyStreak = function () {
    this.currentEnemyAttackCount++;
    this.currentEnemyAttackIndex++;
    if (this.currentEnemyAttackIndex === this.enemies.length) {
        this.currentEnemyAttackIndex = 0;
    }
    if (!this.levelComplete && this.currentEnemyAttackCount < this.levelData.enemyStreak &&
            this.enemies.length > 0) {
        this.beginEnemyAttack();
    }
    else {
        this.enemyAttacksComplete();
    }
}
p.enemyAttacksComplete = function () {
    this.currentEnemyAttackCount = 0;
    this.enemiesAreAttacking = false;
    if (this.battlePanel.waitingToAttack) {
        this.battlePanel.enableButtons();
    }
}
```

The purpose of this function is to increase currentEnemyAttackCount, which was initially declared as 0, and determine if the streak should continue. The length of the streak is unique to the level and is retrieved from the level data. If the current count is less than total streak, the beginEnemyAttack is called again. If the streak should be over, enemyAttacksComplete is called, which destroys the streak and continues the game.

Creating the Check Level Functions

The main application is built to fire a run function on the current scene on every tick of the game loop. This function was introduced when starting the Game class in the "Starting the Game Class and Its Properties" section. As a recap, Listing 14-40 shows this run method.

Listing 14-40. Game.js - The run Method is Called From the Main Application's Game Loop

```
p.run = function (tickerEvent) {
    if (!this.levelComplete) {
        this.checkBattlePanel();
        this.checkEnemyAttack(tickerEvent.time);
        this.checkHeroHealth();
    }
}
```

This function will run three checks when the level is still in progress. Listing 14-41 shows these three functions, plus the checkLevel method that is called after an enemy is attacked.

Listing 14-41. Game.js - The Game's Check Methods Check the Status of the Level

```
p.checkEnemyAttack = function (time) {
    if (time >= this.lastEnemyAttack + this.levelData.enemyAttackWait &&
            !this.attackSelected && !this.enemiesAreAttacking) {
        this.lastEnemyAttack = time + (this.ENEMY_ATTACK_DURATION *
            this.levelData.enemyStreak);
        this.beginEnemyAttack();
    }
}
p.checkBattlePanel = function () {
    if (!this.enemiesAreAttacking) {
        this.battlePanel.update();
    }
}
p.checkHeroHealth = function () {
    if (this.hero.HP <= 0) {
        this.levelComplete = true;
        this.loseLevel();
    }
}
p.checkLevel = function () {
    if (this.enemies.length <= 0) {
        this.levelComplete = true;
        this.winLevel();
    }
}
```

The checkEnemyAttack determines if it's time to start another enemy attack. The time property from the ticker event is passed into it so it can be compared to the sum of the class property lastEnemyAttack and the enemyAttackWait property in the level data. If time is currently greater than this number, the enemies should attack. But only if both the hero and the enemies are not already in the middle of an attack can this happen. If the enemies should start an attack, the beginEnemyAttack method is called. At this point, the lastEnemyAttack value should be set again. Only a few additions need to be added to the current time. This value should be set to the time it will be when the enemy streak is over. You can get this value by multiplying the level's attack streak number by the ENEMY_ATTACK_DURATION constant.

```
this.lastEnemyAttack = time + (this.ENEMY_ATTACK_DURATION *
        this.levelData.enemyStreak);
```

This might seem a little strange, but the ticker's current time will not be in scope within the enemy attack evaluation functions.

The next check method, checkBattlePanel, is a lot simpler. Its only task is to update the battle panel if the enemies are not currently attacking. The checkHeroHealth method is equally as simple. If the hero's hit points have all been depleted, the levelComplete property is set to true and the loseLevel method is called.

The final check function is called after an enemy has been attacked or destroyed. It checks the number of enemies left. If all enemies have been defeated, levelComplete is set to true and the winLevel method is called.

Finishing the Level

If the hero has died, or if all enemies have been destroyed, the level must end. Either the hero wins and the player gets the coins and boost in stats, or the hero dies and the game ends with no chance of saving. Listing 14-42 shows the finishing methods to the Game class.

Listing 14-42. Game.js - The Winning and Losing Methods

```
p.winLevel = function () {
    this.hero.saveStats();
    createjs.Tween.get(this).wait(1000).call(this.leaveBattle, null, this);
}
p.loseLevel = function () {
    var flash = new createjs.Shape();
    flash.graphics.beginFill('#900').drawRect(0, 0, screen_width,
        screen_height);
    flash.alpha = 0;
    this.addChild(flash);
    createjs.Tween.get(flash)
        .wait(1000)
        .to({alpha:.8}, 2500)
        .call(this.goHome, null, this);
}
p.leaveBattle = function () {
    this.dispatchEvent(game.GameStateEvents.LEVEL_COMPLETE);
}
p.goHome = function () {
    this.dispatchEvent(game.GameStateEvents.MAIN_MENU);
}
```

Winning the level will first save the hero's current stats, which is done within the saveStats method in the Hero class itself. A short timeout is created using TweenJS, which will call the `leaveBattle` method after one second. This method will dispatch the LEVEL_COMPLETE event and bring the player to the level complete scene.

Losing the battle creates a simple effect that slowly fades a red shape covering the entire stage. On its completion, the goHome method is called and will dispatch the MAIN_MENU event, taking the user straight back to the title screen. No rewards are given, and nothing that was done or used up in the battle is saved.

There is quite a bit going on in this game. A lot was covered while veering off into different directions while writing different classes. You can find the complete Game class code in the Game.js file along with the other source code. You can download the code from the Source Code/Downloads tab on this book's Apress product page (www.apress.com/9781430263401). Try reading through the methods without getting hung up or lost. When coming across the use of custom classes, take a detour and review the section that created those classes.

Building the Battle Win Screen

When a level is complete, the player is rewarded with a stats increases and coins. The level complete scene will present the player with these new stats and give them the option to spend their newly earned coins. A self-contained magic shop will be created and added to this screen under the level messages. This section will create this level-winning screen.

Creating the Level Complete Scene

The level complete screen will be a container class called LevelComplete. There is seemingly a lot of code, but most of it is messaging and positioning. This class is seen in Listing 14-43.

Listing 14-43. LevelComplete.js - The LevelComplete Class Displays The Level Results and Offer Items for Purchase

```
(function () {

    window.game = window.game || {}

    function LevelComplete() {
        this.initialize();
    }

    var p = LevelComplete.prototype = new createjs.Container();

    p.Container_initialize = p.initialize;

    p.currentPower = null;
    p.powerIncrease = null;
    p.currentDefense = null;
    p.defenseIncrease = null;
    p.currentMAX_HP = null;
    p.maxHPIncrease = null;
    p.currentCoins = null;
    p.coinsIncrease = null;

    p.initialize = function () {
        this.Container_initialize();
        this.updateLevel();
        this.updateStats();
        this.addBG();
        this.addLevelMessaging();
        this.addShop();
        this.drawContinueButton();
    }
    p.updateLevel = function () {
        if (data.GameData.currentLevel ==
            data.PlayerData.player.gameLevel) {
                data.PlayerData.player.gameLevel =
                    (data.PlayerData.player.gameLevel * 1) + 1;
        }
    }
    p.updateStats = function () {
        var player = data.PlayerData.player;
        var currentLevel =
            data.GameData.levelData[data.GameData.currentLevel - 1];
        this.currentPower = data.PlayerData.player.power * 1;
        this.powerIncrease = currentLevel.powerIncreaseAwarded * 1;
        this.currentDefense = data.PlayerData.player.defense * 1;
        this.defenseIncrease = currentLevel.defenseIncreaseAwarded * 1;
```

```
        this.currentMAX_HP = data.PlayerData.player.maxHP * 1;
        this.maxHPIncrease = currentLevel.HPEarned;
        this.currentCoins = data.PlayerData.player.coins * 1;
        this.coinsIncrease = currentLevel.coinsAwarded * 1;
        //update data
        player.power = this.currentPower + this.powerIncrease;
        player.defense = this.currentDefense + this.defenseIncrease;
        player.maxHP = this.currentMAX_HP + this.maxHPIncrease;
        player.coins = this.currentCoins + this.coinsIncrease;
    }
    p.addBG = function () {
        var bg = new
            createjs.Bitmap(game.assets.getAsset(game.assets.MENU_BG));
        this.addChild(bg);
    }
    p.addLevelMessaging = function () {
        var txt;
        var xPos = 30;
        var yPos = 40;
        var vGap = 90;
        var msgWidth = 600;
        var msgHeight = 470;
        var msgPos = {x:20, y:40};
        var msgContainer = new createjs.Container();
        //bg
        var containerBG = new createjs.Shape();
        containerBG.graphics.beginFill('#f7f4ef').drawRect(0, 0, msgWidth,
            msgHeight);
        //title
        txt = this.getBitmapTxt('LEVEL COMPLETE!', xPos, yPos);
        msgContainer.addChild(containerBG, txt);
        //attack
        yPos += vGap;
        txt = this.getBitmapTxt('ATTACK INCREASE_ + ' + this.powerIncrease +
            ' = ' + data.PlayerData.player.power, xPos, yPos);
        msgContainer.addChild(txt);
        //defense
        yPos += vGap;
        txt = this.getBitmapTxt('DEFENSE INCREASE_ + ' +
            this.defenseIncrease + ' = ' + data.PlayerData.player.defense,
            xPos, yPos);
        msgContainer.addChild(txt);
        //HP
        yPos += vGap;
        txt = this.getBitmapTxt('HP INCREASE_ + ' + this.maxHPIncrease + ' =
            ' + data.PlayerData.player.maxHP, xPos, yPos);
        msgContainer.addChild(txt);
        //coins
        yPos += vGap;
        txt = this.getBitmapTxt('COINS EARNED_ + ' + this.coinsIncrease + '
            = ' + data.PlayerData.player.coins, xPos, yPos);
```

```
        msgContainer.addChild(txt);
        //add and position container
        this.addChild(msgContainer);
        msgContainer.x = msgPos.x;
        msgContainer.y = msgPos.y;
        msgContainer.cache(0, 0, msgWidth, msgHeight);
    }
    p.getBitmapTxt = function (txt, x, y) {
        var txt = new createjs.BitmapText(txt, fontsheet);
        txt.letterSpacing = 6;
        txt.x = x;
        txt.y = y;
        return txt;
    }
    p.addShop = function () {
        var shop = new game.MagicShop();
        shop.x = 20;
        shop.y = 550;
        this.addChild(shop);
    }
    p.drawContinueButton = function () {
        var btn = new createjs.Sprite(spritesheet, 'continueBtn');
        btn.x = (screen_width / 2) - (btn.getBounds().width / 2);
        btn.y = 1020;
        btn.on('click', this.onButtonClick, this);
        this.addChild(btn);
    }
    p.onButtonClick = function (e) {
        this.dispatchEvent(game.GameStateEvents.LEVEL_SELECT);
    }
    window.game.LevelComplete = LevelComplete;

}());
```

The very first thing the class does is update the level and stats of the player. The methods updateLevel and updateStats handle this by accessing and manipulating the PlayerData object, which will write to local storage. The current stats values are all referenced and saved to class properties. This is so they can be easily accessed when drawing the messages. The values are then added and saved by being assigned to the player object in PlayerData.

Next, a background sprite is added, followed by the messaging in the addLevelMessaging method. This function creates a series of bitmap text objects to display the proper messages pertaining to what was gained and what the player now has. This includes power, defense, max hit point count, and coins. A little utility function, getBitmapTxt, is used to create and return the bitmap text objects as the messages are built. The complete messaging section of the level complete screen is shown in Figure 14-17.

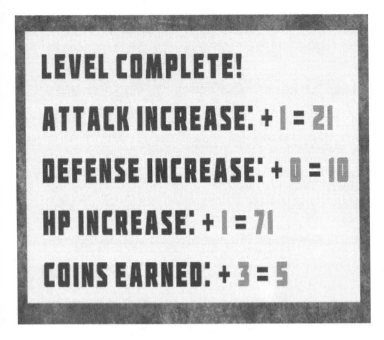

Figure 14-17. *The messaging in the level complete screen*

After the messaging, an instance of the MagicShop class is added and positioned to the bottom of the screen. This class will be built in the next section, "Creating the Magic Shop." Finally, a button sprite is added to the bottom of the screen, which will move the player on to the level select screen when clicked.

Creating the Magic Shop

As previously mentioned, the magic shop is completely self-contained. It's added to the LevelComplete class, but will handle all transactions with local storage within itself. Listing 14-44 shows the entire MagicShop class.

Listing 14-44. MagicShop.js - The MagicShop Class Allows the Player to Purchase Items for Future Battles

```
(function () {

    window.game = window.game || {}

    function MagicShop() {
        this.initialize();
    }

    var p = MagicShop.prototype = new createjs.Container();

    p.Container_initialize = p.initialize;

    p.coinsTxt = null;

    p.totalCoins = null;
    p.magicData = null;
```

```
p.initialize = function () {
    this.Container_initialize();
    this.totalCoins = data.PlayerData.player.coins;
    this.magicData = data.GameData.magicCosts;
    this.addStoreMessaging();
    this.addPurse();
    this.addItemButtons();
}
p.addStoreMessaging = function () {
    var txt;
    var storeWidth = 600;
    var storeHeight = 440;
    var xPos = 20;
    var yPos = 20;
    var vGap = 70;
    var storeBG = new createjs.Shape();
    storeBG.graphics.beginFill('#f7f4ef').drawRect(0, 0, storeWidth,
        storeHeight);
    txt = this.getBitmapTxt('MAGIC SHOP', xPos, yPos);
    this.addChild(storeBG, txt);
    yPos += vGap;
    txt = this.getBitmapTxt('POTION_ ' + this.magicData.potion + '
        COINS', xPos, yPos, .7);
    this.addChild(txt);
    yPos += vGap * .7;
    txt = this.getBitmapTxt('FIRE_ ' + this.magicData.fire + ' COINS',
        xPos, yPos, .7);
    this.addChild(txt);
    yPos += vGap * .7;
    txt = this.getBitmapTxt('EARTH_ ' + this.magicData.earth + ' COINS',
        xPos, yPos, .7);
    this.addChild(txt);
    yPos += vGap * .7;
    txt = this.getBitmapTxt('LIGHTNING_ ' + this.magicData.lightning + '
        COINS', xPos, yPos, .7);
    this.addChild(txt);
}
p.addPurse = function () {
    var coin;
    var xPos = 530;
    var yPos = 20;
    var coinOffsetX = -45;
    var coinOffsetY = -8;
    coin = new createjs.Sprite(spritesheet, 'coin');
    coin.paused = true;
    coin.x = xPos + coinOffsetX;
    coin.y = yPos + coinOffsetY;
    createjs.Tween.get(coin, {loop:true}).to({currentAnimationFrame:8},
        600)
```

```
        this.coinsTxt = this.getBitmapTxt('x' + this.totalCoins, xPos, yPos,
            .6);
        this.addChild(coin, this.coinsTxt);
    }
    p.getBitmapTxt = function (txt, x, y, scale) {
        var txt = new createjs.BitmapText(txt, fontsheet);
        txt.letterSpacing = 6;
        txt.x = x;
        txt.y = y;
        txt.scaleX = txt.scaleY = scale != null ? scale : 1;
        return txt;
    }
    p.addItemButtons = function () {
        var i, btn, btnWidth, prevButton, txt, cost, magicType;
        var btns = ['potion', 'fire', 'earth', 'lightning' ];
        var playerData = data.PlayerData.player;
        var xPos = 70;
        var yPos = 380;
        var btnSpacing = 20;
        var len = btns.length;
        for (i = 0; i < len; i++) {
            magicType = btns[i];
            cost = this.magicData[magicType];
            btn = new game.BattleButton(magicType, playerData[magicType]);
            btn.name = 'btn_' + magicType;
            btn.on('click', this.purchaseItem, this, false, {cost:cost});
            if (cost > this.totalCoins) {
                btn.disableButton();
            }
            btnWidth = btn.getBounds().width;
            if (prevButton != null) {
                btn.x = ((prevButton.x + (prevButton.getBounds().width / 2)) +
                    btnWidth / 2) + btnSpacing;
            }
            else {
                btn.x = xPos;
            }
            btn.y = yPos;
            this.addChild(btn);
            prevButton = btn;
        }
        txt = this.getBitmapTxt('CLICK ITEM TO PURCHASE', 20, 400, .6);
        this.addChild(txt);
    }
    p.purchaseItem = function (e, data) {
        var player = window.data.PlayerData.player;
        var btn = e.currentTarget;
        var item = btn.type;
        var cost = data.cost;
        btn.updateQuantity(1);
        player[item] = btn.quantity;
```

```
         this.totalCoins -= cost;
         player.coins = this.totalCoins;
         this.updatePurse(cost);
         this.evaluatePurse();
      }
   p.updatePurse = function (cost) {
         var xPos = this.coinsTxt.x;
         var yPos = this.coinsTxt.y;
         this.removeChild(this.coinsTxt);
         this.coinsTxt = this.getBitmapTxt('x' + this.totalCoins, xPos, yPos,
            .6);
         this.addChild(this.coinsTxt);
      }
   p.evaluatePurse = function () {
         var i, btn, cost;
         var btns = ['potion', 'fire', 'earth', 'lightning' ];
         var len = btns.length;
         for (i = 0; i < len; i++) {
            cost = this.magicData[btns[i]];
            btn = this.getChildByName('btn_' + btns[i]);
            if (cost > this.totalCoins) {
               btn.disableButton();
            }
         }
      }
   }
   window.game.MagicShop = MagicShop;

}());
```

The player's total coins is referenced from PlayerData and set to the totalCoins property, and the cost of each item is referenced from GameData and set to magicData. These values will be used when determining if the player can buy an item or not. They are also used to build the messaging for the shop in addStoreMessaging and addPurse functions. These messages are built in the same fashion as the level messaging back in the LevelComplete class. A small, animated sprite of a spinning coin is added next to the coins text for a nice visual effect.

Next, the shop items are created in the addItemButtons method. The attack buttons are reused for the shop, and their enablement is determined by the cost of each item and the player's total coins. Their quantity message is set by the current inventory of the player, and their positioning uses the same approach as when added to the BattlePanel class. The complete level complete screen is shown in full with the magic shop in Figure 14-18.

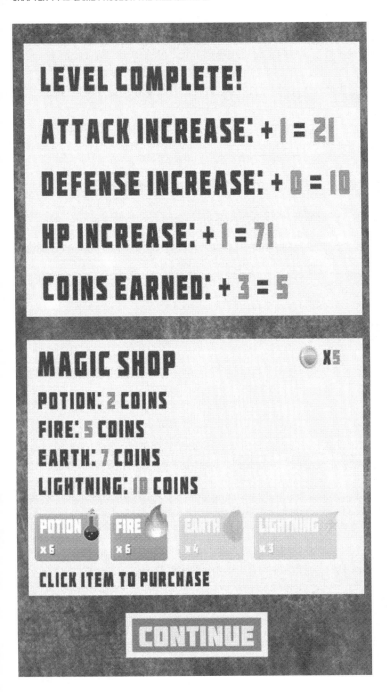

Figure 14-18. The level complete screen with magic shop

If a button is enabled and is clicked, the purchaseItem is called. This event handler is given the cost of the item so it can be subtracted from the player's coins. This is accomplished by using the data parameter in the on method.

```
btn.on('click', this.purchaseItem, this, false, {cost:cost});
```

The button is updated to reflect the new quantity, and so is the property in the PlayerData object. Next, the totalCoins value is updated along with the coins value in PlayerData. The messaging in the store is then updated by calling updatePurse, which will redraw the number of player coins. Finally, the evaluatePurse method is run, which determines what buttons should be deactivated based on the new number of coins the player has to spend.

The Continue button will take the user back to the level select screen where they can advance to the next level or replay previous battles to gain higher stats and coins.

Summary

In this final game project, you combined all of the CreateJS skills that you learned in this book. Graphics were created using bitmap objects, sprite sheets, and the drawing API. Animations were created by utilizing both sprite sheet animation objects and TweenJS. You gained more control over the appearance of your messaging by using bitmap fonts, and other techniques such as cloning and caching were used to help build more efficient code.

Code organization was achieved by creating custom classes that extend sprites, containers, and even events. The asset and state management techniques learned in this book helped mold the game into a readable and reusable structure, and saving game data and state was achieved by using HTML5 local storage.

These techniques, along with the scaling code for various screen sizes, puts this complete game in a position to package for publishing on the Web or even in mobile app stores.

Index

■ W, X, Y

■ Z

Get the eBook for only $10!

Now you can take the weightless companion with you anywhere, anytime. Your purchase of this book entitles you to 3 electronic versions for only $10.

This Apress title will prove so indispensible that you'll want to carry it with you everywhere, which is why we are offering the eBook in **3 formats** for only $10 if you have already purchased the print book.

Convenient and fully searchable, the PDF version enables you to easily find and copy code—or perform examples by quickly toggling between instructions and applications. The MOBI format is ideal for your Kindle, while the ePUB can be utilized on a variety of mobile devices.

Go to www.apress.com/promo/tendollars to purchase your companion eBook.

Made in the USA
Lexington, KY
31 December 2016